THE BLUE GUIDES

Austria
Belgium and Luxembourg
China
Cyprus
Czechoslovakia
Denmark
Egypt

FRANCE
France
Paris and Versailles
Burgundy
Normandy
Corsica

GREECE
Greece
Athens and environs
Crete

HOLLAND
Holland
Amsterdam

Hungary

ITALY
Northern Italy
Southern Italy
Florence
Rome and environs
Venice
Tuscany
Umbria
Sicily

Jerusalem
Malta and Gozo

Morocco
Moscow and Leningrad
Portugal

SPAIN
Spain
Barcelona

Switzerland

TURKEY
Turkey: the Aegean
   and Mediterranean Coasts
Istanbul

UK
England
Ireland
Scotland
Wales
London
Museums and Galleries
   of London
Oxford and Cambridge
Gardens of England
Literary Britain and Ireland
Victorian Architecture in Britain
Churches and Chapels
   of Northern England
Churches and Chapels
   of Southern England
Channel Islands

USA
New York
Boston and Cambridge

Yugoslavia

The 16C Palais de Justice, Rouen

BLUE GUIDE

Normandy

John McNeill

Maps and plans by John Flower

A & C Black
London

WW Norton
New York

First edition 1993

Published by A & C Black (Publishers) Limited
35 Bedford Row, London WC1R 4JH

© A & C Black (Publishers) Limited 1993

A CIP catalogue record of this book
is available from the British Library.

ISBN 0–7136–3730–7

Published in the United States of America by
WW Norton and Company, Inc
500 Fifth Avenue, New York, NY 10110

Published simultaneously in Canada by
Penguin Books Canada Limited
2801 John Street, Markham, Ontario L3R 1B4

ISBN 0–393–30971–1 USA

The author and the publishers have done their best to ensure the accuracy of all the information in Blue Guide Normandy; however, they can accept no responsibility for any loss, injury or inconvenience sustained by any traveller as a result of information or advice contained in the guide.

Please write in with your comments, suggestions and corrections. Writers of the best letters will be awarded a free Blue Guide of their choice.

John McNeill was educated at the University of East Anglia and the Courtauld Institute of Art. He now teaches at London University's Centre for Extra-Mural Studies and Camberwell College of Art, and has extensive experience of devising and leading cultural tours to France, Italy, and Spain.

The author and the publishers gratefully acknowledge Thames and Hudson for permission to reproduce the extract from The Bayeux Tapestry by Sir David Wilson on pages 160–61.

For permission to reproduce the photographs in this book the publishers would like to thank Michael Jenner (pages 2 and 47); the Conway Library, Courtauld Institute of Art (pages 37, 102, 156, 199, 211, 245); the Musée des Beaux-Arts, Dieppe/Bridgeman Art Library, London (page 31); the Musée des Beaux-Arts, Rouen (page 53); the Musée des Beaux-Arts, Le Havre/Giraudon, Paris/Bridgeman Art Library, London © DACS 1993 (page 68); John McNeill (pages 150, 228, 232).

Printed and bound in Great Britain by
Butler & Tanner Ltd, Frome and London

CONTENTS

Acknowledgements

Without the friendly interest and goodwill of all I met in Normandy this volume would have been impossible. I should particularly like to single out Lesley Scouller and Marianne Collopy, who first persuaded me I had an aptitude for the job and whose encouragement was an enduring source of strength. My Richmond diploma class were equally supportive, and kept me bright and far from lazy. Philippe Rabany was magnificent, and his ability to open doors I never even knew existed was a source of continuing amazement. At every point I was helped by curators, parish priests, and local Syndicats d'Initiative, to all of whom I owe a great debt. That I cannot mention them all does not lessen my gratitude. The most historic debt is owed to my parents, who first introduced me to France. My father accompanied me as 'hod-carrier' on the final visit to Normandy, rising above my faults, sociable and generous of spirit. It was an encounter I treasure. Thanks are also due to Ian Ousby for allowing me to absorb the lessons of the introductory format he pioneered in the Blue Guide Burgundy. Finally, I should like to thank Gemma Davies, who was bold in giving latitude to a novice and who is largely responsible for any resemblance between this volume and a comprehensible guidebook.

A Note on Blue Guides

The Blue Guide series began in 1915 when Muirhead Guide-Books Limited published 'Blue Guide London and its Environs'. Finlay and James Muirhead already had extensive experience of guidebook publishing: before the First World War they had been the editors of the English editions of the German Baedekers, and by 1915 they had acquired the copyright of most of the famous 'Red' Handbooks from John Murray.

An agreement made with the French publishing house Hachette et Cie in 1917 led to the translation of Muirhead's London guide, which became the first 'Guide Bleu'—Hachette had previously published the blue-covered 'Guides Joannes'. Subsequently, Hachette's 'Guide Bleu Paris et ses Environs' was adapted and published in London by Muirhead. The collaboration between the two publishing houses continued until 1933.

In 1933 Ernest Benn Limited took over the Blue Guides, appointing Russell Muirhead, Finlay Muirhead's son, editor in 1934. The Muirhead's connection with the Blue Guides ended in 1963 when Stuart Rossiter, who had been working on the Guides since 1954, became house editor, revising and compiling several of the books himself.

The Blue Guides are now published by A & C Black, who acquired Ernest Benn in 1984, so continuing the tradition of guidebook publishing which began in 1826 with 'Black's Economical Tourist of Scotland'. The Blue Guide series continues to grow: there are now more than 50 titles in print with revised editions appearing regularly and many new Blue Guides in preparation.

'Blue Guides' is a registered trade mark.

INTRODUCTION

Normandy has long fascinated the English-speaking traveller, being at once topographically, historically, even socially more accessible than the rest of France. To the early 19C English landscape painter, Richard Parkes Bonington, the Cotentin peninsula was 'remarkably like Worcestershire, although more beautiful', whilst it would be quite uncontroversial to suggest that the events of 1066 are central to the English sense of self-identity. This mutual entanglement extends beyond the sharing of names, or geology, and like the evolving countries of the British Isles the geographical boundaries of Normandy were more or less fixed by the 11C. Neither the acquisition of Normandy by the King of France in 1204 nor the division of the older provinces into *départements* in 1790 affected this geographical definition, and the limits of the Middle Ages are the limits of today.

It has in fact become customary to speak of not one but two Normandies—the sedimentary, limestone country of Haute-Normandie, and the granite country of the west, of Basse-Normandie, with their respective capitals at Rouen and Caen. The local government reorganisation of 1972, which grouped the *départements* into 22 régions, has reinforced this division and the *départements* of Seine-Maritime (with its préfecture, or 'county town', at Rouen) and Eure (with its préfecture at Evreux) were brought together to form Haute-Normandie. Basse-Normandie consists of three *départements*: Calvados, with its préfecture at Caen; Manche, with its préfecture at St-Lô; and Orne, with its préfecture at Alençon. The guide adheres to these definitions, and in keeping with the usual Blue Guide method of dividing the region into a series of routes you will find Routes 1 to 7 deal with Haute-Normandie, while Basse-Normandie is covered by Routes 8 to 17.

The majority of these routes are centred on particular towns, or explore smaller regions unified by topography or historical circumstance. They cover Normandy in a series of interlocking circuits or journeys, and are intended to be suggestive of the main points of cultural interest in any given area. It should be pointed out that the itineraries are not constructed so as to indicate a vital and orderly progression. It is unlikely that their elaborate detours along minor roads would be useful to anyone who is not spending several days in a particular *pays*, or who does not have a specific goal in mind. If you want to follow your own plan there is a detailed index of places (and a separate index of people) to enable you to use the guide in its proper role, as a secondary resource.

Driving is essential if you wish to tour a sizeable area conveniently or in any detail. The headnote to each route gives a brief summary of road directions, with distances between the main towns, and a summary of rail services where relevant (which generally means where available). Detailed road directions are confined to the text itself. The larger towns are described in some detail and the text is accordingly organised with the pedestrian in mind, with the major streets and monuments indicated on the town plans.

The descriptions of places concentrate unashamedly on their art, architecture and history, though without assuming that these belong in some special category apart from contemporary life. Equally, as the current identity and shape of Normandy owes most to its landscape and history the discussion of this is integrated into the main body of the text. For quick reference however, there is a brief chronology of Norman history on page 22. Until the Second World War Normandy boasted the densest concentration of medieval towns in northern Europe, and though the damage sustained in 1944 was real enough the urban fabric of most Norman towns and villages still reflects earlier patterns of occupation. It is even the case that modern agricultural practice, particularly in the west, relies on a landscape whose field systems and balance of woodland and pasture were largely developed in the later Middle Ages. The prosperity of Normandy is a prosperity of the Middle Ages and of the 19C and 20C. Its cultural landmarks are made up of fine churches and manor houses, of late 19C painting and post-war architecture. The 17C châteaux and 18C townscapes which are such familiar features of central France are rare here.

The rest of this section deals with practical matters: ways of getting to Normandy and travelling around it; maps; accommodation; restaurants and food; and questions of access to châteaux, churches and museums. Addresses and phone numbers of the main tourist offices, and of local Tourist Information Centres (Syndicats d'Initiative, Maisons de Tourisme) are listed on pages 16–21.

Getting to Normandy

By car and ferry. Normandy is well served by car ferries, with three major companies offering a choice of routes. **Sealink Stena Line** operate ferries from Newhaven to Dieppe (4 hour crossing time) and Southampton to Cherbourg (5 hours, though overnight crossings can take up to 8 hours). Sealink Stena Line's UK address is Charter House, Park Street, Ashford, Kent TN24 8EX. For reservations phone 0233 647047. **P&O European Ferries** sail from Portsmouth to Le Havre (approximate crossing times; 6 hours day sailings, 7 hours night sailings) and Portsmouth to Cherbourg (5 hours day sailings, 7 hours night sailings). For further information contact P&O European Ferries, The Continental Ferry Port, Mile End, Portsmouth PO2 8QW. For reservations phone 0705 827677. **Brittany Ferries** operate from Portsmouth to Caen (average crossing time 6 hours) and Poole to Cherbourg (all-year service from 1993, average crossing time 4¼ hours). For further information contact Brittany Ferries, The Brittany Centre, Wharf Road, Portsmouth PO2 8RU. For reservations phone 0705 827701. The short sea routes to Calais and Boulogne may also be useful. For information on these the above addresses and phone numbers should be supplemented with: Sally Ferries; reservations on 081 858 1127. For P&O services from Dover phone 0304 203388.

By train. The rail journey from London (Victoria) to Rouen via the Newhaven–Dieppe ferry takes approximately 8 hours, with one morning and one evening departure. Services from London Waterloo to Portsmouth Harbour do not make direct connections with the ferries to Le Havre, Caen or Cherbourg but any train scheduled to depart 3 hours prior to the sailing time would get you there in good time. You can also reach Rouen via the Dover–Calais route (change at Amiens). For southern and western Normandy it may be preferable to travel to Paris (the rail journey from London Victoria to Paris Gare du Nord takes anything from 6–10 hours). Services to Evreux, Lisieux, Argentan and Granville leave from Paris Gare St-Lazare. Further information from International British Rail Enquiries at London Victoria (phone 071 834 2345) and the UK office of SNCF (French

Railways) at 179 Piccadilly, London W1V 0BA (timetable enquiries answered on 071 491 1573).

By air. Air Vendée flies from Gatwick to Rouen and Brit Air flies from Gatwick to Caen. Air France handles all reservations and enquiries (Colet House, 100 Hammersmith, London W6 7JP; phone 081 742 6600).

Travelling around Normandy

Driving is essential if you aim to explore the region in any detail. If you are arriving by boat, both Cherbourg or Le Havre offer a number of car-hire firms, including Avis, Europcar and Hertz, while for those who intend travelling to Normandy by train the same is true for Rouen and Caen. In budgeting for driving expenses remember that petrol prices are higher in France than in the UK. The petrol stations attached to supermarkets usually offer the keenest prices. Unleaded petrol (*sans plomb* or, colloquially, *le vert*) is a bit less expensive than essence, but can still be hard to find away from the larger towns and autoroutes. The road network is generally well maintained, with the larger departmental roads (given the prefix D to distinguish them from the national system, which carry N numbers) offering fast and uncongested journeys.

The rail network is patchy away from the main Paris–Rouen–Le Havre/Dieppe or Paris–Evreux–Caen–Cherbourg lines. A reasonably fast line connects Rouen to Caen via Bernay, but as with most rural services trains are infrequent. Rail services also connect Bayeux to Coutances, Caen to Alençon, and Rouen to St-Valéry-en-Caux, while southern Normandy is served by the Dreux–Granville line. Timetable information can be obtained from any SNCF station, or from the UK office of SNCF at 179 Piccadilly, London W1Y 0BA (071 742 6600).

Cycling is also a popular way of exploring a varied region, though Normandy is hillier than is popularly supposed. Bicycles can be hired by the day or week from some Syndicats d'Initiative and most railway stations. Further information and advice about routes can be obtained from the Ligue Régionale de Normandie de Cyclotourisme, 21, Rue de l'Enseigne Renaud, 76000 Rouen (phone 35 89 45 06).

Walking has received a considerable boost from the development of a series of long-distance footpaths known as Sentiers de Grande Randonée and given route numbers commencing with a 'GR'. The finest are the GR22/223, which follow the western and northern coasts of the Cotentin from Mont-St-Michel to Barfleur, the GR2 along the Seine valley, and the GR221 through the Suisse Normande. All these paths are described in a series of 'Topoguides' published by the Fédération Française de Randonée Pédestre, 8, Avenue Marceau, 75008 Paris.

Sailing has obvious attractions in an area with as exhilarating a coastline as that of Normandy, and a superb selection of ports and marinas. The main harbours are at Le Tréport, Dieppe, St-Valéry-en-Caux, Fécamp, Le Havre, Honfleur, Deauville-Trouville, Houlgate, Ouistreham, Arromanches, Port-en-Bessin, St-Vaast, Barfleur, Cherbourg, Barneville-Carteret, and Granville. Local Syndicats d'Initiative can advise on mooring charges and boat-hire.

Maps

Michelin and the Institut Géographique National (IGN) both produce a good set of maps. The minimum useful scale is 1:250,000 (1cm to 2.5km) if you are to find all villages and most hamlets marked. Michelin's yellow regional maps are excellent at 1:200,000, though number 231 (Normandie) omits parts of southern and north-eastern Normandy and needs supplementing with numbers 236 (Nord), 237 (Ile-de-France), and 60 (Le Mans-Paris). The IGN Série Rouge number 102 (Normandie) covers the area well, though is notoriously generous in its definition of significant ruins and monuments. This again needs supplementing if you are to visit the Pays de Bray (sheet 103 will do the job). If you are walking or cycling you will need one or more of the following series of IGN maps: the Série Verte at 1:100,000 (1cm to 1km), numbers 3, 6, 7, 8, 16, 17, 18; the Série Orange at 1:50,000 (1cm to 0.5 km), or the Série Bleue at 1:25,000 (1cm to 250m). See also the remarks about the 'Topoguides' series above.

Accommodation

Hotels in France are officially classified by a system of stars, running from one to four, indicating the range of amenities offered. There are also many unstarred hotels, particularly away from the larger towns, which provide comfortable and clean accommodation. The star system is only a rough guide to prices, which vary considerably in each category, but as a general rule you would rarely pay more than FF350 for a twin room in a two-star hotel (1993 prices). Prices are usually quoted per room and not per person. Hotels often list their tariffs in the reception area, and are required by law to post the price of each room within the room itself. The figure rarely includes breakfast and in the larger towns hotels might levy a charge for off-street parking. Guests at smaller hotels would be expected to dine, so if you are watching your budget ask what the half-board rate is before commiting yourself. Most such hotels will produce excellent food at reasonable prices, but it is not unknown for modest hotels with good restaurants to charge a lot more for food than for accommodation.

The Comité Régional du Tourisme publishes a brochure listing all hotels in Normandy. This is particularly useful if you are travelling in July or August, when it may be worth booking hotels in advance. At any other time of year you are unlikely to encounter any difficulties in finding accommodation, though it would be advisable to start looking by 6.00 pm. The big hotel chains tend to be represented only in the larger cities, such as Rouen and Caen. Prices here, and in popular tourist destinations like the Côte Fleurie, are higher than in less publicised areas such as the Pays de Bray or Risle valley. Hotels of any sort are also thinner on the ground in southern Normandy, and particularly in the Perche.

The most reliable group of hotels are those belonging to Logis de France, an umbrella network of small, independent establishments rating between one and three stars. Normandy boasts 230 of them, and their distinctive emblem of a yellow fireplace on a green crest makes them easy to spot. Prices vary widely but most rooms cost between FF150 and FF350 (1993 rates). Full details are given in the annual brochure published by Logis de

Normandie, 35, rue du Dr-Oursel, 27000 Evreux (phone 32 38 21 61). The national handbook is published yearly by the Féderation Nationale des Logis de France, 83, avenue d'Italie, 75013 Paris (phone (1) 45 84 70 00). Copies can also be obtained from the French Government Tourist Office in London for £6.50. Other useful sources of information are the 'Michelin Red Guide' and the 'Routiers Guide to France' (available by post from Routiers, 25 Vanston Place, London, SW16 1AZ; phone 071 385 6644). Personal callers at the French Government Tourist Office can consult its computerised register of hotels.

Gîtes, or self-catering accommodation rented by the week, provide a convenient base in rural areas. They are particularly useful for families or groups of more than two people. Typical weekly prices for a gîte capable of housing four people are FF1000–1400 in season and FF800–1200 out of season (1993 rates). You can join the official booking service, Gîtes de France, for a small annual fee and receive its handbook of listings by contacting the French Government Tourist Office in London. Each of Normandy's five départements also has a branch of Gîtes de France which will issue listings and handle bookings. The relevant addresses are: **Calvados**: 6 promenade Mme de Sévigné, 14050 Caen (phone 31 70 25 25); **Eure**: 9 rue de la Petite Cité, BP 882, 27008 Evreux (phone 32 39 53 38); **Manche**: Maison du Département, 50008 St-Lô (phone 33 05 98 70); **Orne**: 88 rue St-Blaise, BP 50, 61002 Alençon (phone 33 28 88 71); **Seine-Maritime**: Chemin de la Bretèque, BP 59, 76232 Bois-Guillaume (phone 35 60 73 34). These services also cover chambres d'hôte (bed and breakfast), fermes auberges (farmhouse inns), campings à la ferme (farm camping), and gîtes d'étape. The Comité Régional de Tourisme publishes a list of all camping and caravan sites.

Restaurants and Food

Normandy's cuisine is less well known than those of, say, Burgundy or Provence, but its approach to cooking is distinctive and there is ample opportunity for eating well at reasonable prices. The whole region is well-endowed with rural auberges, and most larger villages boast at least one restaurant in addition to those cafés which offer snacks throughout the day and a '*plat du jour*' at lunchtime. Any town worth the name will offer a choice of restaurants and will have so organised the '*jours de fermertures*' (all restaurants must by law close on one day per week, traditionally a Monday) that on any given day two out of three will be open. The fixed price menus are almost always a better bet than eating à la carte. All restaurants offer them and most offer three or four, ranging from perhaps FF85–180 in the majority of establishments, though it is possible to spend FF500 for a seven course spectacular at one of the great '*restaurants gastronomiques*'. The choice is greater with the more expensive menus, which will generally include both cheese *and* dessert (rather than cheese *or* dessert). The set price menus are prominently displayed in the windows of most restaurants and, unless otherwise specified, exclude drinks. The service charge is included in the price but it remains the habit, if pleased, to leave a modest tip.

The two best known restaurant guides are the 'Michelin Red Guide' and the 'Routiers Guide to France', the latter offering a more comprehensive picture of the cheaper establishments. It is also worth consulting the locals, who are invariably discerning and well-practised judges. Finally, the old axiom that busy restaurants are good restaurants remains truer in France than anywhere.

Normandy is justly famous for its cheeses, apples, shellfish and poultry, traditionally taken with a bottle of '*cidre bouché*' (corked, rather than flat, cider) and rounded off with a glass of fiery Calvados. Normandy's role as the dairy of France has bequeathed an incomparable versatility when it comes to cream or butter sauces, and the staple '*Sauce Normande*'—a silky, yellow cream sauce—has inspired numerous variations to accompany poultry, eggs, fish and even game. Certain *pays* are equally renowned for particular ingredients or dishes, such as Dieppe sole, Vire chitterlings, or the rich black puddings (boudin) of Mortagne-au-Perche. The list below identifies some of the items you are most likely to encounter.

Shellfish. Coquilles Saint-Jacques à la Crème—poached scallops in a mushroom, onion and cream sauce. Gratin d'Huîtres Chaudivert—oysters with spinach, cider and fresh cream.

Fish. Sole Normande—fillets of sole in a wine, cream and shellfish sauce.

Poultry. Caneton Rouennais—roast duckling stuffed with liver and served in a creamy stock and blood sauce. Canard à la Duclair is a simpler and more rustic version of the Caneton.

Meat. Epaule à la Crème—shoulder of lamb marinaded in dry cider, calvados and onions and served with a cream sauce. Tripes à la mode de Caen—tripe slowly stewed in a stock of calves trotters and cider.

Cheese. Normandy has the distinction of exporting more cheese than any other region of France, one consequence of which is that Camembert requires little introduction. The Petits Suisses of the Pays de Bray, made by mixing fresh cream with curds, are becoming better known abroad, and are usually served in a bowl and accompanied with sugar and fruit. All Normandy cheeses are soft, Pont-l'Evêque being creamier and less pungent than Camembert, while Livarot (known colloquially as '*le colonel*' on account of the banded stripes which wrap each round) is made from milk which has stood and is accordingly sharper and more aromatic. Good unpasteurised farmhouse cheeses are, thankfully, widely available, the most highly regarded being Pavé d'Auge (a richer variant of Pont-l'Evêque) and Neufchâtel, the latter being matured for up to three months.

Pastries and sweets. Given its extensive orchards Norman cuisine has developed a number of recipes using apples or pears. The most commonly encountered are Tarte Normande, an apple pie with the apples sliced and baked, and Bourdelots—stuffed baked apples in pastry. Gourmandise Domfrontaise is a delicious confection of fresh pears baked with pear brandy and cream, but is rarely found outside south-western Normandy.

Cider and Calvados. Many restaurants, and most Normans, will recommend that you drink cider with shellfish, chicken, tripe or lamb. It is, in fact, an excellent accompaniment to most meals and the better restaurants stock an extensive range. The cider of the Pays d'Auge is the most sought-after, and expensive, but for sheer depth of flavour the local ciders of the Bocage are worth tracking down. Traditional cider, *bon bère*, is made from fermented apple juice only, its light effervescence the result of a secondary fermentation in the bottle. This is usually sold as *cidre bouché* (corked cider) and can cost anything from FF15–100 per bottle.

Calvados is an apple brandy, every bit as earnestly discussed in Normandy as is Cognac in its region. The production of Calvados (usually referred to as *'calva'*) is now strictly controlled, and only two methods of distillation are permitted; a single distillation in a continuous still or a double distillation in a pot still. The latter method is confined to the Pays d'Auge and can be identified by the *Appelation Pays d'Auge contrôllée* carried on the bottle. The former method is identified by the term *appelation réglementée*. The spirit is usually matured for up to ten years in young oak casks before being transferred to older casks and blended, although some of the Auge Calvados is aged separately. Generally speaking the singly distilled 'calva' retains a more appley flavour and usually serves to fill the *trou Normand*. This famous Norman hole is to be found in the middle of a large meal, when a pause is announced and a glass of 'calva' taken, as an aid, it is said, to the digestion. Some restaurants now substitute an apple sorbet enriched with Calvados for the old tried-and-tested routine, but the tradition lives on in household Normandy.

Visiting Châteaux, Museums and Churches

Opening times are only given in this guide where they are exceptionally restrictive, and even here it may be worth checking before going out of your way. Up-to-date information can easily be obtained from local Syndicats d'Initiative and from the annual broadsheets issued by each of the five Comités Départemontaux du Tourisme. Their addresses and phone numbers are listed on pages 16-21.

A few general rules should be remembered. Most châteaux and several museums in the smaller towns are closed outside the tourist season, which stretches from Easter to October and reaches its peak in July and August. Tuesday is the closing day for municipal museums and any properties staffed by public employees, as well as for an increasing number of privately owned properties. Smaller properties may only open in the afternoons, or at weekends, and virtually all châteaux, museums and churches close for lunch, usually from 12.00 to 14.00. Smaller village churches are often kept locked and will post a notice indicating where the key might be obtained (instructions are supplied for places mentioned in the text where this is not obvious). If not, then an enquiry at the nearest house or café will usually elicit the address of the custodian, but one should observe the proprieties and the key-holder will not appreciate being interrupted during lunch.

The annual 'Portes Ouvertes' day, usually a Sunday in September, gives the public access to Monuments Historiques (listed buildings and sites) not otherwise open, and organises special events at those that are usually open. Details are available from the Comité Régional de Tourisme de Normandie.

Access to churches and châteaux does vary enormously. The 'Monument Historique' signs which point the way to notable monuments from major roads indicate nothing more than that a building is listed. They do not signify that a place is open, or even generously inclined towards the occasional visitor. Nor, in the case of the smaller privately- owned châteaux which are the norm, do advertised opening hours constitute a guarantee; business, family affairs, or disrepair can cause owners to lock up their premises and abandon visitors to a baffled stroll around the front gate. And when access is obtained it is unlikely that you will be given free rein to wander at will. The guided tour (visité accompagnée) is still the preferred form. These usually last about an hour and tend towards the 'historical-anecdotal', though in summer the availability of bright, enthusiastic and well-informed students can transform a visit. The latter will often speak English, either conducting the tour bilingually or, if the demand is there, taking you round as a separate party. Out of season you will rarely encounter English-speaking guides, except at places such as Mont-St-Michel or Rouen.

Access to churches is more straightforward, the major complications being caused by restoration projects. Guided tours are available to all cathedrals in Normandy, and several of the larger abbeys. Details are usually posted in the west end of the nave. To visit Mont-St-Michel and the crypt and axial chapel of Rouen cathedral a guided tour is obligatory, otherwise one is free to roam, or combine a guided tour with a more leisurely exploration.

Calendar of Events

Normans are not perhaps as gregarious and sociable as the southern French, but they take as much delight in celebrating and sampling the regional fare. The list of markets and festivals below makes no pretence at covering a crowded programme fully, noting only the largest of the local fêtes. Local Tourist Offices will supply fuller details of these events, as well as the precise dates of the moveable feasts. The Comité Regional de Tourisme de Normandie publishes an annual leaflet in English, 'Normandy in your Pocket' (available by post from French Government Tourist Offices), which contains an extensive and up-to-date calendar of events on a département by départment basis.

Markets
The following is a list of the larger markets, most of which start before 9.00 am and are usually running down by lunchtime.

Mondays: Carentan, Pont-Audemer, St-Pierre-sur-Dives
Tuesdays: L'Aigle, Argentan, Soligny-la-Trappe, Villedieu-les- Poëles
Wednesdays: Flers, Le Neuborg, Villers-Bocage
Thursdays: Alençon, Coutances, La Ferté-Macé, Forges-les-Eaux
Fridays: Argentan, Caen (Place St-Saveur), Eu, Vire
Saturdays: Alençon, Avranches, Carrouges (Saturday afternoon market), Dieppe, Louviers, Mortagne-au-Perche, St-Lô
Sundays: Caen (Place Coutonne)

February
Granville: Carnival running from the previous Saturday to Shrove Tuesday

March
Mortagne-au-Perche: Black-pudding Festival (three days in mid-March)

March–April
Caen: Easter fair
Le Neubourg: Palm Sunday Agricultural Fair

April
Bernay: Flower Festival
La Ferte-Mace: Tripe Fair (end of month)
Rouen: 24 hour Boat Race, 30 April–1 May. (International competition of
motor-boats around the Ile-Lacroix)
Vascoeuil: Spring Exhibition of Contemporary Art (until June)
Vimoutiers: Paris–Camembert bike race

May
Coutances: Jazz Festival
Mont-St-Michel: Feast of St Michael on 8 May
Rouen: Festival of Joan of Arc (Sunday closest to 30 May)

May–June
Bernay: Pilgrimage to Notre-Dame-de-la-Couture (Whit Monday)
Honfleur: 'Fête des Marins' (Feast of the Sea and Sailors). Blessing of the
Sea on Whit Sunday, Sailors' Pilgrimage on Whit Monday

June
Balleroy: International Hot-Air Balloon Meeting
Cabourg: International Festival of Romantic Film (mid-June)
Côte de Nacre: Anniversary of the D-Day Landings (6 June)
Fécamp: Festival of the Trinity (9–13 June)
Mortagne-au-Perche: 'Juin Musical' (concerts held every weekend)
Ste-Mère-Eglise/Ste-Marie-du-Mont: Commemoration of the Airborne
Landings of 1044 (5–6 June)
Villedieu-les-Poëles: Festival of St John the Baptist. Procession of
Hospitallers of the Order of St John (last Sunday in June)

July
Carrouges: 'Festival autour d'un Piano' (international piano festival)
Fécamp: Festival of the Sea (early July)
Le Havre: International Regatta
La Haye-de-Routout: Bonfire of St-Clair (16 July)
Mont-St-Michel: Pilgrimage from Genêts across 'Les Greves' to
Mont-St-Michel (late July)
St-Christophe-le-Jajolet: Blessing of Cars beneath the statue of
St Christopher (last Sunday in July)

August
Deauville: Yearling Thoroughbred Sale (early August)
Deauville: Grand Prix de Deauville (major International Horse Race, 4th
Sunday in August)
Granville: 'Semaine de la Mer et grand Pardon des Corporations de la Mer'.
(Procession of the Guilds, maritime events. First week in August.)
Jobourg: Sheep Fair (early August)
St-Lô: Parade of Horses at the National Stud (Haras National. Every
Thursday at 3.00pm)
Lisieux: Foire aux Picots (Turkey Fair, early August)

St-Vaast-la-Hougue: Regattas (mid-August)
Tocqueville: 'Fête de St-Gorgon' (auction sale of church candles, late August)
Valognes: the Valogne Concerts (week-long music festival, mid-August)

September
Alençon: Normandy-Maine Agricultural Show (3 days in mid-September)
Les Andelys: Fair (general fair in mid-September)
Deauville: American film festival (first week of September)
Caudebec-en-Caux: Cider Festival (held bi-annually in even years, last Sunday in September)
Dieppe: International Kite flying Festival (mid-September)
Lessay: Foire de la Ste-Croix. (Horse and dog show held on 'La Lande', the low moor outside the village. Together with the agricultural stalls, amusement fair and subsidiary entertainments it makes for the biggest fair in Normandy. Second weekend in September.)
Lisieux: Feast of Ste-Thérèse of Lisieux (last Sunday in September)
Mont-St-Michel: Feast of the Archangel Michael (Sunday closest to 29 September)

October
Elbeuf: Autumn Festival (gastronomic fair held during the first weekend of October)
Le Neubourg: Marches aux Foies Gras (Wednesday markets in October and November)
Vimoutiers: Apple Festival (three days in mid-October)

November
Dieppe: Herring Fair (weekend in mid-November)
Sainte-Opportune: Apple Market (first Sunday of each month, November–April)

December
Evreux: St Nicholas Fair (Sunday in early December)
Sées: Turkey Fair (mid-December)

Tourist Information Centres and other useful addresses

French Government Tourist Offices abroad

UK: 178 Piccadilly, London W1V 0AL. Phone 071 491 7622; fax 493 6594.

USA, New York: 610 Fifth Avenue, Suite 222, New York NY 10020. Phone 757 1125; fax 247 6468.

USA, Middle West: 645 North Michigan Avenue, Chicago, Illinois 60611. Phone 337 6301; fax 337 6339.

USA West Coast: 9545 Wilshire Boulevard, Beverly Hills, California 90212. Phone 271 7838; fax 276 2835.

USA South: 2305 Cedar Springs Boulevard, Dallas, Texas 75201. Phone 720 4010; fax 720 0250.

Canada, Montreal: 181 Avenue McGill College, Suite 490, Montreal, Quebec H3A 2W9. Phone: 288 4264; fax 845 4868.

Canada, Toronto: 30 Saint Patrick Street, Suite 700, Toronto, Ontario, M5T 3A3. Phone??

For Normandy as a whole

Comité Régional de Tourisme de Normandie, 46 Avenue Foch, 27000 Evreux. Phone 32 31 05 89; fax 32 31 19 04.

For the departments

Basse-Normandie

Calvados: Comité Départemental du Tourisme, Centre Administratif, Place du Canada, 14000 Caen. Phone 31 86 53 30; telex 171 343.

Manche: Office Départemental du Tourisme, BP 419, 50009 Saint-Lô Cedex. Phone 33 05 98 70; telex 170 652.

Orne: Comité Départemental du Tourisme, BP 50, 88 rue St Blaise, 61002 Alençon Cedex. Phone 33 26 18 71; telex 171 556

Haute-Normandie

Eure: Comité Départemental du Tourisme, BP 187, 35 rue du Dr OUrsel, 27001 Evreux Cedex. Phone 32 38 21 61.

Comité Départmental du Tourisme, B.P. 666, 2bis rue du Petit-Salut, 76008 Rouen Cedex. Phone 35 88 61 32; telex 770 940.

Local Tourist Information Centres (Syndicats d'Initiative and Offices du Tourisme

Agon Coutainville 50230, Place du 28 Juillet.
Aigle (L') 61300, Boîte Postale no. 79.
Alençon 61003, Maison d'Ozé, Boîte Postale no. 93.
Andelys (Les) 27700, Boûte Postale no. 31.
Argentan 61200, Boîte Postale no. 62.
Arromanches 14370, Place du 6 juin.
Asnelles 14960.
Auffay 76720, Mairie. Phone 35 32 81 53.
Aumale 76390, rue Centrale. Phone 35 93 41 68.
Aunay-sur-Odon 14260.
Avranches 50300, 2 rue du Général de Gaulle.

Bagnoles-de-l'Orne 61140, Boîte Postale no. 32.
Barenton 50720.
Balleroy 14470, rue du Sapin.
Barfleur 50760, rue Thomas Becket.
Barneville-Carteret 50270.
Bayeux 14400, 1 rue des Cuisiniers.
Beaumont Hague 50440, Place de la Mairie.
Beaumont-le-Roger 27170, Place de Clercq.
Bellème 61130, Boulevard Bansard du Bois.
Benerville 14800, Mairie.
Bernay 27300, BP 29 rue Thiers.
Bernières-sur-Mer 14990, 159 rue V. Tesnières.

Beuzeville 27210, Mairie.
Blainville-sur-Mer 50910.
Blang-sur-Bresle 76340, Hôtel-de-Ville, 76340. Phone 35 93 52 48.
Blangy-le-Château 14130, Mairie.
Blonville-sur-Mer 14910.
Brécey 50370.
Brehal 50290.
Breteuil sur Iton 27160, Bordigny.
Bretteville sur Ay 50430, rue de la Mer.
Bricquebec 50260, Place Sainte-Anne.
Brionne 27800, 6 Place Lorraine.
Broglie 27270, Route de St-Aubin au Thenney.

Cabourg 14930.
Caen 14000, Hôtel d'Escoville.
Canisy 50750.
Cambremer 14340.
Camembert 61120, Mairie.
Carentan 50500, Mairie.
Carolles 50740.
Carrouges 61320, Boîte Postale no. 10.
Caudebec-en-Caux 76490, Quai Guilbaud. Phone 35 96 11 12.
Cerences 50510, Mairie.
Cerisy-la-Salle 50210 Mairie.
Chambois 61160, Mairie.
Champeaux 50530.
Chapelle Montligeon (La) 61400, Mairie.
Cherbourg 50102, 2 Quai Alexandre III.
Clécy 14570.
Clères 76690, S.I. du Haut-Cailly, Mairie. Phone 35 33 23 31.
Colleville Montgomery 14880, Mairie.
Colleville-sur-Mer 14710, Mairie.
Conches-en-Ouche 27190, Poîte Postale no. 59.
Condé-sur-Noireau 14110.
Cormeilles 27260.
Courseulles 14470.
Courtomer 61390, Mairie.
Coutances 50200, rue Quesnel-Morinière.
Criel-sur-Mer 76910, Mairie. Phone 35 50 96 65.

Deauville 14800, Place de l'Hôtel de Ville, Boîte Postale no. 79.
Denneville 50580.
Dieppe 76204, Pont Jehan-Ango, BP 152. Phone 35 84 11 77; fax 35 06 27 66.
Dives-sur-Mer 14160, Avenue du Général-de-Gaulle.
Domfront 61700, 52 rue du Dr Barrabé.
Donville-les-Bains 50350, 80 Route de Coutances.
Duclair 76480, Hôtel-de-Ville. Phone 35 37 50 06.

Ecouché 61150, Place du Général Warabiot.
Elbeuf 76504, CCI 28 rue Henry, BP 465. Phone 35 77 02 16; fax 35 78 98 93.
Essay 61500, Hôtel du Relais Fleuri.
Etretat 76790, Place de la Mairie. Phone 35 27 05 21.
Eu 76260, 41 rue Paul-Bignon, BP 82. Phone 35 86 04 68.
Evreux 27000, Place du Général-de-Gaulle.

Ezy sur Eure 27530, 16 rue Isambard.

Falaise 14700, 32 rue G. Clémenceau.
Fécamp 76400, 113 rue Alexandre-Le-Grand, BP 112. Phone 35 28 51 01;
fax 35 27 07 77. 76400, 12 Place Bellet, BP 4. Phone 35 28 20 51.
Fermanville 50840, Le Château-Houivet.
Ferté Macé (La) 61600, Boîte Postale no. 3.
Feuillie (La) 76220, Mairie. Phone 35 09 68 03; fax 35 09 03 83.
Flers 61100, 4 rue Henri-Véniard.
Forges-les-Eaux 76440, Pavillon Louis XIII, Parc Hôtel de Ville.
Phone 35 90 52 10; fax 35 90 34 80.
Foucarmont 76340, Mairie. Phone 35 93 70 36.

Gacé 61230, 21 rue de Matignon.
Gaillon 27600, Boîte Postale no. 73.
Gavray 50450, 1 rue St André
Gisors 27140, 3 rue Baléchoux.
Gournay-en-Bray 76220, Square Pierre-Petit. Phone 35 90 28 34.
Gouville-sur-Mer 50560.
Grandcamp Maisy 14450, rue du Fort Samson.
Grandes-Dalles (Les) 76540. Phone 35 27 40 74.
Granville 50400, 6 Cours Jonville.
Graverie (La) 14350.

Hauteville sur Mer 50590, Avenue de l'Aumesle.
Havre (Le) 76059, Place de l'Hôtel-de-Ville, BP 649. Phone 35 21 22 88;
fax 35 42 38 39.
Haye-Pesnel (La) 50320, Place de l'Hôtel-de-Ville.
Haye-du-Puits (La) 50250, Mairie.
Hermanville-sur-Mer 14880, Mairie.
Home-Varaville (Le) 14390, Mairie.
Honfleur 14600, Chambre de Commerce.
Houlgate 14510, 26 rue H. Dobert.

Isigny sur Mer 14230, 10 Place de l'Hôtel de Ville.

Jullouville 50610, Place de la Gare.

Langrune-sur-Mer 14830, Mairie.
Lessay 50430, Mairie.
Lillebonne 76170, 4 rue Pasteur. Phone 35 38 06 36.
Lion-sur-Mer 14780, rue Bertin.
Lisieux 14100, rue d'Alençon.
Livarot 14140.
Londinieres 76660, Mairie. Phone 35 93 80 08.
Longny-au-Perche 61290, Hôtel de Ville.
Louviers 27400, 10 rue Maréchal-Foch.
Luc-sur-Mer 14530, Mairie.
Lyons-la-Forêt 27480.

Mauves-sur-Huisne 61400, 11 rue Catinat.
Mele-sur-Sarthe (Le) 61170, Mairie.
Merville Franceville 14810.
Mesnil Hubert sur Orne 61430.
Mont-Saint-Michel (Le) 50116.
Montebourg 50310, Place de Gaulle.

Montmartin-sur-Mer 50590, Mairie.
Mortagne-au-Perche 61400, Place du Général de Gaulle.
Mortain 50140, Mairie.
Moulins la Marche 61380, Mairie.

Neubourg (Le) 27110, Cour du Grand St-Martin.
Neufchâtel-en-Bray 76270, 6 Place Notre-Dame. Phone 35 93 22 96.
Neuve Lyre (La) 27330.
Nonancourt 27320.

Orbec 14290, Mairie.
Ouistreham-Riva-Bella 14150, Pavillon Réception.

Pacy-sur-Eure 27120, Boîte Postale no. 22.
Percy 50410, Mairie.
Perrière (La) 61360, Mairie.
Petites-Dalles (Les) 76540, 'Le Clos de Vinchigny'. Phone 35 97 94 90.
Pieux (Les) 50340, Mairie.
Pirou 50770, Mairie.
Pont Audemer 27500, Boîte Postale no. 405.
Pont d'Ouilly 14690, Mairie.
Pont l'Evêque 14130, Mairie.
Pontorson 50170, Place de l'Eglise.
Port-en-Bessin 14520.
Portbail 50580, rue du Père Albert.
Pourville-Varengeville 76550, Manoir de Pourville. Phone 35 84 71 06.

Quettehou 50630, Place de la Mairie.
Quiberville-sur-Mer 76860, Mairie. Phone 35 04 21 33.
Quinéville 50310.

Rabodanges 61210, Cidex 2608.
Regneville-sur-Mer 50112, Mairie.
Remalard 61110, 'Le Hêtre Pourpre'.
Rouen 76008, 25 Place de la Cathédrale, BP 666. Phone 35 71 41 77;
fax 35 98 55 50.
Rugles 27250, 17 rue Paul-Doumer.
Ry 76116, S.I. des Trois Vallées, Maison de l'Abreuvoir. Phone 35 23 40 74.

St-Aubin-sur-Mer 14750, rue Pasteur.
St-Georges du Vievre 27450, Mairie.
St-Germain-sur-Ay 50430.
St-Hilaire-du-Harcouet 50600, Mairie.
St-James 50240, rue de la Libération.
St-Jean-le-Thomas 50530, Place du Général de Gaulle.
Saint-Lô 5000, 2 rue Havin.
Ste-Marguerite-sur-Mer 76119, Mairie. Phone 35 85 12 34.
Ste-Marie-du-Mont 50790.
Ste-Mère-Eglise 50480, rue Cap de Laine.
St-Pair-sur-Mer 50380, Place de l'Eglise.
St-Pierre-Eglise 50330.
St-Pierre-en-Port 76540, rue de la Mairie. Phone 35 27 42 56.
St-Pierre-sur-Dives 14170, Mairie.
St-Saens (Forêt d'Eawy) 76680, Mairie BP 2. Phone 35 34 51 19.

St-Sauveur-le-Vicomte 50390, Mairie.
St-Sauveur-Lendelin 50490.
Ste-Scolasse-sur-Sarthe 61170, Mairie.
St-Valéry-en-Caux 76460, Maison Henri IV, Quai du Havre, BP 24.
Phone 35 97 00 63.
St-Vaast-la-Hougue 50550, Quai Vauban.
Sap (Le) 61470, Boîte Postale no. 11.
Sartilly 50530.
Sées 61500, Place du Général de Gaulle.
Soligny-la-Trappe, 61380, Mairie.
Sourdeval 50150.
Surtainville 50270.

Thury Harcourt 14220, 2 Place St-Sauveur.
Tinchebray 61800, 49 bis, route de Paris.
Tourouvre 61190, Place de la Mairie.
Tréport (Le) 76470, Quai Sadi-Carnot, BP 27. Phone 35 86 05 69.
Troarn 14670, Mairie.
Trouville 14360, Place Foch.
Trun 61160, Mairie.

Val-de-Reuil 27100, Boîte Postale no. 418.
Vallée-de-la-Saane 76890, Mairie. Phone 35 32 41 58.
Vallée-du-Dun 76740, Mairie. Phone 35 83 03 16.
Valmont 76540, Mairie. Phone 35 28 06 93.
Valognes 50700, Place du Château.
Ver-sur-Mer 14114, Mairie.
Verneuil-sur-Avre 27130, 461 rue Gustave-Flaubert.
Vernon 27200, 36 rue Carnot.
Veules-les-Roses 76980, 11 rue du Dr Giraud. Phone 35 97 63 05.
Veulettes 76450, Maison de la Mer. Phone 35 97 51 33.
Vierville-St-Laurent 14115, Mairie.
Villedieu-les-Poëles 50800, Mairie.
Villers-sur-Mer 14640, Mairie.
Villerville 14113, Mairie.
Vimoutiers 61120, 10 Avenue de Général de Gaulle.
Vire 14500, Square de la Résistance.

Yvetot 76190, Place Victor-Hugo. Phone 35 95 08 40.
Yport 76111, 18 Place J.P. Laurens, BP 14. Phone 35 29 77 31.

Chronology of Norman History

56 BC	Julius Caesar defeats the Gallic tribe of the Unelli near Carentan
298 AD	Emperor Constantius Chlorus expands Coutances
c 386	Bishopric of Sées founded
393	St-Victrice builds a church on the site of Rouen cathedral
c 450	Vandals destroy Evreux
c 485–c 500	Franks, under Clovis, begin occupying eastern Normandy
654	St-Philibert founds a Benedictine monastery at Jumièges
709	Archangel Michael appears to Aubert, bishop of Avranches, ordering the foundation of an oratory on Mont-Tombe (Mont-St-Michel)
800	First Viking raids along the Channel coast
841	Oger the Dane sacks Rouen, Jumièges destroyed
876	Wrolf the Walker leads a Norse invasion fleet along the Seine
911	King Charles the Simple grants lordship of Normandy to Wrolf at Saint-Clair-sur-Epte
c 912	Wrolf baptised at Rouen, taking the name Rollo and adopting the title Duke of Normandy
933	Duke William Longsword annexes the Cotentin to Normandy
966	Benedictine monks introduced to Mont-St-Michel
1003	William of Volpiano arrives to establish monastic reform in the duchy
1027	William, conqueror of England, born at Falaise
c 1045	Lanfranc founds the School of Bec
1047–50	Robert Guiscard captures Calabria
1066	Duke William conquers England
1067	Notre-Dame de Jumièges consecrated
1087	William the Conqueror buried in Caen
1106	Robert Curthose deposed as Duke of Normandy by Henry I, King of England
1120	White Ship wrecked off Barfleur drowning Henry I's heir, William Atheling
1150	Future Henry II of England succeeds Geoffrey Plantagenet as Duke of Normandy
1196–98	Richard the Lionheart builds Château-Gaillard
1204	King John loses Normandy to Philip Augustus, King of France. Duchy of Normandy absorbed into the Kingdom of France
c 1250	Coutances cathedral completed
1315	'Charte aux Normands' guarantees the liberty of the Exchequer of Normandy to raise and spend taxes without interference from the French crown
1333	King Philip VI of France revives the title Duke of Normandy for his son, Jean de Valois
1346	King Edward III of England invades Normandy
1360	Edward III renounces his claims to Normandy at the Treaty of Bretigny, but retains the Channel Islands
1364–84	Du Guesclin campaigns on behalf of the French crown against the Norman ambitions of Charles le Mauvais.

1415	King Henry V of England victorious at Agincourt
1419	Rouen falls to Henry V
1431	Joan of Arc burnt at the stake in Rouen
1437	Foundation of Caen University
1449	King Charles VII of France enters Rouen
1450	English expelled from Normandy after the Battle of Formigny
1494–1510	Georges d'Amboise is Cardinal-Archbishop of Rouen
1504	Jean Cossart completes the north transept of Evreux cathedral
1517	François I founds a new town at Le Havre
1524–30	Dieppe fleet of Jehan Ango engaged in the maritime war with Portugal
c 1530–50	Nave clerestory glass installed at Notre-Dame, Alençon
1594	Nicolas Poussin born at Les Andelys
c 1620–65	Reforming monks of the Congregation of St-Maur begin to repopulate declining Norman abbeys
1668–84	Abraham Duquesne remodels Honfleur
1692	French fleet sunk off St-Vaast-la-Houge
1704	Guillaume de la Tremblaye designs the conventual quarters of St-Etienne, Caen
1789	French Revolution
1793	Defeat of de Rochejaquelin's Vendéen army at Granville marks the end of the pro-royalist 'Chouan' uprising in Normandy
c 1815–25	English colony becomes established at Dieppe
1859	Deauville laid out as a planned resort
1883–1926	Claude Monet at Giverny
1942	Dieppe Raid
1944	D-Day landings and Battle for Normandy
1972	Reorganisation of local government leads to the creation of the *régions* of Haute-Normandie and Basse-Normandie

Dukes of Normandy

911–933	Rollo
933–942	William Longsword
942–996	Richard I
996–1026	Richard II
1026–1028	Richard III
1028–1035	Robert the Magnificent
1035–1087	William the Bastard (known, after 1066, as 'the Conqueror')
1087–1106	Robert Curthose
1106–1135	Henry I (Beauclerc)
1135–1151	Geoffrey Plantagenet
1151–1189	Henry II
1189–1199	Richard the Lionheart
1199–1204	John (known as 'Lackland' after his loss of Normandy to Philip Augustus in 1204)

Further Reading

This is not intended as a bibliography, but as an informal list of suggestions which concentrates as much as possible on works in English.

History. The early medieval duchy of Normandy has understandably attracted the most attention. Eleanor Searle's 'Predatory Kinship and the Creation of Norman Power' (Univ. of California, 1988) is a well-researched study of the period leading up to the invasions of southern Italy and England. David Bates' 'William the Conqueror' (London, 1989) and 'The Rise of Normandy' (London, 1948) give the best accounts of the events of 1066, while John le Patourel's 'Normandy and England 1066–1144' deals well with Anglo-Norman relations. The later Middle Ages are admirably treated by Guy Bois, whose 'The Crisis of Feudalism' (Cambridge, 1984) focuses on the economy and society of the Pays de Caux. A more conventionally political treatment of a significant period can be found in Richard Newall's 'The English Conquest of Normandy 1416–24' (1971). Jonathan Dewald's 'The Formation of a Provincial Nobility' (Princeton, 1980) belies its origins as a doctoral thesis and gives a lucid account of 16C Rouen, while Olwen Hufton's 'Bayeux in the Late 18th Century' (Oxford, 1967) is a superbly detailed case-study, whose lessons might be applied across the region.

A plethora of books dealing with Normandy during the Second World War have appeared since 1944. W.G.F. Jackson's 'Overlord: Normandy 1944' (1978) provides a reasonable overview, while Anne Grimshaw's 'D-Day' (London, 1988) is the most recent of many such surveys. Belfield and Essame's 'The Battle for Normandy' (published in paperback by Pan, 1967) remains much the best general account of the fighting, and makes excellent use of diaries and letters to give a keen sense of the battle at various different levels.

Art and Architecture. Surprisingly little has been published in English, excepting articles in specialist academic journals, a situation which, sadly, is unlikely to change for some time. The two volumes of Lucien Musset's 'Normandie Romane' (Zodiaque, 3rd edition 1987) contain a précis in English and are handsomely illustrated, though the text itself may disappoint the scholarly. David Wilson's monograph 'The Bayeux Tapestry' (Thames and Hudson, 1985) is beautifully illustrated and illuminatingly written, while the relevant entries in Grodecki and Brissac's 'Gothic Stained Glass: 1200–1300' (Thames and Hudson, 1985) and Jean Bony's 'French Gothic Architecture of the 12th and 13th Centuries' (Univ. of California, 1983) might be profitably consulted. The same can be said for Wim Swaan's 'Art and Architecture of the Late Middle Ages' (Omega books, 1982), a seriously neglected area of study when it comes to Normandy. Anthony Blunt's 'Art and Architecture in France 1500–1700' (Penguin, 2nd edition 1981) contains a useful discussion of the patronage of Georges d'Amboise.

There is a considerable body of less accessible material, among which two pieces should be singled out. Sara Jones' article on the ducal tomb at La Trinité, Fécamp; 'The 12th Century Reliefs from Fécamp (Journal of the British Archaeological Association, 1985), and Lindy Grant's doctoral thesis, 'Gothic Architecture in Normandy c 1150–c 1250' (London University, 1987, the unpublished manuscript may be consulted at Senate House Library).

Travel books. Nesta Roberts' 'Companion Guide to Normandy' (Collins, 1980) and the Michelin Green Guides (divided into two volumes: Normandy Seine valley, and Normandy Cotentin) are the only reasonably up-to-date general guides in English. Of the more specialised material Eddy Florentin's guide to the D-Day beaches, 'Gateway to Victory' (Historia/Tallander, 1987) is to be commended.

Works in French. Here you are spoilt for choice. Ruprich-Robert's magnificently illustrated two-volume study, 'L'Architecture Normande' of 1889, was reprinted in Paris in 1971, and remains the best source of detailed architectural drawings. More specialised areas are well-served by the appropriate volumes of 'Le Guide des Châteaux de France' (Hermé) and 'L'Architecture Rurale Française: Corpus des Genres, des Types et des Variants (Berger-Levrault). For ecclesiastical architecture the relevant section of the 'Dictionnaire des Eglises de France' is No. IV—Normandie (Paris, 1968). G. de Knyff's 'Eugène Boudin Raconté par Lui-Même' (Mayer, 1976) and J.P. Crespella's 'La Vie Quotidienne des Impressionistes' (Hachette, 1985) remain the most pertinent treatments of 19C painting in Normandy. Finally, the 'Guide Bleu: Normandie' (Hachette, 1988) must be warmly recommended as a model of clarity and a mine of detailed information.

Glossary

ABACUS. Flat slab seated above a capital.

APSE-AMBULATORY. Semicircular aisle terminating a church to the east, generally used for processional purposes.

APSE-ECHELON. Arrangement of apses forming an inverted V at the east end of a church.

BARBICAN. A defensive work attached to the outside of a town or castle, particularly applied to a double-tower erected over a bridge or gate.

BURH. Early medieval rectangular town enclosure.

COLOMBIER. Dovecot.

CORBEL. Projecting block, usually stone, supporting a beam, roof, or shaft.

DADO. Portion of interior wall between the pavement and the lowest windowsill.

DONJON. Fortified tower (origin of the English term 'dungeon').

EXTRADOS. Outer surface of an arch.

FAIENCE. Glazed earthenware of porcelain.

GRIMOIRE. Manuscript containing a miscellaneous collection of spells, potions, recipes etc.

GRISAILLE. Monochrome painting, the term often applied to lightly tinted stained glass.

IMBRICATED. Covered with scale-like patterns, having the appearance of overlapping roof-tiles.

LOUVRE. Overlapping wooden shutter designed to admit air and exclude rain.

LUNETTE. Semicircular opening beneath an arch or vault.

OPUS LISTATUM. Walling formed of alternating courses of stone, brick or tile; usually arranged in decorative patterns.

PETIT APPAREIL. Small pieces of stone, semi-dressed and roughly coursed.

PILIER CANTONEE. Pier with four attached shafts on the cardinal faces.

REDOUBT. A small forward defensive work acting as an outstation to a castle.

REMOIS PASSAGE. Passage standing above a dado and hollowed out in the thickness of the wall.

RETABLE. Painted or carved screen standing on or beneath an altar.

SOFFIT ROLL. Roll moulding carried round the undersurface of an arch.

SPANDREL. Triangular space between the side of an arch and the adjacent horizontals and verticals.

STRINGCOURSE. Horizontal band dividing one register from another.

TIERCERON. Any rib in a vault, other than the transverse or diagonal, which connects the wall with the crown.

TREFOIL PLAN. East end of a church in which the transepts, as well as the choir, are given apsidal terminations.

TRIBUNE. Spacious gallery, usually situated above the aisles of a church (often mistakenly used to describe any intermediate storey of the elevation).

TRIFORIUM. Arcaded wall-passage found between the arcade and clerestory of a church elevation.

TRUMEAU. Post or statue supporting the centre of a lintel.

VANITAS. Moralising still-life in which objects are arranged to suggest the transience and uncertainty of life.

VOLUTE. Curved scroll or leaf-tip at the corner of a capital.

VOUSSOIR. Wedge-shaped stone around an arch.

1

Dieppe and the Pays de Caux

ROAD (91km): Dieppe, D75, 19km St-Aubin-sur-Mer; D68, 7km Veules-les-Roses; D925 8km St-Valery-en-Caux; 12km Cany-Barville; D50 8km Ourville-en-Caux; D150 7km Valmont; 11km Fécamp; D211 20km Etretat.

The Pays de Caux consists of a weathered chalk plateau covered by a thick layer of clay and alluvial mud, and forming a rough triangle bounded by the Channel coast, the lower Seine valley and the Pays de Bray. Away from either the coast or the Seine valley it is a sparsely populated region, the monotony of its wind-blasted levels relieved by the occasional fortified farmhouse or hamlet. Seen from a distance these farms take on the appearance of walled baileys, planted behind a banked circuit of rubble and earth walls from which sprout great stands of oak or beech. Entry is by a breach, often graced with a monumental porch, which brings you into a spacious grassy court, up to 2.5 hectares (6 acres) in size, where the cattle might be wintered and sheltered from the prevailing westerlies, or indeed protected from the rustlers who in medieval times plagued this area.

The Seine valley (see Route 3) and coastal reaches are, by contrast, characterised by dense pockets of housing which grew on the back of the fishing industry, or the increased trade generated by the commercial skills of such men as Jehan Ango at Dieppe or François I in Le Havre. This stretch of coast, from Le Tréport in the Pays de Bray to the hills above Le Havre, is known as the Côte d'Albâtre, or Alabaster Coast, and its underlying chalk, interspersed with flint and yellowish marls, has conspired with the sea to form an often spectacular cliffscape.

DIEPPE. A port has existed on this site since the 6C when Saxon invaders recognised the advantages to be gained from the deep channel cut by the estuary of the Arques. By the 9C this settlement was known as Bertheville, in deference to Charlemagne's mother who came from the area. The Norse raiders who capitalised on the declining authority of a weak Carolingian monarchy changed this conferring the Germanic word 'deep' on the harbour, and under their Norman and Anglo-Norman successors the town prospered. Philip Augustus considered it sufficiently well-endowed to constitute a serious threat during his campaigns against Richard the Lionheart, and razed Dieppe to the ground, destroying all the shipping at port. After this disaster it was rebuilt as a walled seaport comparable to Saint-Malo. Its fortunes fluctuated during the late Middle Ages, passing into English hands after Agincourt, when retribution was sought for the support the Dieppois navy offered the French crown at the naval battle of 1372 fought off La Rochelle. This particularly brutal yoke was lifted in 1435 when Charles des Marets led a successful uprising and captured both town and castle.

Liberty under an expansively-minded French monarchy clearly benefited the town, and during the late 15th and 16C Dieppe's ships and sailors plied the oceans of the world. Jean Cousin's discovery of Brazil in 1488 offered fresh trading opportunities and was followed by a rash of Atlantic voyages under the brothers Parmentier and the Florentine mariner Verrazano, who sailed up the mouth of the Hudson and named the future New York Le Pays d'Angoulême. The most outstanding of these seafarers was **Jehan Ango**. Born in Dieppe to a family of wealthy shipowners in 1480, Ango succeeded in building a fleet of over 100 ships and, employing Verrazano as his chief navigator, established a far-flung trading estate. Honours and wealth followed, and as maritime adviser to François I, Ango was entrusted with devising a strategy to combat the Portuguese monopoly on trade with West Africa. Ango constructed a fleet of privateers 'such as would make a king tremble', and within six years had captured over 300 Portuguese vessels. Portugal, concerned for the future viability of her merchant fleet, finally compromised on the matter in 1530, and on payment of a hefty sum persuaded François I to withdraw his letters of marque. Ango briefly stepped back from the world of maritime politics and built himself two grand seigneurial residences: a now-destroyed wooden house in Dieppe, and a splendid summer palace at Varengeville. After making the largest contribution towards the ransoming of François I in 1534 Ango was made

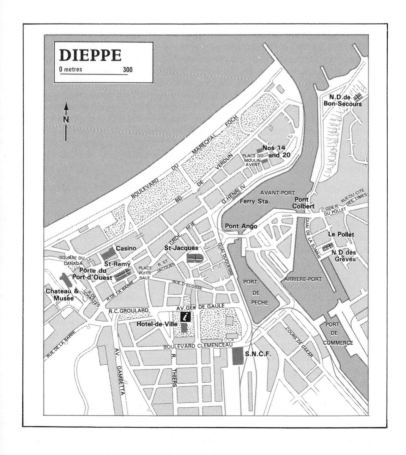

Governor of Dieppe, but the generosity of the gesture crippled his later years and the period up to his death in 1551 was riven by financial crises.

The 17C sadly disfigured the affluent trading port and following the devastating plague of 1668–70, in which between 6000 and 10,000 died, the English fleet under the command of Lord Berkeley bombarded the town. 'If we had been in the town, nobody hindering us, we could not have burned it better' Berkeley reported, and along with the 2000 buildings destroyed in the three-day barrage went the whole of the harbour area and every secular medieval building except the castle.

Recovery seems to have been slow but the establishment of the Channel Packet Service in the early 18C brought a new and lucrative passenger port, albeit one where the ships were under British control. The Quai Henri IV was laid out and a new boulevard, known as the Grande Rue, driven through the town by the engineer de Ventabren. These improvements served the shipmasters John Chapman and Samuel Barton during the Revolutionary Terror when the service between Dieppe and Brighton provided the main escape route to England. The influence of Brighton, and the English, had a marked effect on the development of the town as a fashionable resort throughout the 19C. The emergence of an English colony after 1815 prepared the way for the inauguration of an 'Etablissement des Bains' and the opening of a casino in emulation of those at Brighton. The visit of Marie-Caroline de Bourbon in 1824 ensured aristocratic patronage and the English moved over in force, attaching a library and reading room to the casino and tearooms to the Promenade. Even the broad lawns which separate the Promenade from the pebble beach were initially planned as a Jardin Anglais by the Empress Eugénie in the course of a stay in Dieppe in 1853 with her husband, Napoleon III. The trees were sadly never planted and Eugénie transferred her affections to Trouville and Biarritz, but the lawns and flower beds remain, enhancing the splendid sweep of the beach.

The best place to begin a detailed exploration of the town is in the Place St-Jacques where the parish church of **St-Jacques** marks out a history of Dieppois prosperity, with a 12C nave, 14C porch and early 16C fan of eastern radiating chapels. It was the growth of trade with England during the mid-12C which led to the expansion of the town to the south of the port and thus to the establishment of a new quarter in the immediate vicinity of the church. By a charter of 1182 Henry II undertook the foundation of a collegiate church where the old chapel of Ste-Catherine stood, the choice of titular dedication perhaps motivated by the growing number of English pilgrims travelling to Compostela by way of Dieppe. The burning of the town by Philip Augustus in 1195 largely destroyed this church however, and of the present building only the masonry core of the transepts survives from Henry's foundation. Rebuilding was not undertaken until 1250 and a further humbling blow was struck in 1282 when the college of canons was dissolved and the structure was adopted as a parish church.

Although piecemeal the subsequent building programmes illustrate the responses of a wealthy parish to changing architectural fashions. The nave arcade and aisles take up the Chartrain 'pilier cantonée', and like the lower part of the choir date from 1250. Of interest here is the richer treatment accorded to the choir where the pier profiles are considerably more complex. In 1339 however the lantern tower collapsed taking with it the adjacent bays of the transept and nave. Damage to the choir was seemingly slight and here the superstructure was repaired, but advantage was taken of the situation in the nave which was surrounded by airy batteries of flying buttresses and provided with a new upper elevation (the present clerestory windows are 15C inserts) and west front. It was not until the late 15C that the modest east end was enriched with a glazed triforium and clerestory, the pendant vault being thrown in 1543, by which time the wealthy shipowners of Dieppe were beginning to pour money into their parish church.

The evidence for this wealth lies in the superb displays of stonecarving with which the ambulatory chapels were faced. Their splendour was shortlived for in 1562 a deputation of Huguenots gained entry to the church and, during a nocturnal rampage, smashed the freestanding statuary. The damage was perhaps gravest in the **axial chapel** where eight early 16C figures once stood beneath elaborate baldacchini set between the windows. Nevertheless a delicate stone fretwork of traceries and crockets, reminiscent of that on the west front of Caudebec, frames the mutilated bas-reliefs which depict the Incarnation and Infancy of Christ. Amidst the backgrounds of familiar townscapes evidence of original paintwork testifies to the interaction of architecture, sculpture, painting, and glass which would have seen the chapel shimmer with imagery. As the stone and glass decay before the onslaught of car exhausts and seagulls, this becomes a considerable effort of imaginative projection and the carving on the exterior is now catastrophically eroded.

To the south the **Chapel of St-Yves** was refurbished by Jehan Ango and extended to house an oratory from which he might hear the Mass. Immediately above the flattened arch of the door you can see Ango's crest, a lion above a compass star, carried by two playful 'angelots' or retainers, while towards the base a bearded and pot-bellied Pan plays a viol. Ango was buried in the chapel in 1551, although his tomb has since been lost. He may also have been posthumously responsible for the arrival at St-Jacques of one of the most important examples of Renaissance secular sculpture to have survived in France. This is the extraordinary carved wall separating the sacristy from the north choir aisle. An early tradition has it that after the destruction of Ango's great townhouse in the naval bombardment of 1694 this frieze was rescued and brought to the church, where it was mounted in its present position. It was produced shortly after 1535 and depicts the peoples of Brazil and the East Indies, presumably as witnessed by Ango himself. From left to right the carvings represent: scenes from family life; war and punishment; a child, or perhaps bride, carried on a stretcher towards a fête; music and dance.

Otherwise it is the **west front** which holds the attention. The south-west tower was added in the late 15C and the rose window is a sensitive replacement of that lost in 1694, but the portal and main block were undertaken after 1339. It is thickened out at the base so as to project in front of the aisles and becomes progressively lighter the higher it climbs, culminating in a freestanding gable of open tracery. It is best seen at an oblique angle, preferably to the north-west, for here the continuity sought between the bulky pier buttresses and the later nave supports unfolds with absolute clarity.

Opposite the west front the Rue St-Jacques leads to the Place Puits Salé, at the very heart of Dieppe, overshadowed by the 18C façade of the Café des Tribunaux. A right turn onto the Rue du 19 Août 1942 will bring you to the crumbling east end of **St-Rémy**. Built between 1522 and 1645 it is graced by five radiating chapels which, seen from the north-east, frame a finely calculated arrangement of volumes rising through the rooflines towards an 18C central tower, clearly inspired by that of St-Jacques. The interior is famed for its 18C Parisot and Paul organ but is closed for restoration and unlikely to reopen until 1994/5.

The **Château** is reached along the Rue des Chastes, which climbs to the right off the western end of the Rue de la Barre. The great west tower is all that remains of Duke Richard I's 10C castle and the whole complex has been bombarded, burned and renewed so often that it is difficult to visualise its various states of being. The main rectangular block was built for Charles des Marets, after he had succeeded in expelling the English in 1435. This incorporated a 14C tower, to the north-west, which was originally free-standing. The curtain walls were extended during the 17C, in turn incorporating the late 13C belfry tower of St-Rémy. Following the castle's abandonment as a barracks in 1898 it was purchased by the municipality and has served as the **Musée** since 1923.

The Four Seasons, by J.A. Belleteste (18C), Musée des Beaux-Arts, Dieppe/Bridgeman Art Library, London

The museum's principal concern is to outline the development of Dieppe as an ivory carving centre between the 16C and the 19C. The historian Villaud de Bellefond claimed, in his 'Relation des Côtes d'Afrique' of 1669, that the Dieppois were trading with Guinea as early as 1384, and that by the mid-16C they had accumulated large stocks of ivory. The creation of the 'Compagnie du Senégal' in 1628 certainly boosted this trade and although the majority of the ivories on display in Room 1 are 18C, an ivory working industry was established in the town by the 1530s. By the late 17C this employed 250 craftsmen making ships' models and inlays alongside the staple domestic objects. The displays in the two ground floor galleries aim to locate this industry within the context of Dieppe's maritime trade, and include a model of Verrazano's 'Dauphine' and a replica of the celeb-rated Planisphere designed by Pierre Descaliers at Arques in 1546.

The first floor galleries open with a celebration of the seaside holiday, juxtaposing the general paraphernalia of bathing with several paintings by the late 19th and early 20C artists who observed such scenes. These include Renoir's portrait of Madame Paul Bérard of 1879 and Pissarro's 1902 portrayal of the 'Avant-Port de Dieppe', though much the finest of this group of late Impressionists is Albert Lebourg's 1896 'Vieux Port de Dieppe' with its vibrant sequence of luminous greys.

Beyond, in the old west tower, the main suite of display rooms concen-trates on an exhibition of Dieppois ivories. The range is broad with some good 17C portrait cameos and a varied set of narrative reliefs, expounding religious, mythological and secular themes. As with Belleteste's 18C statuettes of the Four Seasons, copied after Girardon's ensemble in the gardens at Versailles, most Dieppois 'ivoiriers' adapted their compositions from the work of contemporary stone carvers or, more frequently, popular engravings. The only serious exception to this is the work of **Pierre Graillon** (1807–72), who trained in the studio of David d'Angers and, on returning to Dieppe in the 1840s, developed a distinctive repertoire inspired by the mundane and workaday elements of life he observed among the sailors and artisans of the port. The mainstay of the 19C industry was the produc-tion of ostensibly functional items, and the galleries are accordingly crammed with all manner of measuring rules, clockcases, hatpins, cutlery handles, pillboxes, fans, chessmen, rattles, knick-knacks, and fancies, ranging from the mildly practical to the exquisitely unusable.

A room has also been given over to Camille Saint-Saens, sometime organist at St-Rémy, to accommodate the collection of memorabilia he gave to the town in 1889, while a modern extension houses a good collection of lithographs by Georges Braque. This extension also shelters an absorbing series of photographs taken by Henri Cahingt during the 1950s, in the course of an investigation into the history of naval architecture. Cahingt discovered a treasure house of maritime graffiti in the south-west tower of St-Jacques, much of it a response to the battle of Gravelines of 1644. Along with the late 15C ship scratched out beneath the sacristy frieze these ex-votos are a fascinating witness to the uncertainties as well as the shape of seafaring life.

Towards the seaward flank of the castle a path descends to the **Square du Canada**, where a small garden has been set aside as a memorial to those who died in the allied raid of 19 August 1942. Coded Operation Jubilee this subsequently became known as the **Dieppe Raid**, and remains one of the most controversial allied operations of World War Two. The plan involved simultaneous landings by 7000 commandoes at eight points between Berneval and Ste-Marguerite, with the objective of destroying enemy transport facilities and defences and seizing German battle plans believed to be stored at Divisional Headquarters at Arques-la-Bataille. The units were then to use the enemy landing barges in the harbour at Dieppe and take the following high tide to rendezvous with the Navy. Viewed in isolation the raid was a catastrophe. The strength of the German defences had been gravely underestimated and the main landings were subjected to relentless crossfire. The only German strongpoint to be taken was the Ailly battery above Ste-Marguerite, and as the Churchill tanks were bogged down on the beaches under an onslaught from the German artillery they had to be abandoned to protect the re-embarkation. Of the 5000 Canadians who took part in the raid 3379 did not return, of whom more than 1000 were killed and 600 wounded. The naval crews manning the landing craft suffered proportionately even heavier losses, and despite its air superiority the RAF lost 113 aircrew. The landing of tanks persuaded German High Command that the whole episode was a botched attempt to establish a bridgehead on the continent, hastily put together under Russian pressure. Churchill described it as 'a reconaissance in depth', commenting later: 'until an operation on that scale was undertaken no responsible General would take the responsibility of planning for the main invasion'. The official Canadian 'War History' comments soberly that the raid was 'part of the price paid for knowledge that enabled the great operation of 1944 to be carried out at a cost in blood smaller than even the most optimistic had ventured to hope for'.

East of here the Boulevard de Verdun marks out the esplanade which, although laid down in the mid-19C, was extensively and unimaginatively redeveloped after 1945. Just before the casino the **Porte du Port-d'Ouest** is the only survivor of the six 15C enceinte gates, and leads to a pleasant area of small squares and 19C brick terraces. The streets which run off to the right at the eastern end of the Boulevard de Verdun are more promising and bring you down towards the passenger port. The most engaging is perhaps the Rue de la Rade, and, Nos 14 and 20 Place du Moulin à Vent are among the few 16C houses to have survived the bombardment of 1694. This warren of streets also connects with the Quai Henri IV and the pleasures to be had watching the shipping ebb and flow from one of its dozens of cafés or restaurants.

The Quai Henri IV is the grandest of the quays and stands beside the passenger port with the main fishing harbour, the Bassin Duquesne, and cargo dock, the Arrière-Port, beyond. Although both Colbert and Vauban scrutinised several ambitious plans to enlarge the docks, little was actually done until the early 19C when the inner basins were dug out and provided with new warehousing. The Pont Ango connects with these basins, and the tongue of land between the fishing harbour and the main cargo dock, on which the fish market stands. East of here the Pont Colbert brings you into **Le Pollet**, a self-contained quarter whose mostly red-brick buildings house the fishing community. A right turn along the Quai de la Somme leads to Notre-Dame des Grèves, a sailors' barn of a church consecrated in 1849, overlooking the Arrière-Port. Alternatively the Grande Rue Pollet climbs towards the cliff tops, an altogether more bracing experience. On foot the most direct route involves bearing left onto the Rue du Cité des Limes, and after some 200 metres turning left up a flight of concrete steps. At the top an attractive street of red roof-tiled cottages, the Rue Albert Calmette, issues onto the eastern headland above the Avant-Port.

The views of the town are splendid, bracketed between the western cliffs and the narrow harbour mouth, while behind stands a curiously shaped clifftop chapel, **Notre-Dame de Bon Secours**, with its west tower supporting a brick spire flanked by octagonal turrets. Built between 1874 and 1876, it is a scaled down version of the sort of 19C parish church then springing up in the suburbs of Normandy's expanding towns. Inside the reasons for its small scale become clear. It is a place of grief and meditation, sobering in its completeness. The walls support some ex-votos but these are outnumbered by memorials to every sailor from Dieppe lost at sea since 1876. Particularly moving are the crew lists of trawlers '*disparu corps et biens*'.

West of Dieppe the coast road (D75) climbs steeply and for the 34km to St-Valery-en-Caux pitches between the deep gullies which connect the high plateau with the sea, offering exhilarating glimpses of the cliffs, woodland and dairy pasture which are its dominant motifs. At 8km you come to **Varengeville-sur-Mer**, which is neither a coherent town nor by the sea, but a loose collection of hamlets, farms, and spacious 19C villas. Before reaching the one recognisable street a track off to the left leads to the **Manoir d'Ango**, begun as a summer palace in 1530, the year of Jehan Ango's retirement from the maritime war with Portugal. The plan resembles that of the medieval fortified farmhouse favoured in Normandy, and consists of three main wings grouped around an irregular quadrangle which is closed to the north by a stable block. The architectural treatment is, however, not that of medieval Normandy, with the main entrance block made up of a stone arch flanked by a formidable polygonal lookout tower and a delicate subsidiary arch. The two arches have lost their statuary, indeed the whole entrance façade lost its upper two storeys during the Revolution, but the finer detailing is evidence of Ango's determination to import the Italianate decoration favoured by the political contemporaries with whom he did most business: Georges d'Amboise and François I. Ango had the arches, and the splendid loggia which opens onto the inner court, sculpted in Florence, the latter including portrait busts of François I, Henri II, Catherine de Medici, Ango's wife, Anne de Guillebert, and Ango himself. Parts of the house are open to the public and retain some of their original wooden doors and fireplaces, though many of the 17C Flemish tapestries which adorned the lower rooms have been removed for restoration. By the time the house was complete in 1545 Ango had been created Viscount and Govenor of Dieppe, and extracted maximum architectural capital from the fact by embellishing his seigneurial dovecot with a superb display of modulated brick and stone.

The road through Varengeville passes **Le Parc des Moustiers**, a mature landscape garden created by Guillaume Mallet and inspired by his regard for English 18C gardens. These are now open in their entirety, with the formal beds grouped around a house designed for Mallet in 1898 by Edwin Lutyens, dissolving into a wooded valley, planted with shrubs and rare species collected from Asia and the Americas, spilling down to the sea.

Further along the low silhouette of the church of **St-Valéry** serves as a seamark above the cliffs and stands at the centre of the town's cemetery. The contrasts of scale so evident when standing before the church are more readily understood when inside, where it becomes clear that the eccentric south aisle was added to a Romanesque nave in the 16C. Both the richness and the subject matter of its piers, choking with the cables, cockleshells, mermaids, and pirates of maritime Dieppe would suggest that this was financed by Jehan Ango. The site is better known for its more recent patronage however, for in 1949 Georges Braque settled here and produced the bewitching **Tree of Jesse** window in the south choir aisle. He is buried in the graveyard with his wife, Marcelle, beneath a simply designed mosaic headstone, and was by no means the only notable 20C artist to favour the site, for the composer Albert Roussel (1869–1937) is also buried here.

Beyond Varengeville the coast road loops through a landscape which is both beautiful and prosperous, passing at **Sainte-Marguerite-sur-Mer** a handsome parish church with an apse and high altar of c 1140 and a slightly later north nave arcade. 13km further west the aptly named **Veules-les-Roses** boasts the best pebble beach along this stretch of coast. The town itself is equally rewarding, centred away from the sea around a church whose 13C tower acquired a nave adorned with Varengeville-like 'maritime' piers in 1527.

From here the D925 sweeps into (8km) **Saint-Valery-en-Caux**. The town was almost completely destroyed in the fierce fighting which accompanied a rearguard action by the 51st Highland and French 2nd Cavalry Divisions protecting the retreat to Dunkirk. A monument on the Falaise d'Amont commemorates the action and reveals the reconstructed town centre, straddling a large yacht basin which extends well inland. The new centre pivots on the church of Notre-Dame-du-Pont-Port, built in 1963 with an impressive wall of stained glass to the east. Vieux-St-Valery, 1km inland, escaped the carnage and the old undistinguished 16C parish church flanks the road leading to the Franco-British War Cemetery.

12km south-west the pleasant town of **Cany-Barville** lies between two branches of the River Durdent whose meandering waters feed the 19C parkland of the Château de Cany (2km south; closed to the public), itself designed François Mansart in 1640. Beyond, at Ourville-en-Caux, a right turn onto the D150 leads to (7km) **Valmont**.

The town was the feudal stronghold of the Estouteville family whose brick donjon was extended by Jacques d'Estouteville in 1415 and still casts shadows over the river valley. On the opposite bank Nicolas d'Estouteville had founded a **Benedictine Abbey** in 1169 and its ruined and vertiginous choir can be visited. Nothing survives of the 12C church, indeed with the exception of a 13C crucifixion plaque and a superb but mutilated 14C angel, everything is much later. The choir was rebuilt in the early 16C on an evidently colossal scale, with a delicate Renaissance triforium supporting a long-vanished clerestory, and an axial chapel whose survival has preserved something of Valmont's subtle range of effects. This is locally known as the six o'clock chapel (Benedictines often celebrated a Mass at 6pm in the Lady Chapel). Two 15C tombs occupy the side walls: Jacques d'Estouteville and his Navarrese wife; and a posthumous memorial to Nicolas, the founder, beneath a donor's model of the church. But it is the cycle devoted to the Virgin which sets the tone of the chapel—the carved Annunciation at the front of a pictorial stage with a stained glass Annunciation to the Shepherds to the rear. The sculpture is attributed to Germain Pilon, better known for the tomb of François I at St-Denis, while all five windows were given by Cardinal Georges d'Amboise in 1552. The handsome residential block of 1680 remains in private hands and once belonged to a branch of the Delacroix family, hence Eugène Delacroix's panel of stained glass in the west bay of the chapel—not one of his best works.

Valmont is connected to the sea by the densely coppiced gorge of the Vallemont, whose course the D150 mimics, extending a leisurely flow for 11km to **Fécamp**. Until recently the fish docks supported a major deep sea fleet, but their decline has left Fécamp the poorer, though it remains the main market town of this area. Its origins predate Roman Fiscanum but its growth as a religious and commercial centre descend from the foundation of a convent dedicated to **La Trinité** by St-Waninge in 660, where a relic containing a phial of the Precious Blood of Christ was displayed.

Legend has it that Isaac of Arimathea, a nephew of Joseph, concealed the phial in the trunk of a fig tree which he 'entrusted to the sea and the mercy of God', and which was washed ashore at Fécamp. The relic survived the Norse raids of the late 9C and under Duke William Longsword the church was refounded as a Benedictine monastery rededicated, on the miraculous advice of an angel, to the Holy Trinity. Monks replaced the nuns of the earlier foundation, and in 928 Longsword established a fortified hall opposite the church. Fécamp thus became the premier residence of the Dukes of Normandy and before the rise of Mont St-Michel its major pilgrimage centre. The dukes observed Easter here and La Trinité briefly became the ducal burial church, favoured by Richard I in 996 and Richard II in 1026. When in 1003 Richard II persuaded William of Volpiano to leave St-Benigne at Dijon and establish the monastic reform in Normandy, Fécamp was his natural objective. It was also here in 1035 that Duke Robert announced his intention to undertake a pilgrimage to the Holy Land, and assembled a mighty gathering of barons and prelates to witness his vow that his seven-year-old bastard son, William, was to be heir.

The Abbey stands in what are now the south-eastern approaches to Fécamp, to the east of the ruined hulk of the 12C ducal castle, and south of the pink brick and Caen stone dressing of the 18C Hôtel-de-Ville, itself plundered out of the latest, and the last, of the monastic quarters. Nothing survives of the earlier churches, save the relic and a footprint left behind by the visiting angel, now preserved in the south transept. A new church was built between 1082 and 1107 from which some recut capitals, an arcade arch, and two chapels survive off the north choir ambulatory. The chapels are an important survival, and are perhaps the earliest example of an arrangement which was influential in the development of the epoch-making continuous ambulatory at St-Denis. A fire of 1168 however precip-itated a general rebuilding, orchestrated from east to west, and the greater part of La Trinité dates from 1175–1220. The evidence of the one partial choir bay which survives from the earlier church in the choir suggests this represented a considerable heightening. Much of the height is contributed by a majestically spacious tribune, covered by a five-part vault, adding a diffuse and indirect light to that of the clerestory. The tiers of arches are modelled in depth and are sufficiently thick to carry a clerestory wall-passage. It is a remarkably successful design, extracting a sense of gran-deur from the even distribution of height throughout the storeys, and not surprisingly had a profound influence on early 13C builders elsewhere in Normandy, notably at Caen and Bayeux.

The building was tragically stripped and its treasury sacked during the Revolution. Notwithstanding this an impressive body of sculpture remains, though the great late 15C screen which ran between the second and third bays of the nave was broken up in 1802. Two bays survive in situ and some smaller figurative groups have been assembled as a tableau in the north transept. To the other side of the superb lantern tower, in the south transept, a recent memorial slab commemorates the burial of Dukes Richard I and Richard II, whilst set into the east wall a 15C Dormition of the Virgin is alive with incidental detail. The ambulatory chapels, separated from the aisle by exquisitely carved 16C Italianate screens, are an equally rich repository of work. Particularly notable are the tombs of Abbot Thomas of St-Benoît (d. 1307) in the fourth chapel, studded with lively commendatory scenes, and the tomb of Richard d'Argences (d. 1223) in chapel number eight.

The preponderance of late 15C work reflects a desire on the part of the abbey to revive its fortunes in the wake of the Hundred Years War, and is perhaps best illustrated in the rebuilding of the Lady Chapel under the architect Jacques Leroux. This was extended east, though since the opening bay of the earlier chapel was retained it was clearly no higher than the late 12C axial chapel. Its role was to enhance the existing church rather than to break with its spatial norms, and it now acts as a splendid frame for the surviving 12th and 13C glass, coralled into the eastern bays.

The choir is dominated by an unexpectedly successful Louis XV high altar, commissioned by Abbot Montboissier de Canillac from the Rouen

Detail of the Massacre of the Innocents, from a mid-12C tomb chest, La Trinité, Fécamp

architect, de France, in 1751, but its fretted gilt baldacchino now floats above one of the more intriguing survivals of 12C Normandy. This consists of four 12C carved reliefs reassembled as a sarcophagus for the 1979 exhibition 'Trésors des Abbayes Normandes', and representing scenes from the life of Christ. A certain amount of paint and gold leaf remains on the surface, indicating that the work was originally coloured, and though the function and meaning of the chest have excited controversy modern scholarship is inclined to see this as the tomb into which Henry II translated the remains of Dukes Richard I and Richard II on 3 March 1162.

Between the west front of La Trinité and the ruined castle, the Rue Leroux and its continuation, the Rue Legros, lead to the **Musée Municipal de Fécamp**. This is installed in an 18C house to the north of a pleasantly shady garden, and has recently undergone an extensive programme of refurbishment. The ground floor is given over to the ceramic collections, with some good 17th and 18C Rouen faience amidst the Delft and Sèvres porcelain. The first floor displays some Dieppe ivories along with some unremarkable marine paintings by Pierre Le Mettay, and a series of works by the so-called 'Peintres Paysagistes', the latter mostly late 19C depictions of local peasant life. A large canvas entitled 'Filial Piety' stands on the sanctimonious edge of this movement, but equally there are works here which are much closer to the aims of Millais, or even Corot. The second and third floors are similarly devoted to local subject matter, in this case domestic furniture and maritime accessories.

The Rue Legros links the Musée Municipal to the Place de Gaulle, the theatre for the Saturday market, which, with the Place St-Etienne beyond, constitutes the centre of the upper town. The parish church which straddles this scene is an unprepossessing building of c 1500, to which a façade and new central tower were added in the 19C. The interior was stripped at the same time, but it was well treated by the 17C which bequeathed a vibrant wooden sculpture of St-Martin dividing his cloak to give to a beggar, now above the exit to the south transept.

Towards the beach, on the Rue Le Grand, an extraordinary architectural fanfare, blazing with finials and parapets, houses the **Palais Bénédictine.** It was built on the proceeds of the famous liqueur, whose recipe had been rediscovered by Alexandre Le Grand in an old 'grimoire' (spell book) in 1863. The liqueur was initially concocted in 1510 by the monk Bernardo Vincelli, newly arrived in Fécamp from Venice and accompanied by sack-loads of oriental spices destined for the abbey pharmacy. Vincelli hit on the idea of combining these with distilled wild herbs from the cliffs above Fécamp to produce a general tonic and elixir of health. Le Grand's genius was to recognise a good thing when he tasted it, and he used the profits the liqueur generated to indulge his predilection for matters medieval. This, alongside the customary tasting, is the principle reason for visiting the Palais.

Camille Albert, an enthusiastic disciple of Viollet-le-Duc, was engaged as architect and, lacking his mentor's fastidious eye for detail, produced a complex which veers from the 16C as improved by bells and trumpets, to the slightly purer medieval-fantastic. It is a staggering achievement, and doubtless rendered Le Grand thunderstruck with gratitude. Le Grand's medieval connoisseurship was equally promiscuous and his collection, housed in a series of chambers with self-explanatory titles, embraces manuscripts, ivories, metalwork, furniture, sculpture, textiles, panel paint-ing, and sundry liturgical paraphernalia, all of vastly differing dates and quality. Although Le Grand was on the whole quite untroubled by questions of quality or context, he had the wherewithal to acquire several very fine works, particularly in bas-relief, including a Venetian 15C triptych attributed to Taddeo Cigoli, and some Nottingham alabasters. There is also a good late 15C panel painting depicting the Adoration of the Magi by the Frankfurt Master, and the collection of parochial cult objects is an important one as most such items have been destroyed. The rest of the palace is devoted to the production of 'Bénédictine' and its later rooms entice with an ever-strengthening fragrance of herbs and spices, leading you through parts of the old distillery until you reach the last hall and the unmissable tasting.

West of the Palais the Rue Le Grand runs down to the sea, where the Boulevard Albert Ier acts as an esplanade, and gives access to the broad sweep of the pebble beach. Turning to the right you come to the **Musée des Terre-Nuevas**, with the docks visible in the middle ground. The museum houses a specialist exhibition of model boats, fishing tackle, charts, and marine paintings largely drawn from the collections of the Musée Munici-pal. Its great theme is the story of the Fécamp deep sea cod fleet, which has trawled the Newfoundland banks since the 17C, though sadly the opening of the Musée in July 1988 came some eight months after the retirement of Fécamp's last deep sea trawler.

The council has constructed a marina in the old outer dock which, with a flourishing cargo trade to the inland basins, has put the port on a secure financial footing. The inshore fleet has been less affected by territorial disputes and fishing quotas, and still lands its catch in the Bassin Bérigny. And this, naturally enough, is where the best seafood restaurants are to be found, clustered around the Quai de la Vicomté and the Quai Bérigny.

The coastal D211 offers the more interesting route to Etretat, passing at 8km the pleasantly shabby resort of **Yport**, with the beautiful and secluded valley of the Vaucottes beyond. Although the road changes designation to the D11 before the sign announcing **Etretat** this sign is an opportunity for the lazy to introduce themselves to the superlative natural amphitheatre which frames the town. A steep road off to the right leads to the Falaise d'Amont (upstream cliff), from where one of the most celebrated views in Normandy opens westwards to the Falaise d'Aval (downstream cliff) and beyond. To the right the sea has eroded the softer beds of chalk and silex to form an architecture of buttresses, spires, and towers grouped around the colossal porch of the Porte d'Aval and 60 metre Aiguille (needle rock). The effects that light on water can lend this composition are extraordinary and often fracture the cliff face with myriad variations of tone and hue, or flush the chalk with colours which shift dramatically according to the season or time of day. There is a small, modern sailors' chapel on the headland, and an unmistakable parody of the Falaise d'Aval in the shape of a memorial to François Coli and Charles Nungesser. These two First World War pilots were the first to attempt a crossing of the Atlantic, equipped with a Levasseur biplane, on 8 May 1927, taking off from the aerodrome at Le Bourget with the intention of reaching New York. Their plane, *l'Oiseau Blanc*, was last seen breaking through the fog over Etretat. A small museum by the monument also commemorates their fatal daring.

If you decide to walk up the steps connecting the esplanade with the Falaise d'Amont, the coast road passes the large parish church of **Notre-Dame d'Etretat**. This was a dependency of the Abbey of Fécamp, which helps to explain its accomplished design, though perhaps not its size. An early 12C nave, made up of drum piers, was extended two bays westward in the early 13C and provided with a spacious transept and choir. The lantern tower is extremely fine and, with the choir, gives the church the general shape one would expect to find in the English West Country at this date. The handling of specific motifs, notably the arches and responds, also finds parallels at Wells and Pershore, and again raises the question of the nature of Anglo-Norman architectural relations after the loss of Normandy in 1204. The church has been otherwise denuded of decoration and the rather Burgundian-looking west tympanum was added in 1866, of such inferior stone that its embrasures have all but weathered away.

The centre of Etretat has retained some handsome 16C timber houses, notably Le Tricorne and the reconstructed Market Hall, but although it is considered by the French to be an 'elegant' resort it is in danger of finding its piano bars and casinos overwhelmed by postcard racks, pizza shacks and tacky souvenir shops. The esplanade, running above a steep shingle beach and framed by the high promontories of Aval and Amont, remains unimpaired however, beckoning one towards the exhilarating cliff paths of the Falaise d'Aval and westwards past the Manneporte Arch to Le Havre.

2

Rouen

As the capital of Haute-Normandie, and the principal city of the old duchy, **Rouen** might be expected to reflect the history of the whole region; and to an unusual extent the city does indeed fulfil this expectation. The earliest Celtic settlers attracted by the easy river access and encircling range of wooded hills, established a trading station by the banks of the Seine which expanded to become the capital of the Vliocasses. This was taken over by the Romans as *Rotumagos*, probably in the wake of Caesar's Gallic wars and certainly by c 50 BC, acquiring a garrison and a prefect in addition to the westernmost bridge across the Seine.

Medieval tradition holds that the Gallo-Roman city was introduced to Christianity by the Welsh evangelist St Mellon c 260, but the earliest church of which there is documentary proof is that built by St-Victrice in 393 on the site of the present cathedral. The establishment of a bishopric in the 5C made Rouen the pivot of a series of missions to Christianise the surrounding area, successfully initiated under St-Godard in 488 and revived in the 7C by St-Romain and St-Ouen, which led to the foundation of the great abbeys of Jumièges, Fontenelle, and Fécamp. As the administrative centre of a rich, agrarian region Rouen presented an irresistible prize to the 9C Scandinavian raiders then terrorising the coast, and in 841 Oger the Dane sacked the city. Waves of summer raiding parties followed Oger's lead and it was not until the early pirates gave way to settlers that peace was restored, embodied in the *de justo* acceptance of Norse authority conferred by the Treaty of St-Clair-sur-Epte in 911.

Having gained a duchy the Viking leader, Wrolf, adopted Rouen as his capital and was baptised here, Latinising his name to Rollo. He dredged the river, connected the downstream islands to the right bank, and lined it with quays. Even Duke William's foundation of a second administrative capital at Caen had little impact on the city's prosperity, and some time before 1150 Henry II granted the citizens a charter, extending fiscal and judicial privileges. According to Ordericus Vitalis, writing in the early 12C, 'Rouen is extremely rich in population and trade and a very pleasant town with its port, its murmuring streams, the charm of its green fields, and its abundance of fruit and fish and many other things. It is surrounded on all sides by hills and forests, strengthened by its walls and ramparts and fortifications, and enhanced by its great buildings, houses and churches'. It was favoured by the Angevins, Richard I and John being crowned Dukes of Normandy in the cathedral, but after the fall of Château-Gaillard in 1204 Philip Augustus entered the city unopposed. French royal policy was to strengthen the administrative capitals of newly-won dominions, and Philip Augustus enlarged the city walls, the cathedral was rebuilt, and the port extended. In short Rouen shared in the wealth generated by the agricultural and commercial expansion of 13C northern France, and the emergence of a flourishing textile industry brought trade with Champagne and north-eastern France.

The Hundred Years War ill-treated the city however. The Black Death reached Rouen in July 1348, and was followed by a debilitating succession of plague epidemics and famines. There were bloody riots in 1382, and a vicious factionalism scoured the later 14C which was only reversed when Henry V laid siege to the city in 1418. The citizens rallied to Alain Blanchard's calls to resistance, and Henry had to wait six months for famine to decimate the populace before he could finally enter Rouen and make an example of hanging Blanchard. Local opposition crystallised around a policy of volatile riots and plots against specific 'Goddons' (a nickname given to the English occupiers derived from their common oath—'God Damned'), until the arrival of **Joan of Arc** focused the minds of English and Normans alike. Joan had been captured at Compiègne in 1430 by the Burgundian army and, through the mediation of Pierre Cauchon, bishop of Beauvais, was ransomed by the English for 10,000 ducats and brought to Rouen. Richard of Warwick, Captain of Rouen, took Joan as his charge and she was imprisoned in a tower of Philip Augustus' old castle to the north of the cathedral. Warwick reinforced the town against the possibility of popular uprising and on 21 February 1431 Bishop Cauchon opened the first session of her trial on charges of witchcraft and heresy. The trial lasted three months and after further examination in her cell a summary of her statements was compiled. Her visions were declared 'false and diabolical', the summary also being denounced at Paris University, and she was found 'heretical and schismatic' and led to the scaffold in the cemetery of St-Ouen. Encouraged to recant she did so and the sentence was commuted to one of life imprisonment, but Cauchon's determination was not to be brooked and on Trinity Sunday her English captors tricked her into wearing a man's clothes in the prison courtyard, thus breaking a vow she made on recanting her crimes. On 30 May she was led to the Place du Vieux-Marché and burned at the stake as a witch, the terrified English guards throwing her unconsumed heart into the Seine. The zeal with which her captors pursued her death is a measure of the influence she exercised, and the whispered misgivings of the English soldiery that a saint had been despatched corroded their already tenuous belief in an English future in Normandy. In 1449 Charles VII entered Rouen and set in motion the procedures which led to Pope Callixtus III declaring Joan innocent in 1456.

In common with Normandy as a whole the city had suffered grievously and many of her buildings were ruined or decayed beyond sensible repair. As trade resumed the drapers guild augmented the staple linen weaving with silk and cloth woven of silver and gold thread, developing new markets with the help of the Dieppois Fleet. The mercantile classes poured money into their town houses and parish churches, and with Cardinal Georges d'Amboise as an archbishop capable of encouraging active royal patronage, an impressive battery of new administrative buildings appeared, culminating in François I transforming the recently completed Law Courts into a 'Parlement de Normandie' in 1514. Much of this work survives, and it is as one of the finest late medieval townscapes in northern Europe that Rouen is most celebrated.

The population of Rouen in 1790 (approximately 70,000) was only marginally greater than that in 1520, but the industrialisation of the cotton industry in the 19C and the arrival of chemical and process industries around the docks, led to the construction of huge new quarters along the left bank of the Seine. These were twice devastated during the Second World War, first by fire in 1940 and then by bombardment in 1944, but the historic core suffered less except in the area between the river and the axis formed by the cathedral and the Place du Vieux-Marché. The old industrial left bank was largely redeveloped as an administrative centre while an enlightened programme of large-scale restoration was lavished on all major

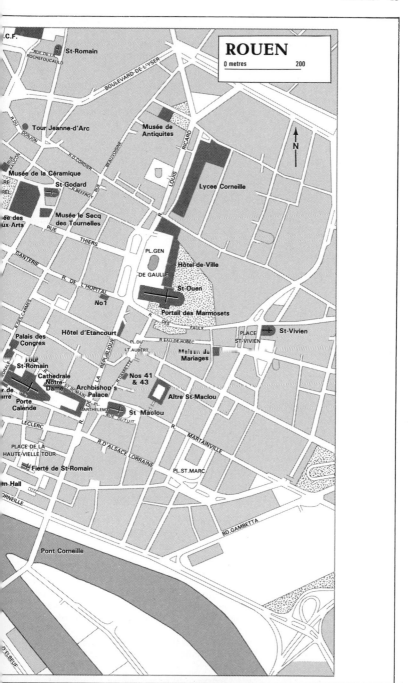

ROUEN

0 metres 200

N

buildings, in conjunction with a policy of conserving those domestic timber houses which had survived the bombing in reasonable shape. This process has been an inevitably piecemeal and long-running affair but must rank, in its slow revealing progress, as one of the most effective programmes of urban renewal undertaken in the last half-century.

Much the best place to begin any exploration of Rouen is the **Place de la Cathédrale**, standing to the east of the point where the two main streets of the Gallo-Roman town intersected. There was a **cathedral** here in 488 when St-Godard was elected bishop, which was enlarged by St-Romain in 638, but the present structure is substantially medieval, the earliest material belonging to a Romanesque church begun by Archbishop Robert at some time between 989 and 1037. This building was consecrated in 1063 with a freestanding tower to the north-west, the **Tour St-Romain**, whose lower stages are now embedded in the later west front. But it was the discovery of the **crypt** in the course of Lanfry's excavations in 1934 that caused the greatest stir, and led to a reappraisal of Norman Romanesque architecture.

Access to this crypt is via the south transept (guided tour only) and brings you, beneath the choir, into a spacious ambulatory with three radiating chapels. The transverse arches were carried on attached shafts and the central vessel was divided into aisles by rows of slender monolithic columns, creating a hall crypt. It is very different from the apse-echelon east ends found in the surviving 11C churches of Basse-Normandie, and suggests that the metropolitan structures favoured by ducal patronage in the first half of the century looked to the designs of Royal France.

These two extremities of the 11C cathedral were joined between c 1190 and c 1240 in a campaign which established the current shape of the building. A new nave had been started to the west of the crossing in the early 1190s when disaster struck, in the shape of a fire in 1200. It is difficult to gauge the extent of the damage this caused, but it seemed to act as a pretext for a wholesale rebuilding and in 1201 the architect Jean d'Andely was engaged to redesign the **nave**. When the 1190s nave had been begun it was as a tribune church, with a thick wall and heavily moulded arches in three orders, a sort of rigorously linear reworking of the nave of La Trinité at Fécamp. Between 1201 and 1220 Jean heightened the clerestory by several metres and removed the tribune floor, continuing the new elevation as far as the west front. The effect was extraordinary, turning the tribune into a flying screen and creating uncertainty as to the limits of the relief plane, indeed as to the very nature of the enclosed space. You can see this most clearly from the north transept, where the north aisle reveals those delicate stands of colonettes above the old aisle responds, whimsically rising in space.

As you move into the **choir and transepts** you become conscious of a shift in architectural language, and the sudden appearance of a new element around the periphery—a passage above the dado arcade. This is known as a Remois passage (after its development in Reims and the Champagne in the 1170s) and it is a sure index of the penetration of mainstream High Gothic thinking. These eastern parts were built between c 1220 and c 1230 by an architect with a close working knowledge of the elevation of Chartres or its derivatives. The arcade is taller than that of the nave and the elevation is supported on slender columnar piers, with an overall flatness of treatment. The choir is also one of the few areas to have retained any of its 13C glass, preserving five windows of c 1235 in the ambulatory. The northernmost of these was given by the guild of fishmongers and depicts the legend of St-Julien the Hospitaller, while the second of two windows devoted to the Old Testament story of Joseph is, unusually and famously, signed as the work of Clément of Chartres, though Grodecki and Brissac's work on 13C glass has thrown up few parallels for Clément's style at Chartres cathedral. The other two windows depict the Parable of the Good Samaritan and the Passion. The ambulatory also contains an uneven though impressive display of sepulchral effigies, dating from a late 13C translation of ducal remains. The most politically important of these was that of the founding duke, Rollo (this a copy), and the most archaising treatment accorded to that of Richard the Lionheart, whose heart was buried here. To the north are a 14C effigy of William Longsword and a splendidly seigneurial image of Henri Court-Mantel, the second son of Henry II (also late 13C).

The **Lady Chapel** was originally built in 1214 but was reconstructed and extended to the east in 1302–20, and now houses two of the finest surviving 16C tombs in France. That to the south was commissioned before 1518 by **Cardinal Georges II d'Amboise** as a memorial to himself and his father, who died in 1510. It was completed in 1525 to the designs of Roulland Le Roux, and sculpted in marble by Pierre des Aubeaux, Regnaud Thyrouin, Jehan de Rouen and Jehan Chaillou. Perhaps the elder Georges would have approved, for it is engorged with all the Lombard arabesques, swags of fruit and candelabra he had introduced into Normandy at Gaillon. To the north the **tomb of Louis de Brézé**, Seneschal de Normandie and husband of Diane de Poitiers (died 1531), was commissioned by Diane and executed in 1536–44. Attributed to Jean Goujon in its lower parts it is a two tiered design, with an effigy of Louis commended to the Virgin by a mourning Diane beneath a rather clumsily figured piece of seigneurial pomp, in which four caryatids support an equestrian figure of Louis—a throwback to 14C knightly tombs.

The **transepts** are dominated by a brilliant lantern tower, a square colossus bathing the crossing with light and which now supports a cast iron spire, put up in 1876 to replace the destroyed 1544 spire. Apart from the 14C stained glass of the north transept rose window, the main interest here is provided by the **Escalier des Libraires** situated in the north-west angle and designed c 1480 by Guillaume Pontis.

The door leaving the north transept brings you into the **Cour des Libraires**, essentially a passage running between the cloisters and the archiepiscopal palace, where the booksellers had their market from the 14C onwards. This is overshadowed by the north transept façade, the **Portail des Libraires**, begun in 1281 by the architect Jean Davy and largely complete by 1300. It is the purest embodiment of Ile-de-France-inspired Rayonnant architecture in Normandy, its forms etched with an almost metallic precision and the tracery run up through the gable heads. Both the rose window and the tympanum are replacements, in the case of the rose a replica, and the jamb figures were destroyed during the Wars of Religion. The subject was the Last Judgement. But at least the figured quatrefoils to either side of the door survived, representing the Creation and Fall along with the Liberal Arts, and a fantastical display of fabulous creatures which includes an exquisite mermaid.

To the west the Cour Albane marks out the confines of the now destroyed cloister and brings you to the **west front**. This may seem an unbalanced and hybrid composition, disturbed by an almost casual overlay of late medieval screenwork, but it is the raw material of Monet and its shimmering variety is capable of throwing off exhilarating contrasts of light and shadow against a turning sun. The lower stages of the Romanesque Tour

St-Romain were heightened c 1160 and subsequently incorporated into the 13C west front, with the two lateral portals dating from c 1240. The north portal is dedicated to John the Baptist and depicts the Feast of Herod, Dance of Salome, and Beheading of the Baptist on the tympanum. To the south the St-Etienne portal embellishes the tympanum with the Stoning of Stephen, and a Christ in Majesty. The central portal acquired a Tree of Jesse in 1512–14, carved by Roulland Le Roux and evidence that he was a better architect than he was a sculptor, however drastic a restoration of 1626 may have been. Above a screen of statuary arranged in two tiers was added between c 1370 and 1420. Finally, to the south, the **Tour de Buerre** balances the situation, though not the language, of the Tour St-Romain. It was begun in 1485 under the architect Guillaume Pontis and completed in 1506 by Jacques Le Roux, rising 77 metres in a virtuoso display of tiered and progressive elaboration. Its name was said to derive, in the 17C at least, from its having been financed out of dispensations granted to the wealthy, allowing them to take milk and butter during the Lenten fast.

The best preserved of the cathedral portals is the recently cleaned **Porte Calende**, framed by two towers of c 1230 and giving access to the south transept. It dates from the first quarter of the 14C, with a rather strangely ordered sequence of episodes from the life of Christ on the tympanum, and a once superb cycle of bas-reliefs in the door embrasures. These are set in quatrefoils and depict the story of Jacob and Joseph, the lives of St-Ouen and St-Romain, and a number of subsidiary themes. Their shallowly carved figure style is derived from Parisian ivories, and treated here with a vitality and finesse which transcends their eroded surfaces.

To the south of the Porte Calende, in the Place de la Haute Vieille Tour, one of the few buildings between the cathedral and the river to have survived 1944 stands in front of the rebuilt 16C Linen Hall. This two storey structure is in fact a chapel, known as the **Fierte de St-Romain**, and was built in 1542 to house the annual ceremony of the Privilege of St-Romain. Each Ascension Day, until the suppression of the ceremony in 1790, the cathedral chapter were given the right to free a criminal condemned to death. This tradition was based on the story that St-Romain himself had employed a condemned man to entice a dragon from its lair, before subduing the bewildered beast by the sign of the cross and leading it to be slain and burned in the city. Legend has it that the grateful townspeople of Rouen insisted that the criminal be pardoned, and it is this action that found reflection in the later 'Privilege'. When the criminal had been chosen the relics of St-Romain were carried in solemn procession to the Fierte, where the prisoner was required to raise the reliquary three times from the open gallery. He was then freed, crowned with flowers, and bore the relics back to the cathedral. Between 1542 and 1790 the relics were raised in this delicate chapel, but the ceremony seems to date from c 1210 when the building of the cathedral was in full swing and powerful relics were mighty raisers of funds.

Turning north the **Rue St-Romain** remains the province of booksellers and print dealers, plying their trade among some of the grandest late medieval domestic buildings in the city. This is one of the most attractive streets in Rouen, with carved wooden figures looking out from doorposts and windows, as in the splendid St-Romain blessing the souls of three supplicants to the left of No. 74. The earliest houses are Nos 52 and 54, dating from the late 14C, but the majority are contemporary with Guillaume Pontis' ambitious Canon's Library of 1464–84 to the right of the Cour des Libraires. The

Late 15C façade of No. 74 Rue St-Romain, Rouen

Archbishop's Palace lies to the east of this and is also substantially late 15C, incorporating the gable window of an earlier archiepiscopal chapel in which the trial of Joan of Arc was held. The main façade of the palace was rebuilt by Le Carpentier in the mid-18C and opens onto the Rue des Bonnetiers.

The **Quartier St-Maclou** lies over the road, handsomely breached by the Place Barthélémy, and takes its name from one of the most accomplished late medieval parochial buildings in northern Europe, the church of **St-Maclou**. The church was begun during the English occupation in 1436 to a design by Pierre Robin, 'maçon du Roi', though the nave remained incomplete until 1470. A second campaign saw the west front redesigned and an entrance porch added c 1500–14. This latter may have been designed as early as 1477 and is usually attributed to Ambroise Havel.

The **porch** is widely regarded as a key statement of late Gothic architecture, its sophisticated geometry the starting point for a speculation on the relationships of surface to space. The porch has five portals, crowned by steep gables, behind which a tall delicately pierced balustrade creates a horizontal link between the gables, and appears to encase the west front in a balcony. The porches themselves are canted outwards and are locked in a diagonal relationship with the western mass. It is a highly-strung dance, impossible of resolution, and this sense of skidding movement, away from the central porch, implies a rhythmic sensibility quite different to that of Rayonnant architecture, with its vertical sequence of parts.

The central doorway, and that to the left, are filled with bas-reliefs attributed to Jean Goujon and added shortly before Cardinal Georges II d'Amboise consecrated St-Maclou in 1521. Superbly executed in wood these depict the Circumcision and Baptism of Christ to the centre, with a medallion representing the Good Shepherd and statues of Samson, Moses, David, and Solomon to the left.

The **interior** consists of a short nave and choir separated by a contained transept. The apse is sprung with an axial pier, and gives on to four chapels (the south chapel was destroyed in 1944), an unusual arrangement which was to prove influential elsewhere in Normandy. The elevation is equally rigorous, with an elegant triforium in which the lower balustrade and upper filigree of tracery are fused in a single design unit. There is sadly little left of the original decoration, though the ambulatory chapels still house some badly decayed 15C glass. Goujon's organ loft, at the west end of the nave, is now reached by a spiral stair originally carved for the choir screen, flamboyantly detailed by Pierre Gringoire in 1515.

Along the Rue Dutuit, to the south of St-Maclou, there are a pair of splendid 16C houses with an industrious Annunciation over the grander of the two, and a fine run of half-timbered buildings along the north flank of the Rue Martainville. A passage to the left of No. 186 brings you into the **Aître St-Maclou**, a rare survival of a facility once common in European cities, a charnel house. The site was used as a plague cemetery in the 14C, and developed as an impressively large charnel house by Denis Lesselin in 1526–33. Lesselin constructed three ranges, their lower storeys originally open walks akin to those of a cloister, and decorated the column shafts with an array of figures performing a Dance of Death. These were mutilated by Huguenot Protestants in 1562, but the double frieze of skull-and-crossbones, interspersed with grave-digger's tools, escaped serious damage. The south range was not added until 1651, closing the quadrangle, and this, together with its present occupation by the College of Art, has made it difficult to imagine the functional arrangements of the 'aître'. The area to the south, in addition to the central space, acted as a cemetery. Demand for cemetery space was always great in crowded towns, and when the corpses had rotted down, the bones were brought to the ranges and stacked on open rafters above the open walks. They were thus aired in the area between the two friezes, which were originally separated by an openwork trellis.

A right turn by the entertaining fountain at the north-west angle of St-Maclou brings you onto the **Rue Damiette**, a largely pedestrianised street which has some fine timber houses, notably Nos 41 and 43. To the left of the Place du Lieutenant Aubert the 17C **Hôtel d'Etancourt** is embellished with wonderfully crude giant plaster statuary, while the **Rue Eau-de-Robec** rises to the east. As in much of Rouen a stream originally ran along the street, here towards the north side. Now conduited and reduced in scale, it nevertheless remains possible to visualise the street as it was in the 16C, for as in Bruges access to each dwelling was by private footbridge. Most of the houses here were built between the 16C and 18C, No. 160 being a particularly fine example, with a spacious courtyard and views over the gardens to the east of St-Ouen. To the right the **'Maison des Mariages'**, now restored to house a specialist educational museum, remains as the grandest of Rouen's late 15C century fortified townhouses. The rue opens onto the **Place St-Vivien**, dominated by a huge and neglected church which unfortunately personifies the early 16C at its most forgettable. A more encouraging vista beckons from the west however, as beyond the gardens above the Rue des Faulx you can make out the eastern buttressing and delicate ascending accents of the lantern tower of the great Benedictine Abbey of **St-Ouen**.

A monastery dedicated to SS. Peter and Paul is known to have existed on the site by 535 which, having been rebuilt at the urging of St-Ouen in 641, received the remains of the saint for burial in 686. This early monastery was destroyed in the Norse raid of 841 and an 11C account ascribes its recon-struction to duke Rollo before 931. Archaeological excavations have brought no structures to light earlier than that begun by Abbot Nicolas in 1066 however, though the existence of a 7th or a 10C church is not in dispute. Romanesque St-Ouen was a transeptal basilica, and according to a contemporary chronicler 'immense', but all that now survives of a clearly significant building, consecrated in 1126, is the two storey north transept chapel known as the **Tour aux Clercs**.

Fires in 1136 and 1248 necessitated extensive repairs but an evidently unsatisfactory state of affairs was only resolved in 1318, when Abbot Jean Roussel demolished the earlier choir and began work on a new church. By 1339 the ambulatory chapels, choir, and east walls of the transept were complete, but even Roussel's legendary wealth was insufficient to bring 'a good beginning to a good and timely end', and it was 1537 before the west bays of the nave were vaulted. Not all is late medieval, however, as the west front is a lumbering 'improvement' of 1845–51, and the Porte des Ciriers, along the south flank of the nave, was added in 1774.

St-Ouen is one of the most conservative late medieval great churches in France, its tone and spatial manner set by Roussel's early 14C choir. This is perhaps not surprising, as French architecture at this date was marked by a certain dryness in the way in which essentially mid 13C Rayonnant forms were pared down. This is noticeable here in the tracery designs, especially in the triforium, which are worked out as self-contained panels. The Hundred Years War prevented any further work until the English occupation of Rouen, concerned to court favour, began to encourage church building projects. In 1422 Alexandre de Berneval was engaged as architect and by his death in 1440 the transepts were complete, the north transept rose window being a design of his son, Colin, of 1441. There was a further hiatus until 1492 when the nave was restarted under Jacques Théroulde, and an initial design for the west front was in building by 1515. Although the nave bays are slightly narrower than those of the choir the later campaigns adhere to the aesthetic predispositions of Roussel's church, and even the flamboyant tracery is held firmly in check by a tendency to square the frames where possible.

The work of the Bernevals is, however, an exception to this, and the south transept window is a masterful whirl of sinuous petals which serves as a matrix for a Tree of Jesse window. The **Portail des Marmosets** (south transept door) is equally inventive and is sheltered by a porch constructed as an eccentric hexagon. The portal gained its name from the marmosets which support the hood mould, or clamber beneath its corbels in a wonder-fully distracting display of animal high spirits. In fact, disregarding the 19C trumeau of St-Ouen, all the sculpture is extremely fine with reliefs repre-senting scenes from the life of St-Ouen in the porch, and a tympanum depicting the Dormition, Assumption, and Coronation of the Virgin.

Of the interior decoration it is the glass which merits the greatest attention, though the choir stalls of 1615 are very fine. The stained glass of the choir and radiating chapels is mostly contemporary with Roussel's building (1318–39), with windows illustrating the lives of saints in all the ambulatory chapels except one, the axial chapel, which boasts a superb cycle devoted to the childhood of Christ. A Crucifixion of 1960, by Max Ingrand, has replaced the great Crucifixion window of the choir clerestory destroyed in the Revolution, but the flanking Apostles to the south, and prophets and patriarchs to the north, remain in situ. These date from the late 1330s and are closely related in style to the series of Apostles carved for Jumièges in 1332–35 (of which an example survives in Duclair), numbering amongst the most important early 14C windows to have survived in France.

The nave windows are variously late 15C and early 16C. Lighter in tone and subtly complementing the linear accents of the architecture, these have been moved so often and so much has anyway been lost that it is now impossible to reconstruct a programme, especially as much of the glass has been lost. These windows may also have been complemented by a series of life-size figures resting under canopies on each pier, as a permanent congregation for the nave.

The late 15C south cloister walk can be reached around the exterior of the apse, passing through Jean-Pierre Defrance's **Hôtel-de-Ville** of 1753–59. This also has the advantage of revealing the crossing tower, a breathtaking 82 metres of spidery stonework shaped into a ducal crown.

Across the Place de Gaulle you pass the charming courtyard of No. 1 Rue de l'Hôpital, built in 1523 to a design by Roulland Le Roux, and, descending westwards, the neo-Gothic Fontaine de la Crosse, reconstructed from a medieval fountain in 1861 by Arsène Jouan. From here the old medieval road north-east, the **Rue Beauvoisine**, climbs out of the Seine valley, past handsome 15–17C town houses to the **Musée des Antiquités**.

The museum is accommodated in the cloister and main monastic block of the convent of the Visitation, which was built in 1680–91. The major rooms open in the north gallery with an eclectic display of medieval objects, which includes some 13C stained glass from the cathedral, usefully juxtaposed with the 16C glass of St-Eloi de Rouen. A good collection of mostly 12–13C Limoges enamels might be compared with the 12C Byzantine enamelled plaque depicting Hosea, but the proficiency of the enamellers' technique is best exemplified in one of the earliest examples of Limoges work, the 11C **Valasse cross**. Among the ivories an 11C Italian oliphant and 14C enthroned Virgin stand out, as do the English late medieval alabasters.

The west gallery contains an arresting group of 15th and 16C Flemish 'Schnitzaltaren'—elaborate retables whose stages are enlarged to often panoramic effect, encompassing Crucifixions, Entombments, and Nativities. When closed they appear as a painted box, but their interiors are animated by gilded wooden figures, deployed across a pictorial stage to enact a religious drama, as in the frozen tableaux of mystery plays. The origin of the form is German, but as a manifestation of popular religion in late medieval northern Europe, they were readily endorsed in Normandy and France, and generally imported from the sculptural shops of Brussels and Ghent. To the left the **Salle des Tapisseries** is famous for the 15C Winged Deer tapestry, woven in Flanders, and hung above an impressive array of 16th and 17C Rouen furniture.

The south walk exhibits some excellent early 16C wooden fretwork from the Palais de Justice, evidence of how inventive small scale tracery design became the province of the carpenters in the late Middle Ages. The **Salles**

des Antiquités are laid out to the west of here, centred around the museum's one outstanding exhibit, the **Lillebonne Mosaic**. This was discovered in 1870 at the bottom of a garden in the centre of Lillebonne and originally decorated the floor of the triclinium (dining room) of a late 3C Roman villa. It is approximately 6 metres square, and shows Poseidon in pursuit of the nymph Anemone in a central roundel surrounded by scenes of stag-hunting and sacrifice at the altar of Diana. Even more remarkably it is signed—'Titus Sennius Felix, citizen of Pozzuoli made (this)'. Despite the extensive restorations, it remains one of the finest late antique mosaics north of the Alps. On a sunny day you can take a chair into the courtyard and gaze on the bewildering array of minor medieval statuary under an open-air pulpit, the Cabinet des Onces.

Downhill from the museum the Rue du Cordier and Rue du Donjon lead to the **Tour Jeanne-d'Arc**, an old free-standing donjon that is all that now remains of Philip Augustus' fortifications of 1205. It originally stood at the north-eastern angle of a huge castle bailey, of which little is known, and housed the exchequer by the mid 13C, while the bailey became the effective seat of judicial government in Rouen until the early 16C. Despite the name, Joan was in fact imprisoned in the destroyed Maid's Tower, and came here only once, on 9 May 1431, when she was shown the instruments of torture before being conducted to the cemetery of St-Ouen (see p 41). The tower is a simple design, comparable to Philip's Talbot Tower at Falaise, with 4m thick walls deeply splayed to form window alcoves.

To the right of the Gare SNCF, on the Rue de la Rochefoucauld, the drab and undistinguished church of **St-Romain** was founded as a convent for Carmelite nuns in 1678. Its chief interest is that it has become a repository for an early 16C cycle of stained glass cannibalised from St-Etienne des Tonneliers. Although this has been poorly releaded and has been placed in windows too small to take more than single scenes, it is of exceptionally high quality. The panels are mostly by Arnold de Nimègue, a Tournai glass painter who settled in Rouen between 1500 and 1512 before moving to Antwerp, and like his work in the transepts of Tournai cathedral seem to share elements of design with contemporary Flemish tapestries, most notably in the scenes of the martyrdom of St Stephen now mounted in the transept ends.

Further south the **Rue St-Patrice** presents a gentle, winding aspect, enlivened with half-timbered houses interspersed among the more elegant 18C stone-built mansions. A church, dedicated to **St-Patrice**, rises above the street, revealing its southern flank. In this situation its spaciousness comes as a surprise, as does its choice of supporting elements—columnar piers mounted on high pedestals. It was begun in 1538 under the patronage of a large Irish mercantile community which had settled in the area. The church is best known for its stained glass which, but for a few obvious exceptions, dates from 1538–1625. The best is in the choir, particularly in the north chancel, which opens with a stunning Italianate Annunciation commissioned in 1540 by Guillaume de Possnes and his wife, who appear as prayerful donors at its base. Next to this are windows dedicated to St-Eustace (1543) and St-Louis. The trio of chancel windows depicting the Passion, Crucifixion, and Resurrection are late 16C, and to their south is a Three Kings window of 1545, but the most insistent piece of vernacular story-telling is dedicated, appropriately enough, to Job, in the north aisle.

Turning back to the Square Verdrel brings you to Rouen's extensive complex of museums, with the Musée des Beaux-Arts flanked by specialist collections of ceramics and metalwork. Entry to the **Musée de la Céramique** is via the Rue Fauçon, to the left of the Beaux-Arts. This was opened in 1984 in the Hôtel d'Hocqueville, an attractive mid 17C classical mansion faced in smooth rusticated Caen stone. A pavilion was added to the right in the 18C, unfortunately unbalancing the symmetry of the tall window bays which strike such a harmonious chord within the design. The museum itself is superbly laid out, opening with a display of faience manufacturing techniques, before moving on to a broadly chronological arrangement of the museum's holdings. Faience manufacture, using an amalgam of heavy red clay from St-Aubin and light prairie clay from Sotteville and Quatre-Mares, was introduced to Rouen in the mid 16C by Masseot Abaquesne. Initially, it was inspired by Mediterranean maiolica ware, using glazed white enamel and metallic colours which owed as much to Valencian as to Italian patterns and best exemplified by the collection of albarelli (pharmicist's jars), and the splendid tiled floor of 1557 from the Bastie d'Urfe.

Before reaching the early Rouen ware you pass through the reconstructed bedroom of Guillemette d'Assy, Abbess of St-Amand (the nunnery was destroyed by the building of the Rue de la Republique after the Revolution), with a delightful sequence of 16C painted wooden panels, arranged around a sturdy fireplace. The last gallery on the ground floor is given over to maiolica from Italy, in which a display plate of 1530, showing the Birth of Adonis and made in Urbino, gives a good idea of the strength of the competition.

A splendid wooden trapezoidal staircase, original to the house, carries you to the upper floors. Here the influence of the fashionable pale blues of 17C Delft, and the impact Chinese porcelain had on 18C Europe is apparent, along with the increasing range of everyday objects. The opposite extreme can be found in a ceramic violin, and Pierre Chapelle's **terrestial and celestial globes** of 1725, manufactured for Madame Lecocq of Villeray.

To the rear of the Beaux-Arts the skyline is broken by an extraordinary pair of late medieval parish churches, St-Laurent and St-Godard. The reasons for the peculiar external silhouette of **St-Godard** become clearer as you step into the north aisle. Both aisles were originally intended to be lower and narrower, the same width as the north-west tower in fact (you can see the aisle window springers take off from the tower's north-east angle). However, during the course of construction, it was decided to enlarge the aisles, so flooding the building with light and creating the feeling of a hall-church. The plastered wooden ceiling is a 19C replacement, as is much of the glass in the nave; it is the earlier glass which dates the building. Glaziers often followed quickly behind the masons, using the same scaffolding, and the **Tree of Jesse** window in the east of the south aisle is by Arnold of Nimègue and was installed in 1506, though that to the north, illustrating scenes from the life of St-Romain, had to wait until 1555. The lancet heads of this later window house a fine, if badly releaded, depiction of St-Romain, accompanied by a condemned prisoner, subduing the dragon. Nevertheless it seems likely that comletion of the choir was in 1506, with Arnold's splendid window a taste of things to come as and when funds and patrons became available.

Its counterpart, **St-Laurent**, was built between 1444 and 1554, with perhaps the most ambitious of all Rouen's parish church towers, added in 1490–1501 to rise in a giddying display of flying buttresses, tracery, and gables, which when finally fused suggest a coronet.

The interior of St-Laurent now houses the finest collection of wrought ironwork in Europe, under the title of the **Musée Le Secq des Tournelles**.

The French 18C ironwork is particularly fine and includes a superb stair-case railing from the Château de Bellevue, and some striking 17–19C inn and shop signs. The medieval holdings are also impressive, with an excellent choir screen door of 1202 from Ourscamp, and an elegant 15C window grille thought to be from the house of Jacques Coeur in Bourges. The locksmithery can be very intricate, as in the 15C Credenza lock, or the marvellous French 18C burglar clamp-lock. Among the domestic items there is also a good selection of late medieval caskets, including an entertaining box where playful huntsmen with their slings and dogs stand beside an improbably picturesque castle.

St-Laurent's grander neighbour, the **Musée des Beaux-Arts,** is entered from the Square Verdrel. The museum is currently housed in an ample symmetrical building specifically designed to hold the collections installed here in 1888, though the creation of a museum of Fine Art dates back to 1801. At the time of writing the museum was still in the throes of a major

Virgo inter Virgines, by Gerard David, Musée des Beaux-Arts, Rouen

reorganisation, and the following description is, therefore, only provisional.

The museum opens with an important collection of works by **Jacques-Emile Blanche**, a frequent visitor to the Normandy coast, who between 1922 and 1932 donated most of the rich collection of studies and portraits on display here. The chief interest of the paintings lie in their portrayal of the major players in the artistic life of early 20C France. Among the portraits of Max Jacob, André Maurois, Jean Giraudoux, Paul Claudel, and a group portrait which includes Cocteau, Poulenc, and Honneger, there is a marvellously languid portrayal of André Gide of 1912.

Beyond this the **Donation Baderou**, consisting largely of 17th and 18C painting and given to the museum in 1975, boasts a strong collection of Dutch and Neapolitan still lifes and a stunning portrait attributed to the

Utrecht master **Gerrit von Honthorst** of a man seen slyly through an octagonal aperture. The best of the later material probably belongs to **Gabriel de Saint-Aubin**, an 18C Parisian painter and draughtsman, whose portrait of the engraver Pierre Chenu is a compelling exposition of grotesque artifice.

A small room is also given over to an excellent display of works by the Rouen born, early 19C painter, **Théodore Géricault**. His 'Cheval Gris' is a magisterial equestrian portrait, in which nothing is allowed to distract from the study of the horse, and the 1818 portrait of Delacroix presents the artist with a countenance so powerful that it seems to draw all light towards itself.

The ground floor gallery devoted to the larger 16th and 17C canvases will be rehung, but for the moment you can admire **Veronese's** 'Barnabus healing the sick', all low viewpoints and Venetian colours, and a somewhat routine **Rubens** 'Adoration of the Shepherds' from the Capucin church in Aachen. Two grisaille paintings by the local artist **Jean de Saint-Igny** reward attention, painted in 1636 to adorn the choir of the convent of Cordeliers in Rouen.

The first floor is largely given over to 19th and 20C painting, but at the head of the stairs a room has been put aside to house the museum's most famous work, **Gerard David's Virgo Inter Virgines**. This is an altarpiece Gerard David and his wife, Cornelia Knoop, offered to the church of the Carmelites at the convent of Sion in Bruges in 1509. One is here within a court of Paradise, David and his wife bearing witness to the vision at the painting's rear edges, where all is meticulously detailed and realised with rich symbolism—the crown of St Catherine shaped with wheels for instance, or St Barbara's tower-shaped cap.

To the right of this is the altogether quirkier work of the **Duchamp family**, anchored around the sculpture of Raymond Duchamp-Villon and teasingly elaborated with mock-ups of work by his younger brother, the brilliant and reclusive agent-provocateur of early 20C art, **Marcel Duchamp**. Beyond another local artist, **Raoul Dufy**, is well represented by 'La Baie de Sainte-Adresse', a work which has become influential among painters currently working in Normandy, and the delightful 'Le Cours de la Seine de Paris à Rouen'. This was originally conceived as a decorative scheme for the bar of the Théâtre de Chaillot in Paris in 1937, and although this kind of imaginary touring landscape has become a common feature of café decor, it is good to see a master laying down the principle. You can also pick out the landmarks—the Seine is flanked by its tributaries the Marne and the Oise.

French 19C landscape painting comes under scrutiny with works by **Daubigny, Boudin**, and a glorious foggy morning in the marshes of Villes-d'Aurey by **Corot**. This tradition of landscape in Normandy certainly contributed to the works by **Claude Monet** on display here, particularly in his studies of the transient effects of mist on the Seine. Appropriately, there is at least one of Monet's series paintings of the west front of Rouen cathedral, seen in grey weather in 1894.

The second floor mixes 16–18C holdings (though again this may change). In a startling portrait of the cynical Antique philosopher Democritus of c 1635, **Velázquez** shows us a court buffoon poking fun at a Mappa Mundi with a looseness of brushwork that is far removed from the tactile realism of **Caravaggio's** Flagellation of Christ of 1606/7. A relatively minor 16C painting, **François Clouet's** Bath of Diana of c 1560, is of interest in that local tradition holds that the central figure is in fact a portrait of Diane de Poitiers. There is certainly a passing resemblance to the representation of

Diane on Goujon's tomb of Louis de Brézé in the cathedral, though Clouet's figure cannot be regarded as being particularly individualised. The painting is so stuffed with visual clichés however, that it seems quite plausible that Clouet may also have seized the opportunity to throw in a provocative flourish.

The Rue Eugène Delacroix connects the Beaux-Arts with the **Palais de Justice**, one of the great set-pieces of late medieval civic building left in northern Europe. The complex consists of three main blocks, that to the east a replacement of 1844. The west wing was the first to be constructed, begun in 1499 to house a merchants' hall and completed in 1509. Work then started on the central block, initially intended to house the Exchequer of Rouen, but the decision of François I to declare a 'Parlement de Normandie' in 1514 led to a change in the building's function. The merchants' hall in the west wing was annexed as the chief judicial court, while the central block was enlarged to house the Salle des Séances du Parlement (parliamentary debating chamber). Work continued on the western part of the central block until 1517, while that to the east dates from 1530–51, the whole much altered complex traditionally attributed to the designs of Roger Ango and Roulland Le Roux, although the involvement of the latter seems most unlikely.

It is best seen from its central court, off the Rue aux Juifs, where excavations have uncovered the foundations of an early 12C synagogue within the present court. The decoration of the central block is virtuosic in the extreme, and clearly intended as a '*tour-de-force*'. The underlying principle, that the higher you are the denser the decorative embellishment, is brought to a brilliant conclusion in the four groups of freestanding stonework which gather round the main attic windows. The full ornamental repertoire of late Gothic architecture is on display here, with arches, gables, pinnacles, finials, and tracery worked into ever more fantastical shapes. Only the mouldings are kept consistently simple, and they are the key to the whole design, for without their linear framework all this complexity would become confusion. The only chamber now open to the public is the **Salle des Pas Perdus**, situated on the first floor of the west wing (open every afternoon). Approximately 48m x 16m the hall is bounded by narrow watching galleries along its short sides, whilst statuary niches impose a definite bay rhythm on the long sides, and articulate the finely calculated volumes. The wooden roof is post-war and evidence of war damage is to be found throughout the palace, particularly in the pitted exterior of the north flank, now sorrowful beneath its bewitching run of gargoyles.

The **Place du Vieux-Marché** lies just to the west and, as its name suggests, was the market square of medieval Rouen. Beginning in 1970 an imaginative redevelopment has seen the place restored to its late medieval ground level, and the area relaid with a triangular lower section from which steps ascend to a northerly garden. The preliminary excavations revealed the ground-plan of the 15C church of **St-Sauveur**, and its foundations have been consolidated to the south—it is from this church that Brother Isambert de la Pierre carried the cross he held out to Joan of Arc. North-west of this, and bounded by cafés and restaurants, is an ambitious complex drawing together a covered fish market, church and a large cross marking the site of the martyrdom of Joan of Arc. The church of **Sainte-Jeanne d'Arc** must rank as one of the finest post-war ecclesiastical buildings in France. It was designed, along with the market, by the consultant architect to Rouen,

Louis Arretche, and completed in 1979. Arretche is best known for his work in reconstructing St-Malo, and when faced with the problem of combining two buildings with quite different functions turned to the vernacular traditions of maritime Normandy. He employed shipwrights to curve the timber beams, and by looking to the roofscape as the principal means of shaping the composition, introduced the imagery of the harbour into the heart of Rouen. The interior of the church is equally surprising, for the fluidity of spatial treatment and liberties taken with axiality are unexpected. The altar is on an approximately SE–NW axis for instance, but this is largely notional as the interior space is arranged so as to suggest a centrally-planned structure. This is most explicit in the ceiling, which seems as if twisted into two keels, kept apart by a lozenge-shaped lantern. Any sense of the raking floorspace suggesting the valves of a modern lecture theatre is dispelled by the handling of the north wall. Arretche's brief required him to house the 16C stained glass fortuitously removed from **St-Vincent** before its destruction in 1944. He resolved the problem of including late Gothic tracery in a building dominated by concerns for volume and tracery by treating the north flank as a gallery for the glass, and recreating the tracery in steel. Housed within a larger frame of glass and bounded by the main supporting piers, the arrangement inverts the medieval orders in a most effective design, with an arched window 'head' forming the base, and an angular 'sill' at the top.

The glass itself was produced c 1515–30 by two quite distinct workshops, the earlier material being undertaken by Arnold de Nimègue, while the later work derives from the shop of Engrand Le Prince of Beauvais. In its new position the glass is brought much closer to eye level, and you can better appreciate the depth of tonal range, so much greater than that of 16C ceramics whose colours it most resembles. The windows are mostly narrative and relate events concerned with (left to right)—St Peter, St Anne, Triumph of the Virgin, Tree of St Anne, John the Baptist, Misericordia, St Anthony of Padua above a multiple saints window, Infancy of Christ, Passion, Crucifixion, Resurrection, and St Vincent.

To the west of the Place, on the Rue de la Pie, the house in which the 17C dramatist, Pierre Corneille, was born and lived for the first 56 years of his life has been opened to the public as the **Musée Corneille**. As the second floor library is closed to all but scholars by appointment, the main interest lies in Corneille's study, retaining his desk and furniture, and with a good portrait of the man at the height of his powers. Also notable to the rear is a maquette of the Place du Vieux-Marché as it was in 1525, as well as plans of the, thankfully, abandoned project of the 1780s for a Place Royale.

The 19C novelist Gustave Flaubert is celebrated a little further to the west, along the Rue de Lecat, in the **Musée Flaubert et d'Histoire de la Médicine**. This is situated in the 18C Hôtel-Dieu, where Achille Flaubert worked as a surgeon and where his son, Gustave, was born in 1821 and lived until 1846. As its name suggests the museum's purpose is two-fold, the subsidiary pavilion which accommodated the Flauberts having been arranged with mementoes of family life, while the main building houses a collection of 19C surgical instruments and 17–18C hospital equipment.

South of the Place du Vieux Marché you are conscious of the damage inflicted in 1944 on the dense webbing of streets which run down towards the Seine. There is, nonetheless, a glorious survival in the Place de la Pucelle where the **Hôtel de Bourgtheroulde** was begun c 1510 for Guillaume Le Roux, lord of Bourgtheroulde and chancellor of the exchequer of Rouen. For most of this century the mansion has housed a bank and is consequently open during business hours. The heavily restored outer gate leads into a sizeable inner court to the west of which is a domesticated version of two bays of the Palais de Justice. The south range postdates 1520 however, and reflects a remarkable change of thinking. It is low and flat, decorated by garlands, urns, and caryatids, with, above the windows, a frieze depicting scenes from the Triumphs of Petrarch. Below you can also make out the meeting of François I and Henry VIII at the Field of the Cloth of Gold, with Guillaume's son, Abbot Aumale, said to be represented in François' retinue.

A path along the Rue aux Ours takes you past the 15C belfry tower of **St-André**, and left to the **Rue du Gros-Horloge**, the main shopping street of Rouen. The street takes its name from its most distinctive feature, a splendid clock mounted above an arch which straddles the road midway between the cathedral and the Place du Vieux-Marché. A belfry had been raised on the site, to the south of the Porte Massacre, before 1382, but was destroyed by Charles VI in retaliation for the town riots of that year. It was rebuilt in 1389–98 under Jean de Bayeux and mounted with an iron clock, forged in 1389 by Jehan de Félains. In 1527–29 the current archway replaced the Porte Massacre, and Félains' clock was moved out of the tower and onto the arch. The tower and balcony can be visited, revealing the clock mechanism as well as a small collection of bells and hour-hands, while a balustrade was run around Nicolas Bourgeois' belfry dome of 1711 specifically to give views over the city.

East of the Gros-Horloge the street passes the old three-storeyed town hall (Nos 60–68), built in 1607–10 by the architect Jacques Gabriel, before bringing you back to the Place de la Cathédrale by the **Maison du Tourisme**. Although this has been denuded of statuary, and seen its window and door rhythms wilfully debased as a result of several changes of use, it remains a telling counterpart to the Palais de Justice. The Maison was begun in 1509 to a design by Roulland Le Roux, then working on the central portal of the cathedral, and completed in 1542 to accommodate the Bureau des Finances. Externally it consists of a shallowly carved rectangular block, overlaid by an astonishingly diverse register of ornament. The intermingling of predominantly late medieval forms, in the polygonal bases and nodding canopies of the niches for instance, with Italianate cherubs and candelabra, has led most commentators to see this building as being in some way 'transitional'. But the dense overlay of all-over patterning is entirely consistent with early 16C architectural forms elsewhere in Europe, most notably in England and northern Spain.

3

The Lower Seine Valley: Rouen to Le Havre

ROAD (103km): Rouen D982, 11km St-Martin-de-Boscherville; 9km Duclair; D65, 13km Jumièges; D982, 15km Caudebec-en-Caux; D81, 5km Villequier; 14km Lillebonne; 15km St-Romain-de-Colbosc; N15 21km Le Havre.

RAILWAY: frequent mainline service from Rouen Rive Droite to Le Havre via Yvetot.

The title Seine is thought to derive from the Celtic 'squan', meaning curve, and the most striking characteristic of the river course downstream from Rouen are those huge winding loops which create the narrow headlands and shelving promontories so beloved of travellers on the river. These meanders describe a consistent pattern, running up against the chalk plateau of the Pays de Caux to form high cliffs before being thrown south again, to carve out convex promontories which bite into the Roumois. Napoléon recognised its commercial value, declaring 'Le Havre, Rouen and Paris are but a single town of which the Seine is the main street', but although he certainly encouraged navigation on the river, the Seine's role as one of the principal highways of France was already well established. During the Bronze Age Cornish tin was carried up the Seine to Burgundy, and the Romans augmented the river traffic by the construction of a road from Troyes to the military base at *Juliobona* (Lillebonne) and *Caracotinum* (Harfleur). With trade came the movement of people and ideas, bringing Christianity into Normandy as early as the 3C, and Norse raiders into Carolingian France in the 9C. The patterns of settlement were largely determined by the contours of the river however, and the safest landing stages were to be found where tributary streams had cut a valley through the chalk cliffs, creating sheltered inlets along the right bank. In consequence virtually all the towns, trading posts, monasteries, and castles which grew above the banks of the Seine, are to be found on its northernmost bank.

You should take the D982 out of Rouen where it climbs steeply to **Canteleu**, throwing off views of the port and city towers, before crossing the narrow neck of land which marks the northern limit of the Forêt de Roumare. As the road hairpins downwards at 11km the cruciform volumes of the former abbey of **St-Georges de St-Martin-de-Boscherville**, stepped deep above the heart of the village, come into view. Excavations have shown there to have been a church on this site since Merovingian times, and a Gallo-Roman temple prior to that, but the secondary dedication dates from an act of seigneurial diktat. At some point between 1050 and 1066 the hereditary chamberlain of the dukes of Normandy, Raoul de Tancarville, replaced the parish church of St-Martin with an Augustinian house dedicated to St-Georges. The canons clearly failed to inspire confidence however, for in 1114 the site was refounded as a Benedictine abbey by Raoul's son, Guillaume, and populated with monks from St-Evroult. The present church dates from this refoundation and, with the exception of some vaults, was complete by c 1130, the parishioners being allowed use of part of the nave.

Like Lessay, to which it is related, the building reveals itself with absolute clarity. A two bay choir carrying high groin vaults is separated from the rib vaulted apse by a quarter bay, the brighter light drawn through two superposed registers of windows further clarifying the relationship between the two areas. The transepts project by one bay, but continue the aisle rhythm with a central pier which supports a transept platform. This area is differentiated from the nave by rich mouldings carried around the extrados of the arcade, and soffit rolls on the under surfaces. It is here that the question of the vaults becomes crucial. Those of the transepts are clearly later insertions, while the diagonal ribs of the nave vaults are uncertainly sprung from corbels or expanded abaci, and are keeled (pointed in section).

As such they would appear to belong to a late 12C remodelling which imposed consistency, at the cost of eroding the careful distinction of parts which must have animated the early 12C church. A difference of perhaps 50 years may not seem much, but ecclesiastical fashions moved with great rapidity during the 12C.

St-Georges was a relatively small abbey, never numbering more than 30 monks, and was thus within the means of the parishioners to whom it reverted after the Revolution. Unfortunately the villagers had little use for the majority of the conventual buildings, although current excavations promise to reveal more information on their disposition, and all that remain are the old precinct wall, chapter house, and a 17C wing of the abbatial lodgings. A gate to the south of the church brings you, via the fantastical capitals of the ambulatory exterior, to the chapter house. Built c 1180 and covered by a sexpartite vault this is an extremely accomplished structure, and carries around its western entry the finest cycle of historiated capitals to have survived from 12C Normandy. The themes are drawn from the Old Testament, with a superb portrayal of Joshua halting the Sun, and Crossing of the Jordan. The much eroded column statues of Benedictine saints which stood on the plinth, and announced the transition from cloister to chapter house, have been temporarily removed to the Musée des Antiquités in Rouen, but plans are afoot to transform the crumbling block to the north into a museum for their eventual display.

Beyond Boscherville the D982 curves to hug the right bank of the Seine, bounded to the north by precipitous chalk cliffs, before sweeping into the ancient market town of **Duclair**. The town spreads upwards from the riverside quays, though you might wish to linger here to watch the flow of ships and barges heading for the larger ports along the Seine, or the small river ferry at work. Above the market square the parish church of **St-Denis** has retained a low 12C belfry tower, surmounted by a slate-hung 15C spire. The interior is notable for the variety of its elements, with a short nave and richly moulded tower bay, both of which employ pink and grey marble half-columns cannibalised from a Gallo-Roman temple. This Romanesque work is surrounded by a 14C choir and 15C aisles, illuminated by mostly 16C glass, with two very beautiful groups of late medieval niche figures framing the entrance to the tower bay. Around the corner, in the north aisle, a solitary denizen of Jumièges lurks in the guise of an Apostle, whose once painted brocades and huddled donor originally formed part of a far grander arrangement at the neighbouring abbey.

Rather than take the direct route to Jumièges you would do better to follow a southwards meander of the Seine, along the D65, passing old quarry workings, apple and cherry orchards, and timber farmhouses, scattered among the fruit trees. There are remains of a 13C manor house at **Mesnil-sous-Jumièges**, but lying at the northern end of the village which grew up to serve its monks, are the ruins of one of the great monastic houses of France, the Abbey of **Notre-Dame de Jumièges**.

The abbey buildings—monumental, roofless, sun-bleached and spare, like the skeleton of some mighty dinosaur—encompass one of the seminal churches of Romanesque Europe. Its formation was complex, if its forms were simple, and the scale and ambition of the major church owed much to the extensive privileges enjoyed by its ancient community. The establishment of an abbey on the site dates from 654 when St-Ouen, bishop of Rouen, encouraged St-Philibert to establish a Benedictine monastery here at the edge of a vast forest. Clovis II donated this forest to the monks, and shortly afterwards we hear of the construction of a monastic complex. As with St Augustine's 7C foundation at Canterbury, where three churches served the monks, Philibert constructed three separate sanctuaries, dedicated to Notre-Dame, St-Pierre, and SS-Denis-et-Germain. Notre-Dame is known to have been the principal monastic church, and to have been cruciform in shape with two towers. Little is known of the dispositions of the other two churches or of the conventual arrangements, and the monastery was razed in 841 by the Norse raiding parties of Oger, intent on attacking Rouen. Further Norse incursions led the monks to carry their relics into exile in 851, founding first St-Philibert-de-Grandlieu, and then passing through Cunault (Anjou), and St-Pourcain (Auvergne), before Charles the Bald gave them the Abbey of St-Valérian at Tournus (Burgundy) in 875, which was subsequently rededicated to St-Philibert. Their odyssey is paralleled by that of the Congregation of St-Cuthbert, also driven by Viking raids, who carried the uncorrupted remains of their beloved patron from Lindisfarne to eventual peace at Durham.

Unlike Lindisfarne, which never regained its former splendour, Jumièges was restored by William Longsword before 942, and reformed by William of Volpiano's appointee, Abbot Thierry, between 1017 and 1027. It thus regained its former pre-eminence and was systematically enlarged, acquiring a new church of Notre-Dame in the mid 11C, a chapter house and conventual quarters in the early 12C, and an expanded choir in the 1270s. The introduction of absentee abbots in 1463 had the usual enfeebling consequences, leading Abbot Gabriel le Veneur to dismantle the spire and strip it of lead several years before the abbey became a Huguenot target. The congregation of St-Maur attempted to reverse the process after 1616, and added the handsome Abbatial Lodge of 1666–71 which stands to the east of the precincts, but by 1790, when the abbey was suppressed, there were only 15 monks in residence. In 1793 the buildings were purchased at public auction by a timber merchant from Canteleu for use as a stone quarry, and the lantern tower demolished. Lord Stuart de Rothesay, British Ambassador in Paris, also took advantage of the situation to ship most of the stone from the cloisters and choir for use in his new mansion at Highcliffe, in Hampshire, between 1825 and 1835. Indeed that anything much at all survives is largely due to the Lepel-Cointet family, who bought the site in 1852 with the aim of preserving what was left.

You enter the site via a 14C '**Porterie**' to the west of the main monastic complex. A large rectangular hall, known as the '**Grand Cellier**', stands opposite, constructed in the late 12C off the west walk of the cloister to serve, in all probability, as the monks' refectory. There is evidence, where it abuts the western massif of Notre-Dame, of a second storey, supported on the collapsed vaulting bays of the main chamber which may well have housed the monastic library and scriptorium. The **chapter house** survived little better but originally carried a rib vault over its main square bay with a semi-dome to the east. Since Abbot Urso was buried here in 1127 the building is usually associated with his abbacy (1101–27), but the violence of Henry I's border wars suggests it postdates 1120. This is all that now remains of the conventual buildings, though the shape of the cloister, the heart of every medieval abbey, can be made out in the void created by its removal.

To the north lies the principal church—**Notre-Dame**. Work began to the east in 1040 under the abbacy of Robert Champart, and the church was structurally complete, save for the arcaded upper storeys of the western towers, by 1066, though given William the Conqueror's then preoccupation with England the monks had to wait until 1067 for Notre-Dame to be consecrated. Comparatively little of the choir survives above ground, and since it was reconstructed in 1278 with a full complement of radiating chapels and a two-storey elevation similar to that of St-Wandrille, it remains difficult to visualise. Champart was favoured by Edward the Confessor with the bishopric of London in 1044, and briefly became Archbishop of Canterbury, before the anti-Norman riots of 1051 forced him to return to Jumièges. He died the following year and was buried to the north of the high altar in the evidently completed choir. It is doubtful whether his exposure to late Anglo-Saxon architecture had much of an impact on the thinking at Notre-Dame, indeed the reverse seems to be true, as the choir of Jumièges had a peculiar distinguishing feature, there were no radiating chapels sprung from its apse-ambulatory. In this it follows Rhemish practice and the arrangement might be paralleled at Brauweiler or Cologne. It is also evident in the scarring of the west wall of the transept that the nave tribune was stepped down a foot or so to issue onto a tribune platform which continued the west–east axis across the transepts. Again the origins of this form lie in Germany, and it was to have a considerable influence on later 11C architecture in Normandy, witness Boscherville or St-Etienne de Caen.

With a lower and thicker-walled choir, and transept platforms, the nave must have seemed lofty and spacious, rising sheer to the clerestory parapet, crisply moulded and elegantly light. It is certainly the triumph of Jumièges, and one of a handful of buildings which might be said to mark the emergence of a mature Romanesque architecture in Europe, alongside St-Michael at Hildesheim, St-Vincent at Cardona, St-Philibert at Tournus, and San Miniato al Monte above Florence. The elevation is in three storeys, with a spacious tribune whose triple arched openings lie beneath tall clerestory windows, and a main arcade made up of alternate columnar and compound piers. This imposes a double bay rhythm on the building, the regular beat of the stronger supports extended up the wall by attached wall shafts which disappear into a mess of scarring beneath the clerestory sills. These transverse divisions cut the elevation into a succession of vertical slices, carving out powerful square bays. This effect would have been more strongly felt before the nave was despoiled, for the wall shafts originally carried diaphragm arches which extended up into the wooden roof, and linked the opposing walls to form a procession of three dimensional spaces. These spaces were sealed to the west by a monumental block, with a tribune chapel, originally dedicated to St-Michel, open to the nave, and twin towers set back behind a projecting three storey porch.

The south transept of Notre-Dame is connected to the earlier church of **St-Pierre** by a vaulted passage, inappropriately called the Promenoir Charles VII, which was refurbished at the same time as St-Pierre was provided with a new choir, in the first half of the 14C. The south elevation of St-Pierre was replaced c 1230 with continuous orders which recall English West Country practice (there are no capitals to mark the transition between arch and support). However, it is the west block and north-western nave bays which most tantalise the scholars. The documentary evidence can be variously interpreted, but the burial of Abbot Ensulbert of St-Wandrille in the church in 993 establishes the existence of the west bays by the late 10C. This makes St-Pierre the earliest surviving truly Norman great church. It possesses a false tribune over the aisles embellished with debased Corinthian capitals, inset roundel decoration, and a handsome western block with a walled-up first storey opening, which originally gave onto a full tribune. It is in all particulars an accomplished late Carolingian building, which one would not be surprised to find in Alsace, or the Poitou, and stands as enduring testimony to an often noted quality of the early Norman settlers—their adaptability and rapid adoption of local 'best practice'.

15km downstream Jumièges was rivalled by an even more ancient foundation, the **Abbey of St-Wandrille**, reached by a right turn onto the D22 just before the D982 passes beneath the Pont de Brotonne. Strictly speaking the abbey takes its title from the valley in which it stands, **Fontenelle**, but it has been known after its founder since the 11C. St-Wandrille studied under the Irish missionary, Columbanus, at Bobbio in northern Italy, and was persuaded by St-Ouen to found a monastery beside the Fontenelle in 649. By the early 9C the abbey was one of the foremost centres of learning in Europe, attracting Charlemagne's future biographer, Einhard, and the reformer, Ansegise, as abbots. The Norse raids of 841–60 destroyed this 'community of saints', and the monastery was not repopulated until c 960 when the relics of St-Wandrille were returned from Flanders by Maynard, who set about rebuilding the largest of the ruined churches on the site, that of St-Pierre. Despite the undoubted eminence of St-Wandrille during the 11C and 12C its reputation as an intellectual centre declined in the later Middle Ages. The Maurist reform contributed a new range of conventual buildings in the 18C, evident behind the **Porte de Jarente**, but the abbey was stripped of most of its treasures, and much of its medieval stonework, after 1790. And so it is to the re-establishment of a Benedictine community here in 1931 that one looks for signs of a renaissance.

Visits are conducted by the monks and are confined to the cult buildings and one walk of the cloister. The most striking is the ruined choir of **St-Pierre**, rebuilt after a fire between 1244 and 1302. It is a colossal two-storey structure, a refined and spare reaction to the Rayonnant buildings of Picardy and the Champagne. The transepts, lantern tower, and north walk of the cloister, date from the abbacy of Guillaume le Douillé, but after his death in 1341 the ambitious plans for the nave never progressed beyond the third bay, and the building remained forever incomplete. The cloister walk is splendid however, with a superb, if mutilated, Coronation of the Virgin portal at the north-east angle, where an angel plays a psaltery, and marmosets support the baldacchini. The cloister also abounds in fragments of earlier stonework, among which is a section of Mozarabic-inspired relief carving from an 8C church on the site.

The monks now celebrate the Hours in a 13C tithe barn, known as the **Canteloup Barn**, which was transported from La Neuville-du-Bosc and reassembled on its present site in 1969, the original cart-worn entrance porch serving as a side chapel.

As was the case with 7C Jumièges, St-Wandrille was equipped with separate chapels to house distinct cults. One such chapel, dedicated to **St-Saturnin**, survives at the north-eastern edge of the abbey precincts, accessible by following the Rançon road and taking the first turning to the right. When you meet up with the precinct walls once more, a woodland track runs along the wall as far as the chapel. It is usually locked and lies in a poor state of repair, but you might at least see the exterior. A cell was established here in the 8C, to house some relics of the Gallo-Roman martyr (better known as St-Sernin of Toulouse), and the present chapel would seem to represent a 10C rebuild, with a trefoil east end supporting a square central tower, and a short nave. It is a rare and beautiful survival, comparable with the chapel at Querqueville (see Route 14), and has embedded in its tower walls sculptural fragments from its 8C predecessor.

4km below St-Wandrille the old Gallo-Roman trading station of **Caudebec-en-Caux** lies at the foot of a breach in the high plateau, where the St-Gertrude valley empties into the Seine. The terrible devastation wrought among its timber houses by a fire in 1940 has denuded Caudebec of its historic core, though the church of **Notre-Dame** escaped serious damage and thankfully remains one of the most intriguing Flamboyant structures in Normandy.

Building began under English occupation in 1426 to a design by the architect Guillaume Le Tellier, and the ambulatory, choir, and eastern bays of the nave were complete by 1484. The western bays of the nave, façade, and bell tower, were added between 1490 and 1539. The apse is canted and supported by an axial column, which part conceals and part reveals the Lady Chapel beyond, an axial beat magnificently reaffirmed by the pendant vault of the chapel. This latter vault is a 7 tonne monolith suspended from a single high keystone, and was considered sufficient achievement to earn Le Tellier a burial place beneath. Suffice it to say, when Henri IV visited the church he described it as 'the most beautiful chapel in the kingdom'.

Much of the internal statuary of Notre-Dame, and particularly the huge 17C figures in the chapel of the Holy Sacrament, were brought here in the 19C from Jumièges, but the glass was designed for Caudebec, and is of a quite different order. It is mostly 15C or 16C, given by noble houses, soldiers, confraternities, or local merchants, who figure as donors at the base of each window. Among many first-rate examples sixteen 15C panels, devoted to St Catherine and St Nicolas in the Lady Chapel, the cycle above the north door given by Fulke Eyton, English captain of Caudebec in c 1440, and the west windows of 1531–34 can be singled out.

The west front, by contrast, depends on a virtuosic display of tracery and fretwork overlaying an initially bewildering geometry. The whole composition is canted outwards, as at St-Maclou in Rouen, but is here seen as an invitation to cover the lower area with small-scale carving. The larger statuary has gone, with the exception of the curious late 16C caryatids in the upper reaches, but the smaller figures that survive—prophets, pilgrims, musicians, and angels, intermingled in a Dance of Death with portraits of the local townsfolk—are provided with exquisite miniature canopies and bases which mimic the carved pendant vaults housing their larger brethren. This ability to resolve stone into unexpected configurations is marked elsewhere on the exterior, particularly above the marvellously dense tracery heads of the clerestory windows, where the balustrade carries the text of the Magnificat, from buttress-head to buttress-head, in letters one metre high.

The other building to have survived the 1940 fire lies along the Rue Thomas Basin, a 13C stone house known, rather enigmatically, as the **Maison des Templiers**. The interior was damaged in 1940, with little more than the capitals surviving, but it has been admirably restored and as a museum of local history contains a valuable portfolio of photographs of early 20C Caudebec-en-Caux.

4km downstream from Caudebec (along the D81), in a bend in the river where the estuary pilots used to take over from the river pilots, the small town of **Villequier** curves three streets deep above the banks. During the late 18C the Vaquerie family, shipwrights from Le Havre, built a long and low brick mansion above the river on the Rue Ernest Binet. This now houses the **Musée Victor Hugo**, a period meditation which concentrates on the tragic affairs of the Vaquerie and Hugo families. Victor Hugo and the writer and critic, Auguste Vaquerie, were great friends, spending long periods together here and in Jersey and Guernsey, and in March 1843 Hugo's daughter, Léopoldine, married Auguste Vaquerie's brother, Charles. The marriage was cut short six months later when the couple were drowned returning from Caudebec, after a freak gust of wind overturned their boat, trapping Léopoldine and driving Charles under in his frantic attempts to save her. The news reached Victor Hugo a week later and provoked him to write 'Les Contemplations', displayed in the house along with contemporary newspaper cuttings, paintings, and photographs. Although the tone is one of sadness the house is warmed by souvenirs of family life and friendship: the cartoon character Fanfan Troussard which Hugo created to amuse his children, the spacious billiard room hung with drawings and paintings, mementoes of Juliette Drouet, Hugo's mistress of 50 years standing, and photographs of the Channel Islands taken by the Hugo-Vaquerie atelier.

The families are buried in the graveyard of the local church—a delightful spot, terraced beneath the 16C nave on a rise above the town. The church itself, dedicated to **St-Martin**, carries a handsome bell tower while inside, below a contemporary wooden roof, a mid 16C window depicts a naval engagement between Jehan Ango's Dieppe fleet and a flotilla of Portuguese galleons.

From Villequier the D81 skirts the huge industrial installations and oil refinery at **Port-Jérôme**, before rejoining the D982 at 14km **Lillebonne**. There are few indications that Lillebonne rose above the ruins of *Juliobona*, named in honur of Julius Caesar, as the ancient port has long since silted up and the street plan has become a mix of the medieval and the 19C. Little of Caesar's town stands above ground, though the ruined **Amphitheatre** gives you a measure of the place. This is situated in the Place de l'Hôtel de Ville (if closed keys can be obtained from the Café de l'Hôtel de Ville), and was designed to accommodate 10,000 overlooking an arena with a diameter of 48 metres. The complex represents a 2C enlargement of a 1C theatre, necessitated by the huge expansion of Juliobona after it became a provincial Roman capital, but its terraces are now grassy banks, and the baths, aqueducts, and forum have vanished, known only from archaeological excavation. The **Musée Municipal** in the Jardin Jean-Rostand displays some of the finds but these are of mostly minor interest, as the major items have been deposited in the Musée des Antiquités in Rouen.

The industrial reaches of the Seine estuary overshadow most of the 36km between Lillebonne and Le Havre, and you might do better taking the D81 to **Saint-Romain-de-Colbosc,** turning on to the N15 for the last 21km into Le Havre.

LE HAVRE was initially planned as a set-piece, and has been replanned as a set-piece, with the result that it has a coherent centre sandwiched between the sea, the commercial docks, and an extensive array of dismal suburbs. No town existed on the site before 1517 when François I decided to construct a port where the estuarial marshes had been stable enough to support an old sailors' chapel, Notre-Dame de Grâce. The fortified harbour basins were designed to replace those of Harfleur, where progressive silting-up of the port approaches had become an intractable problem. The first man-of-war sailed from the Bassin du Roi in 1518 and the town took the arms of the king—a silver salamander on a red field—though the early inhabitants demurred at François' conferment of the title Franciscopolis on the town, preferring to call it Le Havre de Grâce. In 1525 a freak high tide destroyed most of the town, depositing 28 fishing smacks in the streets north of Notre-Dame, and a chequered early history was only redeemed when the exiled Sienese engineer, **Girolamo Bellarmato**, was engaged to redesign the town and consolidate the harbour walls.

Having worked in the unstable marshes of the Venetian lagoon, Bellarmato successfully refounded the harbour fortifications and laid out two new residential quarters, Notre-Dame and St-François. Until Napoléon III ordered the demolition of the walls in 1852, Bellarmato's fortified harbour city contained Le Havre despite its emergence as a major commercial and transatlantic port after the American War of Independence. After that date Le Havre grew quickly, and when the first transatlantic steamship, the *Washington*, docked in 1864 the passenger quays were already becoming as profitable as the trade in cotton, tobacco, sugar and coffee. The great liners, built in the yards of Augustin Normand at Le Havre, which plied the sea lanes to New York, gave the town a cosmopolitan air and the local economy boomed for most of the period between the two World Wars.

Evidence of this is now sadly confined to the archives, as between the 2nd and 13th September 1944, with the Battle of Normandy over and Paris liberated, the continuing German occupation of Le Havre provoked an eight-day Allied aerial bombardment during which the occupying forces sabotaged or blew up every port installation still in existence. Over 19,000 houses were either badly damaged or completely destroyed and more than 4000 people were killed. In the wake of such devastation it took more than two years merely to clear the rubble and reopen the port.

The job of reconstructing the town was given to the 70-year-old Parisian architect **Auguste Perret**, then known for his pioneering use of reinforced concrete at Raincy. Perret envisaged a three dimensional grid, 'a perfect balance of volumes and spaces, of horizontals and verticals', with a new quarter to the west of the old port, and a sequence of monumental public buildings adorning large squares. His initial plan provided for all traffic to be channelled along a network of underground roads, but it was calculated that this would have absorbed the total output of the French concrete industry for the forseeable future and the plan was scaled down. Despite the rebuttal Perret's later designs adhered to the general principles of his earlier conception, a grid of streets interspersed with large public spaces, unified by a stylistic coherence that verges on the neurotic. Most of the large scale buildings and apartment blocks were constructed in the 1950s and 1960s under a team of up to 14 architects, but by the early 1970s a degree of disillusionment had affected the scheme and the most recent buildings in Le Havre represent a departure. Contemporary reactions towards the new town tend be hostile, and it has been anathemised in French political circles as the most desolate urban landscape in the country. This is certainly something of an overstatement, for the net result of Perret's grand design is undeniably airy and spacious, but it is born of a disagreeable architectural generation, and informed by a narrow-minded arrogance. To this visitor it seemed strangely diffuse, removed from the dense sociability common to most French cities, and the insistent rectilinearity and reliance on concrete becomes wearying. One needs shifting, luminous marine light to see it at its most persuasive, for on a dull day it is a dull town, anchored somewhere between Bari and Birmingham.

The **Ile St-François** is virtually all that survives of Bellarmato's town, in

plan at least for little actual 16C building remains standing, and is an appropriate spot from which to begin an exploration of the town as it hosts the **Musée de l'Ancien Havre**. This has been installed in a 17C town house, formerly belonging to the early 18C naturalist Michel du Bocage. Lacking any outstanding exhibits the collections are dispersed over four floors, with watercolours and prints of 'Vieux Havre' on the ground floor, and a section concentrating on the 19C port above. The most interesting area is probably that devoted to shipbuilding, which here means the Augustin-Normand yards, with some glorious photographs of *La France* in dry dock.

Turning along the Rue de Bretagne to cross the Bassin du Roi at the Pont Notre-Dame brings you to the only significant 16C building remaining in the old town—the cathedral of **Notre-Dame**. Built between 1575 and 1630 the exterior is animated by a battery of gargoyles carved as salamander heads and a west front which forms the principal vehicle for an essay in French baroque design. High pedestals support double columns whose banded rings are reflected in the pilaster orders behind, while angels dance above the aisle windows. All this is held in check by the monumental gravity of the upper register, closing the composition with a vast coffered entablature. Given these west front arrangements the interior comes as a revelation. The church is a double-aisled basilica with contained transepts, an unusual and satisfying twist being the subordinate treatment accorded these transepts. They are narrow and separated from the main body of the nave by flying screens which mimic the elevation of the nave. There is thus nothing to interrupt the smooth procession of arches and windows. The building was largely reconstructed after 1944 having been deprived of its original glass, but the organ Cardinal Richelieu donated in 1637 survives to the west.

To the north the Rue de Paris touches on the **Espace Niemeyer**, designed by the Brazilian architect Oscar Niemeyer at the request of the local authority, and completed in 1982. Seen from a distance the square appears to consist of two truncated cooling towers, one of which is asymmetrically sloped, their concrete flanks rising above a sea of cement. Closer inspection reveals that they house the Maison de la Culture, a complex of cinemas, theatre, and open exhibition spaces. Beyond you reach the hub of Perret's new town, the **Place de l'Hôtel de Ville**. It is said to be one of the largest squares in Europe, and short of the vast reaches of Moscow's Red Square few others come to mind. It occupies six units of the grid and is bounded by a series of long rectangular blocks, with six 10-storey blocks breaking upwards to the south. The north is dominated by the Hôtel de Ville, a long, low, reticulated block whose bays are divided by attenuated columns, the only decorative element in the entire square. The flat roofs and continuous horizontals are however interrupted by Perret's tower, 72 metres of concrete cladding, remorselessly patterned into rectangles.

From here you might take the Avenue Foch as far as the Boulevard François Ier, where a left turn brings you to **St-Joseph**, one of the largest post-war churches in France. It was built in 1951–57, and was intended by Auguste Perret as a memorial to those who died in 1944, in addition to functioning as a church. As a building it is a streamlined colossus, a structural skeleton clad in pebbled concrete, with four groups of squared piers acting as a base for a 99 metre high octagonal lantern tower. Perret thought of his tower as a lighthouse dominating both land and sea. But it is an acquirer, not a diffuser, of light, and the architect's abhorrence of curved surfaces is apparent in the thousands of traceried lights, where the glass is set into a systematic panel of lozenges and squares. The colours have been modulated so as to refract the differing qualities of light from east or west, but this seems an oddly naturalistic concession in a building otherwise notable for the aggression with which consistently simple formulas have been deployed.

An arresting site was found for the **Musée des Beaux-Arts** where the Boulevard François Ier meets the Avant-Port, to the right of the P&O building. Built in 1953–61 by Raymond Audigier and Guy Lagneau the museum is essentially a cunningly designed glass box, flooded with natural light which is regulated by a system of shutters and louvres. As the building is arranged to allow flexible displays a room by room account would be inappropriate, but it is best known for its holdings of works by two locally-born painters, Raoul Dufy and Eugène Boudin (for Boudin in Honfleur see Route 8). Among some two dozen or so paintings by Dufy there is a good early Fauve 'Jeanne dans les Fleurs' (1907) and Apollinaire-inspired 'Sirènes', while the later material exemplifies that use of colour blocking and silhouette which is largely responsible for the recent revival of interest in Dufy, notable in 'Le plage et l'estacade du Havre' (1926). Most of the work on display by Boudin dates from the last decade of his life with the finest, 'La Tour Malakoff vue de la jeté', creates a very real sense of imminence in its interpretation of the sky.

The Verandah at Villerville (1930–33) by Raoul Dufy, Musée des Beaux-Arts, Le Havre/Giraudon, Paris/Bridgeman Art Library, London.
©DACS 1993

There is also the opportunity to compare Boudin's late work with that of **Monet**, **Pissarro**, and **Sisley**. The former is well represented by a 1903 canvas of Westminster Palace, picked out in a miasma of evening fog, and one of the 1904 Nymphéas series. Amongst the 19C landscapes of Corot and Courbet a small untitled oil painting by **Constable** comes as a pleasant surprise, as does **Géricault**'s portrait of an old woman. The earlier material contains a broad selection of Dutch 17C still lifes and seascapes, and a heavy burden of 18C Italianate landscapes by Volaire, Hubert Robert and Vien. The finest are usually to be found upstairs, with a portrait of a Florentine goldsmith by **Bronzino**, an arrestingly fresh study of a young man by **Fragonard** and **Luca Giordano**'s gruesome 'Caton d'Utique'.

Graville, Harfleur, and Montivilliers lie along the Seine and Lézarde valleys and fall within the modern catchment of Le Havre, though they were established long before the great port came to dominate the mouth of the Seine. All three are reached by the No. 9 bus which leaves from the main railway station at Le Havre, or via the Rue de Verdun and its continuations.
  Graville is now an industrial suburb above whose modern precincts the ancient priory of **Ste-Honorine** rises on a terrace, offering splendid views over the port and river. The silhouette of its Romanesque nave and lantern tower are unmistakable from the road below, though the fragmentary west front is 13C. There was a Carolingian church on the site dedicated to St-Etienne, but by the early 11C one hears of a relic of the local 4C martyr, Ste-Honorine, enshrined in a golden chest, and displayed here in Graville. The church was initially staffed by a community of secular clerks who

'assured parochial services', but by 1264 this loose constitution was replaced by a college of Augustinian canons. It is they who were responsible for the late 13C choir which greatly enlarged the church and which makes a sensitive transition from the earlier work to the west. Although undated, comparisons with La Trinité at Caen, particularly in the diapering around the low arch leading into the crossing area, suggest the nave belongs in the early 12C. It is drawn up of a simple two-storey elevation, divided into three double bays by wall shafts rising to the clerestory parapet. The south arcade is accorded an altogether richer treatment, with a billet moulded arcade and a splendid array of figurative capitals, that of the jousting knights on the fourth pier being particularly noteworthy.

The former conventual buildings to the south now house a museum, entered via the 13C chapter house. It boasts a motley collection of late medieval statuary and plaster models of vernacular building, descending, via a spiral stairwell, to the 'crypts', where a large barrel-vaulted chamber displays architectural sculpture and damaged tomb slabs.

To the east, upstream of the Roman port of Caracotinum, **Harfleur** developed around a fortified harbour where the Lézarde empties into the Seine. By the late 14C the town had grown into one of the largest ports in northern Europe, trading corn, wine, and textiles from Burgundy and the Ile-de-France in exchange for wool from England, furs from the Baltic, and figs, spices, and sugar from the Mediterranean. It presented an irresistible prize to Henry V after Agincourt and on 17 August 1415 he laid siege, entering the town 35 days later. The 16C was unkind however, and the construction of Le Havre conspired with the silting up of the port to ensure the slow decline of the town into its eventual status as a suburb.

The extent of this decline is made clear in the **Musée du Prieuré**, recently opened in the 15C Hôtel du Portugais. The museum's fundamental concern is the local site history: prehistory to begin with, Gallo-Roman and medieval material on the first floor, all of it admirably presented and animated by reliable models of the earlier towns and settlements. The church of **St-Martin**, a former cell of Montivilliers, is the one other building of note to have survived. This is renowned for its 15C octagonal stone spire, rising 83 metres to act as a navigation mark, but the dilapidated hall church which serves as an interior is frankly disappointing.

5km along the D925 the attractive market town of **Montivilliers** was less affected by the juvenescent stirrings of its grander neighbour, and retains a fine abbey church. This was founded as the convent of **St-Sauveur** by St-Philibert (see Jumièges) in 683. After the nuns' withdrawal in the face of continuing Norse raids the convent languished until the early 11C, when monks from Fécamp were encouraged to settle here. It was refounded in 1035 as an autonomous nunnery by Duke Robert who installed his aunt, Béatrice, as abbess. Subsequent fortunes were mixed. Substantial rents from Robert's endowment throughout the later 11C encouraged the building of a new church, whose nave, separated from the nun's choir by a screen, served as a parish church. By the late 15C however, the wool trade had benefited the parish while the disappearance of Normandy into the kingdom of France had done little for the nuns. This shift in relative status was decisively mapped out in the early 16C when the north aisle was demolished and replaced with a larger and lighter structure, better suited to accommodating the burgeoning population. Inevitably, this was also provided with the most sumptuous entrance to the church.

Of the two building periods the Romanesque excites the greater interest, although the north aisle is handled simply and with great confidence, and most authorities date the main campaign to c 1100, the choir (of which only the arcade survives) a little earlier. The nave marks the adoption of that two-storey elevation favoured by smaller foundations to the north of the Seine at this date, as at Graville for instance. The transepts carry rib vaults however, improvised out of the wall, which may be as early as 1120 and testify to the lack of any systematic thinking about the shape or geometry of high rib vaults in Normandy at this period. As in contemporary England they tend to be handled in an ad hoc fashion. Secondly the voussoirs around the entrance to the south transept chapel carry a series of shallow reliefs, whose apparent date (c 1100) and situation are quite unprecedented.

From the church the Rue Félix Faure crosses the Fécamp road and leads towards the **Brisgaret cemetery**, where a 15C cross and one gallery of the 16C charnel house remain standing, with a splendid grim reaper carved across one of its wooden imposts.

4

The Normandy Vexin: Gisors, Vernon, and Les Andeleys

ROAD (131km): Gisors D10, 8km Dangu; D146, 15km Baudemont; D5, 12km Giverny; 4km Vernon; N15, 14km Gaillon; D316, 12km Les Andelys; D1 and D2, 8km Ecouis; N14, 8km Fleury-sur-Andelle; (D321, 3km Fontaine-Guérard); D1, 10km Vascoeuil; (N31, 6km Martainville); D6, 11km Lyons-la-Forêt; 16km Etrepagny; D14, 13km Gisors.

The suggested itinerary is not as complicated as it appears, and is arranged as a circuit of the Normandy Vexin into which you might dip as you please. It is centred on Gisors, the ancient capital of the Vexin, but you may prefer to base yourself in Vernon, just outside the old county.

The region known as the Vexin was originally formed as a Carolingian administrative area, bordering on the Ile-de-France and bounded to the north and west by the valleys of the Andelle and the Seine. It stretched as far south as the Oise, until the Vexin was split along the valley of the river Epte by the Treaty of Saint-Clair-sur-Epte in 911. In return for a promise of peace and the prospect of his enemies' conversion to Christianity, King Charles the Simple granted the Norse chieftain, Wrolf the Walker, the lordship of all lands north of the rivers Epte and Avre. No formal treaty was ever drafted, the matter being concluded, according to Dudon of St-Quentin, by Wrolf placing his hands between those of the king of France. Wrolf was baptised, took the title Duke, and Latinised his name to Rollo, but although the event saw the creation of 'Normandy' the exact course of its boundaries became a matter of jealous dispute. With the Vexin split along the Epte the whole area grew into a heavily fortified frontier zone. Duke Richard I, William Rufus, and Henry II anxiously surveyed the loyalty of the Vexin barons, and when doubtful of their liegemen threw them out of their castles, and installed nominees in their place. Gisors, Château-sur-Epte, and Baudemont were all provided with castles of the first rank, and when Richard the Lionheart was forced to surrender Gisors to Philip

Augustus in 1196, he immediately set about building the formidable Château-Gaillard to cut off the Seine approaches. This concentration of resources in the major valleys remains evident today, and the chalk scarps towards Ecouis have a sparsely populated and neglected air.

GISORS. Lying in the eastern corner of the Vexin, Gisors was constructed under Norman patronage as its principal town, and although the heart was ripped out of the centre in 1940 it remains a pleasant enough base from which to explore the area. The entire rationale for the town lies with its **Château**, which survives in large part to the west of the market place, and can hardly be missed. The strategic possibilities of the site were first seriously identified by William Rufus, who saw in it the key to a series of castles forming a defensive line from Forges-les-Eaux to Vernon, and west along the Avre valley. In 1097 Rufus raised a 20 metre artificial motte, crowned by a high wall, within which he built a donjon. Henry II may have added two polygonal storeys to this tower in 1161, but the inner complex has the simple clarity of the 11C stockaded keeps depicted in the Bayeux Tapestry, and forms the core of the vastly expanded castle which greets you at the west gate. The view from the top of the donjon reveals the town and explains the subsequent development of the castle. A large bailey was surrounded by an enceinte wall under Henry I in 1125, the walls reinforced and buttressed by Henry II, with a tiny chapel dedicated to Thomas à Becket shoehorned into the space between the inner walls and the donjon in 1184. To the south-east a rectangular tower was raised, known as the Governor's Tower, and connected to the semicircular Prisoners' Tower by a curtain wall. This latter complex was undertaken for Philip Augustus who, having occupied Gisors while Richard the Lionheart languished in a German prison in 1193, began work before his possession was formally ratified by the Treaty of Issoudun in 1196. It is worth asking at the west gate to visit the vaulted governor's hall, where steps lead down to the dungeons of the **Tour du Prisonnier**. Here in the soft stone two inmates have decorated the walls with graffiti, one during the late 15C, the other in 1575, with scenes from the Passion, St George and the Dragon, a tourney, Crucifixion, ball, St Martin, and perhaps final '*Mater Dei memento mei*'.

Below the castle the Rue de Vienne gives onto the church of **SS-Gervais-et-Protais**, founded to serve a rapidly expanding town under Rufus and consecrated in 1119. Some 12C foundations survive beneath the central tower, but the church is now of the 13C and 16C, and a building of considerable merit. Blanche of Castille financed the building of a new choir in 1240 which was completed, along with its lantern tower, in 1249. This 13C work was enshrined in a 16C church and, remarkably, the parish archives survive, recording payments for materials and labour. In 1497 Pierre Gosse and Robert Jumel began the north choir chapel for the Confraternity of the Assumption, the sculpture provided by Pierre Monnier, Mathurin de Lourme, and Pierre des Aubeaux, and the whole complete by 1500. A rectangular screen wall was added to the east of the choir and completed in 1507. In 1515 the Grappin family shop was summoned from Beauvais to begin work on the new transepts—a move which was to result in three generations of Grappin masons and stonecarvers working at Gisors. They were responsible for the transepts (1515–32), nave (1526–42), and the west portal of 1567. The building is therefore substantially 16C, constructed on great church lines, financed by local guilds and confraternities, and deserves an unhurried visit.

The situation of the choir and low central tower is most clearly viewed from the exterior where it becomes evident that the 13C church has been engulfed, remounted almost, by a mass of gargoyles and pyramidal roofs. This 16C work provided a new range of chapels, that to the north with a splendid pair of stags caught up in the fretted lights of a traceried window. The north transept portal retains its great wooden doors with an Adoration of the Magi to the left, and an Annunciation to the right. The arch of stone sculpture has been mutilated however, and the fine traceried hood-mould hacked beyond repair. The wooden doors of the west portal were destroyed by fire in 1940, but were originally framed by a very different type of entrance façade. With the exception of Nicolas Coulle's north tower Apostles of 1536 the west front has been rid of any tendency one could look on as Gothic, and centres on a giant coffered arch enclosing a Grappin-carved Dream of Joseph of 1567. The whole civically generated building programme finally foundered on the classically-ordered south tower, which had to be abandoned in 1591.

On first entering the west door the choir seems shrunken and barely visible. It is considerably lower than the nave and obscured by the crossing piers admittedly, but the spaciousness of these western parts is striking. The nave is double-aisled, and carries considerable real height in both the aisles and clerestory. The piers are articulated with sharp mouldings between concave faces, and rise sheer to the vault, unencumbered by capitals. Both ornament and figurative meaning have been flung to the periphery of the building—the vaults for instance become progressively more fanciful the further you are from the central axis, and reach a crescendo in the pendant-vaulted Crucifixion group in the third chapel off the north aisle. The intermediate piers of the south aisle were commissioned to represent the interests of major donors, that of the Guild of Tanners being the finest, decorated by scenes from the life of St Claude interspersed with details of the working life of a tanner. The guild also employed Engrand Le Prince to provide them with the adjacent magnificent window of St Claude. There is a fine *memento mori* in the neighbouring chapel, but the modest cockleshelled pillar of the Confraternity of St-Joseph has unfortunately lost its statuary.

Blanche of Castille's choir also survives in good order, a square-ended, three-storeyed structure which reflects contemporary architectural styles in north-eastern France. Indeed as Gisors shares its unusual dedication with Soissons cathedral it is tempting to pursue links with the Soissonais, but these links are very generalised, and Gisors is best understood as a local and simplified version of early 13C Gothic, similar to Laon cathedral and probably transmitted via Cistercian churches. Elsewhere Pierre des Aubeaux's bas-relief of the Assumption of 1511 in the north choir chapel is worth studying as is Jean Grappin's tremendous Renaissance spiral staircase of 1575, which gives access up the inner face of the south-west tower and with unrivalled views of the great stuccoed Tree of Jesse opposite.

Leaving Gisors along the D10 brings you into the broad valley of the Epte, the river bed often fed into artificial lakes and reservoirs, above which a number of attractive villages remain grouped around their medieval fortified farmsteads. Rather than taking the direct route to Vernon at the junction with the D181 strike left and follow the D146 through (8km) **Dangu**, past a 12C church renowned for Guillaume de Montmorency's funerary chapel of 1580, and graced in 1589 by a splendid image of the noble lord in grisaille. The road turns swiftly towards the river, where you catch a glimpse of the great château of **Boury-en-Vexin**, over the border in the

Ile-de-France. Further east and opposite St-Clair the striking silhouette of the ruinous castle of (6km) **Château-sur-Epte** stands above a beautifully formed motte, a scaled-down version of its sister at Gisors. The fortified gates are 13C and now give access to a farmyard, but it is possible to obtain permission to stroll within the ruined precincts. The road then curves through (5km) **Aveny**, where the château and 15C bridge make an attractive group, just within sight of yet another Rufus fortification at (3km) **Baudemont** (closed to the public). The road switches designation here to the D5, before catching up with the busy modern pilgrimage to (13km) **Giverny**.

The attraction is the **Fondation Claude Monet**, comprising the house and garden Monet occupied from 1883 until his death in 1926. These were restored in 1966 by van der Kemp, after an appeal brought forward a number of predominantly American donors, and are open to the public from April to October. Entrance is via l'Atelier des Nymphéas, a huge commercial bazaar hung with copies of the 'Waterlilies' series paintings, and which once served as the largest of Monet's studios. The house itself stands to the north of the garden, its low rectangular rooms restored to the vibrant single-colour schemes favoured by Monet, and hung with Japanese prints and reproductions of Monet's work. Much of the original furniture had been dispersed by the time van der Kemp began work, but that of the dining room and kitchen at least survived. The sheer numbers of visitors can make it difficult to appreciate the rhythms of the artist's life here however. Rising at five to eat a large breakfast he worked until noon, either in the gardens or in one of three studios, deliberately avoiding the midday light when he would take lunch followed by a light nap. In the afternoon he would return to the most pertinent of several paintings in hand, all of them fundamentally concerned with the same theme—the effects of light '*sur le motif*'.

In later life Monet's avowal 'I merely let my gaze take in what the world was showing me', was pared down and focused on a narrow range of subjects, as a means of capturing the impressions of light at different times of the day, or the season. It was this concentration that produced the series paintings. Even the most intense tourism cannot overwhelm the beauty of the gardens, particularly on May mornings when the colours are most fresh. The **Jardins des Nymphéas** (waterlily gardens) are now reached through an underpass, remote from the flower beds and official guides to the north. Sensuous and fragrant, redolent of late Monet, they suffice to soothe the most battered visitor, and are the one great triumph of the restoration.

4km upstream of Giverny, and on the left bank of the Seine, **Vernon** is the principal market town of the western Vexin. A Gallo-Roman settlement existed on the site, and as a favoured residence of St-Louis the town prospered during the Middle Ages, although the combined depredations of artillery or aerial bombardment in 1870, 1940, and 1944 have left few reminders of this, and reconstruction has given it an inoffensive, workaday atmosphere.

In consequence little remains of the vast castle undertaken by Philip Augustus in 1196. Fragments of the enceinte walls, mostly incorporated into later buildings, occasionally catch the eye, but a walk along the Rue Ecuries des Gardes brings you to its enduring centrepiece, the **Tour des Archives** (public access currently suspended). In its design this is reminiscent of the Tour Jeanne d'Arc in Rouen, with three floors and a watchpath accessible by spiral staircase. The view from the upper chamber makes it clear that the castle was intended to provide more than a feudal stronghold in Vernon however, for it stands opposite the Château des Tourelles, and thus complements the defences of the medieval bridge which crossed the Seine at this point. A stroll over the modern road bridge brings you into a small riverside park to the left of which rises the **Château des Tourelles**. Although begun in the 12C, the present keep is largely 15C and was extensively rebuilt in 1763. It consists of a square core protected by four round corner towers, the west tower having been destroyed in August 1944. Beyond it another target of 1944 lies in ruins—the section of the medieval bridge which connected the right bank with an island midstream—its piles supporting masses of 15C and 18C masonry, with a forlorn toll-house standing on top of a surviving span.

The majority of the late medieval structures which were left standing are concentrated in the old collegiate quarter, the best being the **Syndicat d'Initiative**, accommodated in a particularly fine 15C timbered house along the Rue Carnot. Immediately south of this, and opposite the 19C Hôtel-de-Ville, is the church of **Notre-Dame**, the one large-scale survival. Begun as a parish church in the late 11C, a college of canons was established here in 1160, under the patronage of William, count of Vernon. It is now essentially a church of two parts—a high and light six bay nave leading, via a dwarf transept, to a low and shadowy choir. The choir arcade is the only area of the 12C building to have been retained, and its modest size suggests that William's foundation was small. The axial chapel was added during the 14C, the clerestory and vault in the 16C, and the ambulatory heightened in the 17C. A final indignity was wrought in 1781 when the altar from the Chartreuse de Gaillon, pure Louis XVI and fine in an 18C church, was installed and flanked by two reliquary chests, one of which reputedly contains a glove of Thomas à Becket.

The nave dates from a late 15C rebuilding, with a recessed triforium and boxy six-light clerestory windows. Little of the glass survives though one of the south aisle chapels includes a fine 16C window, contrasting scenes from the life of John the Baptist with the Nativity and Resurrection of Christ. To the west an excellent **organ loft** is contemporary with this glass, and trembles with extravagant reliefs of angels, virtues, and the inevitable King David playing his harp.

The exterior reinforces these contrasts of scale and ambition, with a squat 13C crossing tower only just breaking above the nave parapet. Nevertheless the north porch must once have been very fine, housing a Last Judgement of which only the angels and elders of the archivolts survive. This stands in sharp contrast to the west front where a 14C Virgin and Child has been reused beneath a routine lintel depicting the Nativity. For the ambition of this western composition is to be found much higher, in the controlled tension exacted from rounded and snaking patterns in the superbly realised rose window.

North of the church, along the Rue Carnot, the **Musée A-G Poulain** has been accommodated in a substantially late 15C house (with a splendid carved wooden corner-post) and extended to encompass a townhouse of 1760 and 19C Hôtel du Cheval Blanc. The museum is named after the local archaeologist Alphonse-Georges Poulain, best known for his excavations at the Neolithic burial site of Mestreville in 1902–04, which has been reconstructed alongside Bronze Age and medieval artefacts, on the ground floor. The rest of the collections are displayed on the upper two floors but the highlight is undoubtedly **Room 10—Artistes de Giverny**. Here amongst a small group of paintings executed at Giverny by **Monet**, his daughter-in-law, **Blanche Hoschede-Monet**, and **Mary McMonnies**, are works by such frequent visitors as **Pierre Bonnard** and **Edouard Vuillard**.

The mighty **Château de Gaillon** lies downstream from Vernon (14km by the N15), a gift of St-Louis to the archbishops of Rouen. Nothing remains of the earlier medieval castle, as in 1502 Cardinal Georges d'Amboise decided to extend the late 15C west wing and add a monumental **Gatehouse**. This latter structure, begun in 1508, is considered by many to foreshadow one of the most far-reaching shifts of identity in the history of French architecture. As a minister of Louis XII, Georges d'Amboise was entrusted with co-ordinating diplomatic support for Louis' claim to the dukedom of Milan, spending long periods in northern Italy. The experience would seem to have produced a particular liking for Italian ornament, if not for Italian architectural design, and when he came to rebuild Gaillon the Cardinal-Archbishop summoned Italian stonecarvers, Pacello da Mercogliano among them, to work alongside his Norman masons. In consequence the Italianate detailing of the gatehouse is the earliest evidence of Renaissance thinking expressly worked into a building in France, and was to have a decisive impact on François I's château at Chambord. Sadly you can see little of either this or the spacious 17C pavilion Jules Hardouin-Mansart built in the grounds for Colbert, as the ten-year restoration programme is unlikely to see the château reopened before 1994.

The direct route to **Les Andelys** (D316, 13km) runs beneath the ruins of one of the most influential fortifications in Europe, Richard the Lionheart's **Château-Gaillard**. Towering over the Seine approaches to Rouen and perched on the edge of the sheerest of those cliffs which rise above the right bank, it is best reached on foot along the path from Petit-Andely (for access by car, the route is well signposted via GrandAndely). Richard was given leave to appropriate the site from the archbishops of Rouen by Pope Alexander III in 1195, after the papacy had brokered a settlement between the English and French crowns, and began actual construction in the following year. His haste was well judged, for Gisors had been surrendered, and Rouen was vulnerable to an attack mounted along the Seine approaches. The undoubted speed with which Château-Gaillard was built gave rise to a legend that it was finished within a year, Richard's reported exhortation—'see my fine yearling'—doubtless enhancing the tale, but the surviving payrolls testify to three building seasons, from 1196–98. Intriguingly among the lists of miners, limeworkers, watchmen, quarrymen, rough masons, free masons, carters, carpenters, and hodmen, there is no mention of an architect, and most authorities are inclined to see Richard as not simply the instigator of the work, but as its designer also. Richard's experience of warfare and siegecraft in the Holy Land, and particularly of the layout of the great 12C Crusader castles, would certainly have been brought to bear on the thinking behind the complex, and it is this world that is the key to understanding the design of Château-Gaillard. He described it as 'my beloved daughter', and when you stand amid its windswept heights, dazzled by the bleached white walls, it is hard to disagree with the chronicler who wrote—'all previous efforts were cast in the shade when Gaillard rose on the rock of Andeli'.

The fortress consists of two parts, the main castle towering above the cliffs, and an advanced redoubt towards the landward side. This redoubt, known as the **Châtelet**, is separated from the main complex by a moat and was itself fully moated and ringed by five towers, of which only one now survives. Entry to the inner defences is via a footbridge, which has replaced the original drawbridge, from where you can make out the casemates, hollowed out of the rock beneath the inner bailey walls to serve as food stores. Within the inner walls a small bailey accommodates a colossal three-storey cylindrical keep, its battered base supporting walls nearly 5 metres thick, and the ruins of a later Governor's Lodge. The fortifications are arranged as a series of concentric defences, forcing an attacker to breach successive rings and rendering him liable to counterattack when exposed within the moats or baileys. This system of concentric lines of defence was in part anticipated by Henry II's construction of the north-east curtain wall at Dover castle, but its origins lie in structures such as Kerak of Moab and are fundamentally and systematically applied here in the manner of Crusader castles. Supremely well-informed and flexible in his thinking, Richard even adopted the circular three-storey donjons his bitter rival Philip Augustus was already developing in the Ile-de-France.

Ironically the castle was in French hands within six years of its completion, falling after an eight-month siege on 4 March 1204. When Philip Augustus learned that the English had provisions to last another year he sent a detachment of soldiers to exploit an unconsidered weak point. They managed to enter the main defences through the latrines, and lowered the drawbridge with such speed that the garrison was forced to surrender 'before they had time to reach the keep'.

The castle was partially dismantled on the orders of Cardinal Richelieu, but the situation remains, surveying a vast sweep of the Seine and casting shadows over the town of **Les Andelys** below. Before Richard began work at Château-Gaillard there was but one Andely, the present Grand-Andely. The smaller **Petit-Andely**, which you see so clearly from the castle, grew out of the shanty town Richard had thrown together to house the masons working at Gaillard. The Rue Richard-Coeur-de-Lion takes you back down from the heights and into Petit-Andely.

Its finest building, the church of **St-Sauveur**, stands amidst half-timbered houses in the central square, an ambitious parochial structure which never received the nave so well-developed an east end calls for. The building mostly dates from 1220–40, with five-part vaults in the ambulatory and a three-storey elevation consisting of a columnar arcade, triforium, and clerestory illumined by Chartrain composed-windows (two lights surmounted by an oculus or foil)—all elements associated with early 13C great church planning. The high vaults are carried on wall shafts, which are in turn supported by grinning figured corbels, and there are ghostly remains of 15C frescoes in the triforium. Along with the battered remnants of some first-rate 15C sculpture in the north transept, and a fine 13C trumeau of a beneficent Christ, there is much to make one regret what has been lost, and perhaps also what was never finished.

From St-Sauveur the broad Avenue de la République leads to **Grand-Andely**, passing the locally famous healing well of St-Clothilde and a pleasant market square, before rising gently towards the collegiate church of **Notre-Dame**. On a grander scale than its counterpart in Petit-Andely, as befits a collegiate foundation, the church was begun in the mid 13C. Although the nave and choir arcades date from this campaign its present appearance owes most to an extraordinarily sensitive 16C programme, which lightened the upper superstructure and widened the aisles into adjacent chapels, developing that sense of amplitude which so pervades the building. Beginning c 1500 the triforium and clerestory of the choir, south transept, and nave were provided with an open lattice of flamboyant tracery. By the mid 16C architectural fashions had shifted, and with a fastidious respect for the established proportions of the church the north transept and exterior of the north flank were rebuilt in a crisp, classically-derived idiom, with an Ionic order on the exterior and beautifully realised Corinthian half-capitals and columns in the transept. This last campaign is likely to have been completed when the superb **organ loft** was installed in 1573 and decorated with female personifications of the Liberal Arts. And this is not the last of Notre-Dame's French Renaissance treasures for in the chapel beneath the south-west tower is a late 16C **Entombment** group from the Chartreuse de Gaillon, and above its door a panel painting of the **Apotheosis of the Virgin**, completed in 1612 by Quentin Varin, Nicolas Poussin's early master. The glass of the south aisle chapels is also late 16C and abounds with portraits of the members of the local confraternities who were their donors.

From Les Andelys the D1/D2 run north to (8km) **Ecouis**, where the 14C collegiate church of **Notre-Dame** enlivens an otherwise drab roadside town. This was founded in 1310 by Enguerrand de Marigny to replace the earlier parish church, and built with an austere twin-towered west front which, unusually, gives onto an aisleless nave. Prior to 1768 the church carried a wooden roof and a fuller complement of the 52 statues Enguerrand commissioned to decorate the building. Twelve of these survive, dispersed throughout the church, and are recognisable by their slightly hunched, lilting quality. The finest are in the north transept, where **Mary Magdalen** stands in prayerful silence and **St-Veronica** holds aloft the piece of cloth which bears an image of Christ. The disquieting **Annunciation Group** in the nave is late 14C, while Enguerrand's original **choir stalls** received their crude and lively rear panelling during the 16C. Although the effigy of his brother **Jean, Archbishop of Rouen**, lies in the south transept, Enguerrand was never buried here, and his fall from grace was spectacular. A close adviser and intimate of Philippe Le Bel he was accused after Philippe's death of practising sorcery by Charles de Valois and condemned in 1315. He was finally hanged in Montfauçon, his corpse left dangling from the gibbet for two years '*pour décourager les autres*'.

   North of Ecouis the N14 bridges the Andelle at (8km) **Fleury-sur-Andelle**, but before crossing the river a short detour along the D321 takes you to (3km) the ruins of **Fontaine-Guérard** (reached along a track which cuts off to the right just beyond Radepont). The site was first occupied by a priory of nuns, founded in 1185 by Robert, Earl of Leicester, but was ceded to the Cistercians in 1219 and raised to the status of abbey in 1253. The main church lies to the east of the spring which lent the site its name. Its consecration in 1218 predates the *de justo* transfer of the priory to Cîteaux, but the situation and austere simplicity of religious observance here were Cistercian in all but name, and required shared manual toil and absolute communal living. Hence the spacious work-room at the southern end of the conventual range, and the relatively unadorned nine bay chapter house, which together support the rectangular dormitory on the first floor. Even the early 15C chapel of St-Michel, standing above the abbey cellars and storerooms, is a model of simplicity. Its modesty may in part derive from its role, for it was built as an act of contrition by Guillaume de Léon, lord of Hacqueville, who arranged the murder of his wife, Marie de Ferrières, after she sought refuge from his ill-treatment in the abbey in 1399. Her effigy lies in the choir, and is the one portable object not to have been removed from Fontaine-Guérard to the parish church at Pont-St-Pierre.

Upstream from Fleury the D1 follows the valley of the Andelle where it grows lush and broad, passing a succession of small mill-towns, before reaching (10km) **Vascœuil**. At the edge of the village a 15C seigneurial residence, known as the **Château de la Forestière**, has been drastically restored but now serves as an exhibition space for contemporary art. The grounds are punctuated with sculpture by Vasarely, Dalí, Calder, and other post-war artists, with the three-storey central block given over to temporary shows. Within this the main stair tower terminates in a splendid octagonal watch-chamber, which Jules Michelet used as a study and where he wrote the greater part of his 'Histoire de France' during the mid 19C. Like most good historians Michelet was sufficiently troublesome to be twice suspended by the Collège de France, but the small museum devoted to his life in one of the outbuildings would scarcely have sufficed to satisfy his vanity. By contrast the 17C brick 'colombier' houses its doves in some style.

Vascœuil is also a good starting point for an excursion to the **Château de Martainville** (6km along N31, mysteriously signposted as N30 in the village). The château was begun by Jacques Le Pelletier in 1485 as a squared castle fortified with angle towers and surrounded by a moat. A 16C desire for comfortable living transformed its outlines however, and led to the filling in of the moat, dismantling of the drawbridge, and provision of a grand façade, creating in the process that picturesque array of chimneys which so enlivens the exterior. The interior remains substantially as it was in 16C, though the rooms themselves have been given over to a series of displays illustrating life in 16–19C rural Normandy. These recreate the interiors of farm or village rooms from the Bray, Vexin, or southern Eure, and provide a rich background for any exploration of remoter rural Normandy. Among the many interesting ojects are a superb Renaissance chest decorated with panels depicting Judith and Holofernes in the library, the 16C tapestry showing apple-pickers bringing in the harvest, and the fine collection of clocks.

You can return towards the Forêt de Lyons by way of **Ry** (4km, D13) generally considered the model for the Yonville-l'Abbaye of Flaubert's Madame Bovary, and an attractive and lively village. Banked above the main street the parish church is emboldened by a magnificent 16C south porch, carved out of local wood by sculptors from Rouen and dressed with Italianate candelabras and arabesques, evangelist symbols, and the instruments of the Passion. Above this the 12C lantern tower is crowned by a late medieval hexagonal spire of a type found throughout Haute-Normandie, hung as usual with slate. At the other end of the village, in an 18C cider-press, the local clockmaker has built an entertaining collection of automata, mostly enacting scenes from Madame Bovary. The whole curious affair is called the **Musée d'Automates** (open Easter to October; Sat–Mon only, 11.00–12.00, 14.00–19.00) but its restricted opening hours may be worth checking before going out of your way.

From Vascœuil the D6 meanders through the ancient beech woodland of the **Forêt de Lyons**, a Merovingian royal forest and favourite hunting ground of the dukes of Normandy. The forest took on its present appearance under the management of the Cistercians of Mortemer, who established clearings and granges throughout the domain during the 13C, and encouraged the building of small hamlets as centres for charcoal-burning and the seasoning of timber in the early 14C. The whole forest is criss-crossed by woodland paths and bridleways, maps of which may be obtained in Lyons. At its heart, in a deep ravine formed by the River Lieure, the one sizeable town of **Lyons-la-Forêt** idles peaceably for much of the year, before its fantastically picturesque timbered houses bring a torrent of summer visitors. The town is bounded by the 12C church of St-Denis to the west, extensively rebuilt in the 15th and 16C, and climbs eastwards along the Rue du Bout-de-Bas to a central square glorying in a 17C covered market hall. Most of Lyons is roughly contemporary with this market as the town was destroyed by fire in 1590, and it makes an excellent centre, out of season, for exploring the surrounding forest and the western corner of the Vexin.

From the central square you should follow the signs to **Mortemer**, a tortuous route along narrow woodland roads which lead to a well-watered glade beneath the headwaters of the river Fouillebroc. It must have seemed an ideal site for the first of the great Cistercian foundations in Normandy, and was colonised with the help of Henry I in 1134, receiving a second, and far greater church, between c 1185 and 1209. Like so many French abbeys it was sold off after the Revolution and stripped of its building stone, leaving a low fragmented ruin which echoes with the cries of one of the many packs of hounds kept for hunting hereabouts.

The main church is an unconsolidated mass of material, thrown up for the most part by recent excavation, but it is possible to gain a sense of the scale and general nature of the building. It consisted of an aisled nave, spacious transepts and choir, and an ambulatory with seven radiating chapels. The north transept wall stands to clerestory parapet level and gives you the height of the main church, as well as a rough idea of its decoration, with waterleaf capitals and provision for a rose window, suitably toned down for the late 12C but hardly austere.

The surviving north cloister walk dates from an extensive rebuilding programme completed in 1691, which also included the abbot's lodging opposite and the 'colombier' down towards the river. This is closed to the east by a long wall, contemporary with the church, whose ground floor arch gave entry to a chapter house. The windows above once lit the monks' dormitory and the arch breaking through into the south transept would have given on to the night stairs. There is in fact a small museum in the abbot's 'logis', recreating supposedly typical scenes from the life of the monks, but the overly sentimental nature of the display is less of an aid to understanding than it might have been.

To complete the circuit and return to Gisors take the D6, passing (14km) a handsome 13C church at **Doudeauville**, before turning left at Etrepagny for a last 13km on the D14.

5

The Pays de Bray: Gournay-en-Bray to Dieppe

ROAD (117km or 73km): D915, 20km Forges-les-Eaux; D1314, 17km Neufchâtel-en-Bray; then take the direct route along the D1, 36km to Dieppe. Alternatively follow the N28, 25km Blangy; D49, 20km Eu, 4km Le Tréport; D925, 32km Dieppe.

The region known as the Pays de Bray separates Haute-Normandie from Picardy and the valley of the Somme. Although it has been regarded as a frontier area, the Bray was neither a significant barrier to the Frankish and Saxon invaders of the 5C and 6C, nor an arena of contention between the Duchy and the Capetian monarchy on the scale of the Vexin. It is however a distinctive region, geologically marking the transition between the high limestone plateau of the Pays de Caux and the sedimentary formations of the Paris basin. To the south lies one of its most distinctive features, 'la Boutonnière de Bray', or Bray buttonhole. This fertile depression, running north-west from Gournay to Neufchâtel, was created by the erosion of undulating ridges thrown up by the repercussive effects of the formation of the Alps. As the limestone was washed away, leaving a sharply defined ridge along the edges of the depression, underlying layers of marly chalk and clay were revealed and deposits of flint built up in the river valleys, accounting in part for the wide range of materials used architecturally.

The Bray was densely wooded, until the 17C brought a policy of clearing the valley bottoms of woodland and giving the land over to pasture. The butters and soft cheeses which were subsequently made found a ready market in Paris and bestowed considerable prosperity on the area during the 19C, though given the damage the Bray was subjected to during both 1940 and 1944, this is less apparent than it is further west.

GOURNAY-EN-BRAY. The town is best known for its *petits suisses* (or *fromage frais*), made by mixing fresh cream with curds. The industry developed after a local farmer took the recipe to Charles Gervais in Paris in 1850, who encouraged Swiss cheesemakers to settle in the area and produce the cheese on a large scale. This became the staple of what remains a lively market town, but the German advance of 1940 denuded Gournay of its old centre and the only building of note to survive is the restored church of **St-Hildevert**.

This was begun in the late 11C on a triapsidal plan and though the nave was provided with a twin-towered west front in the mid 13C and the choir received its east window some 50 years later, the greater part of the building remains Romanesque. An over-zealous restoration of 1875 has had unfortunate consequences for the Gothic work however, replacing the façade with a clumsy replica and renewing the tracery in the choir. It was also less than kind to the main body of the church.

Recent unpublished research has established a relative chronology for the structure, whose chief interest lies with the tantalisingly early display of figurative capitals concentrated in the south arcade. The earliest capital is in the chapel of St Joseph (to the south of the choir), flanked by Celtic derived whirls and bosses and dating from c 1075, but as several of the capitals have been re-used and many recut a fuller assessment is conjectural, and some of the western capitals may be as late as 1140. Whatever their position *vis à vis* the development of Norman architectural sculpture they have lost none of their power to thrill. The variety and exuberance of their decoration and the dramatic shifts of pattern which invigorate the nave arcade must count among the most notable achievements of Norman Romanesque sculpture.

North of Gournay the D915 passes through the fat dairy country separating the Epte and Andelle before reaching the quiet spa town of (20km) **Forges-les-Eaux**. Set on a rise above the Bray 'buttonhole' the central Place Brévière includes an undistinguished Hôtel de Ville, behind which there is a pleasant park. Here are clustered three small museums devoted to local ceramics, rural life, and the Résistance respectively. To the west of the Place, on the Rue de la République, the 18C façade of the Carmelite convent has been preserved alongside the fading charms of the 'Grand Hotel'. While beyond, the Avenue des Sources leads to the ample spaces and agreeable promenades of '*le parc thermal*', relaid by Jean Hebertot in 1950, where the ferruginous mineral waters of Forges have been taken since the 16C.

17km further north **Neufchâtel-en-Bray** is surrounded by the low rolling hills, meadows and orchards which supply the town with the fruit and cheese for which it is renowned. It was the medieval administrative centre of the Pays de Bray and like many of the towns hereabouts was devastated in 1940, though unobjectionably rebuilt and given a large modern theatre to the north of the centre. It remains a pleasant market town, dominated by the silhouette of its parish church of **Notre-Dame**, where a crossing tower of 1130 is sandwiched between a 13C choir and a 16C nave. The western tower-porch was extensively reconstructed after 1940 but the eastern parts were less seriously damaged, and architecturally it is this choir which ranks as the finest achievement. Glowing with exemplary 19C glass it is conceived as a miniature great-church, the wall hollowed out to produce a delicate triforium passage beneath clerestory windows derived from its great neighbour, Amiens. The dwarf transepts were added piecemeal; to the north during the 14C; and to the south when the nave was built. This latter now houses a magnificent painted **Entombment** of 1491, contrasting the gorgeously apparelled Nicodemus and Joseph of Aramathea and the liverish corpse of Christ, his veins swollen by death.

At the bottom of the hill, in the Place de la Libération, the Musée Municipal d'Art Régional has been handsomely accommodated in a restored 16C manor, and includes fine displays of local ironworking traditions, pottery manufacture and cider-making.

From here there are two good routes to Dieppe. A loop north-eastwards to Eu and Le Tréport is described on p 83. The direct route to the coast takes the D1, described here, and follows the Béthune valley which, with its rich dairy pasture, connects Neufchâtel with Dieppe, and thus Paris with the Channel.

Strategically overlooking the old road the present **Château de Mesnières-en-Bray** was begun in 1480 for Louis de Boissey on the site of the demolished family manor house. Louis was a close friend of Georges d'Amboise and keenly aware of the cardinal's new château then being built at Chaumont, hence the appearance here, as at Chaumont, of plain cylindrical towers. The building now houses a Catholic college and is only open on weekend afternoons, so viewing is restricted, but the splendid Cour d'Honneur of 1550 and Salle des Quatre Tambours are always included in the guided tours. This latter is decorated with an allegory of Peace in pursuit of Discord and like most of the internal decoration dates from a refurbishment of 1660–68. The external silhouette of the château is its greatest accomplishment however, cunningly arousing an expectation of symmetry that is never met, in either its elaborate roofscape or its main façades.

4km north one catches a first glimpse of the dizzying broach spire of **Bures-en-Bray**, each octagonal face spiralling upwards to steal the geometric plane of its neighbour. The church contains a plaque in the choir commemorating its dedication to St-Etienne in 1168, the ceremony conducted by Rotrou de Warwick, Archbishop of Rouen. The greater part of the building is 13C however, the west front being replaced after 1940, and it still retains some intriguing late medieval sculpture. Although an amalgam of 13C and 16C glazed tiles extends across both transepts, it is the south transept which contains the worthwhile material. An early 16C Entombment occupies the southern niche with a late 15C Madonna and Child to its right, while a painted relief of the Assumption, locally produced in the 15C, sits in the eastern wall. Their lively iconography may be marred by clumsy execution but given the losses sustained through war, iconoclasm, and local neglect, this represents a rich repository of the sort of minor religious sculpture produced in enormous quantities for parish church use. And there is an unexpected survival, for opposite the Assumption, in an unprepossessing grey wooden coffin, a gruesome surprise awaits the unwary.

Arques-la-Bataille (21km) lies just west of the D1 and on the opposite bank of the river. It acquired its suffix after the beleaguered Henri IV defeated the forces of the Catholic League under the Duc de Mayenne on the 21 September 1589. The battle took place in the early afternoon on the slopes of the great **Château**. Henri had assembled a force of 7000 Protestants here, equipped with every piece of cannon he could lay his hands on, having heard the castle was proof against artillery. The Duc de Mayenne finally attacked from the valley below with an army of 30,000, only for the covering fog to lift, exposing his troops to fusillades of cannon which cut '*belles rues*' through his battalions. It seems the battle was swiftly over and the Catholic forces beat a disorderly retreat to Dieppe.

Henri's great advantage lay in the exemplary position his medieval predecessors had bequeathed. Perched on naturally high ground well above the valley floor, the castle had never surrendered to force of arms, though famine and political negotiation had caused it to change hands. Like most great castles its strength is not merely one of position, but of systematic barriers designed to slow and expose an attacker well before he is in range of the central defences. The most impressive of these is a formidably deep fosse encircling the bailey walls and rising to an outer stockade, but you can best make sense of this concentric system of defences by walking around this stockade and taking in the 14 curtain towers and unimpaired views of the surrounding country.

The whole complex was begun in 1038 by William, Count of Arques and uncle to William the Conqueror, but soon became a ducal possession and was extensively rebuilt by Henry I in 1123. It was finally abandoned and used as a quarry in the 18C. All its internal floors and tower stairs have now gone, and that anything much survives at all is due to Mme. Reiset who purchased the site in 1836. You enter by the outer western gate, where the flanking artillery towers were added by François I in the early 16C. Beyond this is a triple gate, part of the 13C remodelling which saw the bailey wall strengthened with curtain towers. At the rear a low relief carving of 1845 commemorates Henri IV's victory. The 13C work uses brick, occasionally faced with puddled flint, and is easily distinguished from the work of Henry I, which encompasses the storeyed keep of 1123 and the core of the bailey wall. A 12C chevron moulded arch over the entrance to a small watchtower is virtually the only architectural decoration to have survived, but the general shape of the complex, and the military thinking behind it remain discernible.

The reason for the absence of much of the facing decoration becomes obvious if you descend into the town. The handsome 18C houses gathered in the central Place are finished with the same brick and napped flint as is found in the great breaches which so fragment the castle, and their cut stone once adorned the keep. Beyond the Place, and towards the river, the town church of **Notre-Dame** presents a curious spectacle, with a 17C bell tower unbalancing an otherwise delicate west front. The church was begun in 1515 by Nicolas Bédion, master mason, and completed in most essentials by 1633, the nave belonging to the latter part of this campaign and covered by a remarkable wooden vault suspended with heavy pendants. The choir is in fact the only part of the church for which Bédion was responsible, luminous and pale, and separated from the rest of the building by a superbly proportioned Renaissance screen of 1540.

A short detour along the D54e (6km) leads you to the **Château de Miromesnil**, one of the few truly Renaissance buildings in Normandy. The château remains in private hands and visits are conducted by guided tour. The tour starts with the 15C chapel now buried deep in the woodland to the north of the main building. The chapel belonged to the late medieval castle destroyed by the Duc de Mayenne after his defeat at Arques in 1589, and retains three superb stained glass windows commissioned in 1583. The new building began with the south façade, constructed in 1590 to a surprisingly simple, modular design. The principal façade dates from 1640 and is, by contrast, furnished with a giant pilaster order which creates a coherent vertical rhythm, highlighted by the use of Caen stone set against the soft reds of the Varengeville brick. The internal furnishings are mostly 18C or, like the Montebello Salon, Empire style. Strenuous efforts will be made to persuade you that Guy de Maupassant was born here, where he certainly spent the first three years of his life, and not at Fécamp. A display devoted to Maupassant features his birth certificate giving Miromesnil as his place of birth, but this was in all likelihood misrepresented by his mother to put a good address on an important document.

Beyond Miromesnil, at St-Aubin-sur-Scie, you can gain the N27 and thus arrive at (5km) Dieppe (see Route 1).

The more circuitous route from Neufchâtel-en-Bray to Dieppe, via Eu and Le Tréport, takes the N28, climbing steeply out of the Bray 'buttonhole'. East of Neufchâtel you meet a high, chalky plateau, less thickly forested than it used to be and scoured by deep valleys. The most dramatic of these is formed by the Bresle and its high eastern ridge can be seen for miles before you begin the descent to (25km) **Blagny-sur-Bresle**.

Once a significant frontier town astride a major river crossing, the town has been rebuilt in workaday fashion following its total destruction in 1940 and now barely detains the visitor. From here a left turn onto the D49 brings you along the valley of the Bresle which, with the River Epte to the south, marks the eastern boundary of Normandy. Green and broad the valley is shaded by dense woodland on the high ground and liberally scattered with handsome small churches. A 16C spire at **Montchaux** crowns a church which houses a 12C font, whilst at **Soreng** the whole building is largely 12C. At **Gamaches** a wreck of a church retains an intriguing nave of c 1200 alongside a late 15C tower, and at **Gousseauville** a pretty chapel with a 12C bell-cote stands above the road.

Towards the northern end of the valley the river approaches (20km) **Eu**, superbly situated with its collegiate church standing high above the river and visible for miles. The town is built on the ruins of Roman *Auga*, the river port of the larger Augusta Ambionorum 5km south-east. It received its first fortress under Rollo in the early 10C, but it was the creation of the County of Eu in 996 which accelerated its development as an administrative centre and it hosted two of the more dramatic events of the 11C: the marriage of William the Bastard to Mathilda of Flanders; and William's first interview with Harold. Its experiences during the later Middle Ages were less happy. In 1475 Louis XI, fearing Edward IV would invade and make Eu an English stronghold, had the town burned sparing only its churches, and Eu drifted into a gentle decline. Buffeted by the Wars of Religion, its county sold and château derelict, it was eventually acquired by the Duke of Orléans who restored the château and old town in 1828.

The town centres on the **Place Carnot** with the château to the west and church of **Notre-Dame-et-St-Laurent** to the north. The dual dedication of the church refers not to the early Christian martyr but to Lawrence O'Toole, Archbishop of Dublin, who died here on his way to petition Henry II in Rouen in 1180. Widely venerated for his piety, his remains were placed in the Victorine Abbey of Notre-Dame in what is now the Place St-Laurent, where a local pilgrimage began pouring money into the offertories well before his canonisation in 1218. His cult acted as the pretext for the construction of a new collegiate church to the south of the Victorine house, clearly intended to enshrine this lucrative attraction, and begun to an ambitious design in 1186.

The choir and transepts were complete by 1226 and the nave was in hand before 1230, but in 1426 the central lantern tower together with its spire were destroyed by lightning, causing considerable damage to the transepts and choir. Rather than rebuilding afresh a slow and piecemeal refurbishment took place over the following 150 years, which resulted in the bizarre substitution of a seven-light Flamboyant window in place of the north transept rose, and the provision of new windows and flying buttresses around the choir. Little new ornament was added and many of the pier buttresses belong to the original church, and are reminiscent of contemporary early 13C work at Rouen and Bayeux cathedrals.

The interior spaces are characterised by a strongly accented bay rhythm, creating extended vistas which lead the eye along either nave or aisles. Both the length of the nave (at eleven bays it is two bays longer than the roughly contemporary campaigns at Chartres or Reims cathedrals) and the inclusion of a fully-vaulted tribune has led most critics to see the building as a specifically Norman solution to the problems of great church design. But it should equally be pointed out that the height of the clerestory and the unusual method of dividing the bays vertically with an even number of wall-shafts, suggests the architect was aware of recent developments in the Ile-de-France.

The most obvious decorative incursion into the nave is made by the churchwarden's bench, provided with a ponderous baldacchino by Adrien Lejeune of Abbeville in 1731. Behind this, in a niche in the north aisle wall, the tomb of Nicolas de Saint-Ouen, Mayor of Eu from 1482–87, includes a fine Pietà, while to the right of the 16C sacristy door a Burgundian Virgin and Child retains elements of its late medieval polychromy.

These 15C works postdate the collapse of the central tower and the subsequent reorganisation of the canon's choir and shrine of St-Laurent. The latter was moved beneath the tribune platform in the south transept when a spiral column was added as a reliquary marker. This area is now known as the **Chapelle de St-Laurent** and houses a 17C altarpiece showing St-Laurent first setting his eyes upon the town of Eu. The collegiate church is here shown with its majestic 16C spire while the small harbour town clustered beneath the distant cliffs is Le Tréport.

Further east the chapel of the Holy Sepulchre encloses the most famous 15C **Entombment Group** to have survived in northern France. Not in this author's opinion as compelling as that of Neufchâtel, it is nevertheless an extraordinarily moving work of art, richly detailed and vividly observed. It should be seen as in prayer from the level of the railing separating the sarcophagus from the rest of the chapel to have its intended impact.

Although the refurbishment of the choir was not completed until 1584, the proportions and much of the stonework were retained from the late 12C work. This involved renewing the vault, recutting some mouldings, and inserting the distinctive Flamboyant tracery at aisle, tribune, and clerestory level. As the ritual choir extended two bays into the nave, each of the four crossing piers were faced with funerary monuments: Catherine de Clèves (1633) and Pierre de Dombes (1755) to the north; two 19C Bourbonais slabs to the south.

The choir would have looked very different in the late Middle Ages. In 1350 Jean le Bon gave the County of Artois to Jean d'Artois, in whose family it was to remain for 150 years. Clearly alert to aristocratic feeling elsewhere in Europe the House of Artois transformed the choir into a virtual dynastic mausoleum, filling the arcades with family tombs and sepulchres between 1368 and 1472. This ostentatious display became an obvious target during the Revolution, and the tombs were comprehensively desecrated. Their original situation is indicated by commemorative inscriptions set into the floor and thanks to the interest of the 17C antiquarian, Roger de Gaignières, a visual record of the tombs and their settings have survived. Even more remarkably the effigies which originally lay above these sarcophagi escaped complete destruction and were restored and reassembled in the **crypt** in 1828, where they now reside alongside the early 13C effigy of St-Lawrence O'Toole.

The one other focus of interest in Eu is the **Château d'Eu**, opposite the church. The present much restored east façade constitutes the latest and least fortified of a succession of noble residences on the site, dating back to the early 10C. But the space which separates the château and the west front of the church is the result of an unrealised plan. In 1578 Catherine de Clèves, countess of Eu, and her second husband Henri de Guise, employed Claude Leroi to begin a vast palace facing south, flanked by two great wings. The scheme was never completed and the present château is little more than the west wing of the original conception. This abbreviated complex was acquired as a retreat from court in 1661 by Mlle. de Montpensier, 'La Grande Mademoiselle', who employed Le Nôtre to create the splendid terraces which overlook the valley. However, a promenade through its suites of rooms provokes little thought of the 16C and 17C, for in 1828, shortly before he was elected King Louis-Philippe, the Duc d'Orlèans restored and refurnished the house. He used the château as an informal royal palace, receiving Queen Victoria and Prince Albert here twice during the '*entente cordiale*' of the 1840s, and together with Viollet-le-Duc's restoration of 1872–79 the result has been to fill the interior spaces with a banquet of 19C revivalism.

4km along the D1915, at the mouth of the Bresle, Louis-Philippe was responsible for a very different sort of transformation, which saw **Le Tréport** change from a small fishing port into a popular holiday resort. Royal approval in the shape of a summer villa encouraged the building of hotels and ballrooms, and little by little the railway did the rest. By early in the 20C a Parisian's week in Le Tréport was the equivalent of a Londoner's week in Southend, and the keyside now bustles with all the hot-dog stands, carousels and candy-floss you expect from a successful resort. A new fishing quay is being built to the south, but it is still the **Quai François Ier** which constitutes the heart of the lower town and leads, via the casino, to the beach.

Those parts of the old town which survived the 19C expansion are concentrated on the **Musoir**, a rocky promontory which rises above the port. Steps lead up from the Quai François Ier to the Rue de Paris, the old main street, and to the church of **St-Jacques**, built here after the early medieval church was brought down by a landslide in 1360. Rebuilding was troubled by English raids, and it was not until the early 16C that the nave was built and enhanced by an exquisite set of pendant vaults. The most lavish treatment is reserved for the third bay where five pendants are joined by a network of flying ribs and cusped mouldings in a virtuosic display of stonecarving.

From St-Jacques steps lead across the Rue de Paris to a remnant of the 16C town fortifications, now little more than a single gate, which supports an Hôtel-de-Ville of 1882. Beyond this you enter a network of pleasant streets and squares dense with restaurants and cafés, but the Hôtel-de-Ville also stands at the foot of a 378-step climb to the spectacular vantage point of the **Calvaire des Terrasses**. Not only is this a good place from which to survey the varied pitched-roofs of the 19C town but you can also make out Eu, fantastically compacted on a spur above the river. And westwards of here the cliffs of the Côte d'Albâtre, broken only by a few larger rivers, run for 120km to Fécamp and Le Havre.

Although you cannot travel along the coast for the whole 32km which separate Le Tréport from Dieppe, it is worth slipping away from the D925 for glimpses of the small family resorts, favoured by Parisians, which populate the low gaps along the cliff-face. At **Criel-sur-Mer** (9km) the upper town revolves around the predominantly late medieval church of St-Aubin, whose exterior of napped flint and limestone dressing mirrors the underlying geology of the coast. The Mairie is more deeply buried in the village but is handsomely housed in the Château de Briançon, built as a hospice for the orphans of sailors in 1585.

At **Belleville-sur-Mer** (16km) the cliffs are broken by a delightful valley, which descends some 90 metres from the village, though its verdant tranquillity is changing fast as Belleville and its neighbours are being developed as satellites of Dieppe. By contrast, the statelier pleasures of **Puys** (4km) are better observed away from its ugly seafront, and among the 19C villas which climb the valley. The resort was popular in the late 19C, counting Alexandre Dumas and Lord Salisbury among its seasonal regulars, but its maritime charms were destroyed by the brutal fighting which accompanied the Dieppe raid (see Route 1). There is a memorial on the front to the men of the Royal Regiment of Canada who landed here in August 1942, nearly all of whom were killed. To the left of the memorial the Chemin du Camp de César offers a good walk along the cliffs to the **Cité des Limes** (known locally as the Camp de César), a fortified Gallo-Roman settlement now much diminished by the erosion of the cliffs.

Beyond Puys any one of several well signposted roads will bring you to Dieppe (described in Route 1).

6

Evreux, the Neubourg Plain, and Southern Eure

ROAD (194km): Evreux; D543, 9km Sacquenville; D543/D39, 15km
Le Neubourg; D480, 22km Conches-en-Ouche; 14km Breteuil; 11km
Verneuil-sur-Avre; N12, 21km Nonancourt; 12km Dreux; D143, 21km
Ivry-la-Bataille; D836, 17km Pacy-sur-Eure; 30km Louviers; N154,
22km Evreux.

The sparser, acid soils of the southern Eure rise above a vast chalk plateau,
cut to the east by the lush meanders of the River Eure, and bounded by the
frontier country of the Avre valley. The land to the north-east is flatter, and
the scudding horizons of the Neubourg plain command a fertile prairie
which reaches westwards until broken by the warmer contours of the Risle
valley. Almost the whole of this area was once under beech and oak forest,
but the gradual clearance of the plateau from the later Middle Ages
onwards has confined the woodlands to Conches, Breteuil, and the Pays
d'Ouche, with substantial pockets of seigneurial forest still to be found
along the Eure valley and in the area to the south-west of Evreux. The plains
are intensively farmed, though the established patterns of root vegetables,
flax, and sheep grazing have given way to cereal growing towards the
south. It is a predominantly agricultural region, whose towns have become
established along the main tributaries of the River Eure—the Avre, Iton,
and Rouloir—which sustains an unhurried course through the underlying
chalk. Evreux is by far the largest centre and, as the hub of the local road
network, is the most convenient place to stay if you wish to spend several
days in the area, though both Verneuil and Pacy-sur-Eure have much to
commend them as overnight bases. The suggested itinerary is organised
as an uneven and anti-clockwise circuit, centred around Evreux, though,
as ever, it is not intended to be seen as a vital and orderly progression.

EVREUX. A tragic conjunction of the German air raids of June 1940, which
left the town burning for the best part of a week, and the Allied assault four
years later, conspired to destroy much of the centre of Evreux, though the
areas along the river banks have been pleasantly, if unprepossessingly,
rebuilt. The town was in fact no stranger to war and devastation, having
run up an almost unparalleled record of finding itself in the path of anxious
armies, or of courting volatile allies. There are, historically, two Evreuxs—
the ancient capital of the Aulerques Eburovices some 6km east of the
present town, on the high plateau at Le Vieil-Evreux, and the great walled
town established by the Romans on the banks of the Iton. The former grew
into a sizeable Gallo-Roman trading centre, known as Mediolanum, but
was virtually destroyed by the Vandals in the 5C, by which time it had
anyway been eclipsed by the Roman riverside garrison town. This was
occupied by the Franks under Clovis and given the evangelisation of the
surrounding area by St-Taurin during the 4th or early 5C had acquired a
bishop by the mid 6C at the latest.

Recognition came to the apparently growing town in 990, when the
creation of the county of Evreux by Duke Richard I established an administrative buffer zone separating the areas controlled by Rouen from those

of Alençon. This was a mixed blessing, and as the major town of an area where Normandy bordered onto the Ile-de-France, Evreux attracted some unwelcome attention. The alliance between the Count of Evreux and Louis VII led King Henry I to set fire to the town in 1119, and the establishment of a French garrison here during the border wars of the early 1190s led to a massacre of the soldiery by King John, and the swift, retaliatory destruction of Evreux by Philip Augustus in 1194. The Hundred Years War was no kinder, and King Jean le Bon razed the town in the course of a siege in 1356, aimed at smoking out the forces of Charles of Navarre, while most of what remained went up in smoke a generation later, when Du Guesclin led the attack of 1378. This consistent political interest is a measure of Evreux's strategic importance, and one can be forgiven for thinking it surprising that there was much left to target in 1940–44, but a programme of reconstruction during the 15th and 16C had refashioned the town, and it was largely this that was lost during the Second World War.

The **Place de Gaulle** is the main crossroads of the town, with the Hôtel-de-Ville of 1895 standing before a monumental fountain, intended to symbolise the Eure and its tributaries—the Rouloir and Iton. On the opposite side the elegant **Tour de l'Horloge** climbs a flamboyant 44 metres—the work of Pierre Smoteau and Jean Cossart and completed in 1497. From here it is a short walk to the **Cathedral**, a building so straightforwardly renewed where necessary after each fire that it might be used as a primer for students of medieval architecture.

Nothing is known of the earlier churches on the site, and it may be that the seat of the 6C bishopric was situated elsewhere in the town. However, in 923 Duke Rollo gave money towards the building of a new cathedral in recompense for the church he had destroyed in his earlier attack on the town, and documents make it clear that this edifice stood on the present site. Nevertheless the earliest remains uncovered by the 19C excavations belonged to a church consecrated in 1076, and destroyed, with the consent of Bishop Audin, by Henry I in 1119. Henry was constrained on pain of excommunication to build afresh, and work on a new, and almost certainly rib-vaulted, ritual choir began in 1125, incorporating a narrow transept and coming to a halt with the completion of the second bay of the nave. The rest of the nave is later, hence the change from a scheme of unmoulded arches and simple soffit-rolls, to the more complex profiles of the western bays of the main arcade.

The next visible campaign was something of a delayed reaction to the fire of 1194, the hiatus perhaps best viewed in the light of the fact that it had been the nave which sustained the greatest damage. In 1253 Gauthier de Varinfroy, architect of the cathedral of Meaux, was called in to heighten and vault the 'ruinous' nave, adding a triforium and four-light clerestory in a restrained and deeply conservative style. His eschewal of the glazed triforia recently developed at Troyes and St-Denis, and retention of a strip of wall to either side of the clerestory windows recalls the work of Jean des Champs at Clermont-Ferrand, and stands in splendid contrast to the treatment of the choir.

The reconstruction here seems to have followed on from the completion of the nave c 1270, but the choir was singled out for more radical rebuilding. Rather than retaining elements of the earlier work Henry's Romanesque choir was demolished, and the western bay canted outwards to allow for a wider central vessel. The sill lines were raised, jacking up the main arcade, and a glorious filigree of stone laid across the upper superstructure. As Jean Bony (in 'French Gothic Architecture of the 12th and 13th Centuries') has argued it is an architecture designed to exhilarate, a repudiation of the wall in favour of delicate rhythms, uncertain limits, insubstantiality. It is as if the exterior is held in check by little more than the brittle geometry of the tracery, blazing against the rear wall of a glazed triforium which in this guise is almost certainly Parisian in inspiration.

The fires of 1356 and 1378 caused a considerable amount of damage but resulted in little more than the patching up of the affected areas, and the shifting around of the glass. It was not until the 1470s that Cardinal Jean Balue commissioned a new lantern tower, and so instigated the next great phase of building work at the cathedral. The triforium was renewed in all but the western bay of the choir, and a colossal wooden spire was raised above the central tower in 1475. Work then shifted to the transepts and in 1504 the mason Jean Cossart achieved lasting fame when he completed the north transept portal. Later eyes look to the exterior when seeking an explanation for Cossart's contemporary reputation, and this certainly remains one of the supreme statements of Flamboyant architecture, but it may have been the treatment of the interior wall which originally provoked the greater admiration. For here the interest in creating a tiered and modal range of effects is more decisively handled, although tragically diminished by the loss of the lower statuary.

The mid 16C saw the completion of the south transept (largely reconstructed after 1944), and the addition of a string of chapels to the north aisle of the nave, along with the vaulting of the nave aisles and a heavy reworking of the 12C south-west tower. A final, and uncharacteristically insensitive, campaign of 1612–28 saw the construction of the north-west tower, known as Gros-Pierre, under the Parisian architect, François Galopin.

The cathedral is justifiably famous for the quality and range of its **stained glass**, though a detailed account is beyond the scope of this guide, and is anyway rendered provisional by the continuing programme of restoration aimed at making good some of the catastrophic damage suffered after a freak hailstorm in 1983. The diagram below focuses on the subjects and chronology, where known, of the high clerestory windows.

5. Virgin and Child with Bishop Guillaume Cantiers, offered by Cantiers on the occasion of his accession in 1400.

6. Annunciation; second half of 15C.

7. Reused panels; 14C.

9. Rose window devoted to the Last Judgement with, in the triforium, four of the Apostles (complementing the eight in the south transept) and the four Doctors of the Church—Augustine, Ambrose, Jerome, and Gregory; Early 16C.

11. The Three Maries; offered by Robert de Flocques and Pierre de Brézé to celebrate the expulsion of the English from Evreux in 1441.

12. Blanche d'Avaujour, Virgin and Child, Ste-Catherine, Guillaume d'Harcourt; given by Blanche shortly after the death of her husband, Guillaume, in 1327.

13. Virgin and Child, St-Pierre in papal vestments, Pierre de Mortain, St-Denis; given by Pierre de Mortain, son of Charles of Navarre in c 1385.

14. Canon Raoul de Ferrières kneeling at the feet of the Virgin and Child; commissioned by Raoul shortly before his death in 1330.

15. St-Bernard and St-Taurin; given by Bishop Bernard Cariti between 1376 and 1383.

16. Bishop Bernard Cariti at the feet of the Virgin and Child; 1376–83.

17. Annunciation; Bishop Geoffroy Fae (1335–40) represented as the donor.

18. John the Baptist and the Virgin; given by Bishop Jean du Pré (1328–33).

19. Coronation of the Virgin; given, in all probability as part of an intended three part axial composition, by Bishop Geoffroy Fae (1335–40).

20. St-Martin and St-Laurent; given by Geoffroy Fae, 1335–40.

21. Assumption of the Virgin, with Queen Blanche of Navarre; offered by Blanche, wife of King Philip VI and daughter of Philippe III, count of Evreux, in 1349.

22. King Charles VI, accompanied by St-Denis, before the Virgin; mid 15C.

23. St-Taurin and St-Aquilin (legendary early bishops of Evreux) commend Canon Raoul de Molins to the Virgin and Child; given by Raoul in c 1335.

24. St-Foi, St-Vincent, St-Laurent, and St-Aubin; given by Bishop Paul Capranica (1420–27). This may be moved in the course of the restoration programme.

26. Louis XI at the feet of the Virgin; c 1470.

27. Rose window devoted to the Coronation of the Virgin, attended by a vast array of saints and angels. The triforium carries eight Apostles (look to the opposite triforium for the remaining four); early 16C.

31. St Paul and St-Vincent; given by Bishop Paul Capranica (1420–27).

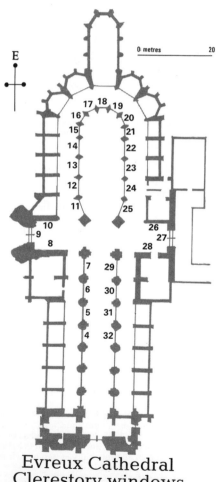

Evreux Cathedral
Clerestory windows

The earliest glass to have survived seems to have been undertaken while the nave was in building, and is usually dated to c 1270. This is now concentrated in the nave chapels and is at its finest in windows such as that devoted to the life of St Jude (bay 32). Comparisons with the transept chapel glass at Rouen Cathedral suggest the active participation of a Rouennais glazing shop here. But it is the choir which offers the most sublime display, with a triforium spangled with heraldic crests beneath a clerestory which holds the finest cycle of 14C glass still to grace a major French choir. Most of the original glass was installed between 1320 and 1350, with that given by Bernard Cariti making good some of the damage caused by the fires of 1356 and 1378, and the two 15C windows the result of a contemporary rearrangement. That depicting Raoul de Ferrières before the Virgin and Child must rank as one of the finest stained glass windows in northern Europe, its extraordinary depth of yellows created by applying 'silver stain' to the glass. This technique was becoming quite commonplace in the glazing shops of France and England by the second quarter of the 14C, but was employed in the choir of Evreux to such effect that in certain circles the colour is described as the *'jaune d'Evreux'*.

The Lady Chapel was added in 1470, a deep, polygonally-ended glass box, largely financed by Louis XI, who appears in the Tree of Jesse window. The chapel also houses a fine 16C painted Pietà, and is enclosed, as are all the ambulatory chapels, by an exquisite early 16C wooden screen. The variety of pattern and figuration inherent in this screenwork, wherein Flamboyant practice is either allied or juxtaposed to Renaissance designs imported from Gaillon and Rouen, merits close scrutiny, and is at its most engaging in the Animals and Virtues.

Immediately south of the cathedral a court opens onto the episcopal palace, designed in 1499 by Pierre Smoteau for Bishop Raoul du Fou. Sheltered beneath steepling dormer windows the L-shaped block is something of an essay in fastidiously applied surface ornament, vertically accented and lending relief to the smooth courses of ashlar. It now accommodates the **Musée d'Evreux**, recently refurbished and enlarged. As Raoul du Fou's palace was built against the Gallo-Roman walls, parts of the cellars have been expanded to reveal the lower ramparts, and create a fitting arena for the display of Prehistoric, Roman, and Merovingian material. Foremost among these objects are two bronze statuettes discovered at Le Vieux-Evreux and contrasting a tousled, fleshy Jupiter Stator with an androgynous Apollo.

The medieval collections on the ground floor are altogether more loosely organised, though the 14C mitre and pastoral staff of Jean de Marigny provide a qualitative focus. Unexpectedly, it is the synthesis of 17th and 18C furniture, ceramics, and painting, brought together on the first floor which creates the most satisfying ensemble. Lacking any single outstanding work, the Rouen faience, French portraiture, fob-watches, tables, and bureaux have been laid out in a suite of rooms which were mostly decorated during the 18C. With their thickly pastelled wooden panelling and tall, shuttered doors the effect is one of cluttered harmony, and an ambience not entirely divorced from that of the 18C.

Above the old episcopal palace, on the Rue de Pannette, the Jardin Public incorporates the **Cloître des Capucins**, part of a Franciscan convent whose southern precincts were built between 1697 and 1701. The cloister's simple, trabeated walks are lined with moralising inscriptions, drawn from the work of the 13C Italian poet and musician Jacopo da Todi and offer a soothing spot for a hot afternoon. A pleasant return, from the cathedral towards the Place Général de Gaulle follows the course of the Iton, where the remains of the medieval ramparts have been consolidated to form a riverside walk.

From the Place de Gaulle a stroll along the Rue Dr-Oursel and its continuation, the Rue Joséphine, brings you past the Palais de Justice, provided with a handsome façade in 1714 to suit its original role as the largest of the town seminaries. A little further west the Place St-Taurin opens invitingly to the right, home since the 10C to one of the major Benedictine monasteries of southern Normandy—the **Abbaye de St-Taurin**. Tradition has it that St-Taurin converted the area to Christianity during the 4C, eventually becoming the first bishop of Evreux. His tomb was subsequently discovered by St-Landulphus, who built an oratory over the site and attracted a small, local pilgrimage. This oratory was in turn expanded, and introduced to a congregation of Benedictine monks who were placed under the authority of the abbey of La Trinité at Fécamp by Duke Robert I in 1035.

Although the abbey was erected in piecemeal fashion, with often bizarre disjunctions of style or spatial handling, it remains a building of considerable interest. The destruction of the town in 1119 seems to have done less damage here than at the Cathedral and the greater part of both the north and south transept chapels were incorporated into the subsequent rebuilding. Whereas the treatment of the major elements of the nave arcade and the two splendid bays of blind arcading in the north aisle are closely related to the contemporary rebuilding at the cathedral (c 1125–40), the transept chapels are clearly earlier and undoubtedly predate 1119.

A substantial refurbishment was nevertheless undertaken by Abbot Gilbert de St-Martin in the mid 13C, when the south porch and trapezoidal lantern tower were added, the latter making allowance for a wider choir and offering a curious parallel to the slightly later decision to enlarge the choir at Notre-Dame. The abbey suffered along with the rest of Evreux during the Hundred Years War however, and an appeal for funds was launched in the 1390s with the offer of indulgences for all those who contributed towards the fabric fund. The choir was rebuilt, in a sort of stripped-down Flamboyant, early in the following century, and the upper storeys of the north elevation of the nave by the late 15C, shortly before the desire for a more classical architectural language lent an element of discord to the opposite wall. Three western bays of the nave were destroyed in 1680, and the present, somewhat academic, west front was thrown up in 1715.

Remarkably the church has not been stripped of all its treasure, and in a chapel off the north transept the abbey's one unalloyed masterpiece, the reliquary **Châsse de Saint-Taurin**, is mounted on a modern plinth. This was commissioned by Abbot Gilbert de St-Martin (1240–55) and executed in Paris some time before Gilbert's death in 1255, being conceived as a miniature chapel whose elegant microarchitecture stands above a base set with enamels and studded with jewels. Its architectural forms are indebted to those of St-Louis' Grande Châsse du Sainte-Chapelle, completed by 1248, and wholeheartedly endorse that mid-13C tendency to update forms by referring them to the norms of contemporary architecture.

The figurative scenes describe the life of St-Taurin, and open on the gable roof with a series of bas-reliefs, depicting the annunciation of his birth by an angel; Taurin baptised as a child by St-Denis and Pope Clement I; his consecration as bishop of Evreux; his miraculous resuscitation of Marinus; and his death. The arcaded scenes narrate stories from the episcopal life of

St-Taurin, with a particularly fine composition depicting the saint before the gates of Evreux, confronted by beasts symbolising the vices of these pagan townspeople. What he would have made of the 14C water stoup opposite the south door, with its human-headed snail, remains conjectural.

The D543 offers a quieter alternative to the major roads of the Neubourg plain, and has the advantage of passing the ambitious seigneurial church of (9km) Notre-Dame at **Sacquenville**. A certain Robert de Sacquenville accompanied Duke William to Hastings, but it was a distant descendant who, in 1521, built the present church, providing it with two doors, and a steeply pitched roof which imposes an identity on the surrounding flat country. The walled-in north door is framed by a once sumptuous portal, whose heraldic plaques and carvings of St Martin on horseback announced the seigneur's entrance. Entry is now gained via a 19C door, bringing one into an unexpectedly accomplished interior. The high notes in an essentially simple treatment are contributed by the vault, emblazoned with elaborately carved escutcheons, on one of which the architect has inscribed *'Andre Coury mason, pries Dieu por li'*.

From Sacquenville the D543 takes you through Bacquepuis, before joining up with the D39 for a level run across the plain to (15km) **Le Neubourg**. As the Roman town of Novus Burgus Le Neubourg has long been the main market centre for the produce of the surrounding plain, and has developed a pleasant and spacious arrangement of large open squares. These open out from the château above the western reaches of the Place Aristide-Briand, and merge, in a splendid succession of public arenas, to frame the church before spilling eastwards into the Place Gambetta. Most of the **Château** has been demolished, though an attractive 13C bay survives to signal the original entrance to the chapel, and to its left a timbered house of 1509 has taken over a part of the castle precincts. To the east the Place Dupont-de-l'Eure is prevented from encroaching on the Place Gambetta by the west front of the parish church of **St-Pierre-et-Paul**.

This had been built and rebuilt several times before the present structure was begun, shortly before 1483, and the eastern columnar piers were set on 13C bases. A simple two storey elevation, made up of a tall arcade and squeezed clerestory, creates the atmosphere of a preaching church, although the handling of the east end rather dispels the initial impression of modest clarity. The choir is triangular and like that of St-Maclou at Rouen generates a considerable tension from the contrast between a high prow-like clerestory and a canted ambulatory. The church has lost virtually all of its late medieval fittings, though a considerable body of 17C wooden sculpture along with a fine late 17C pulpit was moved in as a replacement. The mid 19th and mid 20C stained glass is sadly less successful.

To the south of Le Neubourg the D840 follows an unbending course across the the high plateau, passing the 18C château at Omonville before dropping towards **Conches-en-Ouche**. As you approach the town the vast skies of the plain give way to a darker, undulating landscape, whose thinner soil supports the forests and sheep pasture of the Pays d'Ouche. It is thus not surprising to discover that Conches grew to become the administrative capital of the Ouche during the Middle Ages, though as the eastern outpost of a region centred around the headwaters of the Risle it has been latterly displaced by L'Aigle.

The town owes its curious name to Roger de Tosny, the father of Duke William's standard-bearer at Hastings, who returned from a campaign against the Moors in southern Aragon in 1034, having broken his journey in Conques. At the great Benedictine house of Ste-Foy he acquired some relics associated with the child-saint, and established the cult here in southern Normandy, switching the dedication of the church from St-Cyprien to Ste-Foy, and the name of the town fron Châtillon to Conques, softened by the northern dialect to Conches.

The church Roger retitled **Ste-Foy** was entirely rebuilt in the late 15C, though the north tower was not added until 1620, and the flèche which crowns the south tower is a replacement of 1851. Inside, however, it is the glass which counts. Justly celebrated as one of the finest ensembles of 16C stained glass in northern France, the cycle focuses on the seven bays of the apse, usually attributed to Romain Buron of Gisors. Buron had worked as an assistant to Engrand Le Prince of Beauvais, and like Le Prince was keenly aware of the popular woodcuts and engravings flooding out of southern Germany during the early 16C. Accordingly the upper lights, devoted to the Passion of Christ, are profoundly indebted to Albrecht Dürer's engravings of the subject, and seem to embody a narrative tranquillity at odds with that of the cycle of the life of Ste-Foy beneath. These latter scenes were the first to be commissioned, c 1500, and along with the Passion sequence were the only set-piece programmes to be completed by a single glazing shop.

The life of Ste-Foy was followed by Arnold de Nimègue's Virgin and Child flanked by St-Adrian and St-Romain of c 1510. This lies at the western end of the north aisle and opens a cycle dedicated to the Virgin, leading onto a Presentation in the Temple, Apotheosis of the Virgin, Annunciation (this being a recent copy of the 16C original), Immaculate Conception, Nativity, and, above the altar, Notre-Dame de Bon Secours. The south aisle develops a Eucharistic theme, opening at the west with a Baptism of Christ, and followed by the Sacrifice of Melchisedek, the Miraculous Descent of Manna, the Mystic Wine Press, the Last Supper, and the Celebration of the Eucharist. Above the altar of St Michael a disparate group of panels has been gathered around a central panel of the Archangel.

Virtually all these windows carry either donor figures, or the heraldic insignia of their benefactors. The intense lapidary colours of the Mystic Wine Press and Last Supper are the work of a Parisian shop while the dull opulence of gold, crimson, and purple to be found in the Descent of Manna was probably produced in the royal workshops at Fontainebleau. By contrast, diagonally to the east of this last window, a 13C cult statue of Ste-Suzanne stands as the sole reminder of an earlier structure, and an earlier sensibility.

The most impressive of the many medieval houses which line the **Rue Ste-Foy** are to be found opposite the church, though it is a walk around the south flank of Ste-Foy which affords the most remarkable views. Conches lies on a spur encircled by the River Rouloir, and to the south-east of the church, behind the Hôtel-de-Ville, a small garden has been laid out in which you can look out over the Pays d'Ouche. The gardens also extend to the ruined 12C castle, where a decidedly dodgy set of wooden steps offer a route up into the central donjon.

The road to the south of Conches, the D840, hugs the eastern fringes of the Forêt de Breteuil before catching up with the valley of the Iton at (14km) **Breteuil**, a drab forest town which gathers around a large central square. Its main point of interest lies along the Damville road, where the church of **St-Sulpice** describes a long, low silhouette, with a nave and lantern tower which date from after a fire in 1138.

Breteuil is, however, a good starting place for an excursion to the magnificent **Château de Chambray,** for which you should take the D833 to (6km) Gouville, and then follow the signs to the Lycée Agricole. Standing square above the River Iton, the main rectangular block was built for Gabriel de Chambray in 1590, to the north of an earlier 15C chapel, and finally augmented with corner pavilions in 1881 while under the ownership of the fanatical deer-hunter, Jacques de Chambray. On the death of Edouard de Chambray, the last of the line, the château was left to the State, on the condition that both the main buildings and the extensive grounds were used to found an agricultural college. This finally opened in 1964, hence its current occupation, but it remains possible for small parties to visit all areas of the building, providing arrangements are made beforehand.

Beyond Breteuil the woods give way to wheatfields as the road descends south towards the great plains of the Beauce, and the granary of the Ile-de-France. **Verneuil-sur-Avre** (11km along the D840) effectively marks the border between these two areas—southern Normandy and the Beauce—and as with the frontier towns of the Normandy Vexin was heavily fortified during the Middle Ages. Henry I was so concerned for the integrity of its water supply that he built a canal to connect the town with the River Iton, some 9.5km to the north. He was anxious to consolidate the frontier to the west of the Seine valley, and between 1119 and 1131 built a series of outer ramparts, sufficient, we are told, to defend a town of 25,000 people. This is considerably in excess of the current population, though the numbers are swelled over the summer months as the centre fills with French tourists. Verneuil retains a varied repertoire of domestic buildings, at their most striking around the Rue des Tanneries and Rue Gambetta.

The Place de la Madeleine constitutes the centre of the town, braced to the north-west of a compelling local landmark—the 61 metre high belfry tower of the town's premier parish church, **La Madeleine de Verneuil**. Local tradition has it that, like the Tour de Beurre of Rouen Cathedral, construction was financed out of the proceeds of dispensations granted to those who wished to abstain from the Lenten fasts. There are certainly similarities with Jacques Le Roux's Tour de Beurre, but these are of a general nature and the differences are perhaps more noticeable, in particular the twin crowns of its ornate lantern, and the tremendous vitality of the figures which adorn the lower reaches. The tower is later than the church to which it is attached, having been started in 1470 and completed some 50 years later, and, along with the 18C western porch, avoids using the local grison which is the mainstay of building elsewhere in the town.

The interior is a disappointment. The nave was disfigured by a covering of paint during the 19C, besides which some mediocre 16C windows seem quite attractive. Verneuil became a considerable centre for the production of wooden statuary during the later 16th and 17C and, as with Notre-Dame (see below) La Madeleine fully reflects this. With the exception of a polychromed **Entombment Group** in the south transept, it is the earlier sculpture which catches the eye and there is a splendid 15C **Vierge à la Pomme** in the south choir aisle, and a touchingly intimate 14C Virgin and Child in the north transept.

It is a pleasant town for a casual stroll, and a walk along the **Rue de la Madeleine** takes you past an exuberantly chequered 15C town house on the corner of the Rue du Canon, while a wander down the latter leads to the 13C **Tour Grise**, towering above the remains of Henry I's castle and the now disused church of St-Laurent. From here follow the Rue Notre-Dame, where an alley off to the left reveals the picturesque outline of the parish church of **Notre-Dame**. One of the great features in approaching the church from the town, that revelation of the swelling volumes of the east end, is in fact a relatively recent phenomenon, the choir having been rebuilt between 1872 and 1902. Although the nave survives from the 12C church, the transepts were added during the 15C, and it is here that you see how Notre-Dame became something of an image factory. The majority of the statues are 16C, though there are some medieval works left to reflect earlier modes of religious devotion, and by and large it is these that retain the greatest interest. The finest are a pair of attenuated painted wooden figures opposite the south porch, part of a 13C Crucifixion Group whose central image is sadly lost.

The Rue Notre-Dame eventually winds down to the **Boulevard Casati**, where you might follow the line of the 12C town walls, a pleasant and leafy walk if you head towards the south. The whole circuit is known as the **Promenade des Remparts** and affords constantly shifting views over the town, at their most panoramic along the Avenue Joffré.

From Verneuil the N12 hugs the northern edge of the valley of the Avre, bypassing (10km) **Tillières**, where the parish church of St-Hilaire was sumptuously provided with a pendant vaulted choir, embellished with stuccoed stags and naked putti, by Jean Le Veneur, Bishop of Lisieux, in 1546. 11km further east the N12 also bypasses **Nonancourt**, another frontier town fortified by Henry I, and now overlooked by its ruinous castle.

Beyond Nonancourt the N12 slips into the Orléanais, and to pick up the valley of the Eure you should take the D143, where it is signposted Flonville and St-Georges, on the (12km) northern outskirts of Dreux. Broad, well-wooded, and tranquil, the Eure is fringed by numerous small villages and water-mills, and its high flanks support the isolated farms and hamlets which once lived by timber, and husbanded the building materials to feed the growing towns of Dreux and Chartres. After 7km you come to **St-Georges-Motel**, whose rambling 17C brick-built château was a favourite haunt of Winston Churchill, and where the modest parish church received a fine Tree of Jesse window during the 16C.

To the north the road loops and winds its way to (14km) **Ivry-la-Bataille**, an attractive market town once renowned through all Normandy for its mighty late 10C **Château**. According to Ordericus Vitalis the designer of this castle, Lanfred, was put to death by Aubrey, wife of Raoul, comte d'Ivry, lest he should build another like it for a rival. The finesse with which the rectangular keep was put together is evident even now, among the low scrub which grows out of its truncated walls. A steep path rises to the north-west of the 15C church of St-Martin, to a spur which commands views of both town and river, where sits the ghost of this once great fortress.

An abbey was founded on the banks of the river, lower and less forbidding ground, by Roger d'Ivry, a member of Duke William's household, in 1071. Destroyed by a fire in 1869 the west portal has been reset as a gateway, and is testament to a considerable loss. The voussoirs—among them Abraham cradling souls to his bosom; Christ in Limbo; the Deposition; and the Women at the Tomb—are drawn from more than one portal, but a single jamb figure survives, based on the 'Sheba' figure from the Royal Portal at Chartres. A description of 1726 allows one to reconstruct the original programme, with a central Majestas Domini and four jamb figures representing kings or queens, along with a Passion cycle and scenes from the Last Judgement. It is iconographically indebted to the cycle of column figures at Chartres and St-Denis, and would seem to be the work of a Chartrain group of sculptors, called here during the early 1150s.

17km further north the bustling town of **Pacy-sur-Eure** stands astride a crossroads, humming with the market produce of the surrounding area. Although deprived of any monuments of great distinction, the old parish church of **St-Aubin** makes up for what it lacks in scale by a consistent approach to the handling of modest spaces. Unusually for southern Normandy the building is entirely mid 13C, with the low arcade and tall triforium so favoured in Hainault and Flanders. The north choir aisle carries an unexpected object—an almost jolly Pietà.

The lower reaches of the Eure are skirted by watermeadows and reedbeds, winding amongst a splendid landscape of quiet villages and farms, and passing the occasional château, such as that at (3km) **Menilles**, handsomely coupled with a contemporary late 16C church. At (13km) **La Croix-St-Leufroy**, the old farms and manor of a long-demolished abbey cluster around the parish church, with an abbot's lodge of 1620 turning to face the Eure. The river finally turns to nourish the gardens of (9km) **Acquigny** before skirting the gloomy outskirts of (5km) **Louviers** and emptying into the Seine.

Though once a thriving textile centre Louviers suffered badly during the Second World War, and in the drive to rebuild its industrial base the town has been ringed with modern factory estates. The commercial centre, around Notre-Dame and the Hôtel-de-Ville, emerged relatively unscathed, but the medieval quarter to the south sustained heavy losses, and you must now turn to the area around the Place du Parvis to find much of interest.

On the northern edge of the Place the church of **Notre-Dame** assaults the eye with a giddying display of fretted gables, balustrades, festoons, and gargoyles, pulled together around a south porch where canted bays and pendant vaults play games with one's sense of what is surface and what is space. Though undated the south porch received its wooden doors in 1528, evidence once more that architectural forms we think of as Gothic and sculptural forms we think of as Renaissance (note in particular the Annunciation and Nativity) were never seen as exclusive in 16C northern Europe. The interior of the church makes it obvious that the south flank is in fact a masterful reskinning of a substantially early 13C building. The thickly buttressed west tower was begun in 1428, though never completed, and its basement chapel now houses two very moving 15C Nottingham alabasters, of the **Crucifixion** and **Deposition**. These form a small part of an exceptionally rich collection of 15th and 16C altarpieces, cult statues, and loose sculpture, among which are a wooden group depicting the swooning Virgin, a splendid fully painted 16C altarpiece dedicated to the life of the Virgin, and the reset alabasters of the south-east chapel.

To the north of Notre-Dame, near the junction of the Rue de l'Hôtel-de-Ville and the Place Thorel, the **Musée des Décors de Théâtre, d'Opéra et de Cinéma** has been opened by the Fondation Wakhevitch. This is largely devoted to the work of Georges Wakhevitch (1907–84), a brilliant set-designer whose career encompassed pre-war French film and theatre, the Franco-Italian realist cinema of the 1950s and 1960s, and more recent work for the likes of Buñuel and Peter Brook. After his death the town of Louviers acquired the magnificent collection of stage sets, costume designs, drawings, and paintings from his house at Tosny, and established the museum here as an important historical resource.

For anyone with an interest in the theatre or cinema it is a major collection, superbly disposed around a series of ramps and staircases—sets of headphones available providing a commentary in English. The earlier work, for Jean Cocteau's Ruy Blas, Anouilh's Eurydice, or Jean Renoir's Madame Bovary, takes up the 'poetic realism' which informed French cinema of the time, and ultimately led Wakhevitch into being described as 'the poet of the crumbling warehouse, the creator of tragic and desolate worlds'. To the technically minded the conviction with which he is able to construct artificial decors within existing exteriors, or more riskily, combine real and artificial structures, may signal the creative root of Wakhevitch's ability to thrill; and the later work tends to be freer and more fantastical. As set designers are so seldom celebrated this is a rare memorial to a considerable talent.

Louviers is within easy reach of Rouen and the lower Seine valley, and if that is your destination the N15 via Pont-de-l'Arche is the more pleasing route. If your intention is to return to (22km) Evreux, the N154 offers a fast alternative to the quieter, though otherwise unremarkable, course of the D71 and D155.

7

The Risle Valley: L'Aigle to Pont-Audemer

ROAD (98km): L'Aigle (D13, 14km St-Evroult); D930, 10km Rugles; D830, 11km La Neuve-Lyre; D833/D56, 9km La Ferrière-sur-Risle; D140, 7km Beaumesnil; 13km Bernay; D133, 10km Serquigny (Or D23, 12km Beaumont-le-Roger; D133, 7km Serquigny); D46, 5km Fontaine-la-Soret; D130, 6km Brionne (N138/D39, 6km Bec-Hellouin); D130, 27km Pont-Audemer.

The Risle rises near Planches, to the west of L'Aigle, and with the tributary Charentonne drains the Pays d'Ouche, before settling into a broad valley in the lee of the Neubourg Plain and flowing northwards to empty into the Seine below Honfleur. Its shallow bed and reedy banks readily fragment to form subsidiary streams and meanders, which are often revetted into mill races and canals in the old textile and metalworking towns strung along its course. Above Serquigny, where the valley broadens, the Risle has created a glorious landscape, bequeathing a deep prosperity on the medieval market towns which grew from its abundant fertility. Among the sparser acid soils of the southern Ouche the river is a less dominant feature, though the many feudal domains which clung to its banks testify to its strategic importance and its role as a major line of communication. The most important town of the middle Risle, Bernay, is in fact a few kilometres to the west of the valley, rising above the banks of the Charentonne, and the itinerary described below shifts between these two rivers while relegating the direct route via Beaumont to a subsidiary role. The two other detours, to the ruined abbeys of St-Evroult and Bec, strike off to the east or west of the Risle. The highest of the larger settlements however, at L'Aigle, is an agreeable industrial town with a long history as a metalworking centre, and makes an excellent base from which to embark on an exploration of the valley.

L'AIGLE. An early legend relates that the name L'Aigle (eagle) was bestowed on the town after a bird of prey took up residence above the 11C castle then being built to the south of the river. The medieval occupation of the high ground is the earliest evidence of settlement, though it seems that the town expanded quite quickly to colonise the banks of the river with tanneries and small forges. This movement is responsible for the modern shape of the town and the centre still slides northwards from the château and the Place des Halles towards the river at the Place de Verdun. The latter is sadly no longer what it was, as the late medieval houses which once fringed the Risle along the Rue des Tanneries were destroyed in an aerial bombardment on 7 June 1944. The event is commemorated by a small museum, now installed in a subsidiary pavilion of the Hôtel-de-Ville known as Les Communs in the Place St-Martin.

This was the first museum devoted to World War Two in Normandy and opened in 1953. The waxwork tableaux have themselves become period pieces, but they nevertheless convey something of the atmosphere of reconstruction in Normandy during the early 1950s; and there are intriguing recordings such as that of M. Lescène, the pharmacist from Livarot, describing how the fatally wounded Rommel was brought to him for treatment.

The **Hôtel-de-Ville** was in fact first built as a château by Jules Hardouin-Mansart in 1690 on the site of Fulbert de Deina's early 12C donjon, and together with the parish church of St-Martin forms the main architectural focus of the town. Mansart took advantage of the high ground offered by the medieval motte and developed a bold complex of interlinked square pavilions, which spin off at right-angles to the central block and are ravishingly dressed with pale brick.

To the west of the Place the church of **St-Martin** is, by contrast, less consistent in its handling of volume. The apse and truncated south-west tower belong to a 12C structure built of the local grison, but have been linked by a four bay hall-church, begun in 1494 as a means of expanding the building. The south aisle was not completed until a second campaign of 1545–52, towards the end of which the building was reglazed. Unfortunately this 16C stained glass cycle fell victim to the 1944 air raid and all but two windows were destroyed. The dominant accent of the church is to be found outside however, where the north-west tower rises squarely above its Romanesque neighbour, maturing into one of the most richly animated of all late 15C Flamboyant belfries.

To the west of L'Aigle a 14km detour along the D13 brings you into the parallel valley of the Charentonne. A few kilometres below its source a flat ledge of land supports the ancient abbey of **Saint-Evroult**, though the Gothic ruins that now spill across the lakeside give little clue as to its early importance. The foundation dates from the 6C when St-Evroult established a hermitage on the site, forming the nucleus of a small monastery known as Notre-Dame-du-Bois. As one of the most venerable religious houses in Normandy it attracted lavish patronage from William the Conqueror, and briefly rivalled Bec as the dominant intellectual centre of the 11C duchy, giving shelter to the great chronicler and historian, Ordericus Vitalis, within its cloister. The ruins reflect its latest embodiment and delineate the pier supports and outer walls of a large monastic church, mostly dating from the early 13C. Sadly the entire monastic precinct was abandoned in 1812 and plundered for its stone, hence the rather fine banded ashlar which turns up in several of the houses in the village.

Travelling north-east from L'Aigle the D930 clings to the western edge of the Risle valley before swinging into the attractive small market town of

Rugles. Like many of the towns along the upper Risle, Rugles is an old metalworking centre, which during the 17C learnt to harness the river to drive its newly established textile mills. The water-wheels have long stopped turning but the weirs and mill races remain, surrounded by parkland and provided with footbridges which overlook the town's two churches. The earlier of these lies on the right bank, to the east of the medieval centre, and is known as **Notre-Dame-Outre-l'Eau** (open Tuesday afternoons only). Although subsequently treated to a west portal and high roof the fabric of the building is 10C, with bands of brick tiles and *petit appareil* organised in tightly layered horizontal patterns around a simple two cell nave and apse.

It is impossible to miss the parish church of **St-Germain**, on the Place Foch. Its tall bell tower is a local landmark, and carries an octagonal lantern twisted through 22½ degrees along with more than half of its original niche figures. The sculpture is clearly related to that of the tower at St-Martin at L'Aigle, though the style of decoration is generally flatter, less virtuosic, and more fully early 16C. The *pièce-de-résistance* is the south-east chapel, announced on the exterior by the exaggerated curving of the columnar supports, and on the interior by an attempt to inscribe pilaster orders to the underside of the arcade.

North of Rugles the valley road changes designation to the D830, at least as far as (11km) **La Neuve-Lyre** where you should briefly take the D833 to (1km) La Vieille-Lyre before a right turn onto the D56 takes you across a wooded plateau (8km) to **La Ferrière-sur-Risle**. This was a considerable iron-working centre between the early Middle Ages and the 18C but has since settled to become a quiet market town, centred around a splendid double-aisled wooden market hall dating from the 14C. To the west of this there are a number of fine timber houses separating the main Place and its jovial assortment of cafés from the parish church of **St-Georges**. With the exception of an intimate 14C Virgin and Child the impressive array of altars and statuary date from the 16–18C, and radiate outwards from a superb Louis XIV high altar housing a painting of the **Entombment**. The latter is the finest 16C religious painting still in situ in Normandy. During its restoration in 1963 the Louvre became convinced that it was the work of one of that circle of painters and assistants who gravitated around Leonardo da Vinci during his later years in France. This becomes all the more plausible considering that its astonishing appearance in so modest a parish church would have coincided with the incumbency of Félix de Courteuve, preferred to the parish in 1528 by no less a sponsor than François I.

Above La Ferrière a wide and thinly-soiled plateau divides the Risle from the Charentonne before the two rivers come together near Serquigny, offering a choice of routes northwards. The most direct brings you along the D23 and through the Forêt de Beaumont to Beaumont-le-Roger, while a circuitous path takes the D140 to Beaumesnil and Bernay before cutting back along the lower Charentonne to rejoin the Risle above Serquigny. The latter is the more rewarding but the routes are not mutually exclusive, and are here described consecutively.

Beaumont-le-Roger gained its suffix when ceded to Roger de Vieilles in the mid 11C, though the grievous damage inflicted on its quiet riverside streets in 1944 has denuded the town of its broader charms, and interest is now largely confined to the ruined priory and the parish church. The priory was founded by Roger in the shadow of his castle in 1070 and dedicated to **La Trinité** in 1088, a year after the death of William the Conqueror had deprived the consecration ceremony of one of its intended guests. It was initially populated by a college of canons from Oxford but these gave way to Benedictine monks from Bec in 1141, and it was as a monastic church that the priory was rebuilt in the 13C. What remains of this church is nevertheless impressive, and as the castle had taken advantage of a high scarp to the north-east of the town the priory was built onto a terrace beneath, sharing a postern gate and entrance passage with its neighbour. This entry survives on the Rue de l'Abbaye and gives access to the ruins through a majestic corridor of diaphragm arches which create an ascending rhythm of bays lit by traceried windows. At the southern extremity of the terrace two of the priory walls stand to parapet height. The church belongs to the late 13C and was conceived as a large aisleless chapel with a great east window and walls articulated by a rapid succession of longitudinal window bays. The only major alteration to these accents seems to have occurred in the 15C when a bell-tower was raised against the north wall, though this has been reduced to a mere rump. The priory actually fell into disuse in 1786, before the Revolution, and its relics were transferred down the hill to the parish church of **St-Nicolas**.

This is to be found in the Place de l'Eglise and also rises above a terrace, though one more modest and freshly renovated. The external arrangements are strangely unsympathetic and juxtapose a late 15C nave and north-west tower with a taller and later choir, the latter replacing a choir destroyed in the course of a Spanish attack on the town in 1593. Unfortunately much of the original glass was destroyed in 1944 and what did survive is predominantly in the choir, where to the south, two late 15C windows depict the Raising of Lazarus, and the Apostles and Evangelists standing beneath an image of the Trinity in the tracery head. But it is the **Lady Chapel** which frames the finest of the glass, with a splendid cycle of 1550 centred on the Legend of Theophilus and the Wedding at Cana. The priory (see above) must have been in a poor state when it was deserted because little of note was transferred to St-Nicolas; the last acquisition, in 1826, was the charming regulus figure dressed as a Roman soldier which nods the hours from a niche above the tower clock.

To the north of Beaumont-le-Roger the D133 briefly parallels the Paris to Cherbourg railway as far as its junction with the Rouen to Bernay line at (7km) Serquigny (see below).

The grander circuit from La Ferrière to the confluence of the Risle and Charentonne follows the D140 to (7km) the great 17C **Château de Beaumesnil** (open May–September, Fri.–Mon. afternoons only). This was built on the site of a feudal castle by the Rouen architect Jean Gaillard for Jacques, Marquis de Nonant, between 1633 and 1640, and is that rarest of architectural forms in Normandy—a baroque palace. The château emerges from its moat as an extraordinarily effective essay in richly decorated symmetry, drawing colour from screens of brick and texture from projecting stonework. The orders are broken throughout by rectangular blocks, rusticated on the narrower central block, and thus articulate the play of light and shade which throws the overhanging consoles and pediments into high relief. The larger volumes are stressed from the roofs, imposing a geometrical discipline on the composition and suggesting the underlying triangle which gives the overall design such strength. The novelist Jean de la Varende described it as 'a dream in stone', and the elevations certainly have a visionary quality when seen from a distance, but it would be a mistake to see its rigorously worked programmes as purposely fantastical. Like all

The main entrance façade of the Château de Beaumesnil

great baroque architecture the rich theatre of forms works best when seen from a variety of angles, and it is precisely this quality which is exploited in the superbly wooded formal gardens, said to have been laid out by Jean de la Quintinie, an associate of Le Nôtre, shortly after the house had been completed.

The internal rooms of the château are arranged around a splendid vaulted stairway which occupies the whole central block, and were mostly furnished during the 18C. The last occupant of the house, Jean de Furstenberg, has however created a foundation for the upkeep of Beaumesnil and the retention of his extensive library within its precincts. The basement is now given over to the **Musée de la Reliure**, in which the 16–19C covers of some of the more sumptuously bound manuscripts and printed books are displayed, and complemented by practical displays of binding and stamping on the first floor.

From Beaumesnil the D140 continues over the high plateau to meet the Charentonne by the important crossroad at (13km) **BERNAY**. The word 'Bernay' derives from a Gallic dialect term for a passage over water, though the earliest record of human settlement on this stretch of the Charentonne dates from c 1000, when Duke Richard II received a loose collection of windmills, fishing privileges, and rights to timber as part of the dowry of Judith of Brittany. It was Judith who was largely responsible for the growth of a sizeable town here when, on the advice of William of Volpiano, she founded a Benedictine monastery in the triangle of land between the Cosnier and the Charentonne dedicated to Notre-Dame. The church may not have been started until 1025 but the decision to found a monastery had been taken by 1013, and this led to the building of a donjon, the development of a market, and the establishment of a parish church. By the end of the 12C the town could boast that it had produced the poet Alexandre de

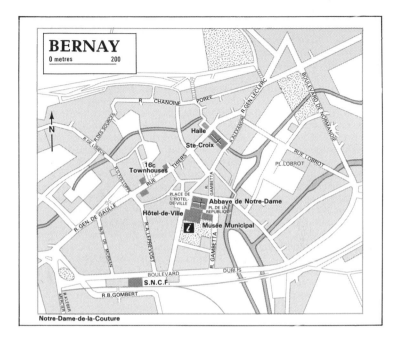

BERNAY

0 metres   200

R. CHANOINE
POREE
R. ALEXANDRE
R. GEN. LECLERC
BOULEVARD DE NORMANDIE

N

R. DE LISIEUX
R. DES SOURCES

Halle
Ste-Croix

RUE L'OBROT
PL. LOBROT

16c
Townhouses

THIERS

R. TOPELONE
RUE

R. GAMBETTA

PLACE DE
L'HOTEL-
DE-VILLE
Abbaye de Notre-Dame
PL. DE LA
REPUBLIQUE

Hôtel-de-Ville

R. GEN. DE GAULLE

RUE DE MOISAN

R. A. LEPREVOST

i   Musée Municipal

R. GAMBETTA

BOULEVARD
DUBUS
S.N.C.F.

R. KLEBER
MERCIER

R. B. GOMBERT

Notre-Dame-de-la-Couture

Bernay, whose Romance of Alexander the Great, told in 12-syllable iam-
bics, evolved the poetic metre henceforth known as the Alexandrine.

The modern town grew on the back of the railway and the textile industry,
but it grew from a substantial base centred around the Place de l'Hôtel-de-
Ville and the **Rue Thiers**. The latter is the main street and where it forms a
junction with the Rue Leprovost acted as the boundary between the
counties of Evreux and Alençon, hence its fine array of 16C townhouses.
The most striking are close to this crossroad: the Bernay residence of the
Dukes of Alençon at No. 6; and along a narrow passage opposite, the superb
courtyard façade of No. 9, impressed with religious talismans and secular
portraits which include a memorable small plaque depicting François I.
Further along at No. 31, in a courtyard to the rear of the offices of L'Eveil
de Bernay, the house of the crown tax-collector is animated by suitably
arbitrary carved wooden colonnettes which lend a rich all-over texture to
the upper storey. The Rue Thiers leads eventually to the parish church of
Sainte-Croix, opposite the 19C market hall.

The exterior here has been disfigured by insensitive restoration and the
addition of a dull 17C entrance portal, but the handsome and spacious
interior houses a collection of sculpture from the abbey of BecHellouin,
salvaged by the far-sighted Revolutionary priest, Abbé Lefebvre. The choir
was begun on a new site in 1374, to the north-east of an earlier parish
church. By c 1430 the nave had been completed, though the south aisle
was not vaulted nor the south-west bell tower raised until the late 15C. The
choir aisles were added in 1863, as were such peculiarities as the plaster-
cast of the 15C Entombment group from La Madeleine at Verneuil, but on
the whole it is the work from Bec that is the most fascinating.

Lefebvre persuaded Cambacerès to allow him to rescue the more notable ecclesiastical fittings from the debris at Bec and install them here in Ste-Croix. These fall into two distinct groups. The wonderfully controlled baroque high altar, and triangular grouping of Saints Maur and Benoît beneath the Crucified Christ, belong to a late 17C refurbishment of the choir of Bec undertaken by Guillaume de la Tremblaye between 1683 and 1699. The second, and more loosely distributed, belongs to the late 14th and early 15C. This consists of a dramatic and gestural cycle of 16 Apostles and Evangelists, mounted on 19C plinths, and a stunning collection of tomb slabs. The latter are life-size inlaid memorial images of the early 15C abbots of Bec, commended to God by a flurry of saints and angels, and caught up in delicate skeins of tracery. The two finest are of **Guillaume d'Auvillars** (d 1418) and his nephew, **Robert Vallée** (d 1430), both of them arrestingly stylised, though the disturbing realism of Guillaume's painted face is due to a late 19C exaggeration of the original paintwork.

Behind the apse the Rue Alexandre weaves past a number of timber houses as far as the Rue Gambetta and the Place de la République. The Place has been extended to the west of the Rue Gambetta by a terrace, which gives onto the east front of the **Abbaye de Notre-Dame** and the recently excavated foundations of a 12C chapel to the south of the apse. The excavations formed part of a larger programme which has seen the old choir of the abbey restored to its original shape, if not in the original materials. The monastic complex is bounded to the west by the Place de l'Hôtel-de-Ville and to the south by the Jardin Publique, and now houses the law courts, town hall, and museum. The church came off worst during this transformation, losing its 11C west front along with two bays of the nave in the 17C, and its eastern elevations in the 19C when it briefly functioned as the municipal corn market. Nevertheless enough remains of the church for it to be accorded the recognition it deserves as one of the seminal buildings of Norman Romanesque. Access to the church is now via the Maurist façade on the Place de l'Hôtel-de-Ville (if locked the keys can be obtained from the Musée).

Judith of Brittany's decision to found a monastery here was due to the advice of the great north Italian reformer William of Volpiano, who at the urging of Duke Richard II had left St-Bénigne at Dijon in 1003 to institute a programme of monastic reform at Fécamp. Although this foundation had been agreed by 1013 there is no evidence of building before Judith's death in 1017, and Richard II's confirmation of the monastery's rights to the Lieuvin in 1025 suggests an unsettled state of affairs. This impression is further borne out by Bernay's peculiar status during the early 11C. Notre-Dame was confided to a series of monastic 'guardians' who had emerged out of the Fécamp reform movement; monks such as Thierry, abbot at Jumièges, and Raoul de Vieilles, abbot of Mont-St-Michel. It was in fact not until another Fécamp monk, Vital de Creully, was appointed shortly before 1060 that Bernay was raised to the status of an autonomous abbey.

Excavations have established that Notre-Dame was furnished with a triapsidal east end, to the west of which a two bay sanctuary lies more or less intact. The north transept was demolished in 1810 but the western elevation of the south transept carries a passage in the thickness of the wall, between the arcade and the clerestory, which originally provided access to the crossing tower. The functional advantages of this are considerable as it does away with the structural enfeeblement implicit in laying a stairwell within one of the crossing piers. To the west the nave is now reduced to five bays and has been re-roofed, with the north and south aisles reworked in the 15th and 17C respectively, but the main elevation is quite unscathed and is treated in three storeys. The main arcade is in two orders with soffit rolls extending the articulation offered by the half-columns to the underside of the arches. Above this paired arches punch openings into the aisle roof space, and are divided by distinctive recessed panels. The decorative potential of these panels is comparable to that of the late 10C roundels at St-Pierre de Jumièges and might, therefore, be regarded as something of a throwback.

Half-columns and soffit rolls are found in several buildings in the Loire valley, for example the crypt of Auxerre cathedral after 1023, but the introduction of a wall-passage is of fundamental importance for Norman architecture and its isolation in the transept here argues for an early date. Modern opinion is divided on the issue, but a date of c 1025–40 for the choir and transepts seems perfectly plausible for such an inventive building, and is equally reasonable for the superb series of shallowly carved capitals and reliefs which decorate the area. The recently discovered reliefs in the south transept are chip carved, but the finest and most famous of the capitals is to be found in the choir where a composition of birds and lions is inscribed, '*Me Fecit Izembardus*' (Isembard made me).

The conventual buildings to the south of the church now house a sizeable administrative complex, and mostly date from the late 17C. Benedictines of the Congregation of St-Maur were installed at Bernay in 1628 and began the usual large-scale reconstruction of the monastic precincts, completing the actual living-quarters in 1694. The last area to be built was the superb refectory, now the **Salle du Tribunal**, to a design by the locally born Maurist architect, Guillaume de la Tremblaye. Further south the old monastic gardens have been opened out as a public garden and overlook the handsome brick and stone-faced block occupied by the **Musée Municipal**.

This in fact predates the late 17C campaign, and seems to have been put in hand as the abbot's lodge before the Maurist reform took hold in 1628. The collections are arranged over two floors, with a recent entrance hall accommodating a grandiose selection of late 19C sculpture, and the ground floor given over to 18th and 19C painting and furniture. The earlier work is concentrated on the first floor, with a fine portrait of 1571 of a **Procurator of San Marco** generally attributed to **Jacopo Tintoretto**, and an engaging collection of Dutch 17C genre paintings. The best of these is **Jan van Goyen's View of Dordrecht**, but the series of small tavern scenes is also entertaining.

The founding curator, Alphonse Assegond, collected ceramics and his bequest of faience has been kept separate and is splendidly displayed in the easternmost gallery of the first floor. Inevitably the accent is on 18C Rouen faience, with some work from centres such as Nevers which were influential in the formation of Rouennais styles. The quality of the collection is outstanding and includes the 1542 tiles of Anne de Montmorency's Château d'Ecouen and a beautiful 18C glazed chess board.

South of the railway, and reached via a pedestrian underpass to the left of the station, the Rue Gombert brings you to the second of Bernay's parish churches, **Notre-Dame-de-la-Couture**. The couture derives from agri-couture and a church was established here by 1340. There is a major procession each Whit Monday to the image of Notre-Dame, and although the present cult statue is post-medieval both the early 16C records and the late 15C stained glass of the aisle windows give accounts of the charitable donations of confraternities to the church. It seems likely therefore that the size of the present building is testament to the prosperity of the cult in the

15C, while its peculiar situation outside the old town reflects its ancient origins.

The earliest part of the existing fabric is the **nave**—spacious and simple, with a two storey elevation and tall aisles which owe much to the design of preaching churches. The transepts were remodelled some time before 1471, when the master-glazier, Pierre Courteys, was commissioned to produce the finest of the windows in the south transept, depicting John the Baptist, Michael, Mary Magdalen, and Christ. Finally, in the early 16C, the choir was completed with a pendant vaulted ambulatory. The barn-like spaces provide an ideal frame for a procession of windows, small in the nave, larger to the east, which were commissioned by the local confraternities. The quality is patchy but the vast majority of the glass dates from the last quarter of the 15C, and offers a fascinating insight into the late medieval social hierarchy of a medium sized Norman town.

From Bernay the D133 sweeps past the rambling outlines and 13C choir of the church at **Menneval**, and follows the fertile lower reaches of the Charentonne to the old railway town of (10km) **Serquigny**. The parish church here warrants a brief inspection, not least for its 12C chevron moulded portal and curious 16C transept, treated as a centralised space with a vaulted crossing in the midst of a nine bay grid. Complementing this extravagance in the chapel of Ste-Anne is a decaying though once fine set of stained glass windows, dating from 1540–41. East of the church an otherwise unsignposted left turn by the Mairie brings you onto the D46 and offers a quiet route northwards towards (5km) **Fontaine-la-Soret**, where a handsome 12C belfry and 16C church choir chequered in limestone and flint lie to the north of a quiet and attractive village. This is also the best place to cross over to the right bank of the Risle, where the D130 hugs the river for the 6km to the old fortress town of Brionne.

A bypass carrying the N138 to the north of **Brionne** is under construction and should reduce congestion in the town, though it has long been a major centre of communication. Traces of a Gallo-Roman settlement have been discovered on the hill overlooking the bridges along the Risle, and a castle was constructed here in the late 10C by Duke Richard I's son, Godefroy. William the Conqueror found the town's strategic importance sufficient to justify a three year siege, from 1047–50, successfully starving the Duke of Burgundy out of Normandy, and the foundation of the abbey of Bec-Hellouin nearby reflected well on the town during the Middle Ages.

The earlier settlements at Brionne were all on the right bank of the river centred around the main squares: the spacious Place Fremont-des-Essarts, and the cramped Place du Chevalier-Herluin. From the latter the Rue des Canadiens gives onto a footpath, the Sente du Vieux-Château, which hairpins up a steep scarp to the keep of a once larger **château**. Just two walls stand witness to the ferocious 12C siegecraft which saw it finally vanquished by Philip Augustus in 1194. The castle was begun shortly after 1090 by Robert of Meulan, count of Brionne, as a square three storey, two bay structure reminiscent of the strongholds being constructed in England at this date, but rare in Normandy before the form was introduced by Henry I. Sadly its facing stone is long gone and it is hard to imagine what detail there might have been, but the position remains—sharply anchored above the town and surveying 20km of the Risle valley.

The reconstructed 15C spire so clearly visible from the castle belongs to the parish church of St-Martin, a building otherwise boasting a battered 13C west front, 14C choir, and 15C nave to which new side aisles were attached in 1870. It does possess one majestic distinction however—a deeply contemplative 15C Virgin and Child, now housed under the central tower but originally from the Lady Chapel of the abbey of Bec.

From Brionne the N138 climbs the ridge which separates the Risle from one of its lesser tributaries—a tiny stream that became famous after 1034 when Herluin, a knight at arms to the count of Brionne, founded the small monastery on its banks that was subsequently known as the abbey of **Bec-Hellouin**. Bec derives from the Old Norse for stream, common to the English 'beck' and a frequent survivor in Norman place-names (Orbec, Caudebec-en-Caux, etc), but so prestigious was Herluin's house that throughout Europe it was known simply as the Abbey of Bec.

The present site of the monastic buildings, 3km along the D39 from the bridge on which the N138 crosses the stream at St-Martin-du-Parc, is a mile or so upstream of the original small and remote foundation envisaged by Herluin. The abbey's fame stems from the arrival in 1042 of the Italian theologian, Lanfranc, weary of his success at Avranches. By 1045 he had established a monastic school at Bec, and was drawn to the attention of Duke William during the long siege of Brionne in the late 1040s. William clearly saw in Lanfranc the man to improve his relations with the Church, and thus began an enduring friendship which witnessed Lanfranc's negotiation of the annulment of William's excommunication in 1059, and his appointment as the founding abbot of St-Etienne de Caen in 1066.

In the meantime Lanfranc attracted the brilliant and saintly theologian, Anselm, from Aosta to Bec, and oversaw the transformation of the monastery into one of the intellectual powerhouses of northern Europe, a position it enjoyed throughout the late 11th and early 12C. Both Lanfranc and Anselm became archbishops of Canterbury, but you need only look to the plaque on the Tour St-Nicolas recording the appointment of novices and monks from Bec to English prelacies between 1070 and 1140 to realise the depth of learning nurtured within the monastic precincts.

Nothing now survives of the first church that was built after the move and consecrated in 1077, indeed little remains of the latest of the medieval churches to have graced the site. This was begun in 1325 and remained incomplete while the Hundred Years War ran its course, being finally dedicated in 1443. You can at least make out the groundplan of a building which stretched 122 metres from the lady chapel to west front. The freestanding bell tower, constructed under abbot Geoffroy Benoît from 1452–76 and known as the **Tour St-Nicolas**, does however stand to its full height and still commands the valley. Elements of the late 15C gatehouse and abbot's lodge also survive, but the greater part of the monastic complex dates from the Maurist reforms. All but a single bay of the nave was demolished in 1645, effectively reducing the church to its choir and transepts while a new range of conventual buildings was constructed, with the infirmary completed in 1661, the cloister in 1666, and the dormitory in 1672. These are on a large scale, with the cloister modelled on Bramante's structure at Monte Cassino, and are articulated by shallow pilasters and tall windows—elegant, modular, and restrained. The refectory followed on between 1742 and 1747, on a scale to rival that of the late medieval church, and was covered by an acoustically determined barrel vault broken into bays by deep lunettes. This now acts as the main monastic church as in 1948 the Benedictine monastery was reconstituted as a thriving community which has also opened the church to the laity during the celebration of the Offices. As an active religious house you may only visit the cloister as part of a guided tour, though there are no restrictions on wandering amongst the ruins and through the splendid grounds.

Beyond Bec the D39 joins the Risle valley road, the D130, running north towards Pont-Audemer and passing the once great seat of the de Montfort family at (9km) **Montfort-sur-Risle**, whose early counts received 114 English manors from William the Conqueror. A few kilometres to the east (via the D124 and D576) the church of **Notre-Dame** at **Ecaquelon** was the victim of a tragic robbery 20 years ago, when the 15C alabasters of its rare late medieval altar frontal were stolen. Understandably the church is now kept locked but Madame La Maire will accompany visitors with the key (from the house next to the café). The church nevertheless retains the frame to the frontal, superbly mounted with painted metal plaques which glow in the low light in the manner of inset enamels. Fortunately the wealth of 16C woodwork was untouched, and the finest carving remains between the nave and the choir in the shape of a pair of retables. Both are mid 16C and depict the Flight into Egypt and Virtue respectively, surrounded by panels of wonderfully curvilinear blind tracery.

2km north of Montfort the road is enlivened by the elegant 16C tower and spire of **Appeville-dit-Annebault**, giving on to a church which contains, in the north wall of the choir, the tomb slab of the local priest, Jean le Senze, who died in 1483 to be memorialised beneath an illusionistically incised hexagonal niche. Beyond Appeville the Risle becomes broader, and the valley floor flatter and less varied, until the last of the chalk hills which rise above its right flank dips to the north of Pont-Audemer and gives way to the marshes of the Marais Vernier.

Pont-Audemer is the northernmost town on the Risle, though still some 16km from where the river empties into the Seine, and is the highest navigable point for the shallow flat-bottomed barges which once plied the river from here to Honfleur, or on up the Seine to Rouen and Paris. The old town is built on an island formed between two courses of the river, and is sunk with small canals and lesser streams which used to be navigated in punts. Despite the damage sustained in 1944 and more noticeable around the fringes of the town, the predominantly 15th and 16C core was less catastrophically afflicted than at nearby Lisieux and Pont-l'Evêque and has been sensitively restored over the last 40 years, in the process becoming one of the most popular inland towns in Normandy.

The town centres around the one large building on the Rue de la République, the parish church of **St-Ouen**, fostered on the back of the booming tanneries of the late 15C. In 1486 Michel Gohier was employed as master mason with a brief to build a new west front and north tower, and demolish the 13C nave, as part of a campaign to replace all parts of the earlier medieval church. By 1506 the north tower and lower façade were complete and the old nave demolished, but the effort depleted the fabric fund more rapidly than expected and after 1506 the work became piecemeal, with entire building seasons seeing little or no work done. The nave chapels and main arcade piers were up by 1520, and the extravagant triforium by 1540, but by this time it was not simply money that was in short supply, but nerve. All work was abandoned shortly thereafter with the result that the inner western screen stops abruptly to the left of the organ, its arches already sprung in anticipation of non-existent responds. The north-west and south-east bays were also left less than half-finished but it is the clerestory which represents the final admission of defeat, inserted shortly before 1545 in order to get a roof up.

The 11C choir remained beneath its 13C vault and truncated eastern wall, with a splendid combat capital to the north, and the tanners and confraternities made do with commissioning the glaziers to produce cycles of the Life of St-Ouen, of Christ, of the Annunciation, and of standing saints, for windows which fill the nave chapels. The earliest of these dates from 1490 but the majority were produced between 1535 and 1556, excepting those of the late 1940s by Max Ingrand. Above all the confraternities peopled these windows with themselves, most radiantly in the serene candlelit procession which lights the second bay of the south aisle. Unfortunately the statuary which originally stood on pedestals corbelled out of the nave piers was smashed during the Wars of Religion, but was undoubtedly made in emulation of the church's great Benedictine namesake in Rouen. However, before lapsing into reflection on what might have been, the 17C managed to enhance the building with an exceptionally fine organ loft, which makes a fitting shelter beneath the west door.

The **Rue de la République** is the main street of Pont-Audemer, linking the Place de Verdun to the north with the Place Victor-Hugo, on the far side of a bridge over the fast-flowing minor branch of the Risle. This bridge is renowned for the picturesque views it gives of half-timbered houses, cantilevered out of the revetting walls and overhanging the river, but there are equally striking late medieval streetscapes elsewhere on the island, for isntance the alley to the north of St-Ouen, or the Rue de l'Eppe beyond that, and on the western side, the busy Rue Clemencin and the narrow courts of the Rue Place de la Ville. The grandest houses are on the Rue de la République, with a particularly notable group opposite the west front of St-Ouen.

The southern bridge once gave onto the town gates, and the old road to the village of St-Germain and on to Caen. **St-Germain** has now merged with the south-western suburbs of Pont-Audemer but was an ancient rival, though none of that once distinct air has clung to it. Nevertheless it is worth making the journey (along the Rue Gambetta and its continuation, the Rue Jules Ferry or N175) to the parish church of St-Germain, whose superb display of weathered Romanesque corbels, dating from the early 12C and supporting the roofs of both nave and transept, amply repays the detour.

8

The Côte Fleurie: Honfleur to the Orne estuary

ROAD (50km); D513 Honfleur, 15km Trouville; D513 1km Deauville; Detour N177 11km Pont l'Evêque; 7km Villers-sur-Mer; 7km Houlgate; 3km Dives-sur-Mer; 1km Cabourg; D514 13km Pegasus Bridge.

This stretch of coast, from the left bank of the Seine estuary to the Rade de Caen, began to change with the mid 19C when the summer pleasures of sea bathing and salt air, liberally interrupted with dancing and gambling, suddenly found favour among the urban aristocracy. The early colonisers of Trouville and Houlgate were careful to landscape their villas with floral gardens, setting the tone for the great planned resorts of Deauville and Cabourg, so that by the turn of the century the whole corniche had become known as the Côte Fleurie.

Parisian society swiftly established summer outposts at favoured resorts: Napoleon III and the Empress Eugénie at Trouville; the Duc de Morny at Deauville and Proust at Cabourg; Honfleur, lacking a beach, was left to Boudin, Monet and the Impressionists. The côte now boasts the most concentrated strand of seaside towns and villages in Normandy, although it has tended to become socially and economically dominated by Deauville, the self-advertised 21st arrondissement de Paris. Strictly speaking the côte proper runs west from Villerville; east of here the Seine estuary throws off too much silt among the shifting sandbars for it to be regarded as a bathing coast, but this is a recent distinction and Honfleur remains much the best centre from which to set out.

HONFLEUR. Before François I founded a new town at Le Havre in 1517 the Seine estuary supported two strategic ports, Harfleur on the right bank and Honfleur on the left. The subsequent rise of Le Havre never reduced Honfleur to that point of economic collapse which so disfigured Harfleur, and its visible prosperity was mostly laid down in the 16th and 17C when its seamen vied with those of Dieppe in establishing a far-flung trading estate. Binot de Gonneville charted the coast of Brazil in 1503 and in 1506 Jean Denis mustered an expedition which followed de Gonneville's to Brazil and then veered north to Labrador and Nova Scotia, which he claimed in the name of France. But Denis' endeavours were not followed up until 1603, when Samuel de Champlain sailed for Canada, founding Quebec some five years later and setting in train its subsequent colonisation by 4000 Normans.

The most durable legacy of this heyday is to be found in the remodelling of the medieval town at the instigation of Louis XIV between 1668 and 1684. The Dieppois Abraham Duquesne was given powers to purchase land and demolish fortifications where he saw fit in order to construct a safe inner harbour. This is known as the Vieux Bassin and its effect on the medieval town was dramatic. As a significant 13C town, pitched into the foreground of Anglo-French hostility after it was taken by Edward III in 1346, Honfleur had developed a system of wards. At its heart lay the fortified 'Enclos', to the south-east of what became the Vieux Bassin. This was separated by a network of deep ramps and ditches which both isolated and protected the faubourg Ste-Catherine to the north and the quartier St-Léonard to the south. Duquesne demolished the north-western angles of the Enclos driving a deep channel of water and light into the heart of the medieval precincts. At the entrance to this harbour, where the old Porte de Caen had grown a 15C mansion, known as the Lieutenance and housing the governor of Honfleur, he cleared an area to act as a small landing stage, and edged the sides of his harbour with two splendid quays—the Quai St-Etienne and the Quai Ste-Catherine. The latter is the most famously picturesque townscape in Normandy and its tall slate-hung houses, fronted by café tables and dappled in reflected light, became a favourite subject among the late 19C painters who gravitated to the Normandy coast.

Duquesne may have opened out the Quai Ste-Catherine but the terrace was already there. In 1630 the medieval counterscarp which rose above the fosse, separating the Enclos from the faubourg Ste-Catherine, was sold off as a series of narrow lots to provide new housing. These were built fairly quickly on steep ground so that their elongated waterfront façades are one

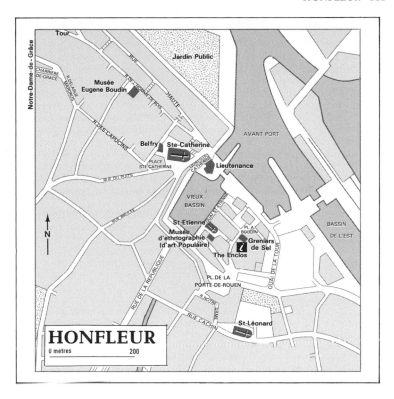

or two storeys taller than the façades giving on to the Rue des Logettes. The decision by Louis XIV to demolish the rest of the town fortifications between 1684 and 1690 reduced the Lieutenance to the status and size of a harbour-master's office and, along with the 18C construction of a new harbour basin in what had been the eastern quarter of the Enclos, was responsible for the modern shape of Honfleur. This latter 18C basin was in turn filled in and now acts as the main town car-park in the Place de l'Ancien Bassin du Centre. From here you might walk along the Quai de la Quarantaine to Duquesne's Vieux Bassin, and thus arrive at the very centre of Honfleur.

The Enclos. A left turn along the Quai St-Etienne brings you to the church. Begun in 1369 as a small aisleless structure **St-Etienne** was the lesser parish church within the Enclos, its larger rival, Notre-Dame, having been demolished in 1811. Nevertheless it was thought worth extending the church two bays westwards in 1432 when the town was under English occupation, and after its deconsecration during the Revolution the building found various uses as a warehouse, theatre, herring market and custom house until it was acquired by the Vieux Honfleur Society in 1897. It now houses the Society's **Musée de la Marine**. The church itself is modest, though it has a fine 16C timber roof, and the main interest lies in the displays of models, old charts, and general nautical paraphenalia. The majority of the exhibits are 19C, centred around a collection of ship's models mostly assembled by their respective crew-members. Around the corner in the Rue de la Prison the **Musée d'Ethnographie et d'Art Populaire** has been installed in the old town prison and an adjoining 17C residence. A 16C seigneurial townhouse, the Manoir Vigneron, was saved from destruction in Lisieux in 1911 and has been reassembled within the precincts of the museum, housing the principal collections of sculpture, leatherwork and armour. The old prison is given over to an account of the lives of various local worthies, but the most interesting is the 'Maison Renaissance', organised as a series of period rooms, each differentiated according to function or class.

From here the Rue de la Prison winds around the apse of St-Etienne meeting the Rue de la Ville opposite the Tourist Office. Immediately adjacent are two of the three enormous salt stores, **Les Greniers de Sel**, which Colbert built in 1670 to warehouse up to 10,000 tons of salt for the cod and herring fleets of Honfleur.

The **Sainte-Catherine Quarter**. A stroll along the Quai Ste-Catherine takes you past the restored Lieutenance and turning steeply left brings you into the **Place Ste-Catherine**. This acts as a beautiful stage for the Saturday market set beneath the wooden shingles of the parish church of the old faubourg. An early church close to this site was ruined by the periodic bombardments, town riots, and factional infighting which marked the Hundred Years War, and so it was decided in 1468 to construct entirely anew. The immediate rebuilding programmes undertaken in the wake of the Hundred Years War focused on the repair and reconstruction of town fortifications and castles, with building stone reserved for military use and stone-masons impressed into service. Consequently at **Ste-Catherine** the decision was taken to employ local shipwrights and construct a timber church. Building began in 1468 when the present north nave was erected, initially flanked by two low side aisles, but in 1496 'to accommodate the growing population' the southern aisle was demolished to make way for a second high nave, in turn furnished with its own south aisle during the 16C. The piers and aisle walls are mounted on stone plinths but the church is otherwise entirely built of timber, plaster, and glass with some, mostly later, slate roofing. Local legend has it that this 15C campaign was intended as a temporary measure, but the quality of the wooden tracery and the handsomely figured corbels which bracket the piers to the upper elevation refute the idea. Furthermore the church was both painted and provisioned for stained glass. The loss of this glass is telling but the most splendid of Ste-Catherine's many 16C aquisitions lies at the west where an organ loft of c 1570 is panelled with reliefs of musicians playing the sackbut, hurdy-gurdy, and serpent among other instruments of the time.

To the west a splendid free-standing belfry is axially aligned to the original northern nave and is contemporary with it. Although you can no longer climb to the loft the first stage is still reachable and is considered an annexe to the Musée Boudin, housing a small collection of religious art.

From the Place Ste-Catherine you can either take the **Rue de l'Homme de Bois** or the **Rue Haute** to reach the Musée Boudin. The former takes its name from the 17C carved head which adorns No. 23, though the latter boasts the grander architecture, a late medieval streetscape interfused by an irregular rhythm of 18C stone-built houses. Any of the steep stepped alleys off to the left will bring you up to the Place Erik Satie, and the **Musée Eugène Boudin**.

The paintings are loosely grouped according to artist, benefactor, or century and are unified by their common subject, which is Normandy, though the emphasis here is on Honfleur and the Seine estuary. The first floor is devoted to a collection of 17th and 18C textiles and costumes along with some paintings and local curiosities assembled by the 19C Honfleur historian Louveau. The floor above houses the core of the museum's holdings, with a room to the right given over to the work of 20C Honfleur painters Jean Dries and Henri de Saint Délis among others. To the left a group of large 19C oil paintings announces the '**Honfleur school**'. The idea that there was a Honfleur school of painters was first put about by **Louis-Alexandre Dubourg** who, in an inspired piece of self-promotion, effectively founded the collections displayed here in 1868, when he gave a small group of paintings by himself and his friends, Jean-Baptiste Jongkind and Eugène Boudin to the municipality for display in the Hôtel de Ville. Their careers, and indeed styles of painting, differed widely but they shared an interest in local subjects and they all came from Honfleur. Few scholars see their work as belonging to a school, in the sense of their sharing a coherent sense of purpose and common identity, and Boudin's work, particularly that of the 1870s and 1880s, is certainly better explored in a wider context.

Eugène Boudin (1824–98) was born in Honfleur, the son of a river pilot and was apprenticed to a papermaker in Le Havre in 1840. During a visit to Holland in 1848 he became aware of, and began to study, Dutch 17th and 18C landscape painting, simultaneously making the aquaintance of Gustave Courbet, and embarked on a series of studies and sketches of the effects of light on low and often watery landscapes. Back in Normandy Boudin began to work '*en plein air*' in oils, developing a very rapid technique which culminated in his showing a group of estuary and coastal scenes at the Salon of 1859. Baudelaire acclaimed him 'the king of skies', adding 'he understands the poetry of clouds, their fluid architecture'. This popularity with the Parisian avant-garde did not last, but back in Le Havre Boudin befriended the youthful Claude Monet and was subsequently invited to exhibit at the first Impressionist show of 1874. His friendship with Monet, which lapsed into periods of cool hostility, has led many critics to see Boudin as a fundamental link between painters of the generation of Corot and Courbet and the Impressionists. While this view may be super-ficially attractive, relating Boudin's luminous skies and his brilliant hand-ling of evanescent light with Monet's later experiments, the working methods, subject matter and underlying ideology of the two artists argue a very much more complex relationship.

The **Salle Eugène Boudin** draws together a range of work from a series of early sky studies, arranged alongside Courbet's evocation of approach-ing dusk at the mouth of the Seine, to a few, mostly minor, paintings dating from shortly before Boudin's death at Deauville in 1898. The finest are to be found among a wonderfully varied series of small oil-paintings depicting the beach at Trouville and dating from the late 1870s and early 1880s.

Above this room is a good collection of works by a more recent inhabitant, **André Hambourg** (1909–), who has lived intermittently in Honfleur since 1936, and with an altogether more anecdotal eye draws from a similar stock of subject matter as Boudin.

The Saint-Léonard Quarter. Although less survives of this quarter than is the case with its counterparts, it nevertheless rewards casual exploration. From the Place de Porte-de-Rouen the Rue Notre-Dame winds around to the church of **St-Léonard**, once the centrepiece of the southern medieval precinct. Originally constructed in the 13C a new stone church was built in 1500, but was in turn destroyed by fire in 1562. This accounts for the most arresting feature of the church, its west front, where a Flamboyant façade is surmounted by an octagonal bell tower of 1760. The interior, bizarrely, relates to neither of these, dating from the main rebuilding campaign begun c 1625, and is by comparison simple, clean and uninspiring.

Since the 11C Honfleur's mariners have sought and found protection through the intervention of **Notre-Dame-de-Grâce** whose cult, like that of so many maritime intercessors, is situated on the high ground above the town. The whole rocky hillside, with a Calvary and chapel on its seaward flank, is known as the Côte de Grâce and is reached, on one's knees if necessary, by a steep haul up the Charrière-de-Grâce, a continuation of the Rue des Capucins. Not only does this offer a panorama of the town and river, but from the Calvary the whole of the Seine estuary becomes visible, from the Pont de Tancarville in the east to the hills above Le Havre. The chapel stands behind the Calvary. With its domed porch and apsidal transepts it presents a picturesque silhouette but it remains a serious, and simple, place of pilgrimage and prayer. It was built between 1602 and 1615 to replace the chapel Duke Richard III had founded some time before 1023, and which had been largely destroyed in a landslide. Miraculously the cult statue of Notre-Dame-de-Grâce had survived in the one standing wall, or so the legend goes, and Madame de Montpensier gave land above the old chapel on which to build anew. The current statue of Notre-Dame is clearly not medieval, though this does not seem to have diminished her powers, and the chapel abounds with ex-votos and deeply felt paintings of ships in distress, made by the crews who survived these tempests.

From Honfleur the D513 never loses more than a few hundred metres on the coast passing, at Cricquebouef, a small ivy-clad Romanesque church, banked above the village duck pond. 7km beyond, as you approach Trouville, the road skirts towards the south along the Boulevard Aristide Briand. Rather than follow it, a right turn onto the Route de la Corniche brings you to the Calvaire de Secours, where you can survey the whole of the Touques basin. The beaches, yachts, and villas spread along both banks of the River Touques, with Porte Deauville moored against the western piers. The whole complex is, practically speaking, now part of **Deauville-Trouville**, which expanded upriver early this century to swallow the old market town of Touques.

TROUVILLE attracted the earlier settlers, inspiring the painter Paul Huet and author Alexandre Dumas to spend the summer of 1829 in what was then a tiny fishing village. Huet also persuaded the marine painters EugèneGabriel Isabey and Charles Mozin to paint here in the early 1830s and Mozin's exhibition of several oils of Trouville at the Salon of 1834 seems to have established the village as a worthy goal for expeditions from Paris. Gustave Flaubert met his long-unrequited love, Mme-Schlesinger, at the Auberge de l'Agneau d'Or in 1836, but it was not until the late 1840s that the first villas, modelled on the Swiss tradition of mountain chalets, were constructed on the hillside. By 1857 it was possible to spend the summer in either of two hotels, hire a wheeled bathing machine and while away the afternoon in the library of the small casino. The following decade saw this nascent resort explode with the arrival of the Empress Eugénie. The number of villas multiplied fivefold, new hotels were built, the Promenade des Plages was laid out and rampant price inflation hit the beach. The arrival of the railway in 1863 further stoked demand but Trouville had become the favoured resort of the court of Napoléon III, and even Eugénie's hasty departure in 1870 aboard Sir John Burgoyne's yacht and into exile, barely slowed the momentum.

All of this has left its mark on a town which retains a late 19C atmosphere, and the idle life now, as then, revolves around the **Casino**. This is housed in a vast Louis XVI-style block on the Quai Albert Ier, and opened for business in 1912. The gambling is now supplemented by a cinema, restaurant and clinic specialising in sea-water therapy. Standing at the centre of the town it separates the old fishing quays from the Promenade des Planches. The former overlook the river and house an excellent fish-market, rebuilt in revivalist fashion as a 'traditional' Norman hall in 1936, while the Promenade des Planches acts as a long wooden beach-walk separating the hotels and restaurants of the sea-front from the bathing area. This latter is more conducive to modern tastes than than that of Trouville's great 19C rival, Dieppe, and is sandy, clean and wide.

Artistic interest in Trouville lies buried in its villas which, with one exception, remain a private domain. The exception is the **Villa Montebello** of 1866, lying off the Rue Général Leclerc above the eastern end of the beach. As its name suggests the villa is dressed with Italianate pilasters and mouldings, marshalled around a canted three-storey central bay. It now houses the town museum. The collections are on the lower two floors with the 19C paintings and prints gathered downstairs and the more recent work of André Hambourg lying off the temporary exhibition space on the upstairs floor. Hambourg's festive beaches and sirens are selfconsciously indebted to two artists from the other side of the Seine estuary, Claude Monet and Raoul Dufy, but lack the directness of his work at Honfleur, and it is the works of **Charles Mozin** on the ground floor which are generally the most interesting. It was Mozin who first popularised Trouville and he later settled in the town, dying here in 1862. He was a moderately successful painter specialising in portrayals of an idealised peasantry at one with the picturesque landscapes in which they lived and worked, but he was also capable of producing the occasionally masterful image. There are two such paintings in the Salle Fernand Truffaut, of navigation along the river Touques, and of a huddle of cottages at Le Quernet, both profoundly influenced by Constable's submissions to the Salon of 1824.

Trouville may be linked with **DEAUVILLE** by the short Pont des Belges but the change of atmosphere is abrupt. The reason for this is that Deauville is a planned resort, conceived and financed by a consortium of businessmen put together by the Duc de Morny and advised by Dr Oliffe, the British Ambassador in Paris. In 1859 the marshes to the west of the Touques were drained and Brunet engaged as architect, having been instructed to design a resort based on a rectilinear grid running parallel to the beach and with a system of diagonally planted avenues meeting at the Place Morny. Free-standing villas were to be set in large gardens along these promenades and a race course laid out to the south. Although the death of the Duc de Morny in 1865 delayed construction, the fact that the railway station had opened two years previously ensured this was no more than a temporary setback and by the turn of the century the resort had become more popular than its established rival on the right bank. The 1920s sealed Deauville's reputation, and it is not difficult to see why. The avenues are broad and the prospects ideally suited to a relaxing stroll. Furthermore the town possesses an intense and aristocratic social calendar based on an accepted 'season'. This opens in July, reaching an international crescendo in early August at the Yearling Sales, and officially closes on the fourth Sunday in August with the running of the Grand Prix de Deauville.

Attempts have been made to extend the season into early September with a festival of American Film, but the price of a parasol on the beach still falls on the Monday after the Grand Prix.

As in Trouville the **Promenade des Planches** consists of a broad walk of wooden boards running between the beach and the seaward-facing cafés, and is where the serious posing is conducted. The beach itself is splendid, sandy and soft underfoot, peppered with an almost pointillist grid of brightly coloured parasols which may be rented by the day. Standing a hundred metres further back is the main corniche, the Boulevard Eugène Cornuché, but as this is Deauville and the cars tend to be larger, it is a four-lane promenade, along which nobody speeds. It is here that the main hotels, casino, and larger villas are to be found. Several of the early villas were loosely modelled on 16C manor houses and the genre was hugely amplified in 1912 when construction of the **Hôtel Normandy** began. Its half-timbered walls, large first-floor windows, steep roofs and sharply pitched dormers give it an unexpectedly picturesque air, and established this essentially decorative vernacular as a major element within the tonal landscape of the town. The Normandy's immediate neighbour was, by contrast, modelled on the Petit Trianon at Versailles and is one of a group of extravagant architectural statements which rise above the more westerly shores of the corniche. These range from the archaeologically-minded Antique and Moorish-exotic, to the frankly incongruous Scottish Baronial, lending this sea-front quarter a more fanciful atmosphere than in the businesslike spaces around the Place Morny.

Recrossing the Pont des Belges and turning upstream the D535 follows the course of the river for 2km to the medieval port of **Touques**. The town has retained several old timber houses, clustered around the central Place, and two parish churches, though its river wharves were abandoned long ago. To the east the church of **St-Thomas** dates from 1164 when the exiled Thomas à Becket laid its foundation stone, an accomplishment which prompted the late 16C window in the apse, depicting Becket's martyrdom. The apse was added during the early 16C but the rest of the building follows on from Becket's foundation, and has suffered badly at the hands of the 19C restorers. Seeking to recreate the 12C windows, only the arches of which were original, new capitals and colonettes were introduced as part of a severe campaign to re-medievalise the church, and just the one western window embrasure came through unscathed.

Further west the earlier parish church of **St-Pierre** now functions as an occasional exhibition space. It, too, is a polyglot structure but the core is substantially late 11C, rising to support a very fine octagonal belfry.

A brief diversion along the valley of the Touques to Pont-l'Evêque passes William the Conqueror's once-mighty castle of **Bonneville-sur-Touques**, now sadly reduced to a ditch and fragments of an enceinte wall. It was here that William launched his diplomatic offensive against Harold's accession to the English throne, strategically linking this with a denunciation of the abuses rife among the clergy, and so enlisted papal support for his invasion plans. Parts of the enceinte towers still stand, enmeshed in a much later manor house. The whole site remains in private hands (open Sat., Sun., and Bank Hol. mornings only) but even when closed it is worth climbing the hill for the ravishing views it commands over the valley.

4km south-east, along the N177, you pass the 15C episcopal manor house of **Canapville**, built to accommodate the bishops of Lisieux in a manner to which their feudal role inclined them, within a sumptuous late medieval seigneurial mansion.

From here it is but 5km to **Pont-l'Evêque**, an important river crossing which takes its name from the bridge built by the bishops of Lisieux in the 11C. The present bridge seems very modest but the river has been tamed and its meanders and flood-plains are corseted within a narrow channel as it passes through the town. Three-quarters of Pont-l'Evêque was destroyed by a combination of allied bombardment and an enemy scorched earth initiative during 1944, with the result that its once rich streetscape is much diminished. There are some fine timbered houses at the western edge of the town along the Rue de Vaucelles, notably No. 68, and a splendid 17C mansion of stone and brick, the Hôtel Montpensier, set back from the Rue St-Michel, but the town has had to be rebuilt around these fragments. Even the Hôtel Montpensier lost the great timber roof which Philibert Delorme designed in 1624. The Place du Tribunal is the one secular corner to have escaped. Set back from the main street it has retained the early 19C Law Courts and the 16C galleried dormitory and cellar range of the Dominican convent.

On the whole the town has retained its more engaging qualities and you can still stand in the very centre and look out over the meadows which have provided the town with its famous cheese since the 13C. There is one building of real distinction, standing against the west bank of the original bridge, opposite the rebuilt town square to the east. This is the parish church of **St-Michel**, built in a single campaign between 1483 and 1519 with a colossally buttressed western bell tower, originally capped by a spire. The interior, indeed the whole spatial frame, bears a close resemblance to St-Jacques at Lisieux, where the choir was going up between 1498 and 1501. The elevation is in three storeys and carried on columnar piers, with a short clerestory and a polygonal apse in which the clerestory sills are dropped to the level of the stringcourse above the main arcade. There are no transepts and no ambulatory but rather a seamless and rapid succession of bays driving the processional axis eastwards, with the choir distinguished from the nave by a pair of quatrilobed piers, carrying the stair vices which give access to the high roof spaces. A subtle late 16C intervention elaborated the respective treatment of the choir by adorning the aisles with pendant vaults. It is a simple, confident, beautifully executed design. The one note which might have jolted this coherence has been masterfully resolved. As the 16C glass had been lost, François Chapuis was approached in 1963 and invited to reglaze the building, resulting in the present cycle of light-sensitive colour and pattern.

From Deauville the D513 sustains its status as the coast road, where possible staying close to a beach of fine sand which stretches for 25km to the mouth of the Orne. **Villers-sur-Mer** is the first of the larger resorts and boasts a casino and a good Museum of Palaeontology, though it lacks the big set-pieces of its grander neighbours. The exhibits in the museum were mostly culled from the **Falaise des Vaches Noires** around the turn of the century by the photographer and amateur geologist Ferdinand Postel, who used the stones and fossils as the basis for elaborate montages. For a complementary walk you should set out just before low tide along the beach towards the foot of the Falaise des Vaches Noires. These strange cliffs were formed by the crumbling of the soft upper strata of marl and clay, eroded and cut into deep hollows by fresh water from the Auberville plateau. The underlying chalk has fractured and great calcarious boulders litter the beach, now dense with seaweed. These are the celebrated black cows. You can also continue along the beach to Houlgate, which is much the best way to get there. The whole walk takes about two hours but should not be attempted within three hours of high water.

The road meanders over the plateau to Auberville from where the Corniche d'Houlgate, or D163, swings past a *'station d'orientation'* offering magnificent views over the whole of the Baie de Seine. **Houlgate** is another coastal village transformed by the mid 19C thirst for sea-air and became, with its neighbour Cabourg, the bourgeois resort par excellence. The villas and gardens which crowd the Drochon valley, along with the residences on the seafront, constitute the finest ensemble of late 19C architecture in Normandy. They are also amongst the most inventive buildings to be found anywhere along the French coast. The star was undoubtedly the **Grand Hôtel**, begun in 1870 as something of a new departure. Rather than the generally favoured hotel style, the château-by-the-sea, the 'Grand' is intended to be seen as a palace, equipped with large reception areas and spacious family suites. This combination of grandeur and practical accommodation made a direct appeal to the Parisian middle-classes, who enthusiastically endorsed the benefits of the seaside holidays pioneered by the aristocracy of the previous generation. Sadly, the Grand Hôtel no longer shares its restaurants and ball-rooms with the merchants and lawyers of Paris and, given that the holiday trade in resorts such as Houlgate and Cabourg is now largely confined to weekend and day trippers, it has been converted into private apartments and renamed **Les Pléiades**. Even the 'American Villas' on the Rue Henri-Dolbert are being turned into flats. Nevertheless this run-down air is confined to the seafront and a walk into the town proper, and the hillsides behind, will reveal many fine examples of late 19C architecture.

Beyond Houlgate the estuarial sands mark the mouth of the River Dives with its medieval port, **Dives-sur-Mer**, crabbed against the right bank. This was the port in which Duke William assembled his invasion fleet, and strove to provision and entertain an army of 7000 Normans, Bretons, and Flemings during the long late summer weeks when poor weather and northerly winds delayed the crossing. The river mouth has silted up leaving Dives a good mile inland, although the river has been recently dredged to facilitate construction of a harbour and marina, the Port Guillaume, which will restore shipping to Dives even if it does not restore the sea.

In 1067, by way of thanksgiving, William provided the town with money for a new church, doubtless much needed to accommodate the swelling ranks of pilgrims who, with the fishing fleet and market, provided Dives with its medieval prosperity. Dives' fame derived from the discovery on the 6 April 1001 of a figure of the Crucified Christ, fetched up in the nets of a local fishing boat. The statue was brought to the small chapel known as Notre-Dame, and a cross was made to suit the figure of Christ. This failed to fit and although several attempts were made to marry Christ to the cross no progress was made until 1004, when fishermen discovered a simple wooden cross on the beach. The two objects fused perfectly and the old Christ *'sans croux'* was raised as a full Crucifix. By 1020 miracles and cures were ascribed to its powers, and Benedictine monks from Troarn were installed to watch over and care for it. Thus the small parish chapel became a local centre of pilgrimage and a suitable object of patronage for the victorious William. All that remains of this ambitious, and important Romanesque building are the distressed and heavily recut crossing piers, along with the north choir aisle entrance, of the church of **Notre-Dame** at the top of the Rue Gaston Manneville.

The rest of the building is an interesting and historically piecemeal structure. The lantern tower was raised in the 13C but in 1346 Edward III destroyed the town, badly damaging the church. A two-bay choir and square-ended sanctuary bay were built soon after, along with a new transept, and in the 15C a strange attempt to build a second transept to the west of this main transept resulted in the bizarre disjunctions now only too plainly visible. These were uncertain times however and during the Hundred Years War it is likely that the church witnessed an upsurge of devotion to the miracle-working crucifix, creating this demand for a larger reliquary display area.

The nave was begun in the late 15C and was intended as a vaulted hall-church, but the money never ran to it, and it is now covered with a flat timber ceiling. The west portal was completed however and remains, aesthetically at least, the most satisfying area of the building. From thereon it was mostly downhill, for the Crucifix was destroyed by Protestant soldiers in 1562, and the church's current state of disrepair urgently requires a programme of sensitive restoration.

Fortuitously the town has preserved much of its medieval infrastructure, particularly along the Rue Gaston Manneville and around the market square. From the church the Rue Paul Canta cuts up to the Place de la République, where the market is still held in a great 15C market hall known as **Les Halles**. This is surmounted by a steeply pitched roof, supported on tall wooden posts which separate a central aisle from two narrow side ranges, and ranks among the larger late medieval timber halls to have survived in northern Europe. The Manoir de la Falaise stands opposite, built as a castellated town house by the Leduc de la Falaise family in 1695, and completing a memorable town square, unfortunately marred by post-war development.

At the bottom of the Rue G-Manneville a famous 16C coaching inn, **L'Hostellerie de Guillaume le Conquerant**, now houses a collection of craft and antique shops but retains the vibrantly picturesque balconies and roofs which Winston Churchill so admired during its previous incarnation, as a pre-war hotel de-luxe.

From Dives the Rue du Général de Gaulle carries the coast road over the river and into **Cabourg**. Conceived as a model resort at the same time as Deauville, Cabourg was laid out in 1860 by Robinet. In plan it resembles a fan, with the 'Grand Hôtel' at its springing point and a system of radiating avenues intersecting with concentric crescents. Around the turn of the century Cabourg boasted a café society the equal of that at Deauville, but its faded gentility is buttressed by a stuffiness now more the equal of a provincial tearoom. This is not without its amusements, and one can readily identify with Mr Hulot's holiday in much of the town, particularly where revolving doors or Byzantine plumbing might become an issue. Cabourg is best known as the favoured resort of Marcel Proust, who was first brought here as a child in 1881 and spent every season from 1907–14 at the Grand Hôtel, in memory of his mother. The town formed the model for Balbec in his '*A l'ombre des jeunes filles en fleur*', and in gratitude the majestically coherent seafront has been renamed the Promenade Marcel Proust. There is little of interest in the town however, save the Grand Hôtel and the symmetries of its avenues, and it remains very much a place in which to swim, eat and rest.

Cabourg marks the western reach of the resorts of the Côte Fleurie. From here you quickly arrive at the huge sandbanks off Merville-Franceville-Plage, before the road swings south to cross the Orne at Pegasus Bridge.

9

St-Pierre-sur-Dives, Lisieux, and the Pays D'Auge

ROAD (141km): St-Pierre-sur-Dives; D511, 20km Falaise; D63/D249, 8km Beaumais; D249/D90, 6km Norrey-en-Auge; D90, 8km Trun; D916, 19km Vimoutiers; D16/D46, 21km Orbec; D519, 10km St-Denis-de-Mailloc; D149/D268A, 8km St-Germain-de-Livet; D579, 6km Lisieux; N13, 17km Crévecœur-en-Auge; D16/D154, 6km Ste-Marie-aux-Anglais; D154, 5km Vieux-Pont; D511, 7km St-Pierre-sur-Dives.

The above itinerary describes a rolling circuit, taking in the main market towns of the Pays d'Auge in anti-clockwise procession. Its apparent complexity derives from a desire to link the towns with the more interesting village churches and châteaux, but it also incorporates a glimpse, at least, of one of the richest agrarian landscapes of northern France. The coastal reaches, very different culturally to the river valleys, are treated elsewhere (see Rte 8). It is still the case however that the medieval towns of the Côte Fleurie—Touques or Dives-sur-Mer for instance—retain a pattern of life akin to that of the pastoral, inland core.

The Pays d'Auge grew prosperous on its ciders, cheese, cattle, and poultry, and the establishment of the great medieval agricultural fairs at Lisieux and Guibray (near Falaise) reflected the development of a rich infrastructure of manorial farms, cultivating the river meadows along the valleys of the Dives, Vie, and Touques. With the exception of the recent industrialisation of the area around Lisieux farming remains the mainstay of the regional economy, and the Camemberts, Livarots, and Pont l'Evêques produced in the Auge are counted among the finest cheeses of Europe. You can savour them in the markets at Orbec and Lisieux, or most spectacularly in the great hall of St-Pierre-sur-Dives, whose Monday morning extravaganza is one of the vital events of Norman life. It is for this event that St-Pierre has been chosen as the base for this route, though Falaise and Orbec are in many ways more attractive, if peripheral, centres. The obvious centre for an exploration of the Pays d'Auge is the regional capital, Lisieux, but as the town was subjected to an unsympathetic programme of post-war reconstruction, and is anyway uncharacteristic of an essentially rural area, most visitors are likely to find the southerly market towns more congenial.

ST-PIERRE-SUR-DIVES. Gloriously situated between the right bank of the River Dives and the chalk escarpments to the west, the town developed during the early medieval period around its large Benedictine abbey and its market. The latter has long attracted subsidiary industries, and now provides the town with its primary employment—making wooden cases and boxes for the cheese producers of central Normandy. The town's early identity, and indeed its name, is bound up with the establishment of a large religious house in the 11C, on the site of the old parish church of St-Pierre at Epinay.

The Carolingian 'burg' of Epinay was sacked during the Norse raids of the early 10C, resulting in the death of Wambert, its much revered parish priest. Out of grief, and in memory of their murdered pastor, the villagers changed the name of the settlement from Epinay to St-Pierre-sur-Dives. The possession of a cult statue, Notre-Dame de l'Epinay, and its association with what was being represented as the martyrdom of Wambert, inspired Lesceline, niece of the Count of Eu, to found an oratory on the site c 1010. This was populated by a congregation of nuns, but their enthusiasm seems to have been short-lived, and in 1040 they moved to the convent of St-Désir at Lisieux. Their place was taken by Benedictine monks from St-Catherine-du-Mont in Rouen, who arrived to find a modest structure, and began building a church on a much larger scale under the leadership of Abbot Ainard in 1046. Lesceline was buried in the choir of this new monastic church in 1058, and in 1067 the building was solemnly consecrated in the presence of William the Conqueror. It is this important early Romanesque structure which underlies the present **Abbaye de St-Pierre-sur-Dives** along the Rue de l'Eglise.

Even the most cursory examination of the emphatic exterior volumes of the building reveals a shape which speaks of the Romanesque, with two square towers to the west and a high lantern tower over the crossing. Although there is evidence of fire damage at the base of the south-west tower which was probably caused by Henry I's destruction of the church in 1106, it seems likely that the lower reaches of this tower originally formed part of the donjon to Guillaume d'Eu's castle, and thus played no role in the early Romanesque church. What is certain however, is that when rebuilding began under Abbot Haimon in 1108 all parts of the remaining castle had been made over to the monks, and were incorporated into the abbey or its conventual buildings. This new church was the same size as the present abbey, and the wonderfully rich half-columns and rolls which articulate the upper stages of the south-west tower date from c 1130–40, the spire from c 1220. Its north-western counterpart, like the lantern tower, belongs to an extensive 13C rebuilding programme, and frames a Flamboyant great west window which was the final flourish in an otherwise unremarkable early 16C refurbishment.

It is evident from the interior that the church was designed to accommodate a sizeable number of monks. The 17C choir stalls will seat 42, but this represents a diminution by one bay of the 13C ritual choir area. On the whole the elevation is substantially late 13C, and is identifiable wherever you see a band of blind quatrefoils stamped above the tall triforium, though both the nave supports and the easternmost four columnar piers of the apse have been mounted on the bases of Haimon's early 12C church. An early 16C campaign ultimately replaced most of the clerestory windows with some routine Flamboyant tracery, and revaulted the building. It is when looking at this nave vault that you become aware of one of the building's major curiosities—for the north and south elevations are out of synchronisation, and would seem to have been purposefully built this way in the 12C.

The choir contains an accomplished 17C altar, and there are four panels of 13C glass remounted in two of the north aisle windows, but the finest of the medieval work is to be found in the **chapter house**. To reach this it is now necessary to walk around the south flank to No. 23 Rue Benoît. The chapter house lies off the cloister and has been laid with a superb 13C tiled pavement, designed and fired by the ceramicists of the Pré d'Auge, which originally decorated the choir. The rest of the precincts have been given over to the **Musée du Conservatoire des Techniques Fromagères Traditionnelles de Normandie**—a well conceived permanent exhibition focused on the making of Livarot, but applicable to most of the justly famous farmhouse cheeses of the Pays d'Auge.

East of the abbey the huge, dusty square of the Place du Marché stretches in the shade of the finest medieval market hall in France, **Les Halles**, whose majestic spaces continue to host the Monday market. Parts of the stonework date from the 11C, but the portals and magnificent roof are 13C, making even the timber hall at Dives-sur-Mer seem a poor relation by comparison. The roof was sadly destroyed in 1944, but has been replicated in all particulars, braced throughout by double beams and bonded solely with chestnut dowelling pegs. It is an exhilarating structure, majestically functional, and pinned towards the edge of a vast, prairie-like tract of ground, in whose windy spaces one might catch a sense of the conduct of great medieval markets and fairs.

From St-Pierre the D511 heads south, hugging the fertile upper course of the River Dives for the first few kilometres towards Falaise. After 4km a well-signposted right turn brings you to the **Château de Vendeuvre**, built in 1750 by Jacques-François Blondel as a summer residence for the Count of Vendeuvre (open early June to mid September afternoons only; Easter to late May, and mid September to 1 November, Sunday and Bank Holiday afternoons only). The main block is set within a formal garden and remains as it was furnished in the mid 18C, with a particularly fine dining room which, as was then the custom, commands the evening sunset. Beyond the château the vaulted **Orangery** houses a collection of miniature furniture, guild examination pieces mostly, and dating from the 16C to the present day. None are more than 75cm tall and, as show-pieces, are chased with bronze, inlaid with ivory, and decorated by miniature paintings—intentionally virtuosic performances which would win the apprentice elevation to his chosen guild of master craftsmen.

South of Vendeuvre the landscape begins to change, as the orchards and rolling pasture of the Pays d'Auge give way to the flat, cereal-growing lands of the Falaise plain, with the small village of (6km) **Perrières** lying on the cusp of the plateau. A priory was founded here in 1075, whose precincts were sold off in lots in 1802, with the parish acquiring the church. This has a modest late 11C nave and transepts which were rebuilt in the 14C. The church is dwarfed by a splendid 12C grange however, whose single pitched roof is supported on thick columnar piers, mounted above high pedestals and spur-bases. Access to the grange is along a winding farm track, belonging in part to a private farm, and you may find it difficult to visit, success being a matter for the persistent. The rest of this delightful village has simply grown up in the grounds of the priory, and scattered among the private dwellings beyond the grange are the priory mill, cider press, precinct gates, and parts of the refectory range.

As you move to the west of the River Dives the landscape levels out to form a long, low-lying plateau, reaching southwards to divide Caen from the granite massifs of the Suisse Normande. This great plain is scored with narrow ravines, one of which, the gorge of the River Ante, lends eminence to the town of (10km) **Falaise**. Both the defensibility of the site and its position at the very centre of the duchy commended the town to the dukes who established the first castle here, and made it one of their principal residences. Its significance was assured when the Faubourg de Guibray grew up to the south-east of the town in the 13C, becoming the site of

Normandy's most important summer fair. Until recently most of Falaise dated from the 15C and 16C, as both the Black Death and a debilitating siege in 1417–18 left the town severely depleted, and reconstruction came late in the Middle Ages. Sadly, between 12 August 1944, when the German 7th Army began retreating from Mortain, and 17 August, when the Canadian 1st Army entered Falaise 85 per cent of the town was flattened. The larger stone structures escaped complete destruction but the domestic timber-built houses vanished, and with them one of the finest vernacular townscapes in Normandy. Given that the German army used the Talbot tower as an observation post, and the Canadians covered it with heavy shell-fire from Mont Mirat across the gorge, the castle stood up amazingly well and remains the best place from which to survey the town.

The Place Guillaume-le-Conquérant leads unmistakably to the **Château de Falaise**, indeed the whole town and most of the surrounding country are surveyed from its complex of towers. You enter by the town gate, to be greeted by a fanfare of donjons which rise above the high ground to the rear of the bailey—for, uniquely, Falaise possesses three connected keep-towers. Not without reason is the whole complex generally regarded by the experts to be one of the most important examples of military architecture in France.

Nothing survives of the castle known to William the Conqueror, and the present structure was laid out by William's youngest son, Henry I, some time before 1123. An enceinte wall, fortified with 15 towers and broken by the one town gate, was constructed to enclose an irregular rectangular bailey, and at its north-western angle a large square keep was raised. This is in three storeys, and divided by a curtain wall which splits the accommodation into two oblong areas.

In the mid 12C however a smaller rectangular hall was added to the valley side, thickly walled but offering more comfortable accommodation, and in 1207 Philip Augustus connected this latter hall with a vaulted corridor to his new pièce-de-résistance—the so-called **Tour Talbot**. This is an inner redoubt—circular, with walls 3 metres thick and a separate water supply via the well Philip had sunk to the valley bed of the River Ante. The tower is arranged over five storeys, with a spiral stairwell within the wall, and intermediate look-out stages. Not only does it survey the valley but it also affords protection against mutiny by the mercenaries who were usually called on to man the defences in times of war and were capable of causing as much injury to their employer as to the enemy. It is, in total, an impressively cogent fortification, whose military logic is abundantly clear and whose roofless spaces command respect.

Below the castle the Rue de la Roche winds beneath the scarp and along the gorge of the Ante to the **Fontaine d'Arlette**. It is an extraordinarily beautiful valley, meandering among the groups of fortified farms and houses which gather along the far bank. And it was here that the 17-year-old younger son of Duke Richard II first glimpsed a tanner's daughter, La Belle Arlette, washing laundery with her skirts drawn high. A plaque has been set up at the natural spring, or '*fontaine*', telling of Arlette's beauty and Robert's prowess, and how in late March 1027 they conceived a child, born at Christmas and destined, as Guillaume le Bâtard, to become William the Conqueror, Duke of Normandy and King of England.

Beyond the Fontaine a complicated network of streets brings you (via the Rue des Tanneries and Rue des Herforts) to the best preserved of the town gates, the **Porte des Cordeliers**, originally raised in the 13C and sub-sequently remodelled after the Hundred Years War. This leads towards one of the smaller of the town squares, the Place St-Gervais. The Place is cut by the main Caen–Alençon road, but its north-east angle is animated by the parish church of **St-Gervais**, displaying a bewildering mixture of styles, something of a feature of this region. The latest is to be found in the choir, which has been largely recreated since 1944. It is out of alignment with the nave and was completed c 1560, supporting an impressive wooden pendant vault from a clerestory wall-passage.

The nave is more of a hybrid. The south elevation is late 11C and sits opposite a late 12C north wall, with a 14C balustrade added just below the clerestory. To the west parts of the Romanesque façade have been incorporated into a shallow 15C baptistery, and chapels were opened out from the aisles to the north and south between c 1480 and c 1560. The richly ornamented lantern tower is early 12C. It is not the most satisfying of interiors. The splendid capital of the south arcade depicting a Norman blacksmith and mounted warrior suggests that the original Romanesque church must once have been very fine.

From the church the Rue St-Gervais leads back towards the Place Guillaume-le-Conquérant, which, in addition to fostering the main approach to the castle, is obliquely addressed by the triangular prow of the western entrance to **La Trinité**—a situation which presumably acted as a catalyst for this otherwise bizarre composition. The porch has been walled up, awaiting the completion of a programme of restoration which has seen the transepts renewed and has now reached the choir.

The transepts are the earliest part of the remaining structure, dating from the mid 13C, and are simpler in style than the nave. This was begun in 1438, a disastrous year which was recorded in the hopeful inscription to the west: 'This year saw many dead from war and famine throughout the whole of France. We pray to God that our new work will be a fine one'. It was not in fact until 1510 that the three chapels giving onto the south aisle of the nave were completed, an event which marked the culmination of the project. These adopt the Renaissance motifs being pioneered in Rouen by Georges d'Amboise, and lie in measured contrast to the prolific late medieval decoration of the north arcade. The best of this latter ornament is to be found amongst the capitals, arranged as sculptural friezes around the heads of the piers, and including both secular and religious themes. On one a crowned bull is led triumphantly to market, on another a banquet unfolds, while to the west an almost heraldic St Sebastian testifies to the vulnerability of the town to outbreaks of plague during the 14th and 15C.

From Falaise the D63 passes the handsome 12C apse of **Notre-Dame de Guibray**, and offers two excursions away from the main road to Trun. The first is to follow the D249 through the wheat fields from Fresné-la-Mère to (8km) **Beaumais**, where the church has an inventive array of Romanesque capitals decorating the blind arcading of the east end. Above the south portal an extraordinary 12C lintel has survived, amply reflecting the resilience of older, Scandinavian traditions in the more rural areas.

The second detour involves following the D249 east for 5km until you reach the D90, and then turning north to **Norrey-en-Auge**. The parish church here has a rare and beautiful nave which is in desperate need of funds to arrest its deterioration. A 15C south porch and early 13C portal give entry to the church. The four bay nave has been divided into two double bays by a pair of columns flanking a central rectangular pier, while the spandrel arches originally opened onto the aisle roof space to give the illusion of a sort of false tribune. Like the crossing this arrangement is early 11C, and almost certainly predates 1039 when the lord of Grandmesnil was killed in a tournament and buried in the church. The rapidly perishing plasterwork of the nave carries fragments of medieval polychromy, and a stunning **Adoration of the Magi** above the north arcade. Stylistically this would seem to date from c 1120–30, but it is positioned here as in the great Early Christian mosaic cycle of Sant'Apollinare Nuovo at Ravenna to act as a processional focus immediately west of the altar. The choir is a 13C extension, also run-down, and carries a few fading traces of late medieval painting.

The easiest way to drive from Norrey to Trun and Vimoutiers is to take the D90 and its derivatives as far as (8km) Trun, and then cut north-east along the D916, though you might also contemplate a brief run along the D13 to (7km) **Chambois**. It was around the ruins of the 12C castle here that the 'Falaise Pocket' was closed on 19 August 1944, and after a brutal battle for possession of Hill 262, some 5km to the north at **Mont-Ormel**, that the Battle for Normandy was effectively won. A monument on Mt-Ormel commemorates the action and offers a superb panorama of the Dives valley, forcibly demonstrating just why the position was so fiercely desired.

The road from Trun to (19km) Vimoutiers sweeps above the valley of the Viette, past the meadows, orchards, and woodland which produce the best Camembert, and much the best Calvados, in Normandy. **Vimoutiers** depends on this agricultural produce for its livelihood, and boasts a Camembert museum on the Avenue Général de Gaulle, along with sundry statues of cows, and of Madame Harel, the originator of the cheese which took its name from her home village of Camembert some 5km to the south. It is a dreary town, and if cheese is your delight then St-Pierre-sur-Dives offers both a better choice and a better background, particularly on market day.

Vimoutiers is however a good base from which to visit the **Musée Fernand-Léger** at **Lisores**. Take the D579 north, and after 2km turn right onto the narrow D268, the museum lying at the end of a well signposted track beyond the village. Léger was a native of Argentan, and the barn and garden which house the museum belonged to his family, transformed as such by his wife, Nadia. The displays are largely confined to reproductions of Léger's better known pre-war paintings and lithographs, though there is a superb three-dimensional maquette of the famous cockerel's head, exploding into a morning reveille. The grounds are also strewn with mosaics based on Léger's work, and a tiled version of the 1948 'La Fermière et la Vache' covers much of the exterior gable wall. A few photographs show the artist at work, mostly in the barn which he used as a studio towards the end of his life, and where he executed seven glass panels for the small chapel he built in the garden. It must have been a marvellous setting in which to work, and it is the immediate environment which constitutes the strongest reason for a visit, with the old buildings banked above a hollow, and surrounded by orchards and hedgerows.

To the north-east of Vimoutiers the D16 is transformed by the departmental boundary into the D46 and leads directly to (21km) **Orbec**, a splendidly unreconstructed market town beneath the headwaters of the River Orbiquet. Its historical credentials are impeccable—successively an Iron Age settlement, Gallo-Roman castrum, Viking trading station, and medieval Viscounty—but it suffered the misfortune of occupation by Charles of Navarre during the Hundred Years War, and in reprisal Charles V dismantled the castle in 1378. Recovery came with the 16C when its tanners, paper-makers, and apothecaries began constructing the sizeable townhouses which dramatise the modern town, and in 1583 Orbec was made the fiscal and legal centre of the largest bailiwick in Normandy. The present population is in fact slightly less than that of the 17C as all administrative functions were removed from the town after the Revolution, and Orbec has reverted to its long-standing role as the lively market centre of a large rural domain.

You approach the town from the south along a gentle curve, as the road struggles beneath the silhouette of one of the tallest belfries of the Pays d'Auge—the north tower of **Notre-Dame**. The base of this tower was built with a view to providing a defensible refuge during the late 15C, but in a more peaceful century it came to support an elegant Renaissance belfry. Unusually the tower lies in a crook formed by the north-west angle of the transept, and so brings one into the church via the north aisle. The reasoning behind this is admirably pragmatic, and the tower was intended to provide a buffer at the southern end of the Grande Rue, and thus serve as a grand town processional entrance.

The main body of the church is slightly later than the lower stages of the tower, though largely complete by c 1500, and consists of an aisled nave and spacious transept, which give onto an earlier square-ended choir. An extensive 19C refurbishment was responsible for the majority of the internal furnishings, though the organ dates from 1526, having been displaced from the abbey of Bec, and three very fine mid 16C windows survive in the south aisle, centred around an excellent Tree of Jesse.

North of the church the historical infrastructure of Orbec unfurls around its principal thoroughfare, the **Rue Grande**, with the Rue des Osiers to the right fringed with 16C tanneries, which gathered their water from the stream channelled along the edge of the street. To the left the late 15C façade of the **Hôtel de Croisy** was built for Viscount Robert de Croisy, and extended during the 18C by the general of the bailiwick, Pierre Fouques. While further on, the unexpected vertical accent provided by a Renaissance brick belfry is the result of a late addition to the 13C **Hôtel-Dieu**. Nothing survives from the original foundation apart from a very ordinary chapel but elements of the present hospital complex date from its 1654 refoundation.

A striking feature of several of the 16C timber houses to the north of the hospital—at Nos 91 or 101 for instance—is the extravagant use of Opus Listatum. At Orbec this involves cutting stone or narrow tiles, and setting these in puddled mortar to create elaborate geometric patterns, enlivening the panels between the timber posts and beams. The most virtuosic performance is to be found at the Vieux Manoir, a superb mercantile house of 1568 which now houses the **Musée Municipal**. The museum houses a display of archaeological finds, rural crafts, and local history, but the central interest is provided by the building itself, ornamented by shallowly carved wooden caryatids, and a complex array of running mouldings and decorative panelling.

North-west of Orbec the fast D519 follows the valley of the Orbiquet to the point where the river flows into the Touques at Lisieux. A more rewarding alternative might be to take the main road as far as (10km) St-Denis-de-Mailloc, and then follow the left of the valley, along the D149, towards St-Germain-de-Livet. The road crosses meadows studded with small coppices and orchards, which occupy the higher ground between the valleys, and descends to cross the River Touques at La Forge de Chambrin. From here the D268A follows the left bank as far as (8km) St-Germain. It sounds complicated, but it is signalled throughout to **St-Germain-de-Livet**, the signposts intended as an enticement to visit the 16C **Château** above the village.

The house was fittingly described by Le Varende as 'a small jewel for an infant princess'—standing as an irregular octagonal island in a broad moat, and spangled with panels of limestone and emerald-painted brick. This picturesque scene dates from between 1561 and 1584, and was inspired by the commercial alliance that Jean de Tournebu and his wife, Marie de Croixmare, forged with the Italian Seghizzo family. The central gatehouse and left wing were constructed during this period, and were joined by an angled passage to the 15C manor house which stands to their right. The additional living accommodation created by this extension was not in fact very great, since the oculi which play so subtle a role in the overall decorative scheme of the façade open onto an extremely fine Italianate loggia, which occupies the whole of the ground floor. The château was made over to the commune relatively recently and its furnishings reflect the tastes of the Pillaut-Riesner family, ranging from Louis XV and Louis XVI furniture in the salons, to the late 19C decoration of the main bedroom. Some of the original decor has survived, with a fragmentary 15C tournament scene in the **Salle des Gardes**, and a late medieval tiled floor in the first-floor salon. These are both part of the 15C manor, and the only 16C internal wall decoration to have come down is also to be found in the Salle des Gardes. Here Judith carries the head of Holofernes on the tip of her sword while, balancing the scene to the far side of the fireplace, the head of John the Baptist lies inert upon a platter.

From St-Germain the valley road drifts gently down towards (2km) St-Martin-de-la-Lieue, where you can pick up the D579 for the last 4km to **LISIEUX**, a thriving regional capital and home to the shrine of Ste-Thérèse Martin. The town has an august past, and was the capital of the Gallic tribe of the Lexovii, who fortified a colossal site to the south-west at Le Castelier. The Roman occupation of northern France moved the governmental centre of the region from Le Castelier to Noviomagus Lexoviorum, whose urban centre underlies the present Place de la République, and enhanced the town with a succession of aqueducts, theatres, and baths. Disaster came early however, and the town was completely destroyed in the barbarian attacks of 275–276, recovering briefly before falling prey to a wave of Frankish and Saxon raids during the 5C. The ruined city was nevertheless of a size to commend itself to Frankish chieftains and the foundation of a bishopric here by the end of the 6C would seem to reflect Lisieux's re-emergence as the most important town of the Pays d'Auge. This role was further enhanced by the choice of Lisieux as the venue for two church councils, held in 1055 and 1106, and in the wake of Geoffrey Plantagenet's sack of the town in 1136 the later 12C seems to have witnessed a rash of new building work. This formed the basis of the medieval town, and until recently Lisieux was renowned for the wealth and variety of its 15C and 16C architecture. This is sadly something of which one is only vaguely conscious when strolling through the town today, and the combined effects of 13 major artillery and aerial bombardments between 6 June and 31 July 1944 have left a generally scrappy and undistinguished townscape, only enlivened towards the north by the survival of several of the grander set-pieces.

At the very centre of Lisieux the **Place Thiers** now hosts a general market, subservient to the great agricultural and food markets of the Place de la République, but nonetheless retaining the seats of municipal administration, the Tribunal and the **Cathédrale de St-Pierre**. Lisieux was in fact deprived of its episcopal status in the 18C, but as the venerable seat of a diocese which included the whole of the Pays d'Auge and the Lieuvin it acquired a new cathedral under Bishop Amoul c 1170. This makes it a design of exceptional interest, roughly contemporary with La Trinité at Fécamp, and undertaken during a decade in which the Gothic styles of Paris and north-eastern France were beginning to find acceptance further afield—at Canterbury in 1174, and Vézelay c 1180.

It is difficult to set a limit and a chronology to Arnoul's building for there is virtually no documentation relevant to the 12C work. Relatively speaking the western and end walls of the transepts are the earliest part of the surviving structure, dating from c 1170. They are thick-walled, hesitant, extensively reworked, and carry a curious triforium passage approximately half-way up the elevation. And it is obvious that a major rethink and change of architect took place between the west wall of the transept, and the next area to be constructed—the **nave**.

This seems to have been built between c 1180 and c 1190, and demonstrates a selective interest in the Early Gothic architecture of north-eastern France. It is true that the Norman predilection for a large tribune storey (subsequently blocked up) has won out. It is also true that the rather even distribution of height between the storeys is not a feature of late 12C Gothic thinking outside Normandy. But the detailed handling of the structure—the perforation of the walls, the faceting of the surfaces, the colonnettes banded with shaft-rings and taken en-délit (against the natural bed of the stone)—all these speak of a new conception of the building which is Gothic. More specifically the architect was acquainted with the shop at Laon cathedral, and indebted therein for more than just the columnar piers.

The doubts about how systematically this north-eastern French architecture was understood begin to surface with the **west front**, which with the superb lantern tower was probably under cosntruction between c 1190 and c 1200. The central portal has been lost, but the mannered ornament of the side portals, where shafts break up through the arch centres, is a straightforward updating of the richer forms of Anglo-Norman Romanesque. You can see similar tricks on the west front of Ely cathedral. Sadly the south-west tower fell in 1554 and was rebuilt between 1579 and 1583 and provided with a spire. The north tower remains however, to give you an idea of the original range of effects, where huge lancets open through the walls to expose the sky.

The two western bays of the **choir** are contemporary with the raising of the lantern tower, but the sudden acceleration of the decorative accent in the rest of the choir and ambulatory, dates from after the fire of 1226. This is by contrast not a freshly imported architecture, but a mature and indigenous style—the early 13C vernacular of Norman Gothic, and the vocabulary of the choir of St-Etienne at Caen. It is a richly moulded and abundantly decorated architecture, with foil figures inscribed over the blind arcades of the aisles, or perforating the tympana of the triforium. The adherence to the earlier spatial formulas has given a coherence and apparent homogeneity to a building which, in actuality, is marked by rapid shifts of language and thinking. This situation is reflected in the axial chapel which was built in 1432–42 by Bishop Pierre Cauchon, otherwise vilified throughout France for presiding over the trial of Joan of Arc. It is an ambitious structure, but being the same height as the other ambulatory chapels, and by having bays which from inner support to inner support are the same length as those of the choir, you move smoothly out of the ambulatory and into the chapel. The chapel retains its own particular range of Flamboyant effects, but they are sensitive to the spatial configurations of the building as a whole.

The **Ancien Palais Episcopal** was built to the north of the cathedral and

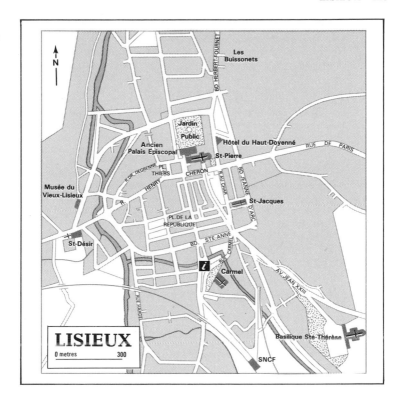

in its present, expanded form houses the law courts. A portal in the 17C range at the north-eastern angle of the Place Thiers opens onto the main court—the Place Matignon. The two-storey southern range was built for Bishop Cospéan during the 1620s, while the mutilated eastern range was refaced under Bishop Matignon some 20 years later, the court being finally closed to the west during the 19C. Léonor de Matignon was also responsible for the opulent decoration of the main reception room, known as the **Chambre Dorée** (to gain entry ring the bell of the conciergerie). This is locally noted for the survival of its 17C decor—consisting of panels of tooled and gilded leatherwork from Córdoba, alternating with grisaille frescoes of 1643 by Calville, and a ceiling by Le Sueur. Hung high on the walls are four paintings described as being from the studio of Nicolas Poussin, though this is not an attribution to be taken particularly seriously.

Steps lead up from the rear of the Place Matignon to the old episcopal grounds, opened to the public as early as 1837, and arranged as a delightfully terraced flower garden. The gardens look over the Louis XVI façade with which the palace was completed, behind which lies the reading room of a first-rate municipal library.

Immediately east of the cathedral apse a flight of steps leads up from the Rue Maréchal Foch to the **Hôtel du Haut-Doyenné**. This was financed in 1769 by the cathedral chapter to serve as a residence for the dean, who in turn employed Le Fresne as architect. Le Fresne produced a mansion sufficiently spacious to house the entire chapter, symmetrically disposed around a canted portal which rises through both storeys, and built of a rose coloured brick set with Caen stone dressings. It is an extremely elegant building, whose clean lines are enhanced by the painted wooden panelling which still survives in several of the interior rooms. The building now houses the school of music but, rehearsals permitting, it is still possible to visit the interior.

South of here the Rue au Char brings you to the late medieval parish church of **St-Jacques**, closed to the public except during the temporary exhibitions held there over the summer. In spite of the damage sustained in 1944, which necessitated a considerable amount of rebuilding around the nave and west tower, St-Jacques remains one of the finest Flamboyant buildings in Normandy. The four bay choir went up quickly, between 1498 and 1501, under the local master mason Guillemot de Samaison, with the nave and western tower following on more slowly, and the whole being complete by 1540. As with St-Michel at Pont-l'Evêque, to which it is related, a smooth and rapid succession of bays drives the eye eastwards, but here the clerestory windows are brought down to the head of the triforium, and form the pretext for a more inventive display of tracery. The west tower is also treated differently and serves as the main entrance, with a sequence of lateral, stepped buttresses framing a tall, sculpted portal. Miserably, the glass was pulverised by flying shrapnel, and the original internal fittings are reduced to little more than a set of routine 16C choir stalls.

From St-Jacques you might take a circuitous route back to the Place Thiers, via the vast reconstructed Place de la République, site of the big agricultural fairs held in Lisieux over the summer. The **Rue Dr-Degrenne** curves down towards the river from the north-western corner of the Place Thiers, passing some of the few timber houses to have survived the war, and with a right turn onto the Rue Henri-Chéron leads to the banks of the Touques. The inner bank was formerly fortified, though only a single, shortened 16C tower remains as a souvenir of the old town ramparts. The greatest reminder of what was lost in 1944 is to be found in the **Musée du Vieux-Lisieux**, situated in a 15C townhouse on the Boulevard Pasteur.

The whole of this quarter west of the River Touques grew up around the 11C abbey of St-Désir, and most of its houses dated from the 15th and 16C. The museum holds an archive of photographs, taken after the dust of 1944 had settled, which might be compared with the display of posters and lithographs of Lisieux in the 1920s by Jean-Charles Contel. It is a profoundly sobering exercise, for Lisieux had been one of the finest late medieval market towns in France. After this the museum's collections seem almost incidental, and in truth there is little of wider interest apart from the ceramics of the Pré-d'Auge, renowned in the 13C for its tiles, and in the 16th and 17C for its glazed ware.

The pilgrimage of Ste-Thérèse of Lisieux should start at **Les Buissonnets**, the family house on the Boulevard Herbet-Fournet where Thérèse Martin lived from the age of four, until admitted into the Carmelite Order in 1888. She was born to a conventionally pious family in Alençon in 1873, and moved to Les Buissonnets on the death of her mother some four years later. Brought up in an atmosphere of deep religiosity Thérèse had already seen her sister join the Carmelite convent when, at the age of 14, she underwent what she described as the complete conversion of her soul, and asked her father for permission to join her sister on the Rue Carmel. The Carmelites refused to accept so young a postulant, and it was not until she went on a pilgrimage to Rome that she obtained papal dispensation, and joined the order in April 1888, at the age of 15. It was a short vocation, undertaken 'to save souls and, above all, to pray for the priests', but it had the heroic quality of a profoundly experienced spiritual journey, and was recorded with stark fidelity in her 'L'histoire d'une Ame', finished a few days before her death in 1897.

The house breathes an air of provincial piety, stultifying to non-believers, but not untypical of late 19C religious feeling. And among the mementoes of family life Thérèse's room has been turned into a small oratory, which with the much-photographed statue of Thérèse asking her father's permission to join the order, has become the focal interest of Les Buissonnets.

The Carmelite convent itself, along the Rue Carmel, had been founded in 1838, but made do with temporary accommodation until the present church was constructed in 1878. After Sister Thérèse's death, as you can see from innumerable ex-voto tablets, many came to pray to her, and in 1925 she was canonised a saint. Her mortal remains had already been translated to the church on her beatification two years earlier, and are housed in a chapel to the south of the nave, while a reliquary chamber was constructed to the north to hold the few personal effects she carried with her into the convent.

Not all of St-Thérèse was reserved for the Carmelite convent however, and her teeth and right arm might be found displayed in a reliquary casket Pope Pius XI presented to the mighty basilica built in her name. A church dedicated to **Ste-Thérèse** was put in hand as early as 1929, on a magnificent site overlooking the town from the south. The initial plans were drawn up by Le Cordonnier, and the work continued under his son and grandson, with Jean and Pierre Gaudin providing a mosaic cycle based around the theme of 'the love and tenderness of God the Father for all humanity'. The main body of the crypt and upper church was completed by 1954, when the consecration ceremony was held, though parts of the monumental Calvary to the east and the curiously remote bell tower were not finished until 1975.

The whole complex illustrates one of the central problems of modern sainthood, for the lack of a continuing tradition of architectural enshrinement led Le Cordonnier to turn to the language of early Christian and medieval reliquary cults. A single model more fully understood might have provided a relevant focus, but plundering motifs from 6C Constantinople, 11C Venice, 13C Rome, and the 19C Sacré-Cœur was only ever likely to achieve the requisite grandeur if inflated to a colossal scale. The equation of size with a position towards the top of the religious pecking order has an ancient pedigree, but Le Cordonnier was no Bramante and one cannot help feeling that a considerable opportunity has been lost.

To the west of Lisieux the N13 climbs out of the valley of the Touques and offers a fast route across the plateau to (17km) **Crèvecœur-en-Auge**. This is best known for its moated **Château**, an important, if over-restored, example of a late medieval feudal complex. Entrance is via a gatehouse, picturesque but an imposter, having been transported here from its previous situation as the late medieval postern gate of the castle at Beuvillers. The underlying shape and organisation of the site is 12C, though this was extensively developed during the 15C. A motte had been raised towards the south c 1150, which originally supported a keep, and was defended by an outer wall and moat. This straightforward arrangement was then supplied with a large outer bailey, which was also moated. With the new space in the outer bailey the keep could be serviced from without, hence the late

12C rectangular chapel. The bailey was also doubtless cluttered with sheds, storage areas, and lean-to workshops, and it was these which were rationalised in the late 15C with the construction of a grange, colombier, and workshop, the latter signalled as the farm. As with the bailey so with the keep, and the earlier structure was demolished to make way for a castle whose accent was less defensive and accommodation more palatial. What is most uncommon about such a complex is its survival, and this is largely due to its later usage as a fairly grand farmyard. The site was restored by the Schlumberger Foundation in 1972, hence the permanent exhibition of the work of the Austrian Schlumberger brothers, pioneers of the electromechanical techniques now used in assessing and drilling oil prospects.

From Crèvecœur the D16 runs directly through the low-lying pasture to (12km) St-Pierre-sur-Dives. For those with an interest in parish churches an excursion might be made along the D154 through the valley of the Viette to **Ste-Marie-aux-Anglais**, whose simple 12C church lies some way from the village. You should take a left turn at the hamlet of St-Maclou and follow the road down, swinging to the right towards the valley bottom. It is not an easy discovery, and if locked the key is kept at the farm of M. Fouques, a good 400 metres beyond the church on the right-hand side. Access is by neither of the chevron moulded portals but through a small door in the southern wall of the choir. The decaying plasterwork of the interior carries a crude and vibrant cycle of outline wall paintings, with a late 12C Nativity in the eastern vault of the choir, and an Adoration of the Magi and Dormition of the Virgin to the west. Along the north wall there is a Last Supper above two 13C tomb effigies, and in the nave the top half of a 13C account of war, mayhem, and siegecraft during the Crusades. It is all some way removed from great church painted cycles, but offers a rewarding glimpse of the work of the itinerant painters often called on to decorate medieval parish churches.

You could also continue south along the D154, to the tiny village of **Vieux-Pont**, whose parish church retains fragments of its pre-Romanesque walling, admirably built of *petit appareil* and banded brick. Both of these materials were also incorporated into the base of a fine Romanesque belfry. And from the bottom of the hill the D511 winds past the tributary streams of the River Dives, before cresting a ridge and throwing off the most splendid of all views of the old market town of (7km) St-Pierre-sur-Dives.

10

The Orne Valley: Sées to Caen

ROAD (129km): Sées; N158, 7km Mortrée; D26, 2km Château d'O; D26/N158, 8km St-Christophe-le-Jajolet; N158, 9km Argentan; D924, 8km Ecouché; 10km Fromentel; D909, 6km Putanges-Pont-Ecrepin; D909/C3, 7km Rabodanges; D239/D21/D301, 10km Roche d'Oëtre; 3km Rouvrou; D43/D167, 6km Pont-d'Ouilly; D1/D562, 12km Clécy; D562, 14km Thury-Harcourt; 14km Laize-la-Ville; D41, 2km Fontenay-le-Marmion; D235, 11km Caen.

RAILWAY service 3 or 4 times daily between Sées, Argentan, and Caen.

The Orne rises a few kilometres east of Sées, near the village of Aunou-sur-Orne, and flows north-west before dipping to the north of Putanges and carving a dramatic gorge through the schists of the Suisse Normande. This latter area marks the point where the Jurassic limestones of the Pays d'Auge give way to the older granite formations of the Armorican massif, and in order to cut a path through the harder rocks the Orne is forced to spin a sequence of rapid meanders before regaining the limestone to the north of Thury-Harcourt. As such the Orne valley has come to describe a cultural boundary, separating the lush meadowland of central Normandy from the sparser soils of the Normandy Bocage, and thus a landscape of self-sufficient villages from the old fortified market towns of the west. Strictly speaking the term Suisse Normande is used to denote the area between Putanges and the Forêt de Grimbosq, which has taken advantage of its curious designation to attract a following among walkers and holiday-makers. Needless to say the region is quite unlike Switzerland, being made up of a group of fractured cliffs and gorges which divide two relatively low plateaux. It is nevertheless an exhilarating and remote area, and one whose precipitous valleys make navigation difficult, hence the rather tortuous list of road numbers (in which respect a good map is essential, Michelin Sheet No. 231 being the most convenient). The upper valley is altogether kinder, and in the ancient bishopric of Sées supports a quiet and restful town.

SEES. Set amid the high watermeadows a few kilometres west of the headwaters of the Orne, the attractive town unfolds around one of the major medieval monuments of southern Normandy. Its present-day tranquillity is due to the decline of its once important convents and seminaries, and belies its significance as a Gallo-Roman capital and seat of a 4C cathedral. The present cathedral of Notre-Dame is the fourth to stand on this site, replacing an earlier structure (dedicated to SS-Gervais-et-Protais) destroyed during the frontier wars of the early 1170s. This in turn was necessitated by an unfortunate accident in 1048 when Bishop Yves de Bellême, attempting to smoke out two opponents who had taken refuge in the church, overplayed his hand and completely gutted the building. The surrounding region had in fact been evangelised by St-Martin of Tours during the 4C, and in its founding bishop, St-Latuin, Sées enjoyed a renowned miracle worker, and the focus of an important early medieval cult.

The existing **Cathedral** (in the Place Général de Gaulle) was unfortunately butchered in the early 19C when, as part of a general restoration programme, the architect Alavoine reinforced the supporting piers with cast iron armatures, and set about painting the interior. Much of the damage was reversed later in the century by Ruprich-Robert, cathedral architect, but it remained the case that the greater part of the internal superstructure had to be replaced. As a result the choir stands as one of the most complete Rayonnant structures in France, while the **west front** decays as a half-remembered, half-brutalised mid 13C composition, its disfiguring buttresses having been added in the 16C and twin spires in the 19C.

The dating of the interior remains controversial, though it is clear that there were two distinct campaigns, contrasting a richly decorated nave with a light and beautifully traceried choir and transepts. The **nave** would seem mid 13C, with a three storey elevation which superimposes wall-passages at triforium and clerestory level, and even hollows out a passage in the south aisle wall above the dado arcade. This interest in passage-making is allied to a congested decorative repertoire, in which the upper elevation is pierced with a variety of foil figures, reminiscent of the similar treatment meted out in the choir of Bayeux cathedral.

The **choir** owes little to Norman versions of Gothic architecture however, and represents an extraordinarily clear-sighted vision of an architectural style usually described as Rayonnant. It seems likely that work began c 1270, and was largely completed during the episcopacy of Jean de Bernières (1278–84), though the cathedral had to wait until 1310 for bishop Philippe le Boulanger to celebrate a general consecration. What is so surprising about the choir is the ratio of glass to stone—or solid to void. The windows have not merely expanded to fill the space made available to them, but have even been run across the rear wall of the triforium. There are long-standing precedents for such a scheme, dating back to the 1230s at Troyes cathedral and St-Denis, but the intimacy of scale at Sées makes the choir feel closer to the exquisite insubstantiality of a glass shrine than is the case with its more august counterparts. This feeling for the small-scale is reinforced by the decision to run the mullions of the triforium down below the balustrade and over the spandrels of the main arcade, creating a further link between hitherto separate storeys, and initiating a tendency towards continuous panelling which was to have a profound impact on English Perpendicular architecture.

More unusually the choir retains a fairly full complement of the original stained glass, adding immeasurably to its iconographical depth. At clerestory level these depict saints, prophets and apostles, whilst the chapel glass relates more directly to the particular dedication of the altars, or locally popular cults. Much of this lower glass was given by aristocratic or guild donors, and their devices indicate that the glazing of the chapels took place between c 1270 and c 1285. Lafond's study of late 13C glass in Normandy led him to conclude that the glazing programme took about 15 years to complete, and employed a single workshop consisting of three glass paint-ers. Their origins are uncertain, with Paris, Rouen, and Le Mans all sug-gested as possibilities, but the subtlety and inventiveness with which many of the scenes are treated is beyond dispute. This might best be seen in the Lady Chapel, where instead of the usual Marian or Christological cycle the windows are composed of figures standing beneath architectural canopies illustrating the history of Sées cathedral.

The great transept windows are of a type known as rose-in-squares, that to the south being late 13C, whilst the north elevation was renewed in the mid 14C. Virtually all of the glass here belongs to an unambitious 19C scheme, and the one cult object which survived both the Wars of Religion and the French Revolution, a 14C Virgin and Child, is now set against the west wall of the south transept.

The **chapter house**, opposite the north flank of the cathedral, contains a small museum of religious art (open mid June to mid September, afternoons only) with a good collection of 13–19C painted statuary, and a splendid 17C chasuble from Carrouges. To the south the Rue d'Argentré gives onto the main façade of the **Palais Episcopal**, built by Brousseau in 1778 around a central courtyard defined by low projecting wings and a symmetrical central block. Continuing south the Rue de la République leads to the intriguing **Place St-Pierre**, where a small garden surrounds the ruined nave and bell tower of the late 12C parish church of St-Pierre. Further west the elegant **Place des Halles** pirouettes around the centrally-planned 19C market hall, appealingly arranged as a series of concentric aisles within an open peristyle, half of which is now given over to the town library.

From Sées the N158 runs south of the Orne as far as Argentan, passing the last vestiges of the town's medieval ramparts, before straightening over the plateau to Mortrée where a well-signposted right turn onto the D26 brings you to (9km) **Château d'O**. Justifiably famous for its picturesque detailing the old seigneurial residence rises from a moat fed by the waters of the Thouanne, and greets the visitor with a gatehouse faceted into myriad angles by steeply twisted, slate-hung roofs.

The existing complex was built over the foundations of an 11C castle for Jean d'O, chamberlain to Charles VII and Lord of O, beginning with the eastern gatehouse shortly after 1484. The **gatehouse wing** is in fact considerably less complex than it appears, consisting of a rectangle embellished with three asymmetrically-treated polygonal projections, and pierced by traceried dormer windows which lend a sumptuous note to an elaborate roofscape. Jean's son, Charles-Robert d'O, was responsible for flattening what remained of the earlier medieval castle and constructing a long two storey southern range, where an Italianate open loggia supports an upper gallery. This in turn connects Jean's east wing with a palatial western block completed c 1590 for one of the 16C's great political opportunists, François d'O.

Château d'O: mid-19C engraving of the gatehouse wing

Assisted by family connections François became successively Governor of Caen, Lieutenant Governor of Basse-Normandie, and Minister of Finance to Henri III. Refusing specific affiliation during the Wars of Religion he grew in the royal esteem and was made First Gentleman of the King's Bedchamber, being retained by Henri IV despite widespread suspicions that he was milking the royal purse. Some of these funds certainly found their way to Château d'O but on his death in 1594 Sully triumphantly noted that he died a pauper, 'It was as if his fortune, in a final act of justice, had to die with him.' Sully was a far from disinterested commentator, but it remains true that no 16C decoration survives at the château, and the greater part of the furnishings are 18C. Much of this later work is very fine, and a splendid 17C *trompe-l'œil* cycle of **Apollo before the Nine Muses** has been recently restored in the drawing room of the west wing. The courtyard is closed to the north by a balustrade which looks over the lawns to an 18C **orangerie**, now used to house temporary exhibitions. This is not the only outbuilding of the château to survive but the estates have been gradually broken up, with the farm buildings to the south-east mostly taken over by a restaurant.

Returning to the N158 at Mortrée points you north-west towards **St-Christophe-le-Jajolet** (a left turn onto the D219 4km west of Mortrée brings you into the village). The interest here is admittedly occasional, and largely confined to the specialised cult which transforms the village every 25 July, when the statue of St Christopher resounds to the sound of hundreds of engines, as the more superstitious local motorists come to have their cars blessed. It puts you on the route to Sassy however (1km south), where the magnificent 18C **Château de Sassy** lies above three descending terraces, overlooking the formal gardens.

The house was begun in 1760 as a rigorously symmetrical rectangular block, whose dusty red brickwork is articulated by vertical stone dressings. Although work was interrupted by the Revolution both the design of the main block, and its furnishings, remain essentially late 18C, despite the embellishments of Etienne-Denis Pasquier who acquired Sassy in 1850. He added a library to house his 30,000 volumes in a room which combines intimacy, opulence and accessibility in equal measure.

Château de Sassy is perhaps best known for its 18C tapestries, the majority from the Aubusson shops, but the finest of which is a Gobelin work, now housed in the small salon on the upper floor. This is one of a series depicting the houses of Louis XIV, in this case Saint-Germain-en-Laye, disposed according to the months of the year, and woven from cartoons by Le Brun. The château's external proportions have been altered by the recent addition of a wing to the east, curving to form a right angle with the 18C work and screening out the stables. But in a sunken garden opposite, the old chapel houses a surprising import in the shape of a 15C carved wooden altarpiece from the great abbey of St-Bavon at Ghent, depicting the Passion of Christ.

A descent to the north of Sassy returns you to the N158 and, following the valley of the Baize, ultimately to (9km) **Argentan**. As an important cattle market, and fiefdom of the counts of Alençon, Argentan has retained the shape of a historic market town, but was so disfigured by air and artillery bombardment between June and August 1944, that over 80 per cent of the town was considered destroyed. Although the subsequent redevelopment is rather drab the town is not without pleasant streets, or entirely denuded of distinctive buildings.

Occupying the high ground to the north of the Place du Marché, the grander of the town churches, **St-Germain**, sandwiches a late Gothic nave between a western bell-tower of 1639–41 and a central lantern tower of 1555. To the east the rusticated outlines of the choir went up between 1575 and 1607, under the architect Guillaume Creste, and culminate in a bizarre display of mannered buttressing which rises above the radiating chapels.

The church suffered appalling damage in 1944, and the painstaking programme of restoration and repair was not completed until 1990.

Building began with the **nave** c 1410, with the polygonal transepts completed by 1464, and the lower stages of the north-west tower and splendid north porch shortly thereafter. These areas exploit the familiar language of Norman Flamboyant architecture, orchestrating a richly balustraded triforium, curvilinear tracery, and a tierceron vault which, though accomplished, seems quite muted when compared to that at Alençon. The oddity here lies in the revival of a much older form, the polygonally-apsed transept, which lends a distinctly north-east French or Flemish air to the exterior elevation. The **choir** is equally surprising for the late 16C architect, Guillaume Creste, has taken up a Norman late Gothic groundplan, whereby a canted four bay apse interacts with a five bay ten-sided ambulatory, and clothed it with classical motifs. The eastern pendant vault was finally locked into place in 1607, by which time Coste had been given free rein to ornament the ambulatory chapels with superposed orders and flattened vault ribs.

Few of the church fittings have survived from the period of construction, though the 18C choir stalls and iron screens of 1741 make an effective foil for the thickly carved stonework. The most striking of the earlier works are the carving of a saddled mule, incorporated into the north-western crossing pier and in all probability a remnant of a fully carved 15C Epiphany group, and a panel painting of 1602 depicting the Adoration of the Magi.

South-west of St-Germain the former chapel of St-Nicolas now houses the **Syndicat d'Initiative** and town library. As the castle chapel it was rebuilt in 1773 and, despite the loss of its windows, still accommodates a fine 17C carved wooden retable. Immediately to the south the **château** itself has been transformed into a fitting arena for the Law Courts, having been originally built c 1370 by Pierre II, Count of Alençon, as a lofty, rectangular keep in three storeys, flanked with two projecting square towers. The system of town fortifications centred on Pierre's castle has all but vanished, though one of its early 13C corner bastions, locally described as the donjon, overlooks the Place Mahé. There is also a later remnant, the 15C **Tour Marguerite**, to the north-west along the Rue de la République.

Beyond the Rue de la République the Rue St-Martin leads to a small and sad square, with at its centre the still-damaged parish church of **St-Martin** (frequently closed). The church was begun shortly before 1450, with a three sided apse, transepts, and northern bell tower, the latter carrying a narrow crocketed spire and lending the building a decisive vertical accent. Though the transepts are entirely 15C everything else above the main arcade dates from the mid 16C, and represents a significant revision. The triforium carries an inventive geometric balustrade and classically derived pilaster orders, while the simple tracery of the clerestory windows floods the nave with light. The most arresting area of the building remains the choir, where the clerestory carries an extremely fine cycle of seven stained glass windows, dating from 1510–50 and depicting events from the Last Supper to Pentecost. The **Last Supper** is particularly intriguing in that it is clearly derived from Leonardo da Vinci's composition in Milan, and offers further evidence of the interest his sojourn in France generated outside the more obvious metropolitan centres.

From Argentan the D924 follows the Orne westwards, bringing you swiftly to (8km) **Ecouché**, where the entrance to the town is marked by a tank commemorating the crossing of the Dreux-Granville road by Leclerc's 2nd Armoured Division on 13 August 1944. The fighting lasted a week, from the 13th to the 20th, during which time French and American forces joined up around Argentan to form the southern claw of a pincer movement that presaged the final stages of the Battle for Normandy. The centre of the town suffered relatively little damage, and its narrow streets and stone houses cluster around an attractive three-cornered square.

To the west of the centre the **parish church** juxtaposes a ruined 13C nave with an unexpectedly spacious choir, which draws on the late medieval forms of neighbouring Argentan. As at St-Germain the transepts are both aisleless and polygonally-ended, creating a delightfully complex and multi-faceted exterior. Though imprecisely dated it seems that work began on the east end before 1480, with the transepts complete by the mid 16C. The later work is clearly indebted to the richly balustraded Renaissance tri-forium of St-Martin at Argentan, while the pendant vaulting presents an equally varied repertoire of forms. All the contemporary glass has been lost, and there is just one, very fine, 15C painted altar frontal still in situ (in the south choir chapel), featuring the Apostles flanking a now headless Christ. The sacristy has some intriguing objects however, and displays a collection of three 15C polychromed wooden tableaux, depicting the Agony in the Garden, Deposition, and Entombment—doubtless part of a larger composi-tion, and in all probability of Flemish workmanship.

The D924 heads west from Ecouché through orchards, woods, and sheep pasture until a right turn at Fromentel takes you back to the Orne at (16km) **Putanges-Pont-Ecrepin**. The town stands engagingly above a weir at the head of the Gorges de St-Aubert, and marks the southern end of the Suisse Normande. There is a tiny 13C cemetery chapel above the town at Vieux Putanges (reached along the first right turning off the D15 to Ménil-Gondouin), crowned by a 16C T-section timber ceiling and in a dangerous state, but Putanges is best known as a base from which to explore the southern Suisse Normande, and has a generous selection of cafés and hotels. To the north-west the River Orne cuts a deep, sinuous path through the primary formations of Armorican Normandy, scouring the rock into defensive headlands, or shattering the looser mica-schists into screes and shelving cliffs. The remote middle course of the **Gorges de St-Aubert** eventually connects Putanges with Pont-d'Ouilly, but can be no more than glimpsed from the road, as this is an area which must be explored on foot, or by canoe, if it is to be seen in its full majesty. Good maps are available in Putanges, Pont-d'Ouilly, and Clécy, but since this is not a hiker's guide the following description confines itself to those areas accessible by metalled road.

Take the D909 north of Putanges and after 2km a left turn onto the C3 passes north of the village of Les Rotours, before dropping down to (3km) a lake formed by the damming of the Orne at the **Barrage de Rabodanges** during the 1930s. This tamed and manmade landscape is a gentle foretaste of the wilder shores to the west and has become the natural habitat of visiting French families, admirably supplied with all the cafés and amuse-ments the visitor from Caen or Alençon could wish for. Beyond the dam the road snakes upwards to the village, passing its small parish church, from where the D239 is signposted to Pont-d'Ouilly. This provides a glimpse, of the exterior at least, of the privately owned **Château de Rabodanges**, built in 1650 of the rough local schist. 5km north-west, by the 19C church of **Ménil-Hermei**, a sharp left turn onto the D21 allows you to cross the Orne and, turning right onto the D301, briefly track the river at the point where the gorge begins to narrow. The road brings you out at (5km) the **Roche d'Oëtre**, a spectacular craggy outcrop standing sheer above the densely wooded valley of the Rouvre some 120 metres below. Like other acclaimed beauty spots in the Suisse Normande the site is provided with a fine timber-floored café, from whose terrace you can observe the shifting patterns of the high pasture as they give way to thick stands of scrubby oak which cling to the steep sides of the gorge.

The road winds down to meet the river at (3km) **Rouvrou**, where the Rouvre exits from its gorge in a series of glorious meanders, before emptying into the Orne. The D43 runs alongside the Rouvre over these final stages, crossing the Orne at Pont-des-Vers, where a left turn onto the D167 takes you beneath a curious rock, eroded into the shape of a lion's head, and into (6km) **Pont-d'Ouilly**. This is perhaps the most charming of the Suisse Normande villages, standing astride a broad stretch of the Orne at a point where the river slows, released from the narrow corseting of the high gorge, and celebrating its weir with hanging baskets of flowers. Downstream of the village, the river shoots a secondary sequence of rapid meanders, and the best way to advance north-westwards is to take the D1 to Le Fresne and the D562 to **Clécy** (12km in total).

The town here is pleasantly disposed around a fine late medieval belfry, attached to an otherwise dull 19C church, and boasts all the facilities to be expected from a tourist centre popular with French holiday-makers. Beneath the town the banks of the river are fringed with café terraces and camp sites, and to the left of the road linking the town with the bridge stands a superb model railway museum, **La Suisse Normande Miniature**. This was begun as a small circuit in 1963 by a local cider-maker, Yves Crué, and has grown to become the largest permanent model railway exhibition in Europe. Its depth, and naturalism, have obvious attractions to anyone with an interest in small-scale working models, but to even the most disinterested of observers the simulated night-time running of trains through darkened landscapes and street-lit towns can be quite stunning.

From Clécy the D562 passes through the decaying industrial town of St-Rémy on the way to an altogether more aristocratic settlement, the old ducal seat of (14km) **Thury-Harcourt**. In 1700 Henri de Harcourt-Beuvon regained control of the early medieval fiefdoms of Thury and Grimbosq, and moved the family seat from Harcourt (near Brionne) on his acquisition of the title, Duc de Harcourt. The town was previously the possession of another branch of a prolific family (see Fontaine-Henry, Bayeux cathedral, etc), and Henri resolved that the **château** should be expanded.

An 11C castle, built by Raoul Tesson, once stood on the site, but its expanded late medieval forms were dismantled by Odet de Harcourt in the early 17C. Odet replaced this with a symmetrical block, fronted by a triangular entrance complex, parts of which survive. Early in the following century Henri set about adding a new wing overlooking the Orne, and refurnished the interior. All this lay on the western edge of the town and was sadly reduced to little more than a fragmentary ruin by a devastating fire, precipitated by the fierce bombardments of early August 1944. It is a major loss, and the destruction was not merely confined to the architectural fabric, for along with all the furnishings over 150 paintings were burned, including an important collection of French 18C work. The right-hand pavilion shows a short video which features pre-war photographs of the interior, and in an oval chapel, modelled on that of Versailles, a 17C tapestry of the Annunciation survives, along with a damaged bust of Louis XIV. The grounds remain quite splendid however, with a group of formal quartered lawns giving way to landscaped rides which rise above the banks of the Orne.

The **parish church** was less severely damaged than the town as a whole, though even here the choir and greater part of the nave aisles required reconstruction. The deeply embrasured west front is 13C and gives onto an extraordinarily hybrid nave, wherein several late 11C arches and capitals were retained in the 13C, when it was decided to cover the nave with sexpartite vaults. The larger polygonal piers are 15C however, and seem broadly contemporary with a general refurbishment which also produced the small wall canopy in the south aisle, carrying an Annunciation and prayerful donor figure around the extrados of the arch.

Beyond Thury the D562 crosses the open wheatfields of the Caen plain, swinging to the east of the handsome bell tower of **St-Laurent-de-Condel** (almost entirely rebuilt in the late 19C), before a right turn onto the D41 at Laize-la-Ville brings you into (16km) **Fontenay-le-Marmion**. The village is renowned among archaeologists as the base for Léon Coutil's excavation of the neolithic tumulus of **La Hogue**, just to the west of Fontenay, undertaken between 1908 and 1918. At most 'reasonable' hours the site guardian will let visitors into a small museum in which an explanatory display is laid out. This in turn gives access to a series of 12 circular burial chambers, linked to an outer revetment by low stone passages. The complex was first in use around 4000 BC, and was reoccupied some 1500 years later, offering a rare physical insight into the often composite and sophisticated burial rites of the neolithic cultures of northern Europe. The village itself possesses a fine early 12C bell tower, richly dressed with chevron moulded arches and scallop capitals. It is just beyond this tower, and its accompanying church, that a left turn onto the D235 offers a quieter route north, and carries you past the 13C belfry at (5km) **Ifs** to (6km) Caen.

11

Caen

When Duke Rollo made Rouen his capital in 911 Caen had peacefully evolved into a small village standing above the confluence of the rivers Orne and Odon. This state of affairs was little altered by the westward expansion of the duchy during the 920s or by the acquisition of the Cotentin in 933, and it was not until Duke William sought to quell the independent-mindedness of a turbulent western baronage that the strategic potential of Caen was recognised. The village had in fact enjoyed an illustrious past, and under Gallo-Roman rule the old Celtic trading station of Catumagos was expanded and equipped with a small river port, its name romanised to Cadomus. But it was William who arrested the early medieval drift towards inconsequence and, after the revolt in the Bessin and Cotentin was put down at the battle of Val-ès-Dunes in 1047, began to make Caen the new capital of Basse-Normandie. By 1058 the town had been encircled with a defensive wall, the castle was raised in 1060, and in 1061 the extraordinary 'Trêve de Dieu' was promulgated in the town, forbidding all warfare in the archiepiscopal province of Rouen between Wednesday evenings and Monday mornings, on pain of excommunication.

Caen's rapid elevation to the status of nominal capital of western Normandy was further enhanced when William and Mathilda chose the town as the site for the twin abbeys of St-Etienne and La Trinité. This single-minded act of generosity was motivated by the diplomacy of Lanfranc of Bec, who in 1059 had successfully pleaded with Pope Nicholas II to lift the order of excommunication which bound William and Mathilda. Having married in defiance of a papal ruling that their wedlock would fall within the forbidden degrees (they were distant cousins), William and Mathilda had been under excommunication since 1051. The lifting of the ban was conditional on their founding two monasteries in expiation for their crime, an Abbaye-aux-Hommes and an Abbaye-aux-Dames. Whatever its merits in terms of Church-State politics the decision had a dramatic effect on the structure of Caen, and the siting of the two abbeys a mile apart extended the town along an east-west axis to intersect with the new commercial quarters to the south of the castle.

William's successors also favoured Caen as a ducal residence and King John's confirmation of a communal charter in 1203 brought an increase in trade and prosperity which was to inspire Guillaume le Breton to compare it with Paris as a centre of 'diverse trades'. The promise of its rich booty persuaded Edward III to pillage the town in 1346, and its population had grown to such an extent that when the English returned in 1417 some 2000 perished in a bloody assault, and over 20,000 were reported to have fled. Although the Hundred Years War resulted in widespread dilapidation, rebuilding was less ambitious than in Rouen and Caen never received as dense a pattern of 15th and 16C mercantile housing as so beguilingly served her rival to the east. Even the foundation of a university in 1437 seems not to have precipitated the wholesale expansion which might have been expected, but then any sense of the structure of Renaissance Caen is necessarily clouded by the degradations of the Wars of Religion, and the devastation wrought during the Second World War. The former saw the town twice sacked by Calvinist militias, an indignity from which it might have recovered, had not the prevailing atmosphere of uncertainty been compounded by plagues in 1584, 1592 and 1631. The town recovered more swiftly from the damage sustained during 1944 but the effect on the actual shape of Caen was radical.

Caen's strategic significance as a major communications centre, standing at the hub of the road and rail network in Basse-Normandie, inclined Rommel to turn it into a defensive stronghold during the spring of 1944 when he moved his frontline 21st Panzer Division into the area. General Montgomery was equally aware of the critical importance attached to control of the town, and the subsequent modifications to Allied thinking over the strategic imperatives involved in Caen has made this one of the most controversial episodes in the Battle for Normandy.

An aerial bombardment was launched on 7 June, and as the town was just within range of the 15 inch guns mounted on British battleships lying off the coast some 16km away, this was supplemented by a naval barrage. The town burned for 11 days, while many took refuge in St-Etienne and an operating theatre was improvised in the Lycée Malherbe. But the German defence of Caen was equally formidable and by the middle of June Montgomery began to see the battle for Caen as a way of sucking the majority of the German armour onto the eastern flank, and away from the American General Omar Bradley's attack on the Cherbourg peninsula. A stalemate of sorts was broken on 26 June when Montgomery launched the 'Epsom Offensive' with the territorial aim of capturing Caen, and the strategic objective of forestalling Rommel's last serious opportunity to launch a decisive counter-attack. After five days of grievously high losses the Allies withdrew to the southern outskirts of Caen, having at least achieved one objective—80 per cent of Rommel's mobile armour was within 10km of Caen. The situation could not last however and on 7 July 276 heavy bombers dropped 2500 tons of high explosives on Caen, and a brutal house-to-house battle began with the result that by 10 July the whole of Caen north of the Orne was in the hands of the Canadian 3rd Infantry Division. But the German forces dug in around the steelworks at Colombelles and on the east bank of the river at Vaucelles, so that the shelling of Allied positions on the perimeters of the town continued up to the very end of the Battle for Normandy on 22 August.

Over 75 per cent of Caen had been destroyed, and in the immediate aftermath of the Canadian advance new roads were simply bulldozed through the rubble. With the exception of St-Pierre the area between the castle and the river Orne was beyond repair and has been largely replanned around a grid of streets which connect the old centre with the station, and the 'Prairie' with the Bassin St-Pierre. A vast administrative complex and commercial centre were laid out to the north, and a new university raised in the shadow of the castle. Those areas of the old town which escaped irretrievable devastation have been sensitively restored, but the extent of the damage has tended to isolate these quarters, creating islands of late medieval streets around the Place St-Sauveur and Rue Froide, or havens of 18C symmetry to the east of St-Etienne. Reconstruction has given the town an airy and spacious aspect, but there is little to punctuate the blandness of much of the modern design. An exception is the remodelling of the 19C **Bassin St-Pierre**, but even here one feels an opportunity to blaze the space with café tables and rigging has been lost. The Bassin does however give onto the **Rue du Vaugueux** and thus offers a sense of the medieval pattern of Caen, as well as providing the consolation of its densest strand of restaurants and cafés.

The town effectively pivots around the **Château de Caen**, with the abbey of La Trinité standing above the hill to its east and the old mercantile quarters spilling away to the west. The main entrance now, as in the 11C, is the **Porte de la Ville**, whose defensive outwork offers a rewarding viewpoint from which to gaze on the 14C spire of St-Pierre. As the castle had been seriously damaged in 1944 it was decided to strip the bailey and the immediate surrounds of most of the post-medieval additions, enhancing one's sense of the sheer amplitude of the inner domain. Although Duke William had established a castle on the site in 1060 the shape of the present complex is largely due to his son, Henry Beauclerc (King Henry I). Henry was reponsible for the square **donjon** to the north of the bailey in 1123, and the building of the first of the expanded enceinte walls. Unfortunately this mighty keep was reduced to its foundations in 1793 but you can still make out its design, and the deep moat Philip Augustus had sunk when he provided it with corner towers after 1204. To the west of the keep a rectangular two storey structure, known as the **Salle de l'Echiquier**, served Henry as the great hall of the ducal palace. Usually dated to c 1100 its functions were never military and it now stands as an extremely rare survival of 12C Norman civic architecture, with a western porch singled out for decorative treatment, and an upper chamber doubtless once resplendent with wall-hangings.

The remainder of this astonishing area was the bailey, bounded by enceinte walls which would have provided rearwards support for lean-to workshops. Three other structures remain within the walls. Towards the

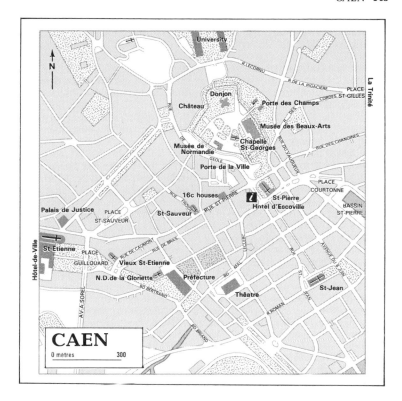

CAEN

0 metres   300

centre the **Chapelle St-Georges** originally served as a place of worship for those who worked in the castle. This refers not to the standing garrison, who may well have used the chapel in the keep, but the servants, laundry women, blacksmiths, cooks, pig keepers, and assorted camp followers who formed the domestic core of castle life. It is a modest 12C structure, whose three bay nave was extended in the 15C by the addition of a new choir. At the same time new windows were inserted into the nave so that the tracery now seen is late Gothic.

Of the remaining buildings only that housing the **Musée de Normandie**, situated in the 15C Logis des Gouverneurs du Château, had a role when the castle was an administrative and military centre. The logis was in fact substantially altered in the 17C when the present façade was built to coincide with its new status as the residence of the Governor of Caen, and in 1982 when the north wing was added. It now houses a disparate collection of material concerned with the archaeology, ethnography, and social history of Normandy, and also acts as a focus for research into Norman social anthropology.

The rooms are arranged chronologically and open with a preliminary section on the geology and prehistory of Normandy, forming the background for an important presentation of Gallo-Roman material. Attempts have been made here to assemble the archaeological data in order to create a putative map of Roman Rotomagus (Rouen), displayed alongside an arresting 1C cult-statue discovered built into the entrance to a 'fanum' at St-Aubin-sur-Mer. An area is also devoted to agriculture, where two models combine to give a clear sense of the very different patterns of farming and animal husbandry which created the landscapes of the Bocage and the Pays de Caux. Most of the upper floor is given over to a display of the development of manufacturing in Normandy, from locally-based craft industries, such as pottery, ironwork, and furniture production, to textiles and shipbuilding. The final room also attempts to extrapolate a social history from the use of a single material—wax, concentrating on the candlestick-makers of the Macé factory at Cherbourg.

The last of the larger structures within the walls is an austere Caen stone pavilion, built in 1967–70 to accommodate the **Musée des Beaux-Arts**. Many of the works here were acquired under Napoléon and the Directoire, which accounts for the surprising appearance of a number of important 16C Italian works, though the museum's undoubted strength is its collection of 17C French painting, much of it dispossessed from the clergy and aristocracy during the Revolution. This core was further enhanced in 1872 when the Caen bookseller, Bernard Mancel, bequeathed to the museum his collection of 50,000 prints, including a considerable portfolio of work by Dürer and Rembrandt along with paintings by Cosimo Tura and Rogier van der Weyden, and it is **Rogier van der Weyden's Virgin and Child** which first greets you on entering. By the time Mancel purchased the panel in Rome in 1845 it had already lost its companion piece, a portrait of the donor, Laurent Froimont (Musée des Beaux-Arts, Brussels), and you are now presented with the left half of a diptych. Hence the Archangel Gabriel on the back of the panel is arrested in the act of making the Annunciation. It is nevertheless a magnificent work, despite the evident splitting of the wooden bands, and you can take the opportunity to examine van der Weyden's saturated colour palette and compare the deep crimson of the Virgin's mantle with that of the unattributed Antwerp **Virgin and Child with St Catherine** nearby.

The 16C work is overshadowed by **Perugino's Marriage of the Virgin**, completed in 1504 for the chapel of St Joseph in Perugia cathedral and removed on the instruction of Tinet and Gros in 1797. The centralised composition and frieze-like development of space were also taken up by one of Perugino's assistants, Raphael, in the more famous Vatican School of Athens of c 1510. The gravity of the painting certainly contrasts with the extravagance of **Paris Bordone's Annunciation**, a splendid Venetian architectural fantasy of c 1545. Along with a fair collection of Venetian painting there is an unusual early work by **Veronese, The Temptation of St Anthony**, commissioned by Cardinal Gonzaga in 1552 and surprisingly mannered when compared to the loose handling and overblown colour of his later **Judith and Holofernes**.

In spite of the intensity of **Guercino's Coriolanus Entreated by his Mother** of 1643, and a beautifully realised small canvas of a female saint by the Genoese artist **Bernardo Strozzi** it is the French 17C painting which catches the eye. The earlier work on show here is clearly indebted to Bolognese painting, and in particular that of the Carracci, although in **Claude Vignon's Portrait of a Young Man** this is given a lyrical twist. You might also detect similar currents in **Simon Vouet's Holy Family,** and as Vouet became court painter to Louis XIII on his return from Italy in 1627 this preference for heightened colour and strong diagonal accents influenced Parisian painting for much of the early 17C, **Charles Le Brun's Charity** continuing the tradition into the early 1640s. This was not the only, nor even the dominant, trend in French painting at this date however, and in **Le Voeu de Louis XIII, Philippe de Champaigne** constructed an austere and scrupulously symbolic environment in which Louis might commend his kingdom to the protection of the Virgin. The painting was commissioned for Notre-Dame de Paris in 1637, the year Louis finally bore an heir, and its harsh lighting and unflinching portrayal of the dead Christ established de Champaigne's reputation as a religious painter. A similarly cool and lucid art was simultaneously developed by one of his best known contemporaries, **Nicolas Poussin**, whose superb **Death of Adonis** is hung close by. The scene represented here dates from the 1630s and shows the moment when Venus pours the scented nectar of immortality over the fatally wounded Adonis.

Dutch 17C painting is represented with a fine pair of lanscapes by **Ruysdael** and **van Goyen**, and a good Vanitas by **Jan de Heem**, while contemporary Flemish painting includes one of **Rubens'** most Italianate canvases, **Abraham and Melchisedek**, painted shortly after his return from Venice in 1612, and a bravura still life by **Frans Snyders** entitled **Intérieur d'Office**.

The 19th and 20C collections are housed downstairs, highlighted by one of **Monet's Waterlilies** of 1904, and **Courbet's La Mer** of 1872. Beyond there is some fairly undistinguished painting from the inter-war period, which contrasts sharply with the execellent alternating display of prints and drawings from the Mancel collection in the **Cabinet des Estampes**.

Leaving the castle by the 15C eastern gate, **La Porte des Champs**, has the advantage of giving you a sense of the depth of defence required of a major late medieval fortification, which remains impressive even as you mentally abstract the 17C outer barbican. A network of paths leads down to the Rue de la Pigacière, where a right turn at the Place St-Gilles brings you out opposite the west front of Mathilda's great nunnery of **La Trinité**, or **Abbaye-aux-Dames**.

Lanfranc's success in having the order of excommunication against William and Mathilda lifted in 1059 does not seem to have precipitated the immediate foundation of an Abbaye-aux-Hommes and Abbaye-aux-Dames (see above), but of the two it was La Trinité that received the earlier attention. Building may have begun as early as 1060, and was certainly underway by 1065, culminating in a dedication of the crypt on 18 June 1066, when William took advantage of the gathering of prelates and barons to further his plans for an invasion of England. This initial campaign established the shape of the eastern limb, with a choir of two bays flanked by deep apse-échelon chapels and separated from the nave by a wide aisleless transept. Although the lower portions of the south wall of the nave had been laid out at the same time, building proceeded slowly and by Mathilda's death in 1083 only the choir was complete, the elevation of the transepts and choir dating from the first quarter of the 12C with the rib vaults being insertions of c 1130.

The **crypt** is one of the more surprising areas of an otherwise spacious building, divided into five aisles by a closely spaced arrangement of 16 columns to create one of the most congested hall crypts of the 11C. The columns in turn support a thickly worked set of volute capitals, occasionally fringed with a lower register of curving leaf-tips, or drawing elements towards the centre of each face to create a console in what are a type of heavily debased Corinthian capital. Immediately above this crypt the **choir** exemplifies the inherently problematical nature of the building as a whole. The site of Mathilda's tomb is marked by a simple slab of black marble towards the centre of a majestic ritual space covered by two bays of groin vaulting. The apse to the east is an early 12C replacement, and the north wall was largely reconstructed by Ruprich-Robert during the 19C when a major restoration campaign was insensitively unleashed on the church. There can be no doubt over the thickness of its north and south walls however, or the fact that there were originally no openings between the choir itself and the échelon chapels (those to the north are modern replacements built on the 11C foundation lines). As such the choir must have been planned for high groin vaults, though the nature of the original treatment of the elevation around the apse is beyond recreation. It so happens that the present apse proved one of the more influential designs of the early 12C and the double-skin treatment of the walls, in which the inner face is opened out into a screen of slender detached arches, was enthusiastically taken up by the early Gothic architects of north-eastern France.

The elevation of the **transepts** is quite different, with the wall divided into three distinct zones which mirror the proportions of the nave. The decorative language is also richer with Greek-key ornament around the extrados of the blind arcade and scallop capitals at clerestory level, all of which suggest a date at the beginning of the 12C. The vaults are later insertions, and though provision was made for vaulting at the same time as in the nave the current vaults, with their five-part arrangement in the outer bays, date from the late 13C. It seems likely that they were replaced at the same time as the splendid six bay chapter house was constructed to the east of the south transept.

It is the **nave** which lays out the early 12C thinking most clearly. Unlike its neighbour St-Etienne, where height is fairly evenly distributed among the various storeys of the elevation, the nave of La Trinité concentrates much of the height in the arcade, and omits a tribune in favour of a blind triforium. Above this a clerestory wall-passage was built into the thickness of the wall and provided with the sort of tripartite arcade developed in Anglo-Norman circles at Winchester and Ely. The opposing walls of this elevation were originally intended to be joined by a wooden roof, but at approximately the same time as it was decided to throw a vault over the nave and transepts of St-Etienne, i.e. c 1130–35, La Trinité was also singled out as a candidate for vaulting. This is handled in distinctive fashion as a pseudo-sexpartite vault, where the intermediate transverse ribs support a section of wall which intersects with the webbing at right-angles rather than forming an arched lunette at the head of the wall.

This interest in offering alternatives to the solutions laid down at St-Etienne is also embraced by the **west front**. Again this has been badly treated and the bull's-eye windows and cumbersome tower balustrades were added in the 17C, while the central block is 19C. But the lower four stages of the flanking towers are original and they are more richly decorated than at St-Etienne, with blind arcading cutting in at the third register to create an emphatic horizontal interest. The church has been denuded of its medieval precincts, as it has its internal fittings, and to the north an immense complex of conventual buildings was laid out by Guillaume de la Tremblaye in 1704, with a splendid cloister modelled on that of St-Etienne now accommodating the Conseil Régional.

To the south of the façade, bordering a small garden above the Rue des Chanoines, an isolated range of late 15C wall chapels marks out the site of the parish church of **St-Gilles**. It makes an attractive setting, with a bench or two laid among the early 12C foundations of the nave piers, below which the street falls gently back towards the Château and the church of **St-Pierre**.

By the time the burghers of Caen had seen to the renewal of the apse in the 16C a legend had grown up to the effect that the mightiest and most ancient parish in the town, that of **St-Pierre**, had been founded as early as the 7C. While this claim is an unlikely one it is certain that a church existed on the site when William began work on the castle, and that the tenure of Theodoricus as priest before 1130 had witnessed the building of a new church. As it now stands the building is substantially late medieval and ranks as one of the more lavish parochial structures in Basse-Normandie.

The most visible expression of this was the construction of a splendid **tower and spire**, sunk against the flanks of the south aisle, and rising deftly to proclaim mercantile ambition in matters of ecclesiastical advertisement. The square base was begun in the late 13C as the support for a freestanding structure, above which a tall intermediate storey serves to launch the main belfry stage past the clerestory parapet and upwards into free space. It is a dramatic composition, completed in 1308 with the squeezed proportions and elongated openings which had so enlivened great Norman church architecture in the later 13C. And as a finishing touch between 1308 and 1317 an octagonal spire was sprung from the balustrade, fretted about its diagonal faces with delicate pavilions and pierced by hexafoils as a means of reducing wind resistance. Although the spire, along with the western rose and nave vault, was destroyed in June 1944, rebuilding has aimed at replicating the original forms, and you remain in a good position to judge the formal temperament of a tower and spire whose reflections can be seen scattered across the villages of north-western Normandy.

The interior is more composite. The western five bays of the **nave** were added in the mid 14C with a curious blind central storey, mimicking the proportions of a tribune church, and a dazzling western rose window floated off from the nave proper behind an open traceried screen. The nave is best known for the relief carvings which adorn the second and third capitals of the north arcade. That to the west shows a group of rabbits hiding in a cabbage patch, while that to the east illustrates a sermon by Honorius d'Autun on the nature of Divine Love, which contrasts Aristotle (saddled and under the whip of his mistress, Campaspe), Virgil (abandoned by the daughter of the Emperor in a basket hauled halfway to her chamber), Lancelot (on the sword bridge), and Gawain (struck by an arrow on his perilous bed) with the Unicorn (whose refuge in the lap of a virgin symbolises the intercessive compassion of the Virgin Mary), the Pelican (feeding her young on her own blood), Samson (breaking the jaw of the lion and prefiguring Christ's conquest of Satan), and the Phoenix (whose love rises from the ashes of death).

The eastern five bays of the nave and choir rest on 13C piers but the decision to rebuild the **Sanctuary** c 1490 coincided with a wholesale remodelling of the choir which transformed the entire nature of the eastern complex. The central zone of the elevation was stripped out leaving a simple wall-passage above the arcade, beyond which an ambulatory with five chapels and a four bay apse hemicycle were planned. Building seems to have been slow, for although the ambulatory chapels had been laid out in 1518 a hurricane two years later destroyed the glass in the surviving central bay of the old 13C square-ended apse, suggesting comparatively little beyond the choir elevation had been achieved. The event seems to have acted as a catalyst and work proceeded on the hexagonal chapels of the ambulatory at the same time as the apse was raised, culminating in a superb pendant vault from which a life-size statue of St Peter is suspended. Finally, Hector Sohier and Jean Masselin were called in to vault the choir, a steady accomplishment which led to their being retained from 1535–50 to weave a giddying tour-de-force of inventive vaulting over the ambulatory chapels. Taken as a whole this new east end represents something of a triumph of patience, but in its revealing use of Italianate ornament it purposefully subjects Renaissance motifs to the controlling power of a late Gothic spatial fluidity.

The area to the west of St-Pierre is the more rewarding having retained its pre-war street pattern, along with the greatest concentration of earlier domestic buildings. One of the most impressive of these stands opposite the south flank of St-Pierre and now houses the Office de Tourisme, being officially known as the **Hôtel d'Escoville**. It was built for a wealthy merchant trader, Nicolas Le Valois d'Escoville, between 1537 and 1550, presenting a relatively plain façade to St-Pierre, behind which a spacious courtyard offers access to the major rooms. The composition of the house is one that was well established in early 16C Normandy and is in two storeys with dormer windows piercing the steeply pitched roofs, an interest in Italian forms being largely confined to ornamental detail and sculptural iconography. In this d'Escoville was not dissimilar from Georges d'Amboise, or even François I, in seeing Italian design as an invitation to enrich the external fabric of a building and retool its interior fittings. To the right he deployed statues of David with the head of Goliath and Judith holding the head of Holofernes, and sited bas-reliefs of Perseus releasing Andromeda and the Abduction of Europa above, all of it taking place beneath the d'Escoville arms. The western elevation is more inventively treated, with an unusual dormer window supported by repeated figures of Tubal Cain, while a spiral stair ascends via an elegant loggia to a splendid cupola, whose upper lantern is crowned by Apollo holding his lyre. There is a warning in all this however, since the mutilated tympanum at the angle of the loggia carries an Apocalyptic message wherein the Great Prostitute rides the Seven-Headed Beast—so be careful when climbing the stairs.

From here the **Rue St-Pierre** runs south-west passing, at Nos 52 and 54, two of the few early 16C timber houses remaining in the town, steeply gabled and studded with wooden statues of saints. A little further on the **Rue Froide** clambers northwards through a streetscape rich with 16–18C townhouses in what is the last unadulterated prospect of pre-war Caen, admirably counterpointed by the church of **St-Sauveur**.

Before 1802 this church was called **Notre-Dame de Froide-Rue**, a title by which it is still sometimes known, and should not be confused with the St-Sauveur in the Place St-Sauveur. This confusion of titles is as nothing, however, to the bizarre and baffling sequence of architectural episodes which conspired to create the least coherent church in Basse-Normandie. The bell-tower is the earliest part of the existing structure, believed to be just anterior to that of St-Pierre (to which it is related, i.e. pre 1308). A seven bay nave and choir were built to the north of this during the 14C, with the effect that the tower abutted the middle bay of the south wall. The 15C nevertheless brought a rethink and it was decided that the church should be enlarged by taking out the south wall of this 14C nave, replacing it with an arch, and raising a second nave to the south of the original. There now existed a twin-aisled church, but the ad hoc nature of these campaigns resulted in the collapse of the apse of the earlier (northern) nave and its replacement some time before 1546. Hence the noticeable shift of architectural language encountered in the apses, whereby the late Gothic detailing to the south gives way to a loosely Italianate ornament. Several authorities believe Hector Sohier to be responsible for this latest work, but be cautioned, this only gives an outline of the leading changes, minor adjustments abound and for good measure a rather splendid and largely redundant spiral stairway leads from the south aisle up the exterior of the aisle wall along the Rue Froide.

Continuing westwards a right turn along the Rue aux Fromages brings you to the **Place Saint-Sauveur**. Even here, in the midst of an area which came through 1944 relatively unscathed, you are continually reminded of the damage which was sustained. The Place is bounded by handsome 18C terraces and overseen by Petitot's statue of Louis XIV in the guise of a Roman emperor, with the ruinous shell of the old parish church of St-Sauveur at its north-eastern angle (under restoration). To the west of the Law Courts on the Place Fontette, you catch a first glimpse of the choir and eastern chapels of one of the great buildings of northern Europe—the abbey church of **St-Etienne de Caen**.

> 'I, William, King of England, Prince of Normandy and Maine, have decided to have a monastery built in honour of God and the blessed martyr Stephen, in the borough commonly known by the name of Caen, for the salvation of my soul, and the souls of my wife, my children, and my parents'.

William's decree of 1067 is commonly taken to mark the commencement of building operations at a monastery he had promised to found as early as 1059 (see above). Planning may have begun slightly earlier, for on 15 June 1066, three days before the consecration of the crypt of La Trinité, Lanfranc had been persuaded from Bec to be appointed first abbot of St-Etienne. Three consecration ceremonies, in 1073, 1077, and 1081, bear witness to William's anxiety to see the building completed within his lifetime. The greatest of these, that conducted by Jean, Bishop of Avranches, in 1077 undoubtedly marked the completion of the ritual choir, and few doubt that by the time of William's inglorious funeral in 1087 the church had assumed its first architectural guise.

The present building in fact reflects the endeavours of three different generations of architects, with an 11C nave and transepts overlaid by early 12C vaults, and a 13C choir. When work began St-Etienne was planned with a two bay apse-échelon east end, shallow transepts, and an eight bay nave culminating in a broad western façade. The choir would appear, on plan at least, to have been similar to that of La Trinité though without a crypt, and it is to the west that you must turn to get an impression of the 11C architectural sensibility underpinning St-Etienne.

The **nave** presents this most forcibly with a three storey elevation whose height is relatively evenly distributed between the arcade, tribune, and clerestory. In its original state the vaulting was confined to the aisles and engaged shafts ran up as far as the clerestory parapet, abutting an open timber roof every alternate bay. These shafts are one of the keys to the whole design, for not only do they impose a set of vertical accents dividing the elevation into tall panels but they establish a subtle secondary rhythm. The major notes are struck by half-columns rising proud of the pilasters which propel them into the nave, while the minor notes are marked by simple half-columns. The effect of this alternation would have been strongly felt before the vault was thrown, as only the major wall-shafts ran as far as the roof and thus framed a succession of ample double bays at the very head of the elevation.

In fact it is when looking at the clerestory that you are reminded of the sheer thickness of the walls at St-Etienne. Although the clerestory wall-passage was first introduced at Notre-Dame de Bernay it is not until it was

The west front of St-Etienne, Caen

taken up here that it was ever systematically exploited, and if you intend riddling the church with passages then thick walls are a *sine qua non*. This progressive lightening of the structure can also be seen to glorious effect in the central lantern tower, where the lower of the inner registers is treated to an open arcade across its inner face in what is the earliest known ancestor of the Gothic triforium. In its way the nave of St-Etienne is not only definitive but immensely influential, having the peculiar distinction of exercising the minds of two quite different generations of architects and patrons. Its exposition of the basic techniques of laying passages through the wall was enthusiastically endorsed in late 11C England, but it was the mid-12C architects of the Ile-de-France who discovered the implications of its approach to the visible system of supposts.

The handling of the various arches, shafts and mouldings which make up the elevation are subjected to a rational set of rules in which every capital or half-column should be balanced by an equivalent responding member, and that each arch should be provided with an equal support. The clarity and logic with which the arrangement of parts is brought together is the enduring achievement of the building, beautifully illustrated by the way in which the nook-shafts which flank the longitudinal faces of the piers find an answer in the angle-roll drawn across the leading edge of every roll. Allied to the light columnar architecture of the Paris basin it gave birth to the Gothic. The vault is similarly precocious and though dated only vaguely to c 1130 is generally regarded as being the first example of sexpartite vaulting in Europe.

The general spirit of rationalism which informed the nave was even extended to the **west front**, where the main lower block is organised to reflect the interior section of the church. This was complete by c 1085 and is divided into three vertical slices by massive strip buttresses which mimic the nave and aisles, and three horizontal zones which accord with the main elevation. The uppermost storey of the towers may be slightly later, c 1100, but the spires reflect a very different order of ecclesiastical imagery. These were probably put in hand shortly after the completion of the choir in the mid 13C, that to the south being the later, and their attenuated aedicules and picturesque spirelets are derived from the south-west spire of Chartres cathedral.

The choir was renewed in two stages after c 1190, but not before the earlier structure had witnessed one of the more gruesome spectacles of the 11C. In July 1087 William the Conqueror injured himself in a fall from his horse while inspecting the damage he had caused in laying waste to Mantes. He was taken to Rouen where his condition continued to decline and on 9 September, having been carried to the priory of St-Gervase de Rouen, he died. It was an unhappy death. His corpse was stripped by his servants and left untended for days while his sons and the local barons squabbled over his effects. It was thus some time before he was brought by ship, in accordance with his will, to Caen. A large crowd had assembled to meet the cortège but as the funeral procession began to move through the town a fire broke out and the crowd caused the mourners to panic into changing their route. Even when the choir of St-Etienne was finally entered the ceremony was interrupted by a petitioner, Asselin, who demanded restitution for the land on which the crossing stood, arguing that it had been stolen from his father. The bishop of Bayeux and assorted nobles raised 60 sous on the spot with the promise of more to come, and William's body was lowered into a grave under the lantern tower. As the ropes were released the bloated corpse burst, releasing a rank fetor which caused all but the monks to leave and the final obsequies were conducted without a congregation.

The dating of the present **choir** is uncertain, and while many scholars are agreed that the design was substantially changed in the course of construction, there is less of a consensus on the question of dating. Building started to the east with the apse hemicycle and ambulatory chapels, probably around 1190, where it is apparent that a thin walled structure akin to the great churches of north-east France was intended. The evidence for this lies in the way in which the piers and upper elevation of the apse hemicycle have been thickened out to accommodate a clerestory wall-passage. Despite its being intended as a tribune choir from the outset this thickening of the wall had a decisive impact on the handling of the elevation. The hiatus which precipitated the rethink is likely to have been the Anglo-Norman warring which preceded King John's loss of Normandy in 1204, and it is doubtful whether work restarted much before c 1210. When it did the sculptural possibilities raised by the decision to broaden the masses of masonry were splendidly realised in the enrichment of the moulding profiles, and the excavation of the arcade spandrels with spiky rosettes. The ornament was further refined around the hemicycle where the tribune was singled out for extravagant cusped mouldings and sunken roundels. The architect of this second campaign was rewarded with a burial plot within the monastic precincts, and a heavily defaced inscription on the outer wall of the apse recalls the event—'Here lies William, he excelled in working stone; he brought this work to a successful issue. May God reward him. Amen.'

The choir has sadly lost all its medieval furnishings, variously replaced by a marble altar of 1771 and a fine set of choir stalls of c 1625. Even Duke William, his tomb desecrated during the Wars of Religion, makes do with a simple modern epitaph in front of the high altar. Towards the north-west of the nave, however, a spacious chapel, known as **La Chapelle Halbout**, was built shortly before 1315 and now houses Claude Vignon's mid 17C Adoration of the Magi.

To the south of the church **les bâtiments conventuels** were rebuilt by the Maurist architect Guillaume de la Tremblaye after 1704, being finally completed to his plans in the late 1760s. They enjoyed a brief monastic occupation, for in the wake of the Revolution the buildings were turned over to accommodate Napoléon's imperial Lycée Malherbe in 1802, and since 1965 have housed the **Hôtel-de-Ville**. There are restrictions on the areas which can be visited but the compulsory guided tours offer a compelling insight into some of the finest early 18C architecture in Normandy. Beyond the rigorously symmetrical 27 bay façade of the eastern range a superb 'Escalier d'Honneur' brings you to the point where the guided tours begin. To the left the Salle des Moines was rebuilt in the 19C while opposite, the **salle capitulaire** is hung with 17C paintings which include Sébastien Bourdon's Crossing of the Red Sea, and a portrayal of Moses Striking the Rock attributed to the studio of Mignard. Beyond this, and parallel to the south aisle of the church, lies a magnificent **refectory**, built in 1752–66 and panelled throughout in oak. This is hung with 18C paintings, with Lépicié's melodramatic Duke William embarking for England of 1765 farcially representing William as a latterday Roman emperor. The heart of this complex is nevertheless the cloister, whose clarity and restraint makes an excellent foil for the adjoining **parlour**.

There is one medieval survival in all this. To the rear a building known as the **Salle des Gardes** dates from 1315 and came through the Wars of Religion reasonably unscathed, though the present rose window is a 19C insert. Modelled on 13C episcopal halls, it was used as a reception chamber by the prior, becoming the centre of excited comment in 1974 when remains of the Gallo-Roman village of Cadomus were discovered under its north wall.

The more interesting route back to the town centre takes you through the Place Guillouard, where the ruined silhouette of the church of **Vieux St-Etienne** completes the north-east angle of the square. The church was decayed before the nave was destroyed in 1944, and though closed the 13C choir rewards a cursory examination of its exterior. The most interesting adjunct is to be found to the south of the east window, where a damaged 12C equestrian relief has been remounted, presumably originally forming a pair with the beggar to whom St Martin gave half his cloak. Continuing east the Rue de Bras passes the 16C Collège du Mont with a 12C doorway from the Maison Dieu picturesquely reset in its grounds, while off to the right **Notre-Dame-de-la-Gloriette**, consecrated in 1689, in Rue St-Laurent is neo-classical.

The centre might also be regarded as a good starting point for an excursion to the one outstanding attraction of suburban Caen, the **Musée Mémorial** on the Esplanade Dwight-Eisenhower (open every day 9.00–19.00. The No. 12 bus from the Place Courtonne offers a direct service). This is an exceptional museum, and although an overview of modern warfare is the basis of its achievement, the building also acts as a documentary and research centre in addition to being a place of commemoration and a 'symbol for peace'.

The main exhibition is conceived as a journey through history and you descend a ramp which opens with the First World War and the failure of the post-war peace. Brief commentaries on the rise of Fascism and the Great Depression of the 1930s are accompanied by newsreel footage of the Japanese invasion of Manchuria and the Nuremburg rallies. This serves as an introduction to the two major sections, the first dedicated to French experience from 1939–44 and entitled **France: The Dark Years**, the second called **World War: Total War**. Both of these include showings of relevant short films and interviews, while the main displays are labelled throughout in French, English, and German. Above there are shorter sections on D-Day, the Battle for Normandy, and L'Esperance—Hope for the Future. The museum authorities recommend that visitors allow two hours for a reasonable exploration, though if you intend to watch the collages of newsreel footage covering D-Day and the Battle for Normandy, which are both extremely moving and masterfully put together via a split-screen presentation, I would recommend a whole morning or afternoon.

12
Bayeux and the Bessin

ROAD (122km): Bayeux D6, 8km Douet; D33/D178, 3km Mondaye; D178/D73, 13km Balleroy; D13, 8km Cerisy-la-Forêt; 19km Deux-Jumeaux; N13, 14km Tour-en-Bessin; 6km Bayeux; N13, 8km St-Léger; D82, 6km St-Gabriel-Brécy; 2km Creully; D22/D141, 5km Fontaine-Henry; D170, 2km Thaon; 12km Norrey-en-Bessin; N13, 16km Bayeux.

The route suggested above describes two unequal circuits which loop to the west and east of Bayeux respectively. The dense pattern of secondary roads makes them complicated but none of the places mentioned is more than 25km from Bayeux, and you can easily use the text as a gazetteer for gentle excursions to just one or two places at a time.

The area covered here is that to the south of the Côte de Nacre, from Caen to Isigny-sur-Mer, consisting of a low plateau undulating between 200 and 300 metres above sea level, cut by the meandering and marshy valleys of the rivers Aure, Drôme, and Seulles. Superficially the whole of this region, known as the Bessin, seems to mark the transition between the limestone heights of central Normandy and the older granite formations of the Cotentin peninsula. The landscape to the west certainly has the banked hedgerows and intimate scale encountered in the Bocage, but the thick overlay of clay lends the whole region a distinctive air. The area was quite densely populated during the Middle Ages and has retained its pattern of closely distributed villages, fortified farmhouses, and large parish churches, which provide a stable base for the staple dairy farming. At its centre the ancient city of Bayeux was respectively the Gaulish capital of the Bajo-casses, a Roman town fortified by Augustus, and the centre of Breton, Saxon, and Viking occupations. Duke Rollo married Popa, the daughter of the governor of Bayeux, in the town and their son, the future Duke William Longsword, was born here in 905. After Rouen was made chief city of Normandy Bayeux stayed in close contact with Scandinavia, and was the last of the old Viking centres to adjust to the feudal Christianity of northern France, remaining Norse speaking well into the 11C.

As the first large French town to be liberated, on 7 June 1944, Bayeux escaped the damage which so disfigured neighbouring Caen, and retains much of the unhurried bourgeois atmosphere described by Balzac in 'Une Double Famille'. It is not only an obvious centre from which to explore the Bessin but also the Côte de Nacre and D-Day beaches, and though its hotels are busy with visitors between June and September, out of season there is little that disturbs its unselfconscious and businesslike ways.

BAYEUX. The old town lies in the cradle of a gently shelving valley formed by the River Aure, and was effectively divided by its one main street (the Rue St-Martin and its continuations), with a mercantile quarter to the north, and the main organs of civic and ecclesiastical jurisdiction to the south. The prosperity of the 17th and 18C led to the building of ambitious townhouses in the area to the west of the cathedral, but the town still pivots on the cathedral church of Notre-Dame and this remains the best place in which to begin an exploration of the town.

A Gallo-Roman temple stood on the site now occupied by the **Cathedral**, adapted for Christian use by Bayeux's first bishop, St-Exupère, c 360. However, none of the existing fabric predates the mid 11C, and as a composite, and important, building the following account takes an essentially chronological approach, moving from the deepest recesses of the church outwards.

The 11C cathedral was begun c 1040 by Bishop Hugues II and was completed under his successor, Odo de Conteville, half-brother to Duke William. The increase in Odo's wealth and prestige after the Conquest seems to have speeded up the building programme so that the new cathedral was solemnly consecrated by the Archbishop of Rouen in 1077, in the presence of William the Conqueror, Lanfranc, Archbishop of Canterbury, and Thomas of Bayeux, Archbishop of York.

The town fire of 1105 destroyed much of this church, but the crypt and central core of the two west towers sustained little damage and remain in situ. The **crypt** extends beneath the later choir and gives an idea of the 11C work, being divided into aisles by two rows of slender columns which carry foliate capitals in two registers. Several of the capitals were recut in the

19C, but the majority are original and compare with those in the crypt of Rouen cathedral, securely dated to before 1063. Unlike Rouen, 11C Bayeux was designed with an apse-échelon east end, a feature which clearly antagonised the authorities responsible for planning the 13C choir who had it filled in, and the crypt was only 'rediscovered' in 1412 when it was decorated with a lively late Gothic fresco cycle, depicting musical angels in the vaults and saints in the aisle niches. And at least one canon, **Gervais de Larchamp**, took advantage of the august space to be buried against the north wall, his damaged effigy complemented by a commendatory wall painting.

The damage caused by the 1105 fire seems to have been confined to the area west of the crypt and choir, but the ructions of Henry I's reign were not conducive to large-scale ecclesiastical building projects and the **nave** was not rebuilt until the episcopacy of Philippe de Harcourt (1142–63). Again this is a composite structure and only the main arcade of de Harcourt's work survives, its two western bays replaced during the 13C and its eastern bay a 19C rehash. This is generally considered to be one of the finest examples of the Norman decorative tradition, restless with a compellingly varied exhibition of architectural ornament which overwhelms every surface with variations on a theme of chevrons, lozenges, and interlace. Some of the fanned motifs here may derive from Middle Eastern textiles, a suspicion which finds support in the spandrels, where a series of sculpted plaques, depicting fantastically patterned lions and serpents, are clearly indebted to Sassanian designs. The rest of the sculpture also merits close attention, with a notably austere relief of a bishop and a curious plaque showing a man stroking his beard.

By the end of the 12C it was the turn of the collegiate buildings to receive attention, and c 1200 a magnificent **chapter house** was constructed to the north of Odo's west front. Sadly this is rarely open to the public, but if the opportunity to visit the building arises it should be seized. The vault was renewed in the 14C, shortly before the decaying fresco of the north wall was painted to illustrate the college chapter lying at the feet of the Virgin, but the supporting array of fabulous and imaginary animals remains from the earlier work. The floor is laid with an extraordinarily rare survival—a 15C tiled pavement centred around a splendid labyrinth.

With their new chapter house complete the chapter embarked on a spate of new building which was to transform the choir, nave, and transepts, and establish the present architectural shape of the cathedral. The result was sufficiently dramatic for it to seem like a controlled and continuous programme of works, planned from the outset, but there were in fact four separate and consecutive 13C campaigns each prone to their own problems and revisions.

The first area to be resolved was the **choir**, where work began c 1230, probably in response to the new and spacious choirs recently undertaken at St-Etienne de Caen and Lisieux cathedral. It is Caen which offers the closest parallels and the problems must initially have seemed similar: how to reconcile the chapter's desire for an aesthetically appropriate 13C choir with the necessity of joining it to a Romanesque nave and transepts. Although this is now difficult to visualise the answer was precisely that offered by St-Etienne. The old apse-échelon east end was pulled down and a new and larger apse-ambulatory design built in its place, mimicking the three storey elevation of the 11C work to the west. This latter point is important as it casts light on one of the oddities of the choir at Bayeux. The middle zone of the elevation may be handled as a triforium, with a closed

Bayeux Cathedral: south elevation of the choir

rear wall, but it is given all the height to be expected from a tribune and its arrangement of arches, subdivided beneath a single relieving arch, echoes that of a tribune church. The effective substitution of a triforium for a tribune allowed the Bayeux Master to indulge his predilection for running passages through the thickness of the wall, superimposing a clerestory wall-passage over that of the triforium. And this interest is not confined to the main elevation, for above the aisle dado arcade a passage is disposed around the radiating chapels, breaking through the buttresses in the manner of Henry III's later choir at Westminster Abbey. The architectural embellishment of the choir was originally part of a wider treatment, though most of the glass, and all the liturgical fittings, have been lost. The south-western aisle window retains panels of two bishops but this is all that remains of the 13C glazing, though the choir stalls of 1588 are a worthy addition.

The renewal of the **nave** took place under quite different circumstances, and began c 1250 with the removal of the upper superstructure of Philippe de Harcourt's work. This was replaced by a tall clerestory, its massive two-light windows repeated by heavy tracery in two layers, and a thickly worked balustrade which sits above the 12C arcade and allows another wall-passage to connect up with the choir. At this date the transepts still carried 11C tribune platforms, but the successful completion of the choir and remodelling of the nave seem to have persuaded the chapter to rid the cathedral of its darkest central area.

The **north transept** was begun first, perhaps as early as 1265, with a delicate trefoil arched balustrade supporting a seven-light window, and blind traceried walls. The **south transept** is later and is accorded a very different treatment. Here the wider end bay is divided by a free-standing pier, enabling a double chapel to be constructed in the thickness of the wall.

This is now filled with some hideously vapid 19C painting but to the south a register of scenes from the life of St Nicolas of Bari dates from the 15C.

With the exception of a beautifully consistent east end the **exterior** of the cathedral is very uneven in quality. The twin towers of the west front belong to Odo's 11C building and received their spires in the late 12C, but the heavy stepped buttresses and division of the façade into five portals are mid-13C, and the two surviving tympana bear undistinguished representations of the Passion of Christ (North) and Last Judgement (South).

The **south transept portal** is more lively, despite its worn condition, and is dedicated to Thomas à Becket, showing the return of Thomas from exile, his murder, and the act of expiation undertaken by Henry II at his tomb. This stands parallel to the oddest, and at a distance, most striking feature of the building—the **crossing tower**. In the course of the late 15C, and above a square 13C base, Bishop Louis d'Harcourt raised a lavish octagon, whose original lead roof was unfortunately destroyed by fire in 1676. The subsidence caused by its replacement began to cause serious concern by the mid 19C however, and the railway engineer Crétin was called in to shore up the foundations. His evident success was roundly applauded, but it was also greeted as a pretext to add an upper storey and inappropriate Louis-Philippe dome.

To the north of the cathedral a venerable plane tree, known as l'Arbre de la Liberté, was planted in the Place des Tribunaux in 1797, offering shade to the Place and shelter from the crowds who congregate to the south and west. Beyond its westerly branches the old bishop's palace now plays host to the **Musée Baron-Gérard**, named after the 19C collector Baron Henry Gérard, whose bequests to the town of Bayeux so swelled the earlier small municipal gallery that the museum was moved here in 1880.

The museum is rich in two particular areas: local ceramics, and French 18th/19C painting. The ceramics are gathered on the ground floor, where a notable collection of 17th and 18C faience apothecaries' jars is allied to a patchy display of Bayeux porcelain. The kilns closed in 1951, but the pottery's heyday was the early 19C and among some otherwise poorly executed and derivative work the Chinese-inspired ware of **Joachim Langlois** (1812–30) is quite outstanding. A small archaeological section houses two archaising 17C effigies of **Jacques and Marie de Ste-Croix**, seigneurs de Ry, while the first floor is devoted to a chronologically arranged display of painting and furniture. Among the unattributed and minor 15C panel paintings there are some excellent Renaissance carved wooden chests, but the overall strength of the collection lies more in its intermingling of paintings by local artists with those of **Boudin, Caillebotte**, and **Lebourg**. There is one undoubted masterpiece however, **François Boucher's 'Le Cage'**, whose vibrant brushwork outshines an otherwise impressive group of 18C paintings.

Balancing the Musée to the south of the cathedral an ostentatiously carved portal of 1697 leads to the 18C **Hôtel du Doyen**, the residence of the Dean. A plain rectangular block with a chapel to the east, the ground floor now accommodates a small museum of religious art and a lace conservatory. The former consists of a collection of 17–19C liturgical objects—ciboria, pyxis, priestly vestments etc, centred on a superbly panelled room hung with historicising portraits of the bishops of Bayeux. The lace conservatory is more modest, with a brief display of lacemaking indicative of the somewhat tentative revival during the 18C of the predominantly floral Bayeux patterns.

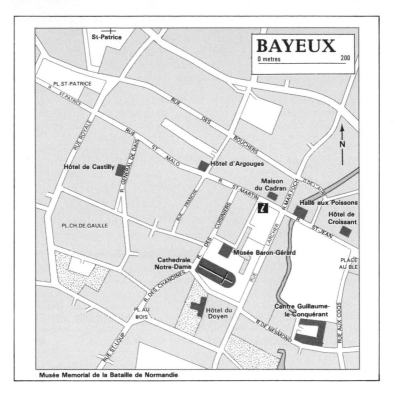

Musée Memorial de la Bataille de Normandie

To the east of the cathedral the Rue de Nesmond climbs alongside a handsome 17C watermill, beyond which Nesmond's seminary of 1693 has been transformed into **Le Centre Guillaume-le-Conquérant** and now houses the **Bayeux Tapestry**.

The remounting of the tapestry in 1983 occasioned a scholarly re-examination of the work, which resulted in the publication of a number of studies and photographs whose findings can be seen in the excellent preliminary audio-visual display which elucidates the background to the tapestry.

The tapestry is made up of eight strips of linen, varying in height and stretching 230 metres from the opening scene of Edward the Confessor to a frayed and premature ending depicting the English in flight after Hastings. In fact to call it a tapestry is a misnomer as the episodes are recounted by means of woollen embroidery, using five principal colours which would appear to have suffered very little fading, as the colours on the back of the linen have an almost identical depth of tone to those on the front. These colours are not intended to be seen naturalistically (the horses are often rendered in a deep blue for instance), but are capable of endowing the scenes with an extraordinarily vivid sense of pace and movement. The main narrative takes place in a broad central strip, fringed by two borders which punctuate the events with ornaments, fables, and sub-plots, and often comment on the story in an allusive and wry voice. The tale itself is well known but it is well known precisely because our perception of the events of 1066 owes much to the tapestry. As a historical source its portrayal of Harold in Normandy during 1064, William's initiatives to claim the English throne, and the Battle of Hastings, adds enormously to what is known via the contemporary histories of William of Poitiers, William of Jumièges, and the Anglo-Saxon Chronicle.

As an object it find few parallels and is the only large-scale wall hanging from the period to have survived, though both its date and provenance are open to question. The tapestry was in Bayeux in 1476 when it is mentioned in a cathedral inventory, and by the 18C had become popularly attributed to William's wife, Queen Mathilda. Modern scholarship favours Odo de Conteville, William's half-brother and the Bishop of Bayeux, as patron. He features prominently in the embroidery and two other named characters, Vital and Wadard, have been shown to have been among Odo's retainers. Furthermore the controversial scene in which Harold swears an oath to support William's claim to the English throne in the event of Edward's death, is situated in Bayeux in the tapestry, and not at Bonneville-sur-Touques as recounted by William of Poitiers. The central position given to this event, a solemn oath sworn on the relics of Bayeux, has led many to see the tapestry as a religious object. However, not only does it seem almost inconceivable that it was designed for display in the 11C cathedral, but the story is one of worldly conquest, of castles and feasts and bloodshed. The manner in which events are narrated in the tapestry also evokes the world of Old English poetry, where the 'losing side' is shown with dignity, and embodies the heroic ideals shared by all the participants. Criticism of Harold is confined to the oath, and even here we are made aware of a dilemma, for Harold is fated to forswear the wishes of the dying Edward if he is to keep his oath. Although the tapestry was displayed at the feast of relics in the cathedral from the 16C onwards, its context is almost certainly secular, and would most comfortably fit a building such as the early 12C salle de l'Echiquier in Caen. As such one is inclined to imagine the great hall of the warrior-bishop Odo in Bayeux as the most likely theatre for its display, hung around its walls when feasts were held, and songs composed extolling the actions of all at Hastings.

If Odo was its patron the question of where and by whom it was made remains. The epigraphy tell us that it was scripted in England, with a crossed D in Gyrth and the abbreviation 7 for et. The closest stylistic parallels for the treatment of figures, buildings, and the unusual trees which are often used to frame particular scenes, are also to be found in mid 11C Anglo-Saxon manuscripts such as Aelfric's Hexateuch, illuminated in Canterbury c 1030. Odo's estates in Kent and southern England could have provided the wherewithal to commission the work, probably at a nunnery with Canterbury or Winchester connections, but whether or not they were attached to a convent the embroiderers would certainly have been female. If it was made for Odo it must have been made some time between 1067 and 1097, though as Odo was imprisoned by William in 1082 it is likely to have been made before this.

Many more questions remain unanswered. How were the stories translated into pictorial form? Were the embroiderers provided with a cartoon, or did they rely on an oral account? How was the narrative decided on, and by whom? It is a testament to the power of the tapestry that these questions suggest themselves so forcefully.

The following description of the 55 scenes which make up the main body of the work simply repeats the tapestry's own inscriptions (adding bracketed interpolations where it is felt these may be helpful) and is indebted to Sir David Wilson's translation (The Bayeux Tapestry). Scenes 1–22 are set in 1064, scenes 23–55 in 1066.

1   King Edward (instructing Harold in his palace, Winchester?)
2   Where Harold an earl of the English and his soldiers ride to Bosham.
3   The church (at Bosham).
4   Here Harold sailed the sea and, the wind full in his sails, he came to the country of Count Guy (Harold feasts on the upper floor of his manor at Bosham, and departs with the hawk that remains his frequent companion in Normandy).
5   Here Guy arrests Harold (Wido is Guy of Ponthieu).
6   And led him to Beaurain and kept him there.
7   Where Harold and Guy talk (note one of William's spies to the right of the tree).
8   Where the messengers of Duke William came to Guy. (William's messengers demand Harold be released into the Duke's hands while the bearded dwarf, Turold, holds their horses. William of Poitiers states that William paid a large ransom to Guy in order to secure Harold.)
9   The messengers of William.
10 Here Guy brought Harold to William Duke of the Normans (Rouen castle beyond).
11 Here Duke William came with Harold to his palace.
12 Where a certain cleric and Aelfgyva (the explicit male nude below makes it likely this records a sexual scandal, well known to the contemporary audience but alas now lost to us).
13 Here Duke William and his army came to Mont St-Michel (William was accompanied on his 1064 campaign against Conan II of Brittany by Harold. In the background is a marvellously economical view of the abbey atop its mound).
14 And here they crossed the river Couesnon. Here Harold pulled them out of the sand (Harold rescues soldiers of the Norman army from the notorious quicksands).
15 And they came to Dol and Conan turned to flight.
16 Rennes.
17 Here Duke William's soldiers fight against the men of Dinan and Conan surrendered the keys (it is worth noting the superb depiction of a classic motted castle).
18 Here William gave arms to Harold.
19 Here William came to Bayeux.
20 Where Harold made an oath to Duke William (the famous scene also notable for the depiction of two architecturally detailed reliquaries).
21 Here Duke Harold returned to the English country.
22 And came to King Edward.
23 Here the body of King Edward is carried to the church of St Peter the Apostle. (This is Westminster Abbey, its choir newly completed, but the sequence of Edward's counsel, death and funeral have here been reversed. The action has switched to January, 1066.)
24 Here King Edward in bed talks to his faithful followers.
25 And here he is dead.
26 Here they have given the crown of the king to Harold.
27 Here sits throned Harold, king of the English. Stigand, archbishop.
28 These men marvel at the star (Halley's comet was at its brightest from 24–30 April 1066, and was thought an ill omen).
29 Harold (probably informed of William's invasion plans).
30 Here an English ship came to the country of Duke William (difficult to interpret but may be the bearer of the news of Harold's coronation).
31 Here Duke William ordered ships to be built.
32 Here ships are hauled to the sea.
33 These men carry arms to the ships, and here they pull a wagon with wine and arms (quite superb!).
34 Here Duke William in a great ship crossed the sea and came to Pevensey.
35 Here the horses leave the boats.
36 And here soldiers have hurried to Hastings to seize food.

37 Here is Wadard (one of Odo's tenants).

38 Here the meat is cooked, and here it has been served. (A scene made famous of late when the tapestry was argued to be a fake on the grounds that kebabs of cubed meat did not arrive in western Europe until the 17C. The argument is essentially preposterous, and cooking on a spit was ubiquitous in the 11C. The fact that a very few items of food look faintly squared is the result of the nature of the embroidery and the thick gauges of wool used.)

39 The servants. Here they made a meal.

40 And here the bishop blesses the food and drink.

41 Bishop Odo, William, Robert (of Mortain, William's other half-brother).

42 This man has commanded that a fortification should be thrown up at Hastings (also mentioned by William of Poitiers prior to the battle, who attributed the Norman victory to their using cavalry and being castle-builders).

43 Here news is brought to William about Harold (Harold having engaged with the invasion of the North by an army led by his brother, Tostig, and Harold Hardrada, King of Norway. This culminated in the bloody battle of Stamford Bridge, outside York, on 25 September, 1066, three days before the landing at Pevensey).

44 Here a house is burned (William's scorched earth initiative).

45 Here the soldiers went out of Hastings and came to the battle against King Harold (14 October, 1066, preparations for battle).

46 Here Duke William asks Vital whether he has seen Harold's army (critical scene as several sources suggest that Harold's original plan was to take the Normans by surprise, and that this was foiled by Norman scouts).

47 This man tells King Harold about Duke William's army.

48 Here Duke William exhorts his soldiers that they prepare themselves manfully and wisely for the battle against the army of the English. (Let Battle Commence!)

49 Here were killed Leofwine and Gyrth, the brothers of King Harold.

50 Here at the same time English and French fell in battle.

51 Here Bishop Odo holding a wand encourages the young men.

52 Here is Duke William. Eustace (of Boulogne).

53 Here the French fight and have killed those who were with Harold.

54 Here Harold has been killed.

55 And the English have turned to flight (the evident fraying here leaves the tapestry incomplete, though it is unlikely that much has been lost. This author's opinion is that we might have been deprived of William's march on London, his retirement to Barking while the first Tower of London was built, and a final scene of William's coronation at Westminster Abbey on Christmas Day 1066, thus matching the opening image of King Edward with a closing image of King William).

From the Centre Guillaume the Rue aux Coqs runs down to the **Place au Blé**, notable for its recently restored 15C merchant's house, and an excellent place in which to get a measure of vernacular Bayeux. The domestic architecture is predominantly 17th and 18C, of rendered '*petit-appareil*' with rectangular stone-dressed windows and a commitment to simple, modular forms. These buildings form the background rhythm to a splendid townscape, occasionally punctuated by a fanfare of medieval houses or 18C 'hôtels particuliers'. To the west of here the **Rue St-Jean**, and its continuations the Rue St-Martin and Rue St-Malo, run together as the main street of Bayeux. At No. 53 an alley gives onto the Cour de **l'Hôtel de Croissant**, an ambitious but derelict 15C tower-house so-called from the crest of a starred crescent-moon carved above an alley window.

A wide 18C bridge crosses the river and carries the contemporary covered hall of the old fish-market, as well as affording views of the mostly 16C houses which fringe the banks of the medieval tanners quarter. The Rue St-Martin boasts a fine late 18C mansion, the **Maison du Cadran**, built in 1794 on the site of the ruined parish church of St-Martin. While further up the hill the **Maison du Tourisme** has adopted an early 14C half-timbered lodging house, one of a handful of pre-Hundred Years War domestic buildings to have survived in Normandy. Diagonally opposite the Rue Franche the late 15C **Hôtel d'Argouges** carries a conscientious display of 14 wooden statues, including images of the Virgin and Child, Joseph, Christ, and 11 saints. The **Rue Franche** is nonetheless the most exhilarating street in an exacting town, bordered by 16–18C hôtels particuliers standing to the rear of spacious courtyards, and articulated with a sharp and linear restraint which, unusually, complements the austerity of the 15C tower-houses down towards the cathedral. Running parallel, and to the west, the **Rue Général de Dais** reveals a similar density of grand houses though, in spite of the 18C splendour of the **Hôtel de Castilly**, it lacks the coherence of the Rue Franche. The Rue St-Malo continues as far as the huge market spaces of the **Place St-Patrice**, to the right of which the elegant Renaissance clock tower of St-Patrice, completed in 1548, has been unsympathetically juxtaposed with a 19C church.

South of the town centre, along the Boulevard Fabian Ware, the **Musée Mémorial de la Bataille de Normandie** provides an account of the development of the Normandy Campaign between 7 June and 22 August 1944 (see also the Musée du Débarquement at Arromanches, which focuses on D-Day, and the Musée Mémorial at Caen, which is concerned with an overview of war and occupation). The displays of maps, propaganda, contemporary news reports, and military uniforms are arranged in sectors which roughly correspond to British, Canadian, American, or German military experience. There is a small cinema which shows 25-minute films, drawing together newsreel and archive footage of the Battle, and which complements the main photographic displays. The most impressive of the actual exhibits are to be found among the captured or abandoned hardware—tanks, personnel carriers, artillery, and ammunition—and the extensive display of uniforms.

To the south of Bayeux the **Abbaye de Mondaye** can be reached along the D6, taking a right turn at (8km) **Douet** onto the D33, and then following its northern spur, the D178. On the outskirts of (3km) **Juaye** the abbey rises above a site originally occupied by a small Premonstratensian monastery, founded in 1212, and of which nothing now survives. Between 1706 and 1743 the prior, Eustache Restout, planned, laid out, and painted what must rank as the finest neo-classical church in Normandy. The cruciform piers of the nave support crisply moulded arches and a simple clerestory, with the clerestory sills dropped to within 3.5 metres of the pavement in the choir, beneath which the soft wooden panelling provides seating for 46 monks. The painting, sculpture, and woodwork is contemporary, and the north transept chapel of the Virgin houses an extremely fine terracotta **Assumption**, executed by Verly to the designs of Jean Restout, Prior Eustache's nephew. The conventual quarters are gathered around three sides of the 18C cloister, and the resident monks are happy to conduct visitors to the famous library, reached along a monumental staircase still balustraded with its splendid wrought-iron screen.

Continuing along the D178 takes you past the 18C abbey gatehouse, now the centre of a long farm range, and onto the D572 at (7km) **La Tuilerie**. A quick left turn onto the D73 is much the best route (6km) to the **Château de Balleroy**, bringing you over a ridge and onto the main street of a village which serves the château as an architectural guard of honour. The house itself was built between 1626 and 1636 for Jean de Choisy, Chancellor to Gaston d'Orléans, and is the earliest building firmly documented as being the work of François Mansart. It consists of a three storey central block flanked by two smaller pavilions and surrounded with a now dry moat. Mansart was careful to use the local schist, concentrating the colour and texture which he derived from its reddish-browns and greys in the flattened panels of the major elevation, and the two long outhouses and church which followed on from the main building before 1651. Although the house remained the possession of the Marquises de Balleroy until relatively recently, it was acquired by the American publisher Malcolm Forbes in 1970, who indulged his passion for hot-air ballooning in the grounds. Hence the museum of balloons and ballooning now installed in the southern outbuilding.

The main block is raised above an austere arrangement of formal parterres, laid out by Le Nôtre, which form an admirable contrast to the rich interior decoration. The rooms themselves are disposed behind a central stairwell with salons on both ground and first floors, the lower of which is hung with clumsy hunting scenes painted by Albert Balleroy, the mid 19C owner of the château. The centrepiece of a carefully worked-out programme of interior decoration is to be found in the first floor drawing-room however. Remarkably, this has survived as an unrestored example of a 17C salon, staggering under luxuriant swags of stuccoed fruit and marbled paintwork which form a splendid setting for a series of portraits by **Juste d'Egmont**. These depict the leading players of the French Court—Louis XIII, Mademoiselle Montpensier, Anne of Austria, Philippe d'Orléans, and Marguerite de Lorraine.

The area to the west of Balleroy is mostly given over to what survives of the medieval 'Forêt du Bur', a tract of beech forest now known after the venerable abbey which lies at its heart, the church of St-Vigor at **Cerisy-la-Forêt** (8km along the D13). The oddities of the complex are apparent as soon as you approach the truncated nave, the west front having been walled in when the western four bays were demolished. A 13C arch to the right brings you into the remains of the old abbey precincts, overlooking a field which once supported the cloisters and conventual buildings. Cerisy had suffered badly under its 17C *ad commendam* abbots and after the Revolution the monks' quarters and cloister were sold for building stone. The monastic church was made over to the parish but proved too large for their needs, and in 1812 the west bays of the nave and mid 13C twin-towered west front were pulled down, leaving little more than the pier bases and a foliated blind arcade.

However, a considerable portion came through, and what survives of the church is substantially Romanesque. Cerisy was originally founded c 510 by St-Vigor, but having lapsed was refounded by Duke Robert in 1032. In 1034 relics were brought from Jerusalem by Robert's chamberlain, and a new church was started in the following year. This early 11C work was probably confined to the choir, which has been subsequently replaced, and the earliest surviving work is to be found in the three bay **nave**. This is thought by most authorities to date from the late 11C, with a single-arched arcade, double-arched tribune, and triple-arched clerestory wall-passage. The chevron-moulded tribune arches are richer to the north, where two carry studded relieving arches, but with a judicious disregard for stylistic or iconographic unity the capitals of the south arcade are much the more varied. The present **choir and transepts** were completed c 1110, and unusually at so late a date carry a full transept tribune, rebuilt in the 18C to the north and given a delightful 15C balustrade to the south. Unlike most early 12C architecture in Normandy, however, Cerisy persists with the roughly equal proportions of the elevation of St-Etienne de Caen, allowing a spacious tribune in the choir. The 14C apse vault is supported on figured corbels which depict monk-musicians and the simply carved wooden choir stalls were complete by 1400, but the greater part of the abbey's few surviving furnishings are to be found in a small museum to the west.

This is housed in the undercroft of an ambitious two storey **Abbot's Chapel** built c 1260, and amongst the litter of sculptural fragments lies a superb 13C polychromed mitre, part of a larger statue, and sections of a 14C glazed tile pavement. The private chapel above received new tracery and vault bosses after the battle of Formigny in 1450, and the area behind the altar has retained a 15C Nativity cycle painted directly onto the stone. As was often the case the Abbots of Cerisy exercised feudal jurisdiction over the demesnes de Cerisy, dispensing justice from the small '*salle de jugement*' beyond the chapel's west wall. This also acts as a small museum and to the rear of the furniture a rare 12C wooden reliquary chest, denuded of the jewels and enamels with which it was originally decorated, once enshrined the abbey's most precious relic of St-Vigor.

North of Cerisy you can select a number of routes through the small fields and high hedgerows of the Bessin to cross the N13 at **Longueville** (approximately 18km, D145 is the best option for the greater part of the journey). To the north of the main road an attractive small hamlet clusters around the remains of the ancient priory of **Deux-Jumeaux**. A monastery was founded here c 550 and destroyed during a 9C Norse raid, but in the course of the late 11C Deux-Jumeaux became a dependancy of Cerisy-la-Forêt, and it seems likely that the aisleless choir and lower stage of the crossing tower date from this period. The conventual buildings to the south belong to the 17C and are now incorporated into a farm, but the oddly mutilated western part of the priory church is due to the 18C demolition of the nave and subsequent infilling of many of the openings to the north and west. The north transept is notable for its billet-moulded circular windows, and although the interior is badly decayed it retains a good set of Romanesque volute capitals, alongside a late medieval south chapel and a fragmentary glazed ceramic tomb slab.

From here the N13 speeds east to Bayeux bypassing (5km) the site of the **Battle of Formigny**, where on 18 April 1450 a French army under the command of the Comte de Clermont defeated Thomas Kiriel's English troops, and evicted the English from Normandy. Clermont erected a small chapel alongside the old road west of Formigny, which he had dedicated to St-Louis in 1486, and whose modest interior accommodates a few trophies of battle. 9km further east, at **Tour-en-Bessin**, one of the finest parish churches in Basse-Normandie lies beneath an octagonal stone spire, visible for miles from the north or east though easily overlooked as you approach from the west.

The Romanesque nave was deprived of its aisles in 1751 but the 12C **west portal** still dazzles with its complex display of geometric ornament, arranged around a plaque depicting the Apostles, Peter, James, and John. The transepts and spire were added at the beginning of the 13C and open onto a **choir** which is quite astonishingly inventive for so rural a parish church. Though little known this is one of the more significant early 14C choirs in northern France, consisting of two bays with a squared eastern wall. Two slender freestanding piers create a sort of triumphal screen across this east wall, allowing the architect to cant the windows at the angles, and play elaborate games with the vaulting. The delicacy and spatial ingenuity of the choir is further enhanced by a wall-passage which runs behind a continuous balustrade above the high dado. The dado is also embellished with an engaging cycle of the Labours of the Month above the stalls to the south, and a carefully worked pair of piscinas. Unusually for a French church the officiating clergy were also provided with a three bay sedilia which reinforces the suspicion that the general design of the church owes much to English West Country practice. The choir finally acquired a quirky postscript in the shape of two late medieval plaques depicting Christ in Judgement and the Torments of Hell jammed between the mullions of the north-western dado arcade.

An excursion into the prosperous country of the western Bessin might begin at **Rucqueville** (8km east on the N13 as far as St-Léger, 2km north on the D82). Just below the road as you pass through the village, the tiny church of **St-Pierre** (key next door if locked) houses what may be the earliest set of Romanesque historiated capitals in Normandy. These are grouped around the crossing and, clockwise from the north-west, depict—the Flight into Egypt, a Combat, Addorsed Lions, the Ascent of the Soul, the Adoration of the Magi, a Tonsured Cleric and Angel, Corinthian-derived Acanthus, and the Incredulity of Thomas. They are quite unprecedented in Normandy though their appearance in a minor parish church may be explained by Rucqueville being in the possession of Turstin Haldup, the founder of Lessay, at the likely date of their execution. The unusual Ascent of the Soul is most readily paralleled in northern Spain however (at Jaca for instance), and suggests a date of c 1100 and an awareness of the sculptural styles of the pilgrimage roads to Compostela.

From Rucqueville continue along the D82 for 1km until a left turn onto the D158C brings you to the **Château de Brécy**. The main house was built shortly before 1650 as a simple two storey block surmounted by dormer windows, which alternate rounded with pedimental forms. There is a slightly later entrance gate, which glories in a thickly carved repertoire of acanthus scrolls and fruitful abundance, but the greatest interest is to be found in the **formal gardens**. It is thought these were created to celebrate the marriage of François Lebas to Catherine Roger in 1653, their family initials L and R entwined in the wrought-iron gate standing at the head of the uppermost terrace. Their son married into the Mansart family in 1685 and, given the great friendship enjoyed by these two families during the 1650s, the design of the garden, as well as the gatehouse, is usually attributed to François Mansart. If so he is revealed as a master of the mannerist garden, creating formal lawns and parterres which are terraced across five levels, and divided by richly balustraded walls and urn-capped revetments. Seen from the house the terraces give the illusion of rising evenly and continuously, but the gardens are full of perspective tricks of which the wonderful reversal of curved steps in the middle flight, over-looked by a pair of deeply drilled whiskered lions is merely the most blatant.

West of the house a small medieval church acted as a family chapel, with a separate parishioners' entrance via the 13C western porch. The timber roof is modern but the greater part of the stonework at least is 13C, and much altered as a result of a locally popular 17C pilgrimage attracted by the curing waters of the walled spring to the north of the church.

2km north of the Château de Brécy, along the D158C, the remains of the medieval priory of **St-Gabriel-Brécy** lie towards the edge of a village to which it lent its name. The priory is now used as a horticultural college, and successive building phases have left the complex arranged as an irregular rectangular court to which a monumental 13C gatehouse gives entry. A priory was founded here by Richard, Comte de Creully, in 1058 and placed under the authority of La Trinité at Fécamp, an affiliation doubtless inspired by Richard's son, Vital, who enjoyed the life of a monk at Fécamp before William the Conqueror appointed him Abbot of Westminster.

Nothing survives of the 11C church, and successive waves of construction and subsequent demolition have left a peculiar group of buildings, of which the church, south-west precinct tower, and refectory are the most significant. The **church** has lost its nave and transepts but the aisled two bay choir and apse is the most ornate mid-12C sanctuary in BasseNormandie. The arches carry chevron moulding and an outer frieze of palmettes, while the stringcourses are cable-moulded and the apse arcade crawls with beak-head ornament. In addition, the wall beneath the triforium stringcourse is reserved for some fantastically reordered second cousin to a Classical egg and dart frieze. This decorative luxuriance was broken by a three light window inserted into the apse during the 14C, and a pseudo-sexpartite vault, comparable to that at La Trinité de Caen, which though improvised is a little later than the main elevation. The interior has been comprehensively stripped but a 15C effigy and Romanesque piscina have returned to grace the unnaturally stark spaces, and the altar reuses an upturned Merovingian tomb slab.

To the north-west the students have planted a herb garden on the site of the original kitchen garden next to the 15C twin-aisled refectory which forms its western border. A slightly later tower gives access to the upper chamber of this refectory, known as the Salle de Justice, whose magnificent fireplace of 1615 is engraved with graffiti depicting three caravels. St-Gabriel was certainly the seat of a priory court but pressure on space, as well as uncertain demand, lent a dual purpose to the south-western precinct tower. This was erected in the late 15C and is called the **Tour de Justice**, combining a prison in the lowest storey with a defensive retreat for the monks above.

From St-Gabriel the D35 takes you (2km) to the handsome Caen stone village of **Creully**, set above a sharply defined ridge overlooking the valley of the River Seulles. The early 12C church in the market square was so ferociously recut during a 19C 'restoration' as to have been utterly denatured, and now stands as a sad relic of 19C 'Romanesque Correctness'. Happily a gate to the north of the church gives onto the silhouette of broken towers and battlements that outline the **Château de Creully** (open during July and August only). This was originally fortified by Henry I and given to his illegitimate son, Robert of Gloucester. The enceinte wall is largely 12C and you can make out, particularly to the west, that above a batter wall the square central block retains much of the 12C masonry which saw it elevated as the main keep. The square tower to the north was added in 1358 and the grandest of the vertical accents, the high polygonal tower, during the 15C. In the 1530s, however, the whole complex was transformed into a comfortable and sunny 16C mansion by the simple expedient of adding a gracefully pilastered semicircular 'tourelle', and knocking steep windows through the thick walls and into the central block. Although Colbert bought the château in 1650 he seems to have left little mark on the fabric, and the most significant internal features remain the two 12C vaulted chambers at the base of the old keep.

From Creully take the D22 to (2km) **Pierrepont** where a left turn onto the D141 brings you to (3km) **Fontaine-Henry**. The village took its name from the 13C lord of the Manor of Fontaine, Henry de Tilly, who extended an earlier fortified site overlooking the valley of the Mue c 1250. Parts of this complex survive as the underpinning to the startling pitches and roofs of the Renaissance **Château de Fontaine-Henry** (open afternoons only, closed Tues. and Fri.). The earlier castle was acquired by the Harcourt family and, following its partial destruction during the Hundred Years War, a wonderfully piecemeal rebuilding programme was instigated. The lower storey of the mid 13C work was banked and revetted so that the six bay vaulted lower hall and adjacent cellars (signposted Salles Basses) could serve as a substructure for what became a vastly expanded château. Work began in 1450 and continued periodically until 1537 when the house was effectively complete, though a terrace and gallery were added to the rear in the early 19C. Within this prolonged building campaign you can detect sharply differentiated architectural styles, running like a series of vertical tidemarks from right to left as you face the main façade. The earliest work is confined to the gable wall and squared stairtower, which is both austere and eminently defensible, but these practical throwbacks to English occupation soon gave way to the balustraded flamboyance of the narrow central range. This is late 15C and runs as far as a second tower, beyond which a distinct building break marks an equally distinct change of architectural language. Here the shallow pilasters sport cartouches of intertwined urns and masks alongside roundels of François I and his wife, and date from the second decade of the 16C. Around the corner paired columns frame tall windows, above whose lintels rise busts of Judith and Moses, while Adam and Eve lean forward from an illusionistic window. This northern wing was finally completed in 1537 and given a superb slate roof, pitched at 75 degrees to soar above all else, and in total higher than the main elevation itself.

The freestanding **chapel** to the south also formed part of the 13C castle but was extensively remodelled during the 1530s, when a low columnar-supported ceiling was inserted into the nave, breaking across the earlier window lines and creating a private upper chapel.

The interior was mostly furnished in the 17th and 18C and you enter by what was the main kitchen, lined with three splendid chimneys. Beyond this, in the Grand Salon, are paintings by Poussin and Philippe de Champaigne, along with a piece of serious whimsy—a painting by Mignard of the child Louis XIV as the God of War.

If you continue south past the gates of the château the gently winding road makes its way to (2km) **Thaon**, justifiably renowned for the decorative splendour of its Romanesque parish church of **St-Pierre**. (At the time of writing the church was closed for restoration, though it is hoped it will reopen in early 1993.) This is gloriously situated on the banks of an idling stream, surrounded by woods and cow pasture, and is reached along a track which rolls down from the Fontaine-Henry road just before you enter the village proper. As it now stands the church consists of a long aisleless rectangle, surmounted by a pyramidally-roofed central tower and articulated with a dense profusion of chequered billet mouldings and fantastical corbels. It is undated though you can easily distinguish three architectural campaigns which rapidly followed on from each other.

The base and lowest register of the central tower is the earliest extant part of the building, its capitals comparable to those of the crypt of Bayeux cathedral, suggesting a date in the 1060s or '70s. This received a narrow two bay choir c 1100 with a flat east end and tall exterior blind arcading, the whole being narrower in relation to the tower on the north side than it is to the south. Finally, c 1120–30, the south wall of the choir was reconstructed, extending the structure several metres to the south, and the nave built. Unfortunately the aisles fell into disrepair during the 18C and were demolished, leaving the capitals half-visible around the blocking stones used to seal the church. These capitals have been simply and effectively varied, and together with that virtuosic display of chequered pattern and blind arcading which enlivens the exterior elevation of the clerestory, constitute an impressive body of Romanesque ornament. Above this the roof is supported by a run of figured corbels which clamour for attention, and amply reward both the casual visitor and the specialist.

From Thaon you can follow the D83 south to (12km) **Norrey-en-Bessin**, its central square endowed with a breathtakingly accomplished **parish church** (the key can be obtained from Mr Yves Hué at the Marie in St-Manvieu-Norrey, Tel. 31 80 70 38). The core of the building is to be found in the choir and transepts, which are treated as a miniaturised great church and draw extensively on the language of the choirs of Rouen and Coutances cathedrals. The whole eastern limb is of a piece and dates from the mid 13C, with double columnar piers around the apse hemicycle, a 'Chartrain' triforium, and a low clerestory wall-passage. Badly damaged in 1944 the building has been carefully restored with the new stonework precisely emulating the original richly moulded profiles. The relief sculpture is extremely elaborate, encrusting the frieze above the aisle dado with a frenzied band of inhabited vinescroll, richly worked foliage, and animal masks. There is a lively account of the Judgement of Solomon and Adoration of the Magi in the north aisle, and a fine pair of musicians flanking an ambulatory window to the east. The nave is earlier, aisleless and of a far more modest cast of mind, but the overall consistency of purpose and confidence with which such small spaces are handled offers a salutary object-lesson to historians of the 13C.

13

The Côte de Nacre: Pegasus Bridge to Isigny-sur-Mer

ROAD (81km): Pegasus Bridge (Bénouville); D514, 4km Ouistreham; 6km Lion-sur-Mer; 9km Bernières-sur-Mer; 16km Arromanches-les-Bains; 11km Port-en-Bessin (D514/D206, 5km Etréham); 10km St-Laurent; D517, 4km Vierville-sur-Mer; D514, 11km Grandcamp-Maisy; 10km Isigny-sur-Mer.

The stretch of coast between the estuary of the Orne and the great salt marshes of the Baie des Veys has become known as the Côte de Nacre (Mother-of-Pearl coast), reflecting the propensity of the shallow reefs and rock pools to nurture an abundant supply of shellfish. Towards its extremities the estuaries of the Orne and Vire distribute their silt across a wide area, creating a landscape of mudflats and dunes, which give way to low, scrubby coastal hills where vegetation has begun to consolidate the sand. The central reaches, around Arromanches and Port-en-Bessin, possess a very different character and are overshadowed by dramatically fissured cliffs where the chalks and flint of the Bessin give way to the sea. These areas are linked by a common theme, cultural, historical, and topographical, in that all 70km of shoreline from Riva-Bella westwards to

Grandcamp glory in an almost uninterrupted strand of golden sand. It was this which first encouraged the growth of the small seaside resorts which hug the coast in a succession of '*sur-mers*' and lend a brighter face to the older market towns just inland. The larger resorts around Courseulles and Lion-sur-Mer remain popular with Parisian holidaymakers, while local visitors flock to the fishing ports of Port-en-Bessin and Grandcamp during fine weekends. And it is the beaches which have seered a place in the modern consciousness, since this stretch of coast has become inevitably fused with the events of D-Day. The suggested itinerary is thus much concerned with battle, though it should be pointed out that the text largely confines itself to what can be seen, and it is recommended that any visitor with a serious interest in Operation Overlord use this in conjunction with one of the more specialised accounts of June 1944. A few titles are given in the suggestions for Further Reading on page 24.

After the Allied Joint Planning Staff finally decided that the invasion of Normandy would take place on 6 June 1944, D minus 1 (5 June) witnessed the gathering of ships from the 'forming-up' areas in the western Channel before nightfall, in preparation for a night crossing through the mine-swept channels. The first air offensive consisting of 1056 bombers was on the wing before midnight, and both the British 6th Airborne Division, and the American 82nd and 101st Airborne Divisions had landed to the east of the Orne and Cotentin respectively by 02.30 on 6 June at the latest. The Western (US) Task Force began landing on Utah and Omaha Beaches at 06.30 and the Eastern (British) Task Force scrambled ashore Gold, Sword, and Juno Beaches at approximately 07.30.

The German 7th Army was initially slow to react. The 716th Division was taking the threat posed by the British 6th Airborne Division's paratroopers seriously by 01.30, and Rommel's Chief of Staff was told at 02.15 that engine noises could be heard off the coast of the Cotentin, but it was not until 06.00 that it was realised that the increasingly frantic reports from along the coast might portend something more than a series of nocturnal raids. Two Panzer regiments from the 21st Panzer Division were called up to move on the 6th Airborne Division around Pegasus Bridge, and two divisions were moved into the field against the American Airborne Divisions around Ste-Mère-Eglise, but mostly it was left to the coastal defence forces to at least hold the immediate hinterland. This they did with varying degrees of success, with the fighting around Omaha Beach perhaps the bloodiest and most desperate. Nevertheless by the evening of D-Day the beaches themselves had been taken, and a string of inland villages liberated, creating a cushion between Omaha Beach and Colleville, and extending south of the eastern sector beaches to Creully and Douvres- la-Délivrande. The situation was still precarious, particularly so around Omaha Beach, and the 6th Airborne Division's hold on the east bank of the Orne looked as though it would crack, but a foothold had been gained. Churchill subsequently described it as 'the most difficult and complicated operation that has ever taken place', and by nightfall, quite astonishingly, over 130,000 troops and their assorted stores, vehicles, weaponry and ammunition had been landed. The stage was set for the anticipated and much desired build-up to be launched. All this was not achieved without loss, and the cemeteries of this coast contain, among those who died in the subsequent Battle for Normandy, the graves of the 2500 Allied lives lost on 6 June 1944.

One might see evidence of the earlier elements of the D-Day campaign at **Pegasus Bridge**, some 10km downstream of Caen. One of the strategic objectives of the British 6th Airborne Division was to isolate Caen from the coast by obtaining command of the ship canal, silencing the Merville battery to the east, and capturing the bridges over the Orne river and canal at **Bénouville**. At 22.00 on the night of 5 June and under the command of Major Howard, the gliders and paratroopers of the 6th Airborne Division landed on the right bank of the Orne, having been blown well east of the planned landing areas by high winds and, more crucially, dispersed across a wide tract of ground separating Troarn from the Orne. This had the unintentional effect of confusing the German 716th Division's commanders who failed to realise until 01.30 that paratroopers had landed in force. By this time Howard's forces had taken the bridge at Bénouville and, regrouping, managed to silence the Merville battery by 04.30. These early successes were the prelude to some of the grimmest fighting encountered in the first few days of the campaign, and the Airborne Division was soon forced onto the defensive, managing to retain the position as the artillery of the British I Corps was deployed in their favour. Nevertheless the area upstream of the bridge offered the German forces a network of strong defensive positions, and the northern approaches to Caen became the *bête-noire* of British Divisional commanders, offering a continuous barrage of fierce resistance well into August.

In honour of the initial action the Bénouville bridge has been renamed after the divisional insignia of the Airborne troops—the Winged Pegasus. And where the bridge touches the west bank the first house to be liberated in France, the famous café of Mme-Gondrée, continues a worthy tradition which dictates that free drinks must be offered to anyone who took part in the airborne assault of the night of 5–6 June 1944. In addition there is a small museum a little further inland, the **Musée de Pegasus Bridge**, which recounts the story of this action with models explaining the dropping zones, and displays of military uniforms and weapons.

North of Bénouville the D154 tracks the west bank of the canal as far as the once important port of (4km) **Ouistreham**. The construction of a deep canal capable of taking ships of up to 25,000 tons has compromised Ouistreham's role as the ancient port of Caen, and though the car ferry service to Portsmouth has reinvigorated the lower basin the greater part of the harbour has been given over to yachts and pleasure boats. At the very mouth of the river the town has merged with the seaside resort of **Riva-Bella**, renowned as the 6 June landing ground for Captain Kieffer's 4th French Commando Brigade. A monument at the edge of the town commemorates the role of the French commandos, and a small museum in the Place Alfred Thomas has gathered together a collection of photographs, documents, and memorabilia from the action.

Further inland, in the old centre of Ouistreham, the 12C parish church of **St-Samson** stands as a reminder of the town's significance as a medieval port. The foundation is early and was made a dependency of the abbey of La Trinité at Caen by William and Mathilda, which accounts for the calibre of the building undertaken c 1150. An unfortunate late 19C restoration has wrecked the nave, replacing the original ornament with a lack-lustre arrangement of machine cut stonework only loosely based on the 12C design. The west front failed to attract so radical an 'improvement' however, and remains one of the more impressive Romanesque parish church façades in an area notable for its inventive displays of geometric decoration.

To the west of Ouistreham the D514 courses through the most concentrated stretch of beach resorts to cling to the Côte de Nacre. As the main coast road it also retains this designation for the whole of the 66km to

Grandcamp, and unless otherwise specified this is the road referred to in the text. The eastern coastal reaches, between the Orne estuary and Lion-sur-Mer, became operationally known as **Sword Beach** during 1944, and were provided with an artificial sea wall off **La Brèche d'Hermanville** where the old French battleship, *Courbet*, was scuttled. There is an imposing Allied war memorial on the seafront, beyond which the otherwise drab resort merges with the more agreeable promenade at (6km) **Lion-sur-Mer**.

Further west, in the Canadian sector, **Juno Beach** more or less centred on Courseulles-sur-Mer, though there was much activity to the east, along the urban strand which runs from Langrune to Bernières. Away from the seafront the old centre of **Langrune** pivots around the unexpectedly handsome 13C tower of the parish church, crowned by a splendid Norman spire whose octagonal faces are punched with foil figures designed to lessen the wind resistance of the tower.

A comparable, and closely related, tower and spire is to be found 5km west at **Bernières-sur-Mer**, where the base rises two full stages clear of the nave roof, embellished by the elongated blind lancets which are the stock-in-trade of 13C tower design. The octagonal spire here is unpierced, but a date of c 1220 would place Bernières at the forefront of the burgeoning Basse-Normand interest in towers and spires. The nave, though over-restored during the late 19C, retains some of its splendid original architecture—namely the four eastern bays, with their fully alternating piers and pseudo-sexpartite vault (a vault where the intermediate transverse ribs support a section of wall which intersects with the webbing at right-angles, rather than forming an arched lunette at the head of the wall). This probably dates from the second quarter of the 12C, and was extended westwards by two bays during the late 12C.

The choir is an equally composite structure, with two mid 13C western bays and two early 14C eastern bays, but it is dominated by an accomplished high altar in the style of Louis XIV, dating in fact from the late 18C and the reign of Louis XVI. There is also, in the north choir aisle, an intriguing panel painting of 1570, describing the Crucifixion with a heavy and carefully deliberated perspective foreshortening.

The next resort you come to, **Courseulles-sur-Mer**, was an old fishing port on the estuary of the River Seulles, famous for its oyster beds, but has been almost entirely redeveloped since 1944. A monument by the aquarium recalls the visit of Général de Gaulle to the landing beaches on 14 June 1944—one of a succession of VIPs who used the supply base at Courseulles, before the establishment of the Mulberry harbour at Arromanches made the crossing less hazardous. These also included Winston Churchill on the 12 June, and King George VI on the 16th. To the west (5km) **Ver-sur-Mer** is a pleasant village. At its crossroads is a memorial to the British regiments who fought in this sector, forged in the shape of a ship's anchor, and where a left turn leads to the parish church of **St-Martin**. This carries an impressive late 11C tower in four storeys, though sadly the sculpture has gone, to be replaced by an undistinguished post-medieval tympanum depicting St Martin dividing his cloak to give to a beggar.

Between Ver-sur-Mer and St-Côme the D514 straddles a low ridge, throwing off views of the sweeping sands of **Gold Beach** before rising to the beautifully situated Romanesque church of (7km) **St-Côme-de-Fresné**. West of the church, and just before the road drops down towards Arromanches, a *table-d'orientation* affords a magnificent panorama of the massive, crumbling breakwaters of the 'Mulberry' harbour which became affectionately known as **Port Winston**. The need for an infrastructure of artificial harbours was recognised at an early stage in the preparations for D-Day, and two sites were chosen—one to serve the Western (US) Task Force off St-Laurent, on Omaha Beach, and a larger facility here, off the coast of Arromanches, to serve the Eastern (British) Task Force. The Mulberry harbour at St-Laurent had to be written off after the tempestuous storm of 19–22 June 1944 (nerve-racking days for the Allied forces, and often described in the official histories as 'the great set-back'. It was the most violent storm to have hit the Channel for 40 years). The main break-water at Port Winston held however, and work continued on building up its capacity, so that by 30 June 850,000 men, 149,000 vehicles, and 570,000 tons of stores had been shipped across the Channel to Normandy, more than half of it passing through Arromanches. Work began immediately after D-Day, when 18 old merchant ships and a cruiser crossed the Channel under their own steam and were scuttled by their crews nose to tail on the rocky shoals, known infamously as the Rochers du Calvados. Then, from 9–18 June, huge concrete caissons, each known as a 'Phoenix', were towed from southern England at a sedate three knots, arranged as three sides of a rectangle, filled with water, and sunk. The largest of these weigh up to 7000 tons and are 67 metres long, but the most enduring testimony to their effectiveness is witnessed by the survival, through almost half a century of winter gales, of more than 40 of the original complement of 115.

All this is well illustrated in **Arromanches-les-Bains**, where the **Musée du Débarquement** houses a small film theatre which runs a copy of the official Admiralty film, detailing the actual construction and assembly of the Mulberry harbour. The museum is situated on the seafront of an otherwise unremarkable resort and has been handsomely laid out, drawing on the resources of the modelmakers to provide a keen sense of the shape and character of the harbour installations here.

To the west the road climbs past (3km) the robust 13C pyramidal spire of the church at **Manvieux** before intersecting with the old crossroads at (3km) **Longues-sur-Mer**. The village's modern and medieval emplacements straddle the road, with the ruined abbey of **Ste-Marie-de-Longues** to the south (open Thurs afternoons only) retaining its 13C choir and north transept, along with the refectory, chapter house, and three splendid late 13C tombstones commemorating the lords of Argouges. To the north the Longues coastal battery, a key emplacement within the German Atlantic Wall, survives in surprisingly good condition. Four ferro-concrete case-mates house the 152mm guns, which were directed by a range-finder from the command post set in a two-storey bunker above the cliffs. They fired in anger on 6 June 1944 when their 18,000 metre range was turned on the American cruiser, *Arkansas*, and British command ship, *Bulolo*, before the combined firepower of HMS *Ajax* and the French cruiser *Georges Leygues* silenced the guns. The battery had been abandoned by the time Allied troops moved up to take control of the position on 7 June, and although one gun had been knocked out by a direct hit and a second casemate damaged, the result of several near-misses with high explosive shells had been to wreck the sighting gear and radar units, effectively disabling the guns.

Longues lies towards the western edge of Gold Beach, but the responsi-bilities of the Corps commanders ran as far as the gap in the marly chalk cliffs where the fishing village of (5km) **Port-en-Bessin** lies. Its situation is reminiscent of the smaller coastal resorts of the Pays de Caux, fringed by cliff walks which offer extensive views of the surrounding coastline, and it was accordingly given a high priority on D-Day. The German resistance was stronger than anticipated and the town was not finally cleared of enemy snipers until the night of 7 June, but despite a heavy naval barrage the major part of the town remained relatively undamaged. In consequence it thrives as an attractive small working port, mustering a sizeable fishing fleet which lands scallops from the Baie de la Seine, or whiting, mullet, and skate from the coast of Devon, gathering the boats in a harbour along the Quai Félix Fabre. Plans were put in hand to build a naval base at Port in the late 17C, and though little came of it Vauban's circular defensive tower of 1694 still protects the right flank of a splendid outer harbour, sheltered within two pincer-like granite jetties.

Inland from Port-en-Bessin the village of **Etréham** (5km along the D206) centres around a 15C manorial farmstead, splendidly framed by the banked walls of the parish cemetery opposite. The parish church itself boasts a weathered, and curious, late 12C west front, and a gable-topped 13C bell tower supported on the interior by four grotesque corbel heads from which the central vault ribs spring.

To the west of Port-en-Bessin lay the American sector, running from Ste-Honorine to the distant beaches of the south-east Cotentin, and most readily approached from (7km) **Colleville-sur-Mer**. The village church, with winged chimeras on its southern tympanum, is one of the few medieval buildings to have survived in an area scarred by perhaps the bloodiest of all memories of the D-Day landings. Just before the church, a narrow side road leads down towards the beach before curving back along the shallow scrubland formed by the collapsing cliff faces, and rising to a monument erected in honour of the US 5th Engineer Special Brigade. The monument stands above a half-ruined blockhouse (part of German strongpoint Wn 62), and surveys the gently curving strand of the whole of **Omaha Beach**.

It is easy to get a measure of the problems confronting the 5th US Corps from such a vantage point. For in contrast to the beaches to either side of Omaha, the shoreline is protected from the farmland beyond by a steep grassy bluff which rises over 30 metres, and is riddled with trenches and hollows. This natural disadvantage was compounded by an element of appalling bad fortune. Shortly before the landings, and unbeknown to the Allies, the German 352nd Division had been moved from St-Lô to the coast here in order to practice a series of defence manoeuvres. In consequence, at 06.30 on the morning of 6 June the first American troops to wade ashore were met by a fully armed and mobile front-line Infantry Division. As the 29th US Infantry Division on the right flank and the 1st US Infantry Division on the left tried to move into position on the shore, they were met by a withering volume of German fire and, catastrophically short of their own supporting tanks and artillery, were pinned down on the beach itself. By 07.30 it was realised that the situation demanded any support that could be mustered, and a flotilla of destroyers closed in on the beach at speed and opened up on the German positions at close range. By 09.30 Strongpoint Wn 62 was finally knocked out by naval fire and the Colleville gap was stormed, but the casualties were heavy, and the fighting remained murderous throughout the day. A much quoted remark of Colonel Taylor designed to rally his troops may catch something of the conditions on the beach: 'Two kinds of people are staying on this beach, the dead, and those who are going to die—now let's get out of here'.

It was considered fitting that the dead should be honoured by the grandest of the Norman war cemeteries, and the **American Military Cemetery** lies just to the west, overlooking the beach from the clifftops, wherein are buried 9386 of the American servicemen who fell during the Battle for Normandy, many on that dreadful first day. It is an impressive sight, maintained with the precision of the White House lawns, and pivoting around a circular chapel whose saucer dome carries a mosaic symbolising America Blessing Her Departing Sons.

To the west of Colleville, beyond St-Laurent, the D517 offers the more interesting route to (6km) **Vierville-sur-Mer**, hugging the beach as far as the monument to the American National Guard, before looping back into the village itself. Although substantially restored after 1944, the church here supports a fine 13C tower and spire, built in a straightforwardly local style, with a good set of 14C capitals in the now aisleless south nave arcade.

Between Vierville and Grandcamp the road tracks inland, passing the magnificent gateway and round, fortified stair towers of the late 16C manorial farmhouse of **Englesqueville**. Half a kilometre before, by another commodious and handsomely portalled farmhouse, the D125 twists a pleasant back route to Grandcamp, via the dumpy early 13C spire of (1km) **Englesqueville-la-Percée**. This sits in the midst of a splendidly unreconstructed farming village, boasting a couple of grand 16th and 17C farmhouses, whose main yards are graced with the decorated high-arched gateways which were the preferred tradition of the Bessin. The D194 continues this inland loop to Grandcamp, curving around the impressive 13C choir of (3km) **Cricqueville-en-Bessin**, before sloughing through the marshy fields south of the coastal bluff which were flooded by Rommel in 1944 as part of his Atlantic Wall improvements. Grandcamp is then reached along a last kilometre of the D514.

The direct route stays close to the coast, offering a glimpse of the roofs and towers of the Renaissance château at **St-Pierre-du-Mont**, before a right turn along a short track brings you to a rocky outcrop known as the **Pointe du Hoc**. A natural stronghold commanding 180 degree views over the Côte de Nacre, the rock was strongly fortified by the German forces in 1943, forming one of the larger naval batteries in the Atlantic Wall. The task of taking this position on 6 June 1944 fell to a force of 225 Rangers under the command of Lieutenant-Colonel James Rudder. In effect his mission was akin to scaling a fully armed and fortified feudal castle, and he trained his men on the cliffs of the Isle of Wight. In spite of the intense enemy fire which killed 15 of his troops on disembarkation, and led to the abandonment of the initial plan to scale both sides of the headland simultaneously, the first Ranger reached the top within five minutes of landing. By 07.30 they began the brutal job of clearing enemy troops from the intersecting passages of what they had discovered were in fact dummy casemates, the big guns having been moved half a mile to the rear several weeks previously. Not only did the Rangers thus have two sites to deal with, but by 09.00 they attracted a sizeable counter-attack. The fighting here was extraordinarily intense, and by the time the Rangers were relieved at midday on 8 June no more than 90 remained.

There is a small museum on the seafront at (5km) **Grandcamp-Maisy**— the **Musée des Rangers**—devoted to retelling the history of the corps, from its formation as a specialist American unit in Ulster in June 1942, until its virtual obliteration between 6 and 8 June 1944. The promenade on which the museum is situated is pleasant enough, and turns south to meet the old fishing quays, but like so many of the coastal settlements hereabouts Grandcamp was badly damaged in 1944 and has been unimaginatively redeveloped. West of the town the vast estuarial salt-marshes of the Baie des Veys separate the Bessin from the Cotentin peninsula, and the road finally cuts south to join the N13 above (10km) **Isigny-sur-Mer**. Renowned for its creameries, over 60 per cent of the town was destroyed during the bitter attack of 8 June 1944, and excepting a late 18C château since adopted as the **Hôtel-de-Ville** little of distinction survived. Much else has changed besides, for with the reclamation of the mudflats and marshes to the southern end of the Baie des Veys, Isigny's traditional role as a refuge for the 'fen tigers', who made their living from fowling, banditry and guiding travellers across the wastes, has been usurped, though it remains the main gateway to the Cotentin.

14

Cherbourg, Valognes, and the Northern Cotentin

ROAD (251km): Valognes (D2, 5km Colomby; 8km St-Sauveur-le-Vicomte); D902, 15km Quettehou; D1, 2km St-Vaast-la-Hougue; 11km Barfleur; D901, 27km Cherbourg (N13/D352, 10km Tollevast); D45, 31km Auderville; D901, 5km Jobourg; D37/D904, 43km Barneville-Carteret; D903/D50, 8km Portbail; D650, 23km Lessay; D900, 10km Périers; D971, 19km Carentan; N13/D913, 10km Ste-Marie-du-Mont; D913, 6km La Madeleine and Utah Beach; D421, 14km Crisbecq; D14/D15, 10km Ste-Mère-Eglise; N13, 10km Montebourg; 7km Valognes.

The culture and landscape of Normandy's remote north-western prow sees the province at its most Atlantic, removed from that quiet pastoral efficiency which characterises the eastern and central lands. In part this is due to the shape of the Cotentin peninsula, propelling the Armorican massif sharply northwards into the path of the prevailing oceanic westerlies. But it is a product of the underlying granite as well as of the sea, and it shares its primary formations with those of Brittany, lending a harder edge to the country. Geologists describe the whole area as Armorican Normandy, extending this description to all those sub-regions in which the principal rocks are impermeable crystalline mica-schists, granites and gneiss. The geology is fundamental to the general appearance of the Cotentin, but the local effects of erosion by water, wind, and ice have conspired to create a subtle and varied landscape which ranges from the lush meadows of the Val de Saire to the wild, wind-blasted heights of the Cap de la Hague.

Agricultural practice along the Vire and Sée valleys has also moulded a distinctive landscape of deep hedgerows, encircling the small pastures with a dense thicket of orchard green. This beautiful country is known as the Bocage and stretches north from Avranches and Mortain as far as St-Lô and the south-western Bessin. It is separated from the northern end of the peninsula by the Cotentin 'Pass', a low-lying plain of marshes and open parkland whose cattle and sheep supply the agricultural markets of Carentan and Périers. This trough of land divides the Cotentin into two dissimilar halves, and the southern reaches are treated in the following chapter.

The north is a considerable area in its own right, and its attractions, along with its population, tend to be widely diffused. As a consequence the itinerary is arranged orbitally, but whether you stay in Cherbourg, Barneville-Carteret, or any one of the smaller towns on the peninsula all the places mentioned are easily accessible by car, though if you are cycling it might be better to keep switching overnight accommodation. As the major road junction and geographical centre of the northern Cotentin Valognes is the obvious place to stay if you intend to spend several days in the region, and is a very much more accommodating town than it at first appears.

VALOGNES. Sadly, more than three-quarters of the town was destroyed in 1944 and the centre has been extensively rebuilt in the austere reticulated vernacular of the region, contrasting the grey local granite with rectangular limestone-dressed windows. The town had in fact been destroyed previously, during the Hundred Years War, and it was the predominantly timber late medieval core which vanished in 1944. As most of the larger stone buildings lay among spacious walled gardens they were less catastrophically affected, and it is still possible to assess the architectural development of the town as it expanded in the 18C. By this date Valognes had become the favoured resort of the Cotentin aristocracy, many of whom built large townhouses to host the salons and dinners which earned the town the self-conscious appellation—Le Petit Versailles.

The centre remains anchored around the Place Vicq-Azir with the parish church of **St-Malo** at its heart, tragically denuded of its late Gothic nave and fanciful lantern tower during General Bradley's assault on Cherbourg at the end of June 1944. The late 15C choir was less badly damaged and has been substantially rebuilt, retaining a fine balustrade which was unusually corbelled out of the wall to create a succession of progressively deeper relief surfaces. The nave and tower which replaced those earlier counterparts are avowedly Modernist, their reinforced concrete derived from the school of thinking which inspired Auguste Perret's rebuilding of Le Havre, but have been provided with a finely judged stained glass window in the south transept to relieve the otherwise stark interior surfaces.

Beneath the church the Rue l'Officialité joins the Rue du Petit Versailles, before crossing the River Merderet to enter the old tanners' precinct. The whole of this medieval quarter was pulled down in the 18C to provide larger garden plots for the town mansions of the gentry. The river, however, had already been revetted and as you follow its picturesque course through, and under, the town there are dozens of projecting rectangular flues which once attached to household latrines, and emptied into its now clear waters. The only 15C stone-built house to have survived here, the Maison du Grand Quartier, presently accommodates the **Musée du Cidre** and luxuriates in an extensive display of rural mashing troughs, stone grinders, casks, jugs, and pails alongside two tremendous wooden cider presses. The house itself was built on a large scale as a dyer's shop, and is modelled not so much on the medieval town workshops common in Haute-Normandie but on the late medieval rural manor houses prevalent locally.

Opposite, on the Rue Barbey d'Aurevilly, the **Hôtel de Beaumont** is both the largest and the finest of the surviving 18C mansions, built for Pierre de Beaumont c 1760 by the architect Raphael de Lozon. To the rear a simple pedimented garden façade complements the landscaped terraces with an arithmetically divided rectangular grid efficiently composed of string-courses and projecting wings. The main façade is more showy, and sports a convex entrance pavilion rippling with classical orders and superposing the Doric with the Ionic.

Returning along the Rue du Petit Versailles you pass a good museum of distillation, the **Musée de l'Eau de Vie**, housed in the 17C Hôtel de Thieuville and twinned with a second smaller collection in the same building devoted to tanning and leatherworking. The **Rue des Religieuses** offers the most concentrated display of 18C building however, with a splendid succession of spacious and crisply detailed houses often, as in the case of the Grand Hôtel du Louvre, giving onto large stabling yards. The best known is the **Hôtel de Granval-Coligny**, built to an H-shaped plan and provided with the elaborate garden front favoured in Normandy.

An interesting afternoon's excursion might take in St-Sauveur-le-Vicomte and Colomby. Both lie on the D2, **Colomby** being 6km south and boasting an unusual 13C parish church. This was built without transepts or aisles—a sleek rectangular hall with a single central tower bay supporting a simple octagonal spire. The tower bay has a marked effect on the interior in that the buttressing necessary to carry the tower and spire projects inwards, and thus divides the west–east axis into two distinct but equal areas, a four bay nave and a four bay choir. The greater part of the surviving statuary is fairly vapid 19C work, but a quantity of more eye-catching late medieval work has been retained with a fine 16C Pietà opposite the south porch, and an accomplished 15C Christ, bound and crowned with thorns, in the tower bay.

Eight kilometres to the south the pleasant fortified town of **Saint-Sauveur-le-Vicomte** lies more or less at the very centre of the peninsula, on a low rise to the west of the River Douve. The seigneurial lords of St-Sauveur generally allied themselves against their immediate feudal overlords, and Néel II's participation in the revolt of the western barons against Duke William in the 1040s was followed by Geoffroy d'Harcourt's championing of the claims of Edward III to Normandy. It was Geoffroy who was also understandably responsible for the north-east enceinte tower of the most impressive surviving monument in St-Sauveur, its great medieval **château**.

This is now the subject of an ambitious programme of restoration which has already stabilised Geoffroy's early 14C enceinte tower and the later 14C barbican. The greater part of the castle was built between 1375 and c 1430, after an Anglo-Navarrese army had seized the town. Edward III made over the castle to Sir John Chandos, who was responsible for building the vast square keep, some 24 metres high and clamped with heavy external buttresses. This now stands between the inner and outer baileys, as by the early 15C two round towers had been linked with the keep to form an inner enceinte wall. The entrance to the inner court takes you beneath a 16C gatehouse, built over the truncated entry towers and known as the Herse. Since Louis XIV had created a hospice within the castle the damage sustained to the complex in 1944 was seen as an opportunity to construct a new Maison de Retraite within the inner court, hence the somewhat discordant architectural effects at the castle's heart. The cemetery was untouched however, and below the western walls you can still gaze on the grave of the now unfashionable 19C author and critic, **Jules Barbey d'Aurevilly**.

Barbey d'Aurevilly divided much of his life between St-Sauveur and Valognes, and in recognition of this and his immense late 19C popularity a bronze bust of the author by Rodin stands before the castle entrance. You can also follow this up at No. 66 Rue Bottin-Desylles where a museum devoted to his memory has been installed in the Aurevilly family home, recalling the life and work of a dandyish author best known for the 'Chevalier des Touches'.

To the east of the town, along the Rue des Petits Pavés de l'Abbaye, the abbey of **St-Sauveur** has become the mother house of the Congregation of

Sisters of St Mary Magdalen Postel, who run a large co-educational college on the site. Mère Postel selected the ruined medieval abbey as a future mother church in 1832, and summoned the architect François Halley to repair and rebuild where necessary. Despite the collapse of the crossing tower in 1842 the enterprise was successful and the church was consecrated in 1855, giving the congregation a permanent home.

The earliest church on the site had been collegiate, but in 1049 Benedictine monks from Jumièges established a monastic community and began work on a new church in 1067. As the early 19C engraving displayed in the nave makes clear, by the time Halley began work little more than one face of the crossing tower, the choir, and the south wall of the nave remained. As such virtually all the stonework in the building is either 19C or post-war though the general shape of the major elements has been retained. The nave was late 11C with square piers, chamfered with recessed quarter-columns at the angles and articulated by attached half-columns on the cardinal faces. The elevation carries a triforium arcade, and a high clerestory which was added after 1451 when a programme of refurbishment was inaugurated which saw a new, and fairly dull, two storey choir completed. The 19C rebuilding was harshly reviewed by Yves Froidevaux, who spent much of his time from 1945–50 repairing the damage sustained during 1944, but this starkness has been in part reversed by the acquisition of a lively and quite splendid 15C wooden altar frontal depicting scenes from the Infancy and Nativity of Christ.

From Valognes the D902 runs north-east to Barfleur, passing the striking 12C octagonal bell tower of (3km) **Tamerville**, whose church shelters a group of decaying Romanesque capitals around the crossing and a 16C polychromed Pietà in the south chapel. Five kilometres further on a left turn takes you through a mossy wood to **Montaigu**, unusual in northern France in that the huge walled enclosure accommodating the village church of St-Martin also houses a medieval ossuary, or bone pit. These were used to maintain the remains of the dead, skeletons and odd bones mostly, on consecrated ground when old or abandoned graves were cleared. Common in England and the Low Countries they are quite an exception in France, and though the rectangular pit here has acquired two medieval statues at the diagonal ends, the original corbelled steps still run up its western face.

Some 8km further east the road rises to the church at **Quettehou**, before descending into the village. Begun with an aisleless nave and choir in the 13C, the building was provided with aisles in the 15C and a tower in the 16C, disturbing those uncluttered qualities evident in the composed windows of the purely 13C choir. From the cemetery the land falls away quite steeply to St-Vaast and the rocky shallows of the coast, all clearly visible on any day when the mist clears. Although the valley of the River Saire is a few miles to the north the whole of this north-eastern corner of the Cotentin has become known as the Val de Saire, its rolling pattern of hills and hollows broken by thick hedgerows. It is the most fertile area of the whole peninsula, with a balmy climate to encourage the growing of early vegetables, and a granite coastline which slides away into the quartzy sands around St-Vaast, and is usually regarded as a distinct sub-region.

The simplest way to explore the coast here is to take the D1 to (2km) **St-Vaast-la-Hougue**, whose picturesque quays reflect the easy co-existence of the fishing port with a yachting harbour. To the right a long breakwater runs away towards the rocks of La Hougue, offering protection to the broad main street and stretching south to the recently restored

Chapelle des Marins the early 12C rump of a parish church whose nave was demolished in the 19C. The breakwater was heavily fortified in 1944, forming a key link in the German Atlantic Wall, but the later relics now seem an unsurprising adjunct to the great 17C defences protecting the harbour. These were built in reaction to the naval disaster of 1692 when a French fleet under the command of Admiral de Tourville, sailing to assist in a landing aimed at reinstating James II, was intercepted and annihilated by an Anglo-Dutch flotilla in the battle of La Hougue. The defeat showed up the inadequacy of the Channel coastal defences and certainly worried Louis XIV's advisers. Benjamin de Combes, a colleague of Vauban, was called in and undertook the construction of two new forts: the first overlooking the oyster-beds on the **Ile Tatihou**, and a second above the rocks of **La Hougue**. Both were begun in 1694 and centred on thickly-walled and vaulted high circular towers, fringed with cannon emplacements and built above independent cisterns. That of La Hougue remains within a military zone but in summer you can take a boat out to the smaller fort on Tatihou.

North of St-Vaast the high banks which protect the D1 from flooding have been planted with tamarisks, which seem to thrive in the salt air particularly above the sandy shallows of the Saire estuary. Just beyond the river bridge a granite outcrop supports a striking configuration of gables and roofs, topped with an octagonal spire, belonging to the church of (3km) **Réville**. The nave is 12C, but successive campaigns added a 13C tower and a late medieval aisled choir to produce a building whose external silhouette is quite memorable, but whose internal spaces bear the marks of a gloomy and over-zealous 19C restoration. From here the D1 winds inland, before cutting back towards the coast at (8km) **Barfleur**.

You regain the sea via the wide main street of Barfleur, the **Rue St-Thomas**, bordered by solid houses of granite whose tall windows and sleek chimneys are best exemplified by No. 16, now the Hôtel Le Conquérant. At the top of the street the **Mairie** gives onto a courtyard with a splendid roofscape originally belonging to the conventual quarters of the Augustinian priory, built in 1739, whilst to east the Rue opens onto the fishing quays of one of the finest small working ports in western Normandy.

Despite its dangerous reefs and strong currents Barfleur was long the major port of the Cotentin, favoured by Romans and Vikings alike, before the Anglo-Norman kings established the town as the principal means of communication between England and Normandy. Tradition has it that William the Conqueror's flagship, the *Mora*, was built here, and it was from Barfleur that Henry I's son and heir, William Atheling, set sail in November 1120, only for his *White Ship* to be blown onto the offshore reefs. William and his sister drowned along with many of the royal court and it was left to the sole survivor, Bérold the butcher, to carry the dismal news to England. 'Jacob did not grieve more bitterly for Joseph' than Henry for his son, and the event soured English court life for the rest of the decade.

Before Edward III razed the town in 1348 Barfleur had a population of around 9000, approximately three times its present number, but it never recovered its earlier medieval pre-eminence and with few exceptions the greater part of the present town was remodelled from 1842–65. This wholesale renewal of the port was responsible for the granite quays and jetties of the fishing harbour, which are the town's livelihood and greatest attraction. None of the medieval buildings have survived, though the low and cruciform church of **St-Nicolas**, perched above the Quai Henri Chardon, has the shape of a modest 13C village church. Surprisingly the choir and transepts belong to the late 17C, and the mid 19C nave did little to alter the aesthetic temper of the building. Its character derives from the larger volumes, rather than from any details of handling, for as it was built of the local granite little carving was attempted, and even the simple dentil-moulded capitals of the choir made use of limestone. There is a fine 16C Pietà in the south transept beneath a decaying Flemish painting of the Annunciation, but the situation of the cemetery to the north is of extraordinary beauty. Sited on the headland it is surrounded by reefs and water, shaded by a tiny cupola over the axial chapel and looking over the inshore fishing smacks, the families of whose crews are buried within its walls.

The direct route from Barfleur to Cherbourg, the D901, is dull but fast, relieved by the handsome outlines of the 13C church at (5km) **Tocqueville**, family home of the 19C historian and philosopher Alexis de Tocqueville, and the curious church of (5km) **St-Pierre-Eglise**. This is predominantly 17C but its bell tower has an early 12C portal which is all that remains of the earlier church.

Just before the D901 picks up the eastern suburbs of Cherbourg a left turn is signposted (14km) Château des Ravelets. This is more properly known as the **Château de Tourlaville** (interior open during July and August only), and was begun in 1562 for Jean II de Ravalet as an essentially rectangular block articulated by four asymmetrically-disposed towers—the two round towers of the main elevation, and the shallow oblong and polygonally accented central stair towers of the rear façade. The latter is called the Tower of the Four Winds and is the main corridor of circulation, its steps elegantly supported by slender columns on high chamfered bases. The late 19C landscapes surrounding the château were decimated by the hurricane of 1987, although the lake, which laps at the rear elevation, gives you an idea of the grandeur of René de Tocqueville's gardens. However, Tourlaville is less known for its Renaissance architecture, good though this is, than for the celebrated scandal of the love of Julien and Marguerite Ravalet.

In 1575 Jean II Ravalet gave the château to his nephew, Jean III, on the occasion of his marriage to Madeleine de la Vigne. The marriage produced eight children, among them Julien, born in 1582, and Marguerite, born in 1586. They were very close throughout childhood, but were separated in March 1600 when Marguerite was married against her wishes to Jean Le Febure, a man 30 years her senior. Julien was sent to Paris, and there followed a series of snatched meetings before Marguerite left Le Febure and was reunited with Julien at Fougères, where they lived secretly for six months. Charged to return to Tourlaville they moved to Paris, where at the insistence of Jean Le Febure they were arrested, tried on counts of incest and adultery and, in spite of Jean III Ravalet's petition for clemency, beheaded in December 1603. There is a celebrated painting of 'Marguerite et ses Amours' in the salon on the first floor, showing her gazing wistfully into space before the main façade of Tourlaville, the legend *'Un me sufit'* above the house. It is usually attributed to Nicolas Mignard but was not painted until 1658 for the new owner of Tourlaville, Charles de Franquetot—though it did him little good, as he was assassinated in the same room in 1661. With this exception the internal decoration is either 19th or 20C and mostly incongruous, though the views from the upper windows over the 16C belfry and later farm buildings to the south are really quite splendid.

A return onto the D901 brings you swiftly into Vauban's 'Channel Inn'—the once great port of **Cherbourg**. Known to the Romans as Coriovallum, the

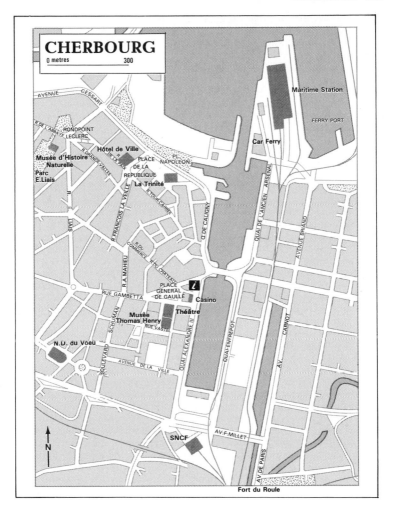

valley in which Cherbourg lies had earlier been settled by the Megalithic peoples of northern France. Fragments of prehistoric monuments have been uncovered beneath the modern town, as have the foundations of 2nd and 3C villas, but the present shape of Cherbourg is almost wholly due to more recent developments. Sunk within the arc of a broad and shallow bay the town was dangerously exposed to north-westerly gales, and was never seriously considered a viable port before Vauban began to proselytise on its behalf. To Vauban its strategic potential, offering easy access to the Atlantic and the possibility of stationing an advance guard for a French fleet fearing English attack, outweighed its physical disadvantages.

Nevertheless it was three-quarters of a century before La Bretonnière designed the first breakwater. Work began in 1776 on a barrier which was intended to stretch 4km from the Pointe de Querqueville to the Ile Pelée, supported by a foundation made up of 90 timber cones which were to be sunk to a depth of 18 metres and filled with rubble and mortar. Early optimism gave way to a sporadic pattern of work as the winter seas scattered or fractured the cones, and it was not until 1853 that the undertaking was complete. It is no longer known how many cones were finally sunk, but the accumulated debris was fashioned by the tidal currents into a stable artificial island which now supports the main *digue*. With the main breakwater complete and moles driven out towards its eastern and western extremities, the outer roads, or Grande Rade, could be used for loading and unloading larger vessels at anchor, while an inner pair of jetties protected the harbour basins themselves. Cherbourg's massive growth as a transatlantic port culminated in 1933 when the dredging of a deep water channel allowed the big liners to berth along the quaysides, rather than leaving them to lie at anchor in the roads and tender their passengers aboard. The contribution of this infrastructure to the Allied campaign during the Battle for Normandy was critical, hence the bitterness of the fighting around Cherbourg in the late June of 1944. When the American First Army finally entered the town on 26 June they were faced with a port whose facilities had been systematically destroyed, and which bristled with mines and booby-traps. Despite this PLUTO (Pipe Line Under The Ocean) was pumping petrol from the Isle of Wight to the town by 12 August, and by early 1945 the harbours were handling a greater tonnage than any other port in mainland Europe.

Despite the demise of the great liners which once plied the Atlantic from its quays, Cherbourg remains a prosperous and attractive town, drawing much of its wealth from the huge nuclear submarine-building sheds of the arsenal. Relatively undamaged in 1944 the old town is made up of a collection of narrow streets, clustered and slanting unexpectedly to provide shelter from the prevailing westerlies. The townscape is predominantly 18C and 19C, its houses built of local schist or slate with stone-dressed window reveals, and stretches from the largest of the open spaces on the Place de la République west to the Rondpoint Leclerc, and south to the Place Général de Gaulle. The latter provides the most handsome of Cherbourg's public spaces, centred around an ambitious 19C fountain and closed to the south by a theatre that epitomises popular French design during the 1880s.

Behind, in the Rue Vastel, the **Musée Thomas Henry** has been housed in a specially constructed cultural centre which opened in 1983. It was founded by Thomas Henry, adviser to the royal museums in Paris, who between 1833 and 1835 gave a collection totalling 163 paintings to the town. Although the museum has subsequently been expanded by substantial bequests of work by Jean François Millet and the local sculptor Armand Le Véel, Henry's original donation forms the core of the displays.

The entrance to the museum proper is on the first floor, the whole of which is given over to temporary exhibitions—a spiral staircase leads to the permanent collections on the floor above. The greater part of the available space is given over to Thomas Henry's collection. Henry was primarily interested in French and Flemish painting, and his acquisition of 17th and 18C Italian paintings seems perfunctory by comparison. But unusually for an early 19C collector he was not averse to buying 15C work when it became available, and the collection opens with three important, and sharply contrasted, paintings from this period—an enthroned **Virgin and**

Child by the **Master of the Legend of St Ursula**, an unusually bulky and disproportionate rendering of the **Entombment** by **Filippo Lippi**, and a magnificent predella panel by **Fra Angelico** showing St Augustine seated in a quattrocento garden wrestling with the question of faith.

These paintings are isolated as a sort of prologue to a display broadly organised according to national schools. The most eye-catching are the Dutch 16th and 17C works, and although **David Tenier's Monkeys' Ball** has become a standard illustration for 20C inn walls its grotesquely populated tavern interior, full of rat-arsed, rat-footed monkeys retains its power to shock as an emblem of the world turned upside down. By contrast **Jan Massys'** portrayal of drunkenness is more straightforwardly menacing. Here called **Joyeuse Compagnie**, it depicts a group of leery-eyed peasants, weaving disconcertingly from right to left. Opposite is a striking portrayal of a woman of unknown identity by the Hague portraitist **Adrien Hanneman**. Of the rest of the Flemish work the allegorical painting by **Hendrik van Balen** and **Jan Brueghel** stands out as a notable co-production of a type popular in early 17C Antwerp, with van Balen responsible for the allegorical figures and Brueghel for the landscape. One of van Balen's pupils, Sir Anthony van Dyck, is represented further on.

An untypical array of southern European painting separates the Flemish from the French 'schools', with **Murillo's Christ on the Road to Calvary** the undoubted highlight. Beyond this you reach the substantial holdings of French 17C–19C work, within which a dark and roughly painted still-life by **Jean-Baptiste Chardin**, **Nicolas Poussin's** unsettling **Pietà**, and an unidentified portrait by **Philippe de Champaigne** can be singled out. In fact taken as a whole the museum has a fine collection of French portaiture, with a slickly professional rendering of the financier **Montmarel and his Wife** by **Hyacinthe Rigaud** but a few feet from one of the heroic images of Revolutionary art—**Girodet's** portrayal of the **Man in a Blue Jacket**.

The museum's collection of the work of **Jean François Millet**, was donated in 1915 by the uncle of Millet's wife, Pauline Ono. Millet was born just down the road in the village of Gréville-Hague in 1814, and after spending several years in Cherbourg departed for Paris to study under Delaroche. The interest of the paintings and drawings on display here is that you can readily compare Millet's early work with the superb small sketches and drawings he did after he had established himself at Barbizon in 1849. The early portraiture reveals a diffident and often clumsy artist, far removed from the active poses and simple shapes of the drawings from the 1850s and 1860s.

North of the museum you can take any one of a number of winding streets to reach the **Place Napoléon** and the beach. The former hosts an equestrian statue of the emperor, erected in 1858 and cast by Le Véel, which resounds with the hopeful despatch—*'J'avais résolu de renouveler à Cherbourg les merveilles de l'Egypte'*. This seems particularly ironic as you turn from the plinth towards the careless indignities all too apparent in the adjacent parish church of **La Trinité**.

The present building stands on the site of a church founded before 1065 by Duke William, though nothing was retained from this earlier structure when rebuilding began in 1412, except for a section of apse wall where it abutted Philippe le Bel's early 14C town fortifications. Building continued throughout the 15C, the three bay choir being completed in 1450 and the transepts and nave before 1504. Although subsequent construction was confined to the addition of a south porch in 1525 and Le Sauvage's insensitive and block-like tower porch of 1823, the church has rarely been out of the hands of the restorers. The combined effects of salt air on delicately carved stonework and changing attitudes to worship, led to the replacement of most of the exterior facing stone in the 17C, the expansion of the north aisle in 1751, and the renewal of the tracery along with the painting and repaving of the nave during the late 19C.

The most striking feature of the church is its nave, whose columnar piers are backed by short colonettes offering independent support to the aisle vaults. Above the arcade a balustrade forms the ground for a series of carved panels, representing the Passion of Christ to the south and the Dance of Death to the north. By 1784 these were reported to be worn and mutilated and they were eventually hacked out to be replaced by the present sequences, which were based on drawings of the originals. Stylistically they do not ring true, but they suffice to give an idea of the sort of narrative imagery that once featured here. One further battered remnant has come down to us, for embedded in the south-eastern crossing pier are five Nottingham alabaster panels. The centrepiece is an Adoration of the Magi but the now disparate arrangement would appear to be made up of fragments of a late 14C altarpiece.

West of the church the Place de la République gives way to the Rue de la Paix and eventually, through a gateway on the Rue de l'Abbaye, affords access to the **Parc Emmanuel Liais**. These secluded gardens, planted with semi-tropical trees and shrubs and murmuring with fountains, are a delightful place in which to while away the heat of a summer afternoon. When tired of the tranquil shade you can also retreat to the main house of Liais' 19C estate. Liais himself was a naturalist and mayor of Cherbourg who left his property and collections to the town in 1900, with a view to creating a **Musée d'Histoire Naturelle**. This has been accommodated on the ground floor of the house, a large and eclectic display of geological specimens, stuffed birds and mammals, sea-shells, reptiles, butterflies, and insects, all maintained in the manner of a mid-19C collection—that is to say generically and in depth. The upper floor has been given over to a department of ethnography, divided by room into Oceania, Asia, Africa, and Egypt. The displays mostly consist of mementoes brought to France by returning travellers—grass skirts, lanterns, musical instruments and so on, arranged in cluttered cabinets. Individually there are some interesting items, the collection of Polynesian spears and harpoons, and the Samurai suits of armour for instance, but these tend to be overwhelmed by an inclination to cram every available space with artefacts, although an exception has been made for a sumptuous Chinese funerary shroud, beautifully mounted above the stairwell.

On the edge of the town the **Musée de la Guerre et de la Libération** is appropriately accommodated in the old **Fort du Roule**. This lies to the south-east, off the Avenue Lecarpentier, but if walking you should allow 30 minutes to negotiate the steep and winding approach. Strategically positioned above the port, the fort was completed in 1857 but was extensively reinforced by the German command in 1943–44. Architecturally it is of scant interest but the terrace throws off stunning views of the town and the harbour roads, and is a pleasant spot from which to watch the shipping below.

Since 1954 the fort has housed a museum of the Second World War, arranged over two levels, with a single room downstairs devoted to French experience of war, and a more extensive display spread across the entrance storey. To the left a collection of photographs of the entire Normandy campaign is laid out, with a moving case of individual photographic portraits of Allied soldiers. Elsewhere a map room shows the progress of

Operation Overlord and the situation as it developed in Europe between 6 June 1944 and 8 May 1945, complemented in the rooms beyond by displays of armaments, munitions, and propaganda leaflets.

West of Cherbourg the bleak moorland of the north-western corner of the Cotentin seems utterly remote from the fertile valleys of the Val de Saire and the southern peninsula, and given its isolation and shape the whole area is known as the Presqu'île de la Hague.

From the western rim of Cherbourg the D45 runs all the way to the headlands around Goury and the Hague, climbing initially to the old Norse town of (7 km) **Querqueville**. Here to the north of a dull, mostly 19C, parish church and casting majestic views over the whole of the Rade de Cherbourg stands the chapel of **St-Germain de Querqueville**. The St-Germain celebrated here is not the great early Christian churchman from Auxerre but one baptised by him, St-Germain of Cornwall (known as d'Ecosse), who evangelised the Bessin and was martyred along the banks of the Bresle by the Saxons c 480. The chapel consists of a short nave, trefoil east end, and a square tower whose exterior was entirely refaced and heightened by one storey during the 17C. During the archaeological dig of 1975–77 four Early Christian sarcophagi were discovered obliquely underlying the choir, one of which is displayed in the tiny north transept, making it evident that the choir is later than the Early Christian burial rites here. It was further established that the nave walls are pre-Carolingian, possibly 6C, and originally gave onto a small rectangular eastern cell as well as supporting a shallow narthex. All this is well explained in the excavation reports and diagrams displayed in the nave. The dig did not throw much light on the trefoil east end however, considered of importance since these early medieval terminations are most commonly found along the Rhine and in northern Italy. The use of *petit appareil* laid in herringbone patterns at Querqueville would suggest a date in the late 10th or early 11C, but as this type of stonework was still locally practised well into the 12C and the only comparable structure is the undated chapel of St-Saturnin at St-Wandrille, the speculation remains undimmed.

Five kilometres further west, to either side of Urville-Nacqueville, there are appealing châteaux, with that of **Nacqueville** just to the east (open afternoons only, excepting Mon. and Fri., Easter to October). This is sheltered from the coast amidst a secluded wooded park and entertains a splendid arrangement of late 16C granite walls and rose-tinted roof tiles, restored to their current shape by Hippolyte de Tocqueville during the 19C. Just beyond the village the **Château de Duc-Ecu** (open 11.00–18.00 except Mon. and Tues., April–September) was built in a more exposed position, banked above the sea and fed by the waters of a clear stream, its great schist walls concealing the verdant lawns and courts of the outer baileys. It should more correctly be termed a manor house, as its arrangements and fortifications are those of the local seigneur and landowner, Thomas de Lesdo, bailiff of Cherbourg under Henri IV. Although heavily restored after the Second World War, the late 16C composition of circular schist towers to the right of the great look-out tower and magnificent colombier happily remains unaltered.

West of Duc-Ecu the D45 meanders along the cliff-tops and up among the narrow valleys which fracture the underlying granite in this part of the Hague, passing through François Millet's home village of (5 km) Gréville-Hague before dropping to the sea once more by the handsomely restored spaces of (6 km) **Omonville-la-Rouge**. A low aisleless church is set in a cemetery above its twisting 17th and 18C streetscape, with a rectangular bell tower and spacious north porch. Despite the date of 1171 incised above a window in the north nave wall the church was built in a single 13C campaign, and given a splendid chamber over the north porch. This is decorated with a fresco depicting the martyrdom of Thomas à Becket, to which the date of 1171 doubtless refers. Access to the chamber is difficult, but the church boasts an equally unusual survival in the shape of an unparalleled 16C **Abbot's Throne**, the back of which carries a fully painted cycle of relief carvings depicting the Mysteries of the Rosary. There is also a small harbour to the north of the village, embraced by low houses and cafés, beyond which the coast road rises and falls alongside the wonderfully remote beaches of the far west. A tiny harbour at (6km) **Port Racine**, supposedly the smallest in France, is the last shelter before the peninsula runs out at the **Cap de la Hague** in a welter of hamlets grouped around St-Germain-des-Vaux and Auderville. **Auderville**'s simple 13C church is also an unexpected locale for two very beautiful 15C alabasters, mounted in the choir walls and depicting St John Trampling the Beasts, and an unidentified bishop.

South of Auderville the D901 runs across the blasted heights to (5km) **Jobourg**, whose naked church was compared by Millet to some prehistoric dolmen rising out of the bleak moor. It is certainly an unadorned and striking silhouette, concealing a fully rib vaulted late 12C choir and offering sanctuary from the dizzying grandeur of the cliffs at the **Nez de Jobourg**. The horizons hereabouts throw up shifting views of the vast nuclear reprocessing facility of Cogema-La-Hague, sited between Jobourg and Beaumont.

To the south of Beaumont take the D37 and D118 to **Biville** (14km from Jobourg), just inland from the desolate sand dunes of the Anse de Vauville. The village has attracted a considerable local pilgrimage, animated by the obscure cult of the Blessed Thomas Helye, a priest and teacher who was buried in the cemetery here in 1257. By 1260 his miracle-working powers were sufficiently well attested for a new four bay choir to be built to house his relics, and his corpse was duly exhumed and translated into the church. His remains are still displayed, albeit in a modern shrine, in the 13C choir, along with a chasuble reputedly owned by the Blessed Thomas which is now to be found in the south chapel. The cult was reinvigorated early this century by the local priest, Father Le Coutour, who between 1923 and 1926 built the nave which he had modelled on the Salle des Chevaliers at Mont-Saint-Michel. The architectural virtues of the church as a whole are modest but there is interest in the six 15C reliefs adorning the choir wall, remnants of an earlier tomb cycle perhaps.

Le Coutour was also responsible for another curiosity in an otherwise bleak area, the building of a granite cross, known as the **Calvaire des Dunes**, at the centre of the majestic sweep of the Anse de Vauville (Vauville loop) facing westwards to Jersey and the nearby Channel Islands.

The inland route along the swooping D904 soon brings you to the splendid fishing port and bathing resort of (30km) **Barneville-Carteret**. The commune consists of three distinct entities: the port of Carteret on the right bank of the estuary of the Gerfleur, the tiny settlement of Barneville-Plage on the opposite bank, and the old inland market town of Barneville.

Apart from a short modern main street **Carteret** is mostly a town of 19C villas which climb the slopes of a rocky headland known as the Cap de Carteret. To either side of this headland are magnificent sandy beaches, the Plage de Carteret between the fishing harbour and the cape, and the

Plage de la Vieille-Eglise to the north. The latter is named after the 11C church of St-Germain, abandoned in 1689, and of which little now remains.

The character of **Barneville** is very different and its rectangular market square lies on a rise some 2km above the beaches, with the parish church of **St-Germain** higher still. The Romanesque core of this church was much altered by the addition of a north aisle and fortified tower during the 15C, and a restoration programme of 1893 which involved the complete reconstruction of the south aisle. In spite of the harsh recutting of most of the sculpture the nave retains some fine mid 12C capitals, mostly concentrated at arcade level. These are largely decorative, though two accomplished historiated designs stand out—a Baptism of Christ on the eastern respond pier of the south arcade, and Daniel in the Lion's Den on one half of a capital above the northern wall shafts.

Eight kilometres south by the D903/D50 the small fishing port of **Portbail** is but a ghost of the great Gallo-Roman town which once existed here, its ramparts then a mile in circumference. The most striking views in what has shrunk to a handsome village, are to be found alongside the broad reach of water which separates the old quarter from the little ferry station where the summer boats for Jersey come and go. There, on the inland bank, the fortified tower of the church of **Notre-Dame** rises shimmering in the low marine light, or dappled in reflections of the setting sun of a fine summer's evening. A dependent priory of Lessay once stood to the north-west which has long since collapsed into the sea, but it seems likely that Lessay was also responsible for the construction of the present parish church. The splendidly crenellated tower is late medieval and was intended as part of the town defences, but the main body of the building is Romanesque—with two fine choir capitals depicting a combat between the Lion and the Unicorn to the north, and an Abbot to the south, probably dating from c 1120. The north transept dates from the 17C and the nave roof is 16C, the latter evidently a period which saw a considerable amount of work undertaken, as the choir piscina, painted Virgin and Child, and north transept St James all date from around this time.

The nave of Notre-Dame was built on Gallo-Roman foundations, but the most significant Early Christian survival in Normandy was discovered, quite unexpectedly, 100 metres away to the north-east. Excavations in 1956, intended to clear the ground for the footings of a new school behind the modern Mairie, uncovered the lower walls and central font of a hexagonal **Baptistery** dating from the 6C. The remains were considered to be of sufficient importance for the area to be roofed over, and the structure can be visited on enquiry at Notre-Dame. The bases of two *absidioles*, flanking a western door now give entry to this extraordinarily rare relic, its floors sloping downwards towards a central sunken font in what is evidence not only of the Mediterranean traditions which underpinned the early Christianity of the Channel coast but also of the exceptionally high quality of its ritual buildings.

From Portbail the D650 skirts the coast as far as the estuary of the River Ay, where a left turn onto the D652 brings you (23km) to **Lessay**.

The quiet and pleasant village which lies to the south of the church is the result of a decision by Turstin Haldup, Lord of La Haye-du-Puits, to found a Benedictine abbey by the banks of a Roman dyke (exaquium or 'essay') in 1056. Although this was populated by monks from Bec-Hellouin under Abbot Roger, the abbey's foundation was not confirmed by William the Conqueror until July 1080 and it is extremely doubtful that any of the present building predates this act. It is not until February 1098 when

Turstin's son, Eudes au Capel, was buried in the choir that documentary evidence of actual building on the site is found, and even here considerable doubt must remain as to whether this choir is in any way embodied in the present structure. The issue is further clouded by the serious damage sustained in two attacks on the church in the 14C and 20C respectively. The first came in 1356 when the Navarrese army of Charles le Mauvais destroyed the greater part of the nave, a situation rectified between 1386 and 1420 under the supervision of the monk Pierre Le Roy. Le Roy reconstructed the western six bays of the nave reusing the Romanesque capitals and stonework wherever possible, in what amounts to a replica of the earlier building, with the only selfconsciously late Gothic notes being struck in the high vault bosses. The bombardment of June 1944 had a more devastating effect on the fabric, particularly to the east, but between 1945 and 1958 Yves Froidevaux laboured to piece the building back together.

Froidevaux sees Lessay as a building striving to adjust its frame to incorporate newly developed vaulting technologies while in the course of construction. Few would dispute this, nor the order by which earlier designs were updated, but the improvisatory way in which the high rib vaults are handled makes this a building of considerable importance.

It seems likely that the first campaign at Lessay involved laying out a two bay choir and apse échelon east end, transepts which project one bay beyond the aisles, and the two easternmost bays of the nave. The subsidiary chapels were contained (i.e. they were squared on the exterior and semicircular to the interior), and the transepts were intended to carry a transept platform which would act as a tribune to either side of the crossing, hence the peculiar capital islanded towards the base of a half-column which runs up the south wall of the south transept. As a detailed examination of the handling of the minor elements here makes it unlikely that the choir was begun much before 1100, the reconciliation of the archaeology and documentation has become particularly problematic. In spite of the discovery of the tomb of Eudes au Capel it remains the case that if Eudes was buried 'in medio coro' in 1098 then it is unlikely to have been in this choir, and a benefactor as important as this would surely have been translated whenever new circumstances necessitated the move. Considerable changes were made to the design of these eastern parts in the course of their construction, and it seems likely that at some point building work came to a halt, probably during the Anglo-Norman war of 1106. The most obvious of these alterations was the decision to abandon the transept platforms, and as at Ely they remained unbuilt. It is here that the question of the vaults becomes crucial. Those which cover the transepts are quite obviously grafted onto an elevation which was never intended to take them, but what is the status of the vaults over the choir? The rib profiles are similar to those of the Promenoir des Moines at Mont-Saint-Michel of c 1120, and their uncomfortable springing suggests they were improvised well after the elevation had been completed to clerestory parapet level, but there can be no certainty in the matter. As with the choir so with the nave except that here the opportunity was taken to subtly alter the treatment of the elevation during this second campaign, and the five western bays continue the general shape of the triforium elevation but arrange it under two arches rather than three. Taken as a whole the building has in a sense become a facsimile of itself, but this is not to cast aspersions upon its pedigree and it remains one of the most enduringly beautiful monuments of Norman Romanesque.

If the aim is to return towards the northern Cotentin from Lessay you could take the D900 to the small market town of (10km) **Périers**, provided with an imposing parish church dedicated to **SS-Pierre-et-Paul**. As a major landmark and a considerable vantage point from which to survey the low-lying marshes of the Cotentin Pass the church was left as little more than a shell-blasted hulk by the close of 1944. The greater part of the existing church is 14C, work having begun after Pope Urban V issued a Bull in 1364 granting 140 day indulgences to all who contributed to the fabric fund. The scheme was ambitious, with a polygonal sanctuary, shallow transepts, and a six bay nave, all lit by large windows to the east and west which supplemented the indirect light of the aisles. Périers was in English hands at this date, and English habits were adopted, with a delicately carved sedilia and piscina to either side of the sanctuary and a handsome north porch whose trumeau now supports a 15C Virgin and Child. The spire dates from the restoration and stands in sharp contrast to the hexagonal tower which lodges in the angle between the sanctuary and south apse. By the 16C, if not before, this seems to have been used as a Lanterne des Morts, whereby a torch was placed in its spirelet on the death of a parishioner.

From Périers the D971 runs more or less straight through the low marshy landscape of the Vey to (19km) **Carentan**. This was once an important fortified medieval centre, controlling both the salt marshes of the Cotentin Pass as well as navigation across the Baie des Veys. It has latterly become a significant livestock market with facilities to auction up to 1600 cattle per day, though it had long been a thriving market town, and has also established a marina at the head of the Canal du Taute-Dick which connects it with the sea. In consequence Carentan has an airy, spacious atmosphere animated by the large squares which once housed its many markets. The finest of these, the **Place de la République**, is also the most central, flanked by the open arcades of four late 15th and early 16C stone houses, and stands at the junction of the town's two main streets—the Rue du Château and the Rue de l'Eglise.

The latter leads past a row of handsome two storey townhouses to the church of **Notre-Dame**, processionally aligned to channel the visitor through its late 15C south porch, where an emaciated corpse cautions the living to consider the dead. The church was first mentioned by Ordericus Vitalis, who reported that Henry I assisted the bishop of Sées at the Easter service here in 1106. The heavily restored crossing piers are all that survive of this church, carrying a lively series of capitals at their best in the sirens and wrestlers of the south-west pier. Although the west portal is late 12C the greater part of the church was rebuilt during the 15C. The south aisle was begun in 1443, while the town was still in English hands, and the 12C nave piers were dutifully recut to receive the high arches and vault. Nevertheless it was not until 1466 that a more comprehensive rebuilding programme was countenanced, after Guillaume de Cerisay, bailiff of the Cotentin and Lord of La Haye-du-Puits, provided funds for a new north aisle and choir in gratitude at seeing the back of the English. The construction of the spire continued into the 1480s, and the axial chapel was added in 1519, but Guillaume's generous benefaction produced a church ready for consecration in 1470.

The difference in the quality of ambition between the 1443 and 1466 schemes was doubtless responsible for the relative darkness of the nave in relation to the high two storey choir. The south transept window is nevertheless a work of fine sensitivity, and its expensive cycle of stained glass dates from 1450–55. There is in fact a considerable body of late 15C glass concentrated in the choir aisle windows (to which the parish has provided an exemplary short handbook) though much of it is in a poor state of preservation.

The exterior is far less integrated than the interior, the south aisle being covered with transverse gabled roofs and surmounted by musical angels in an uncomfortable arrangement which epitomises the piecemeal approach to the handling of the external elevations evident elsewhere. There are some entertaining carvings along the north aisle however, with a jester among the corbels which support the outer gargoyles, and a pair of headstops representing a puzzled husband gazing across the arch as his wife pulls on his trousers—a commonplace of late medieval comedies. Above all the spire is a majestic composition, breaking above an open balustrade to clear eight alternating aedicules, and ornamented in stages by the arches and foils that had provided Normandy with its sky-borne vernacular since the 13C.

Further south, on the old main road through the town, the **Hôtel-de-Ville** occupies the imposing and symmetrical 17C residential block of the old Augustinian convent, and brings you back onto the main route north. The N13 here offers a fast return to Valognes, via Ste-Mère-Eglise and Montebourg, taking advantage of the early 12C church at **St- Côme-du-Mont**— beautifully articulated by a Romanesque apse and chevron-moulded western portal, and possessing an odd pedimented lintel of Reynard the Fox, remounted on the western exterior wall of the Gothic south aisle.

A more circuitous route taking in Utah Beach involves following the D913 as it strikes north-east just before you come to St-Côme-du-Mont. This also passes a Romanesque church at (10km) **Ste-Marie-du-Mont**, bizarrely surmounted by a hemispherical dome of 1843, which is the dominant landmark in the surrounding country and guided in the American paratroopers of the 101st Division on 6 June 1944. Although the transepts and crossing are of a fairly routine early 13C construction, the nave arcade was retained from a building begun before 1060. Among the contemporary carved capitals a crude Christ in Majesty, uneasily seated amidst the prevailing beasts and foliage, is virtually the only example of early Romanesque figurative sculpture still to be seen in Basse-Normandie.

Five kilometres north-east the D913 finally disappears into the shifting sand dunes beyond the hamlet of **La Madeleine**, at the southern end of what became known operationally as **Utah Beach**. There is a small **Musée du Débarquement** installed alongside the remains of a German blockhouse, part of a standard defensive position (No. W5), which has drawn together a collection of models, documents, and photographs. A small film theatre within the museum also shows compilations of mostly Army and Navy footage taken in 1944. The building stands next to the Monument to the American 4th Infantry Division, which in turn marks the southern end of the military beach road and the point from which it cuts north, now known as the D421, to (8km) Ravenoville-Plage. On a ridge some 2km inland the German coastal battery of **Crisbecq** still survives and was a key obstacle to Allied advances in this sector during the week following D-Day. Despite the dropping of 600 bombs on the site over the night of 5–6 June the battery opened fire on the landing fleet after dawn, sinking a US destroyer, and held out until 12 June when in a desperate attempt to hold position the Crisbecq battery commander ordered his opposite number at Aumeville to fire on the emplacement in order to repel an American attack. The American attack succeeded.

From Crisbecq a combination of the D14 and D15 takes you past the handsome Romanesque tower of the church of (1km) **St-Marcouf**, strikingly hung with 12C relief sculpture, to one of the prime objectives of D-Day—the village of (9km) **Ste-Mère-Eglise**. The eponymous church stands in a spacious square at the centre of the village, its 13C bell tower hung with a model of the paratrooper who remained tragically suspended throughout the night of 5–6 June, his parachute caught on the balustrade. The tower has been extensively restored after sustaining considerable damage from the assault on the German snipers who took up residence within the louvred belfry windows. The rest of the church was only lightly damaged however, and boasts a fine 13C nave, rippling with clustered shaftwork, and a late 11C crossing. To the west an early 15C portal carries a splendid and salacious pair of label-stops while above, and best seen from the interior, the master glazier Gabriel Loir was commissioned to make a west window in memory of the landings of 6 June, interpreted here by a Virgin and Child between two descending paratroopers.

Across the square a substantial museum, the **Musée des Troupes Aéro-portées** (Airborne Museum), has been established around two large-scale exhibits—a restored WACO glider, and an American C-47 Transport Aircraft, more commonly known as a Dakota and affectionately referred to as 'the willing slave'. The museum is perhaps the most intimate of all the specialist World War Two collections in Normandy, and abounds with personal mementos, photographs of unguarded moments, and the common or garden artefacts with which hard-pressed troops tried to maintain a semblance of domestic order.

The ancient market town of **Montebourg** some 10km to the north (along the N13) was the scene of a more bitter assault, and the fighting which blazed around the abbey of Notre-Dame-de-l'Etoile from 10–19 June left both town and abbey in ruins. Although the abbey had been founded in 1080 by William the Conqueror it fell into disrepair after the Revolution and was rebuilt in a dull and academic manner by the Brothers of the Misericordia during the later 19C. Nevertheless the abbey had an enduring impact on the town early in the 14C, when the monks replaced a small chapel dedicated to Thomas à Becket with the large parish church of **St-Jacques**. This stands on a rise above the town centre, having been laboriously and accurately restored since 1944, and is a straightforward cruciform building with a large area of blank wall in the lunettes of the vault, and no clerestory. There is little reason to doubt that it was finished in time to be consecrated by Guillaume de Thieuville, bishop of Coutances, in 1329, and is the sort of austere and ample structure which found favour among 14C parochial congregations. A 14C statue of its patron saint now stands above the west door, and against the north-east crossing pier a 15C alabaster of St James the Pilgrim is adored by seven headless figures, probably the members of a local confraternity. The only other portable medieval object in the church is altogether more enigmatic. This stands in the south aisle in the shape of a splendid Romanesque font, richly carved with interlaced strapwork and articulated, in the manner of a crude capital, by four powerful heads. Its date remains as much of a mystery as its origins, for there is no particular support for the presumption that it was made for a parish at Montebourg, or indeed for William's abbey, and a date of between 1070 and 1150 is still the best that one can manage.

To complete the circuit to (7km) Valognes the N13 takes no more than a few minutes, sweeping one into the centre of the town along the old road to the north of the Place Vicq-Azir.

15

Villedieu-les-Poêles, St-Lô and the Southern Cotentin

ROAD (180km): Villedieu-les-Poêles (D9/D51, 12km Abbaye de Hambye); D524, 26km Vire; N174, 26km Torigni-sur-Vire; 15km St-Lô; D972, 27km Coutances; D971, 30km Granville; D973/D580, 12km La Lucerne; D335/D35, 12km Genêts; D911, 10km Avranches; N175, 22km Villedieu-les-Poêles.

The suggested itinerary here spins a circuit around the southern Cotentin, a sort of parallel orbit to that of the northern peninsula, and has elected Villedieu-les-Poêles as its hub. The advantage of this old metalworking town is not simply that being cradled in a loop of the River Sienne it lies at the very centre of the region, but that it is one of the most congenial towns in western Normandy. Those with a liking for small cathedral cities, or maritime resorts, might equally consider Coutances or Granville as sympathetic bases, and both give ready access to the sunken lanes and small fields which are the distinguishing features of the Normandy Bocage.

Descending from the northern Cotentin you will notice a gentle shift in the landscape, as the low marshes of the Vey give way to the twisting valleys and dense orchard plots to the north and west of Coutances. This change gathers pace as you move south-east, and although the underlying geology of the southern Cotentin is similar to that of the north, the slow transition from the moorland and rough pasture of Valognes, to the greenwoods of the Sienne valley masks a larger transformation in the nature of the landscape. This pattern of open woodland, made up of small meadows sheltered beneath deep hedgerows, is known as the Bocage, and its criss-crossing of hedges has led to it being characterised as a linear forest. It is perhaps the most glorious of all the manmade landscapes of northern France, and acts as both a larder and a garden for the larger market towns of an otherwise sparsely populated region.

VILLEDIEU-LES-POELES. A 'poêle' is a copper pan and since the 17C Villedieu has been renowned for the production of domestic copperware, its once fantastic array of small forges and workshops now rationalised into the industrial manufacture of boilers and pipework on the one hand, and the making of specialist kitchenware and souvenirs in beaten copper or brass on the other. Accordingly it has all the bright and brassy shops expected of a sizeable tourist centre. But Villedieu is also a business-like market town, rotating the rich agricultural produce of the southern Bocage amidst the 18C mercantile houses of the Place de la République and Rue Carnot, and its ambience is that of a hardworking and unselfconscious small town.

There was an early medieval settlement here, known as Siennêtre, but it was the decision of Henry I in the early 12C to grant land adjoining the town to the Knights Hospitallers of St John of Jerusalem that led to the growth of a more sizeable town. The Knights founded one of their earliest Commanderies on the site, named Villa Dei de Santa Caprioli (or, in Norman French, Villedieu de Saint-Chevreuil), and obtained exemption from episcopal jurisdiction and feudal taxation, along with a succession of valuable trading privileges. Louis XIII and Louis XIV pared back these exemptions but by then the forges and foundries which had shaped Villedieu in the 13th and 14C were well established along the banks of the river, and the specialised nature of the town's economy carried its own momentum. It thrived during the 18th and 19C, and at one time boasted over 400 metalworking shops.

Most of these were grouped around the great communal courts which run off the Rue du Docteur-Havard, sheltered precincts such as the **Cour de l'Enfer** or the **Cour de la Luzerne**. Towards the top of the hill, along the Rue de Général-Huard, the Cour de Foyer is another and houses the **Musée de la Poeslerie et Maison de la Dentellière**—devoted to brass and copper-work, and lacemaking respectively. Like many such courts the houses are interlinked, and the 17C forge which guards the metalworking collections gives directly onto the 15C dwelling which now accommodates a small lace display. There are some interesting exhibits, notably the late medieval spouted ewer said to be for warming bath water, but a better sense of Villedieu's specialist traditions is to be found to the west of the church, on the Rue du Pont-Chignon.

The **Fonderie de Cloches** (Bell Foundry) here occupies the site of the Hospitallers Commanderie, its industrial sheds set in an overgrown garden teeming with lilac and wild roses, and can be visited during working hours. During the Middle Ages bells were usually cast by itinerant founders, who dug their pits and built the moulds wherever they happened to be employed. As was the case when firing ceramic tiles for church pavements, furnaces and kilns were put together on site, and the establishment of a permanent bell foundry at Villedieu during the 13C is thus something of an unusual occurrence. There have been several foundries since, but the town has sustained the tradition of lost-wax pit casting without interruption up to the present day. The refractory materials of brick, and a paste made up of clay, horsehair, and dung remain the most effective, and the only substantive difference between the techniques you currently see in action and medieval practice lie with the furnaces. Even so the molten bronze for a 500kg bell must be poured within one minute for the cast to be even and the note true.

Back over the river the granite belfry of the parish church of **Notre-Dame** overlooks both the Place des Chevaliers de Malte, and the splendidly elongated market square, the Place de la République. The greater part of the church is late 15C when the parishioners decided to rebuild the Hospitallers' 12C structure, Notre-Dame de l'Ospital, which had been extensively damaged during the Hundred Years War. Granite from the quarries at Gast was already being assembled in the late 1450s and by 1460 building began in the choir, the nave and upper parapets of the crossing tower being complete by 1495. The nave is both taller and marginally lighter than the east end, having been unsympathetically reconstructed after a fire in 1632, and it is the choir which holds the surprises. While the crossing tower is richly ornamented the choir is purposefully severe, break-ing the ribs of the vault sharply at the keystones and getting rid not only of the capitals but also of any residual corbels, so that the vault springs directly from the wall. Beneath the modern windows of the apse an unusual, and remarkably graceful, 18C canvas depicting the **Adoration of the Sacrament** has been installed as an antependium to the altar. Along with a good pulpit of 1683, bearing a representation of Christ with the Woman of Samaria, this is the most notable of the church furnishings, though a considerable body of statuary has been assembled in the aisles, including the early 16C Pietà which once stood above the west door.

Villedieu is also an excellent base from which to mount an excursion to one of the more significant monastic foundations of Basse-Normandie (reached along a combination of the D9 and D51)—the **Abbaye de Hambye**. This was founded in 1145 by Guillaume Paisnel, Lord of Hambye, and settled by monks from the abbey of Tiron, in the Perche. The embryonic Order of Tiron shared the austere reformist ideals of Cîteaux, and though it was never formally absorbed into the Cistercian Order its links with St-Bernard and his successors remained strong. As such, Hambye was designed very much as a Cistercian house. The roofless church is accordingly severe with a colossal choir soaring above tall columnar piers, bereft of ornament and lit by sharply pointed lancet windows. The north transept would appear to be late 12C, but is the only remnant of a building which was almost entirely rebuilt during the 13C. The general frame of the choir draws on two quite distinct traditions. On the one hand it incorporates that most Cistercian of elements, the containing apse wall, which had found favour at the important Burgundian abbey of Pontigny (i.e. the apsidal chapels do not project beyond the continuous outline of a polygonal containing wall). Yet the treatment of the main volumes suggests that the choir was conceived as a suitably toned-down version of the east end of Coutances cathedral, with vaults at three levels creating a tiered arrangement of space. The language has been simplified, with simple holes punched through the wall between the arcade and clerestory, where at Coutances there is a balustraded wall-passage, but it remains the case that however austere the treatment it was the space-frame of this nearby cathedral which provided Hambye with its model. The chapels were probably laid out by 1228, when a document mentions that work was proceeding on the church, but it is unlikely that the main body of the choir predates c 1240–50 or that the transept windows were in place before c 1280.

The conventual quarters thankfully remain in large part, and, as one of the most complete arrangements of monastic buildings to have survived in north-western France, have been extensively restored over the past 20 years. The **gatehouse** is partially Romanesque, though Guillaume Paisnel's coat of arms above the double opening has been all but obliterated, and the main monastic complex is grouped in three ranges to the south of the church. Those to the east and west gave directly onto the now vanished cloister. The important **east range** is mostly late 12C and consists of a barrel-vaulted sacristy, chapter house, parlour, warming-room, and subsidiary cellars, all of which originally supported the monks' dormitory. There is a crude but moving 15C wooden Pietà in the sacristy and some 13C painted decoration on the vaults of the parlour (in this case the room where the dead were laid out), but it is the chapter house which is perhaps the most significant structure. This was completed in 1230 and is twin-aisled, with tripartite vaulting cells around the eastern return. This plan was taken up in the chapter house at Norwich Cathedral, and as the bishop of Coutances sold the parish church of the village of Hambye to the bishopric of Norwich in 1232 the assumption must be that the links are direct.

The western lay-brothers' range is late medieval and though the refectory has gone the great 13C **kitchen** remains intact at the southern end, its segmentally-arched fireplace supported by a system of notched stones which are joined in a manner more familiar in vernacular building, and known as 'Trait de Jupiter'. The monastic farm buildings which close the complex to the south are the rarest survival as with their stabling, store-room, and cider press they remain pretty much as adapted in the 16C, and alone give a sense of the innate balance of the Benedictine Rule.

East of Villedieu the D524 strides above the low ridges of the southern Bocage, offering glimpses of the wooded hedgerows and intense greenery of this most profoundly rural of areas. To the north of the Forêt de St-Sever the ancient abbey town of (13km) **St-Sever-Calvados** sustains remnants of the church which grew above a small monastic cell founded by St-Sever before 565. This was refounded as a Benedictine abbey in 1070 but the present buildings are substantially later, with a 15C west portal and 13C choir, neither of great distinction. The choir retains some fine stained glass, the best of which is to be found in the eastern lancets where a 13C Tree of Jesse is mounted alongside scenes from the life of Christ and of St-Sever. There is also an accomplished 16C window in the south-west bay devoted to the monastery's early abbots. What little else survived is concentrated to the south-west where the 18C Mairie was originally built as a palatial abbot's lodging, though the strangely autonomous belfry of 1697 to the west had nothing to do with the abbey, and was rather the bell tower of the now demolished parish church.

13km further east the old walled town of **Vire** rises proud of a meander in the selfsame river, demanding fealty of the Bocage from its perch above a granite massif. Sadly the town was decimated by aerial bombardment in June 1944 and has been almost entirely rebuilt in a uniformly austere and reticulated style. The medieval town was in fact quite small and you can follow the path of its walls northwards along the **Rue des Remparts** where two truncated defensive towers still stand. The old town gate, the **Porte Horloge**, has at least survived in better order, giving onto the modern centre of Vire and providing the town with its most distinctive motif. The two great drum towers which frame the portal were constructed in the early 13C, but it was the decision in 1480 to raise a tall belfry above the gatehouse and furnish this with a clock which provided the structure with both a new name and a new silhouette. The present clock is more recent but the gate continues to give access to the medieval main street of Vire, the Rue Saulnerie, and brings you swiftly to the restored granite surfaces of the church of **Notre-Dame**.

This was the major medieval town church and it reflects the determination of an ill-served populace to unseat a castle chapel and transform it into a spacious parish church. Henry I was responsible for building the earlier chapel in the 1120s, but shortly after Normandy was absorbed into the kingdom of France in 1204 an agreement was reached with Philip Augustus, and having been demolished the chapel was replaced by a larger parochial building. The nave and inner aisles as far east as the transept screen belong to this church, work having started c 1230, and though the building's completion was not marked by a consecration ceremony until 1272 it seems that the early 13C design was followed throughout. The treatment is unostentatious and strangely articulated by a narrow triforium in which arches are simply punched through the wall to look into what was originally the aisle roof space. In 1373 the south transept and **Porte aux Sabots** (Clogmakers Door, adjacent to the south transept) were built behind the existing 13C elevation, and the restrained central tower was raised in 1390. The grander works were reserved for the end of the Hundred Years War however, when the Corporation of Drapers financed the north transept, and the Fishmongers paid for the now walled-in door in the north choir aisle. The nave was also furnished with outer aisles between 1511 and 1545, and a new choir designed, plainly wrought with a three bay apse, and elaborately carved and painted high vault bosses. The Wars of Religion and the Revolution succeeded in destroying any liturgical or cult objects, but the uncluttered interior has a serenity which marks it out as one of the finest town churches of southern Normandy.

To the north the Rue Geôle extends to a belvedere commanding views of the old industrial village of Vaux de Vire, whence the drinking songs of the 15C native poet, Olivier Basselin gave rise to the term 'Vaudeville'. While to the south the ruined shell of the 12C keep nestles above a deep V-shaped gorge formed by the river, though it is now somewhat removed from the rest of the town by the dismal spaces of the Place du Château. The two surviving walls are all that remain of a much larger castle raised by Henry I in 1123, and substantially dismantled on Cardinal Richelieu's orders in 1630. The views are understandably majestic and following the river round to the east you can make out the shape of the 17th and 18C town, as its expansion was channelled along the water course. The only vestige to have escaped the 1944 onslaught here is the handsome 18C Hôtel-Dieu, at the bottom of the Rue Gasté. This has long ceased functioning as a hospital and now houses the **Musée de Vire**, primarily concerned with the crafts and traditions of the Bocage. The collections are arranged over three floors and include reconstructions of forges, saddleries, and clogmakers' shops, il-lustrative material on the history of the town, collections of Norman furniture, and an extensive display of work by the local painter, and illustrator, Charles Léandre. The latter was a sharp observer of life in southern Normandy and the portraits and caricatures offer a compelling commentary on social mores between the 1890s and 1930s, drawn in a very different style to that of the better known illustrations of Flaubert and Courteline.

The N174 follows the path of the River Vire as it flows north, switching away from the narrow gorges to track the flatter heights, before returning to the valley at (26km) **Torigni-sur-Vire**. An ancient crossroads, the town now centres on the bruised remains of the late 16C **Château de Torigni**, built by François Gabriel for Jacques de Matignon, Maréchal de France, in a rich purpley granite known as pudding stone. Two further wings framed the central block, creating a large Cour d'Honneur open to the north. These were demolished in 1813 to provide building material for a new road from Vire to St-Lô, and the central range was itself gutted by fire in 1944, but what could be salvaged was restored and the old residence now serves as the Hôtel-de-Ville. The remaining block is architecturally unremarkable—rhythmically modulated by alternating niches and windows at first floor level, massive and rusticated, but a part of the interior (open afternoons only, 1 June–15 September) houses an excellent collection of 17C and 18C Brussels and Aubusson tapestries.

15km north-west the river supports another fortified town in the shape of **St-Lô**, massively ringed by the towers and ramparts which separate the early medieval enclosure from the sprawling industrial town below. There was a Celtic settlement here, known as Briovère (Bridge over the Vire), but on the death of St-Lô, the late 6C bishop of Coutances, the town acquired a portion of his relics and adopted his name. The town's distinctive shape emerged as early as the 9C, when Charlemagne enveloped the high ground with an enclosing wall in the manner of a rectangular Saxon burh. This was subsequently rebuilt by Philip Augustus after 1204 and variously refortified during and after the Hundred Years War. In spite of the demolition of its eastern perimeter in 1812 the walls define the character of St-Lô, restricting the centre to a rectangle formed by the Rues des Noyers to the north, de la Poterne to the west, Torteron to the south, and the Place de l'Hôtel-de-Ville to the east.

As a major road and rail junction the town was regarded as the essential hinge linking the Landing Beaches with the southern Cotentin. Accordingly, it was heavily defended and only fell when the American 8th Corps entered the town on 19 July 1944, after a fierce battle which had begun some 16 days earlier. The damage was grievous and with 95 per cent of the town destroyed St-Lô became known as the 'Capitale des Ruines'. This necessitated a monumental programme of reconstruction which involved some large scale replanning, most readily exemplified by the impressive ranks of administrative offices in the Place de la Préfecture. To the south the Rue des Près runs from the heavily rebuilt rampart towers which overlook the river, to the Place Notre-Dame, where the extraordinary west front testifies to the ferocity of the artillery ranged on the town.

Notre-Dame itself was an eclectic building before 1944, and the decision to restore the south tower of 1464 while leaving the corroded stump of the late 13C north tower isolated in front of a modern central screen, is vindicated by the church as a whole. The interior is vast and irregular, disconcertingly so to the south where the nave aisle becomes progressively wider. The greater part of the building is 15C, beginning with the replacement of the nave between 1400 and 1420, the bizarre south choir aisle being added in the following decade. An elegant and airy double aisled choir followed in 1490–1510, with the north elevation of the nave finally acquiring a second aisle for all but its westernmost bays shortly before 1544. The effect of a double ambulatory in the choir is to transform freestanding columnar supports into quasi-central piers, with each responsible for four bays of aisle vaulting superbly sprung direct from the body of the pier. Given the problems the building has faced with its glass is now somewhat patchy, though the so-called Royal Window, given by Louis XII in 1470 and depicting St-Louis, St-Rémy, St-Denis, and St-Geneviève, has been reassembled in the south nave aisle. A particularly fine window devoted to the legend of Thomas à Becket was commissioned in the 1950s for the main south choir chapel.

To the east is a modern shopping area centred around two large squares— the Place Général de Gaulle with its Hôtel-de-Ville and the sole surviving relic of the eastern perimeter wall, the Tour Poudrière, and the Place du Champ de Mars. The latter houses the **Musée des Beaux-Arts**, recently opened and fronted by a changing display of sculptural installations. The interior spaces are impressively organised, with ramps and partitions creating a set of loosely related displays which bring together pre-war images of St-Lô and interweave these with the museum's holdings of French painting. The best work is 19C with some excellent portrait miniatures by the local artist, **Daniel Saint**, and two fine canvases by **Corot**—a sketchy and atmospheric late work entitled 'L'Etang—souvenir du marais de Beauvaisis' juxtaposed with the 1845 'Homer among the Shepherds'. A good study of a sunset beyond Le Havre painted by **Boudin** in 1884 is oddly allied to an academic portrayal of a male nude by the young **Millet**, and leads to a collection of 20C work which includes sculpture and objects in mixed-media by **Picasso, Man Ray, Léger**, and **Miró**. Nevertheless the highlight is to be found in a small circular room designed to accommodate a series of eight tapestries woven in Bruges shortly before 1600, illustrating the **Loves of Gombaut and Macée**. These idealised cycles of shepherd life were popular in the 16th and 17C, and their forms can be traced to the prefatory miniatures of 15C Books of Hours, but so extensive and textually based a cycle is rare. You can easily follow the story—Gombaut and Macée are variously shown chasing butterflies, playing tiquet (an ancestor of croquet), dancing, and eating a picnic prior to their betrothal and marriage. The final scene represents Gombaut, in stupified old age, caught in an animal-trap, but there is additionally a ninth, woven later and by a different shop, held in the reserve collection which illustrates the death of Gombaut.

Further east, towards the outskirts of St-Lô, the **Haras de St-Lô** was created as a national stud by Napoléon in 1806. This now accommodates 135 stallions— thoroughbreds, trotters, Norman cobs, and percherons—in vast 19C stableblocks centred on a quadrangular parade ring, where you can watch the driving displays on summer mornings, or more spectacularly the galas held every August.

West of St-Lô the D972 rolls coastwards for 27km, its later stages silhouetted by the airy spires of **Coutances** cathedral. The attractions of the site were recognised early and the Gallic tribe of the Unelles established their capital here, calling the town Cosedia. But it was the Romans who realised its strategic potential for controlling the region and in 298, under the Emperor Constantius Chlorus, the growing city took the title Constantia (the surrounding country becoming known as the Pagus Constantinus, corrupted in the 7C to Costentin and ultimately Cotentin). At what date this Gallo-Roman city developed a sizeable Christian community is uncertain, but the earliest mention of a bishopric is in 511 and it seems likely that St-Lô was one of the earliest, though not the first, of its bishops. The clergy fled before the Norse invaders of 866 destroyed the city, bearing the relics of St-Lô to Rouen, and by 900 the ruinous fabric was the seat of a permanent Norse-speaking population.

The **Cathedral** does not seem to have been rebuilt before 1030, and then on a site to the north of the earlier structure (thought to underlie the present church of St-Pierre), but received a substantial boost on the election of Geoffroy de Montbray as bishop in 1048. The area to the east of Coutances was the cradle of the Norman dynasties of southern Italy, and many of the 12 sons of Tancred de Hauteville (Hauteville-la-Guichard, 15km north-east of Coutances) were encouraged by earlier Norman successes to descend on the old Byzantine Exarchate. Between 1047 and 1050 one of the eldest, Robert Guiscard, captured Calabria, while the youngest, Roger, became count of Sicily. As stories of incomparable wealth began to filter back Geoffroy undertook a journey to Calabria, and secured the promise of generous funding for his new cathedral from Guiscard and the Hauteville clan. The result was a resounding success and the cathedral was considered sufficiently complete to merit consecration by the Archbishop of Rouen, in the presence of Duke William, in 1056. Although work was evidently still in progress in 1066, when Geoffroy despatched funds from England towards the completion of the building, few authorities would dispute that what survives is substantially a design of the 1050s.

Given that the cathedral was rebuilt in the 13C, it is far from immediately obvious that much of Geoffrey's church survived at all. In fact when work began on the nave and west front, in all probability after the town had been seriously damaged by fire in 1218, the Romanesque cathedral was treated as a frame which could be recut, or reclad, in 13C clothing. The Gothic nave does not merely mimic the proportional system of the earlier building but

Coutances Cathedral: interior of the crossing tower

actually encases it, so that the relative dispositions of the arcade and tribune one now sees are the same as those of the 11C. As Geoffroy's nave was wooden-roofed the first step was to redesign the inner elevation to receive the clustered wall shafts which support the vault. The old square cored piers were provided with larger octagonal bases, and triple shafts were added to the longitudinal and aisle faces. Above this the Romanesque arcade originally consisted of plain semicircular arches in two orders, the central unmoulded order sprung from a pilaster attached to the face of the pier. These were reworked by cutting the surface with deep mouldings, broken at the head to form a pointed arch, but one remains conscious that the V-shaped profile still reflects the twin orders of the earlier arrangement.

The tribune was similarly treated, though here it was a question of laying a balustraded screen across the previously open storey, to create a zone of blind relief in two layers, subsequently blocked by a third. This becomes clearer if you follow the guided tour of the high spaces organised twice daily by the Amis de la Cathédrale. The tour starts with the north aisle roof space, and allows you to examine the unmoulded arches of the 11C tribune, walled in where they originally gave onto the nave. The Romanesque windows also survive at this level, deeply set to the rear of an outer wall thickened by a segmental blind arcade, but although this exterior wall is indeed relatively thick that of the main elevation is not, and the suggestion that the nave originally carried a clerestory wall-passage must be discounted.

In addition, the main block of the two west towers is 11C, its exterior skin of blind lancets put up in the early 13C. Once above the aisles the towers were divided into two chambers, that on the first floor carrying a barrel vault, where the upper room now opens sheer to the octagonal tower vault and makes clear the manner in which the Gothic wall simply recoats the Romanesque. Most of the earlier work here dates from the 1090s, for after the crossing tower had been struck by lightning in 1091 the damage seems to have been used as a pretext to make good any deficiencies encountered elsewhere in the building. This included an extensive restoration of the mid 11C transepts, apse, and sanctuary, the evidence for which is nothing like as comprehensive as it is for the nave and western façade.

The chronology of the 13C cathedral is more conjectural. There is little doubt that work began with the nave and that, as described earlier, this was conceived as a relatively modest remodelling of the earlier fabric, drawing on the rich vernacular of late 12C tribune churches pioneered at Fécamp and in the nave of Rouen cathedral. Although it is possible to argue that this was begun before the town fire of 1218 it is unlikely to have been much earlier, and the rash of rebuilding elsewhere in Coutances remains much the most probable catalyst. The closing off of the tribune by a rear screen of blind arcades brings the nave into line with the choir of Bayeux cathedral of c 1230 and is a minor though telling testament to the radical rethink which must have occurred before work began on the choir.

There are few commentators who are not struck by wonder at the amplitude of the choir at Coutances, at its sense of being apart from the rest of the building, of embodying a more refined, more humanist sensibility. Whose sensibility this might be is an open question. The presiding bishop at the likely date of the commencement of work on the nave was Hugues de Morville, a nephew of one of the murderers of Thomas à Becket. He was present at the dedication of two chapels in the transept in 1233, and when he died in 1238 he was buried by the crossing, suggesting that the transepts must have been largely complete by this date, and implying that the choir may have been begun. His successor, Jean d'Essey, was certainly responsible for the completion of the choir, but was he also its prime instigator? One would be inclined to see so dramatic a shift as exists between the design of the transepts and that of the choir as coinciding with a change of patron; it certainly demanded a change of architect, but it is difficult to gauge the level of involvement pursued by the bishops in their cathedral.

You can examine the nature of this change in the **transepts**. The transept ends are enlivened by three lancets, splendidly sunk with stained glass, while the lower walls are articulated by the type of subdivided blind arches which are often encountered in Norman 13C tribunes. In the crossing the Romanesque western piers were colossally thickened, and matched to the east, in order to provide a platform from which to launch a dazzling **lantern tower**. This is scooped into a giddying sweep of light-fractured cells by massive squinches, laid like the steps of some mighty inverted pyramid, before breaking upwards into a coronet of open lancet windows. It is one of the triumphs of Norman architecture, and from the exterior towers even higher as the 16-ribbed vault supports an octagonal belfry chamber from which, sadly, no bells will again be heard.

The transepts in a sense represent a culmination of the thinking which inspired the nave, and they develop an essentially regional style of architecture, a language to be found at Rouen, Caen, and Bayeux. The **choir** does not unfold in these terms, and both its forbears and its imagery came from further afield. As you step down east of the crossing the rhythms of the building are inexorably changed, the sweeping verticality of the high spaces tempered by a lateral movement, away from the centre and towards the low recesses of the outer ambulatory. The main arcade has also grown taller and gives way to an inner aisle which carries its own three storeyed elevation and its own clerestory. The area is thus illuminated by light from three levels which suffuses three different zones of relief. This arrangement of staggered volumes applied to a double-aisled building was introduced towards the end of the 12C at Bourges cathedral, and Coutances is one of a small number of great churches which drew on this model during the first half of the 13C, along with St-Martin at Tours, and Le Mans and Toledo cathedrals.

If this imagery is both sophisticated and exclusive, the detailed handling is more eclectic and the choir draws on an extraordinary wealth of resources. The decorative treatment and play of blind arcading and wall-passages, extravagantly and purposefully extended to the clerestory of the inner aisle, is entirely Norman in handling. The treatment of the arcade is very different however, and the tremendous depth and elevation derived from the paired columns of the apse hemicycle is indebted to the revival of early Christian forms undertaken in north-eastern France, most notably in the choir of the now destroyed cathedral of Cambrai. Even the vaults find unexpected parallels. The beautifully sprung five-part vaults in the inner aisle are reminiscent in form to late 12C practice, but with a stilted fifth rib which looks as if it might have walked here from Lincoln Cathedral, and a high vault which carries that most English of features, a central ridge rib. In this, as in much else, the choir must be regarded as a synthesis of often divergent trends in late 12th and early 13C thinking, and the clarity and invention with which these were resolved is a measure of the building's achievement.

The only significant alterations to the 13C structure were concerned with the provision of additional altars, hence the addition of a set of lateral chapels in the nave c 1300, and the enlargement of the axial chapel in the late 14C. Squirrels are carved on the capital frieze of this latter structure, loosely comparable in the way in which woodland and domestic creatures have been invited into the building with the north-east cloister door at St-Wandrille. The chapel also houses an intimate, and very graceful, 14C marble Virgin and Child known as **Notre-Dame de la Circata**, which became an object of great veneration during the Hundred Years War in its original locale at the parish church of St-Nicolas.

A considerable quantity of 13C glass survives, although much of it is in poor condition, but the vast majority of the furnishings and portable objects have gone. There are exceptions, notably in the south choir aisle, where a 14C painting of the Trinity, above an Annunciation, St Michael, and Commendation of the Virgin, illuminates the area beyond a heavily restored parclose. In the **Chapelle de St-François** (south-easternmost of the nave chapels) a 16C wooden retable depicting the Betrayal has been mounted in a superb 14C piscina. To the right of this a bas-relief devoted to the Infancy of Christ looks mid-14C and includes an excellent Flight into Egypt, adjacent to which two battered reliefs depict a bishop offering up a relic, and a fragmentary Assumption and Coronation of the Virgin, both of them very fine.

The best of the glass is concentrated in the transepts, where the three lancets to the south were filled with a Last Judgement in the early 16C. This was releaded and extensively restored in 1916 but for the most part the glass remains original, with a saturated colour range shot through with pale canopies and flickering grisaille images of the souls of the blessed and damned.

The majority of the surviving 13C compositions are concerned with the lives of saints, and would seem to be the work of three, perhaps four, different teams of glaziers. The north transept is the earliest with three lancets devoted to Thomas à Becket, St George, and St-Blaise, probably completed shortly after 1230. The figurative compartments are large and the compositions rather schematic, particularly in the central light, betraying a reliance on the large-scale forms of the choir clerestory windows at Chartres. The next group of windows to be undertaken were those of the radiating chapels of the ambulatory where, in the surviving windows to the south of the axial chapel the themes revolve around the legends of purely local saints. The finest represents the life of St-Lô, showing him invested by royalty, being consecrated bishop at the age of 12, celebrating the Mass, and his ultimate death. (L. Grodecki sees the hand of a Rouen shop of glaziers at work here and dates the remnants to 1240 and 1250.) The last of the 13C work lies in the choir clerestory, where to the north a badly corroded group of lancets may depict Saints John the Baptist and Evangelist, and a Life of Christ, with a slightly more legible series in the hemicycle given over to the Childhood of Christ, Glorification of the Virgin and, again, local saints.

The 13C sculpture is, unfortunately, a lost cause. The cathedral was transformed into a Temple of Reason at the Revolution and the reliefs of the Virgin which decorated the central tympanum of the west front were destroyed, as were the niche figures reputedly containing portrayals of Tancred de Hauteville and six of his 12 sons amongst other statues. The **west front** remains a memorable composition however, with its 11C towers used as a scaffolding for the 13C work. A screen was laid across the front, connecting the projecting stair towers, and the Romanesque fabric refaced with tall blind arcades. This central screen was provided with its upper balcony in the late 14C, but the topmost stage of the towers and spires form part of the 13C campaign—airy, graceful, fantastically worked about with attenuated turrets, and capped by a pair of spires whose faceting of form suggests a purposeful interest in the possibilities of the broken silhouette.

The west front is best seen from what is the highest point in a deceptively steep hill town, the **Parvis Notre-Dame**. This also serves as the market square, bordered to the south by the Hôtel-de-Ville of 1907. Coutances sustained considerable damage in the course of 1944, necessitating a wholesale reconstruction of the quarters to the north and west, and the results of this are clear whenever you move away from the narrower streets at the centre of the town. To the west of the square the **Musée Quesnel-Morinière**, on the street of the same name, is housed in the 17C Hôtel Le Poupinel and along with an adjacent cider press forms the main entrance to the glorious terraced walks of the **Public Gardens**. The ground floor of the museum is mostly given over to temporary exhibitions, but upstairs the predominantly local collections have been rearranged with three rooms given over to a routine display of 17–19C painting, among which are a few highlights—a loosely worked oil painting of a returning fishing fleet by **Claude-Joseph Vernet**, and a small study of a combat between dogs and lions by **Rubens**. Beyond these are some cabinets devoted to popular local art, with the rural earthernware pottery much the most appealing, and a room of medieval religious sculpture, the grand 15C statue of a Knight of Malta being from the Commanderie at nearby Villedieu.

From the musée the Rue Daniel leads you to a huge mid 19C complex, known as **Les Unelles**, which was built as a seminary on the site of an earlier Dominican convent. The rebuilt 19C chapel stands behind the diocesan offices, but the greater part of a set of tall ranges have been converted into a first-rate socio-cultural centre, the Centre d'Animation. The town library and council chambers are also housed here. Striking east along the Rue St-Maur brings you through a haphazardly revamped area to the spacious and dull parish church of **St-Nicolas**. The building has been deconsecrated and there are plans to turn it into an agricultural museum, but in the meantime its part-restored interior remains entirely uncluttered. The church is substantially late 15C, with an austere western tower porch giving access to a broad two-storeyed nave. The choir and transepts suffered considerable damage during the Wars of Religion and were rebuilt in the 17C, acquiring an octagonal lantern in the process.

The Rue Tancrède connects St-Nicolas with the cathedral and with its various continuations constitutes the main commercial street of Coutances, its rhythm of granite houses sadly disrupted by the depredations of 1944. On the whole those vernacular buildings which remained structurally sound were saved, hence the uneven terraces of 19C shops and town houses, but the more studious restoration projects were reserved for the architectural set-pieces. Even so several of these schemes were essentially makeshift and a second wave of architectural renewal is underway, at its most visible as one moves south along the Rue Geoffroy de Montbray to the parish church of **St-Pierre**.

As one of the finest Flamboyant churches in Basse-Normandie this has finally received the attention it long deserved, with an exterior whose lower volumes are virtuosically overshadowed by two strongly contrasted towers. A Romanesque church existed here, and the site may have hosted St-Lô's 6C cathedral, but the present structure dates from 1495 when bishop Geoffrey Herbert began work on a new church intended to replace a building damaged during the Hundred Years War. The choir, transepts, and nave were completed early in the 16C, with the western bell tower raised before a stone clock face was placed against its northern elevation in 1550. The more sober classical entablatures of the lantern tower were begun in the same year, 1550, but not completed before 1580 by which time the design had developed to reveal a soaring interior octagon, disguised on the exterior by the addition of corner towers. The internal spaces were recently restored but the largely undecorated stonework now reflects too much light without the original stained glass. This is particularly unfortunate at St-Pierre as the calculated extravagance of a sumptuously carved balustrade was intended to be seen sandwiched between the two main fields of glass. Three distinct patterns are used, supported throughout by a delicately carved frieze of vinescroll and naturalistic foliage, and serve to contrast the main areas of the building, with the transept balustrade given an almost wave-like fluidity. The piers and aisle walls also carry a number of 16C funerary inscriptions, testimony to the mostly bourgeois patronage that featured here.

Behind the apse the Rue St-Pierre retains some attractive 16C houses and descends steeply, past the hospital on the Rue de Morville, to the **Rue du Pont-de-Soulles**. Although its terraces are mostly redeveloped you can catch occasional glimpses of the late medieval workshops and houses which once animated what was the main street of a small industrial village. The dyers and tanners of Coutances had settled here by the 13C, but it was the 16C which brought the greatest prosperity, when the newly established binders and papermakers grew rich on the back of diocesan demand. Despite the incursions of suburban Coutances the area retains that sense of being apart from the town, seeming to belong to the valley of the Bulsard and the Bocage, and points one south towards Granville and the Baie du Mont-Saint-Michel.

The direct route to Granville follows the D971, passing just to the east of a low ridge which supports the important priory of (4km) **Orval**. The documents make no mention of a priory here before the late 11C, when it is listed as a daughter house of Lessay, and the crossing tower, crypt, and eastern bays of the nave may well date from this period. The presence of archaic elements, notably the narrow rectangular capitals visible around the lower storey of the crossing tower, have provoked speculation as to earlier buildings on the site however, suspicions which are reinforced by the nature of the crypt. Orval was the birthplace of the widely venerated 7C bishop of Thérouanne, St-Omer, and it is clear that the crypt here housed a reliquary cult. Entrance was originally from within the church, via doors in the east wall of the transept, but as these were blocked up during a 15C refurbishment of the transepts and choir you now enter through an external door in the north wall of the choir. The crypt consists of two rooms, that to the west supported by a central pier (it is now used as a repository for an assortment of medieval stonework which includes a Romanesque font). The eastern chamber is a later addition but this type of short, flat-ended crypt, accessible from the transepts, has Carolingian precedents and, coupled with the pre-Romanesque nature of the incised decoration of the tower capitals, suggests that earlier forms were either being reused, or being deliberately invoked. As the church is always open during daylight you might also take a look at the fine octopartite vault thrown above the crossing in the late 12C.

Regaining the D971 to the south of Orval allows you to cross the River Sienne and steer a line between the coast and the western reaches of the Bocage, measuring out the distance (26km) to Granville. **Granville** is very much a town of two parts—a flat and breezy lower quarter which expanded rapidly in the 19C between the railway station and the port, and a fortified 'haute ville' enclosed by granite walls on a rocky spur which pushes the town out into the Atlantic. Its eminence dates from 1439, when English impatience with the continuing success of the French garrison on Mont-Saint-Michel led the Earl of Warwick to construct a fortified base, encircling the 12C chapel of Notre-Dame-de-Lihou on the rock here. A ditch, known as the 'Tranchée aux Anglais', was excavated across the isthmus linking the rock with the mainland, but the fealty of this new fortress was short-lived and in 1442 the Governor of Mont-Saint-Michel, Louis d'Estouteville, succeeded in expelling the English. The early fortifications were demolished in 1689 by the Marquis de Louvois, Louis XIV's military adviser, but the French corsairs who used the harbour beneath the southern cliffs provoked an English naval bombardment in 1695, by way of retaliation at their habit of picking off Atlantic-bound ships. In consequence the greater part of the upper town dates from the 18C, enfolded by partially recon-structed ramparts, and largely self-contained.

You enter by the **Grande Porte**, a much repaired early 16C gatehouse and the key point in the surviving defensive systems. This carries a plaque commemorating the action of 14–15 November 1793, when a Vendéen army under the command of Henri de la Rochejaquelin laid siege, only to be repelled after 28 hours by an unsympathetic populace and garrison, the defeat effectively marking the end of the Chouan uprising in the Cotentin. To the right the old Logis du Roi houses the **Musée du Vieux Granville**, and gives access to a glorious terraced garden from which you can survey the fishing quays sunk beneath its eastern flanks.

The museum provides a stimulating prologue to a stroll around the upper town for, as with Granville itself, it reveals a minor, vernacular history, strangely remote from metropolitan forms. The main displays concentrate on Granville's illustrious past as a major fishing port, whose boats once plied the Newfoundland banks and whose oysters were eulogised by medieval pilgrims to Mont-Saint-Michel. The deep sea trawlers have disappeared and the oyster-beds were wiped out by disease in 1923–24, but a small inshore fleet still works out of the harbour here, complementing the ferries and supply boats which serve the Iles Chausey. A floor is also devoted to 19C Norman dress, particularly the elaborate bonnets of net and lace, called coiffes, bizarrely favoured in some of the windiest towns in Basse-Normandie—the Papillon in Avranches, the Grande Volante of Coutances, and Granville's Bavolette.

East of the Logis flighted steps, known as Les Degrés, lead along the Rue Lecarpentier to the breathtaking panoramas of the **Place de l'Isthme**, where views reach across the great strands sweeping north to Barneville, or south across the mudflats of the Baie du Mont-Saint-Michel to the Brittany coast, and the reefs and islands of the Chausey archipelago. The Place also overlooks a handsome casino, built in 1910, which persuaded the municipal authorities, and the SNCF, that henceforth Granville should be seen as the Monaco of the North. Towards the square's western perimeter the modern Musée Richard-Anacréon plays host to temporary or touring exhibitions of contemporary art, and it is from this corner, at the eastern limit of the old rectangular enceinte, that the upper town is most visible. Two long streets, the Rue St-Jean and Rue Notre-Dame, run the length of the town, linked by narrow lanes and bordered by handsome terraces of mostly 18C houses, whose projecting granite stringcourses maintain the storey lines in an undulating townscape. The favoured building material is a quartzy granite quarried on the Iles de Chausey, at its best in the sharp light which follows spring showers, when the moist crystalline nature of the stone lends a sparkling quality to the elevations. This works particularly well in buildings such as **L'Hôtel dit Ganne-Destouches**, at No. 45 Rue St-Jean, where an elegant late 17C façade is articulated into panels by shallow pilasters and lintels. There are some grand houses set beside courtyards along the Rue Notre-Dame, notably No. 76, and the 19C **Hôtel des Le Mengnonnet** (No. 54) sheltering behind a fine wrought-iron screen of 1850. Beyond the small central **Place Cambernon** the ground level rises to meet the unusual façade of No. 3 Rue St-Jean, sporting two terracotta reliefs of Adam and Eve, and the bell-hung spire where the church of **Notre-Dame** marks the western limit of the town.

This was probably the site of a Romanesque chapel 'sur la Roque et

Montagne de Granville', where a cult statue of the Virgin, Notre-Dame de Lihou, was venerated, having been raised by fishermen off Cap-Lihou some time before 1133. The cult is still observed in the north transept chapel, though the present statue is 15C, and as a new church was begun in 1440 this later cult object may be directly connected with the current structure. The construction of the church eventually stretched over 300 years, though the all-embracing Chausey granite tends to merge any more distinctive phases. The crossing piers and choir aisle walls date from 1440–45, the choir proper from the mid 16C, and the nave was completed c 1600. A classical west front was added between 1767 and 1771 but the maintenance throughout the interior of columnar piers, quadripartite vaulting, and short clerestory windows welds the church into an airy and unified complex.

To the west of Notre-Dame, and beyond the limits of the old town, some 18th and 19C naval batteries are revetted into the cliffs of the western headland, **La Pointe de la Roc**, whose lighthouse traditionally marks the northern limit of the Baie du Mont-Saint-Michel.

The lower town is considerably less interesting, and you might either follow the coast road, the D911, past the great sandy beaches of St-Pair-sur-Mer south-east to Genêts and Avranches, or take an inland detour, along the D973 and D580, to the abbey of **La Lucerne**, some 12km distant.

A Premonstratensian abbey had already been founded in the forests of the Thar valley in 1143 when, on the advice of the great schoolman, Achard, the community moved to the present site in 1161. This was downstream of the original foundation, in a well-watered glade beneath the wooded slopes of the Cortils. The south nave arcade, transepts, crossing tower, and choir, along with parts of the conventual buildings, escaped demolition during the 19C, and since 1959 the Association des Amis de l'Abbaye de La Lucerne has undertaken an extensive programme of consolidation and repair, enabling a reconsecration to take place in 1970.

Achard was a well-travelled scholar, having been Abbot of Bridlington before accepting the immensely influential abbacy of St-Victoire at Paris. His elevation to the bishopric of Avranches in 1160 does not seem to have dulled his interest in the relatively contemplative life of the Premonstratensians (a non-monastic order of canons regular, also referred to as Norbertines or, in England, White Canons)—and he was buried, in accordance with his wishes, in the choir in 1171. The church itself was built in a single campaign between 1164 and 1178, with a square-ended two bay sanctuary, aisleless transepts, and a long two storeyed nave. Both its design and its rigorous eschewal of ornament have much in common with contemporary Cistercian practice, and the only serious concession to architectural decoration is to be found in the blind arcading of the west front. The **crossing tower** is a different matter however, and was not raised until 1180–1200. It carries three deeply moulded lancets, covered by wooden louvres, and is the seminal essay in an approach to the design of bell towers which was to have profound consequences for Norman architecture during the 13C. For it was with La Lucerne in mind that the churches of the Bessin and Cotentin began to embrace these tall staged lancets and square belfries.

The cloister arcades were rebuilt from 1700–12, though not an arch remains standing, but the 12C **lavatorium** is in situ in the west walk and supports a billet-moulded arch. More curiously the foundations of the **chapter house** show this to have been a rectangular hall divided by an arcade into two aisles, rather in the manner of the slightly earlier chapter house at Cistercian Kirkstall. Again the pattern proved influential and was picked up locally at Mortain and Hambye. Further south the late 12C **refectory** is underpinned by a handsomely vaulted cellar range, its surviving bays currently serving as a template for an ambitious reconstruction. By contrast, work on the southernmost reaches has been completed, imaginatively clearing and reinstating the pond between the claustral buildings and the privately-owned 17C Abbot's Lodging. On the whole the Abbaye de La Lucerne de l'Outre Mer (the outre-mer refers to the support Lucerne gave to English claims to Normandy) has been neglected by historians of medieval architecture, surprisingly so for a building which could shed light on Anglo-Norman relations during the later 12C, and even stranger in view of the beauty of the site.

From La Lucerne the D105 takes you south as far as **Sartilly**, from where the D35 continues down to the sea at (12km) **Genêts**. The village itself languishes above the salt meadows which fringe the Baie du Mont-Saint-Michel, and is often flooded by the higher spring tides. It is best known as a point of embarkation however, where pilgrims would undertake the treacherous 9km crossing over the flats at low tide to Mont-Saint-Michel, leaving Genêts by the banks of the Bec d'Andaine. Mont-Saint-Michel can be seen from the stone benches behind the Mairie, clear in the foreshortening light, invitingly within two hours' walk—but be warned, for many pilgrims perished in these sands and heard their last Mass not in the mighty spaces of the abbey, but in the modest parish church at Genêts. What remains of the Romanesque parochial accommodation is fairly typical of the smaller 12C granite churches of the Cotentin, with a transept and square crossing tower, appealingly quartered by a ranting gargoyle, to which a 13C choir and late medieval nave were appended.

The shoreline of the bay was once peppered with religious foundations such as at St-Léonard or Ardevon, but those of **Avranches** (10km along the D911) were the earliest and much the most important. The town now centres around the Place Littré, to the south of the high ground on which the town originally grew. The **Hôtel-de-Ville** stands to its rear and houses, in the second floor library, the 203 manuscripts from the abbey of Mont-Saint-Michel which were packed into carts after the French Revolution and driven across the sands to Genêts. They were bound, according to law, for the literary depôt at Avranches, and now form one of the major collections of French medieval illuminated manuscripts still to be seen outside the Bibliothèque Nationale or larger university libraries. A dozen or so are usually to be found under glass display cases, identified by library press-marks—so that Avranches 237, for example, turns out to be a late 12C copy of Boethius' treatise 'De Musica'. The library is best known for its important holdings of early Romanesque manuscripts, reflecting a bias in the mid 11C scriptorium at Mont-Saint-Michel towards the production of Early Christian texts. Many of these carry large illuminated initials inhabited by beasts or masks, though occasionally, as in the superb frontispiece to St Augustine's 'Dialogue Against The Manichean Faustus', the manuscripts are enlivened with full or half-page illustrations. The 11C works were mostly written in an angular miniscule, but as many of the books had been acquired as gifts and been made in different scriptoria, the range of textual and illustrative styles is enormous. For sheer clarity look at the rounded capitals of an 8C Anglo-Saxon Gospels (MSS 66 and 71) written in an almost bouncy style.

Until recently the manuscripts were kept at the **Musée**, reached along an avenue to the left of the Hôtel-de-Ville, but a general reorganisation of the municipal collections has focused the museum into three, rather than four, sections: medieval, local, and lithographic. The actual museum building was an outhouse of the former bishop's palace, built in the 15C to provide additional cellarage, but having served out the 19C as the town jail it has been extensively modified. In the course of the most recent refurbishment it was clearly felt that the medieval material deserved the deepest gloom, and all metalwork and stone sculpture is now displayed in the cellars. With the exception of two 12C Limoges reliquary caskets, and a damaged 14C Crucifixion in translucent enamel, the material is of mostly local workmanship—at its best in the 14C limestone relief of the Martyrdom of St Apollonia. There is also an extensive section concerned with the social and commercial aspects of life in the Avranchin during the 18th and 19C, climaxing with an entertaining account of how the humble maid's working bonnet was transformed by lace, and heroically elaborated into the great coiffes favoured by the 19C petite-bourgeoisie. The museum's core is its collection of 19C lithographs however, and representative examples of the work of every major French lithographer have been mounted in the largest gallery.

To the west of the museum the **Palais de Justice** stood until 1790 as the main block of the bishop's palace, having been rebuilt by Bishop Louis de Bourbon in the 15C. Sadly the damage wrought by a fire in the late 19C has denuded it of most of the late medieval rooms, though a splendid rib vaulted kitchen survived both the fire and the rebuilding. Contact with the cathedral was via the western gates of the palace, but as these now give onto a grassy ledge, known as **La Plate-Forme**, you are left to gaze across the steep drop to the estuary of the River Sée, with the rock of Mont-Saint-Michel the looming element in a vast horizon. The site was recently excavated, uncovering material from the 5th, 9th, and 11C cathedrals, and has been regrassed, leaving a chained paving slab and upturned column as the only visible reminders of the church. The paving stone was placed by the west portal to commemorate Henry II's act of penance on 22 May 1172, when barefoot and dressed only in a shirt Henry abased himself before the cathedral, and asked forgiveness for his part in the murder of Thomas à Becket.

From the Plate-Forme the old town unfolds along the high ground, parcelled between the cathedral and the castle. The municipality has compiled a recommended itinerary, indicated by green arrows: a section from here, along the **Rue de Lille**, takes you past the rear elevation of the late medieval dean's mansion. A right turn onto the cobbled Rue Engilbault leads to the Rue de Geôle, and thus follows the line of the 12C ramparts as far as the Place d'Estouteville, bringing you face to face with the system of fortifications at its strongest point—where the walls meet Henry I's early 12C **Donjon**. This was mostly destroyed in the 19C but elements of the 13C enceinte walls remain in place, encompassing a sheltered garden where an enceinte tower has been transformed into an immitation mini-keep. The castle overlooks the rear elevations of the Hôtel-de-Ville, returning you to the Place Littré, but it also looks onto the pair of large 19C churches which renewed the religious life of Avranches after the destruction of its cathedral. The huge structure high on the south-western horizon is the Gothic Revival **Notre-Dame-des-Champs**, while the neo-Renaissance bell tower towards the east belongs to **St-Gervais**.

The latter stands a couple of streets behind the Place Littré and was built between 1843 and 1863 as a replacement for a much smaller church, marrying a ponderous Doric arcade with a disturbing triforium. The south-west tower houses a small treasury which displays several 13–14C enamelled, or engraved, gilded copper reliquaries, and a very beautiful

15C Virgin and Child—simply carved in stone and no more than 30cm high. It is best known however for the skull of **St-Aubert**, holed towards the top of the right lobe where, according to legend, the finger of the Archangel Michael left a mark of impatience that Aubert required a third visit before he would agree to found an oratory on the rock of Mont Tombe (subsequently known as Mont-Saint-Michel). Of such powerful magic are great cults made.

The second of these churches, Notre-Dame-des-Champs (Place Carnot), is of less interest, but it stands opposite the superlative **Jardin des Plantes**— planted in the grounds of the old Franciscan convent by Professeur Perrin during the late 18C, and subsequently expanded by the cultivation of exotic species from Japan and south-east Asia. Its terraced walks incorporate a Romanesque portal from the 11C chapel of St-Georges-de-Bouillé, surrounded by gingko and heliotrope, and are perhaps the most pleasant of all situations from which to muse on the marshy flats and sweeping shoreline of the Baie du Mont-Saint-Michel laid out below.

16

The Southern Marches: Mont-St-Michel to Alençon

ROAD (159km): Mont St-Michel; D976, 9km Pontorson; D30, 15km St-James; 20km St-Hilaire-du-Harcouët; D977, 14km Mortain; D907, 9km Barenton; D907/D217, 15km Lonlay-l'Abbaye; D22, 9km Domfront; D908/D335, 19km Bagnoles-de-l'Orne; D916, 6km La Ferté-Macé; D908, 17km Carrouges; D2, 26km Alençon.

It may seem a little perverse in the context of this guide to see Mont-St-Michel as a beginning rather than as a goal, to reverse the experience of pilgrims and wayfarers to whom the abbey signified a stage in the ascent of the soul towards Judgement, and instead turn eastwards on a journey across the southern belly of Normandy. But most pilgrims must at some time return, and Mont-St-Michel is not only a spiritual haven for the penitent, it is also a frontier, a border zone where one might look south to Brittany and western France, or survey the Marches before turning back towards the heart of the duchy. To many English pilgrims the mount was but a stage in a longer and greater pilgrimage, and having saluted the arm of St James at Reading they would navigate the Channel to Barfleur and race across the Cotentin, bound for Compostela. To the monarchs of 13C France Mont-St-Michel was more importantly a fortress, and one which might be said to complement the older, feudal castles stretching out eastwards as far as the Normandy Perche.

This line of fortifications protecting the south-western flank of Normandy was not the result of a concerted programme of building, such as under-pinned the defensive structures of the Vexin or Avre valley, and in truth the threat posed by Brittany and Maine was most keenly felt by the local baronage. Nevertheless the castles at St-James and Mortain were raised by Duke William and his half-brother, and the formidable donjon at Domfront was brought under the control Henry I. These defensive works stand above the hill towns of the southern Marches, and the predominantly Bocage landscape of this area is broken by a series of prominent ridges, running west to east, which command the main vantage lines over the valley of the Mayenne or the Alpes Mancelles. In fact the whole area was once quite densely wooded, but the most extensive stands of oak and beech are now to be found towards the east, in the forêts des Andaines and Ecouves, and the southern reaches of the Cotentin conform to the same pattern of mixed farming as has shaped the land to the north of the Sée valley. The low-lying western shores, particularly around Mont-St-Michel, were originally renowned for their treacherous quicksands and shifting river courses, but even the notorious Couesnon has now been tamed, and the old salt-marshes have given way to sheep pasture.

MONT-ST-MICHEL. The association of this isolated granite outcrop with religious, cultic, or funerary rites is an ancient one, and it seems that before the early 8C the island was known as Mont Tombe, derived from the low Latin 'Tumba', and signifying either a tumulus or tomb. The islet to the north carries a distant echo of this in that it is known as Tombelaine, though it remained unoccupied until 1137 when the monks established a small priory there. It is believed that in prehistoric times Mont Tombe may have acted as a sea-tomb, whither, according to Celtic legend, the souls of the dead were ferried by an invisible barque, and that equally this was annexed during the Gallo-Roman period to act as a shrine to the cult of Mithras. But the primary source for the study of the early history is the 'Revelatio Ecclesiae Sancti Michaelis', written by monks from the abbey during the late 10C, and its legendary account soon entered the medieval canon.

According to this the Archangel Michael appeared one night in 708 to Aubert, bishop of Avranches, instructing the bishop to build a church in his honour on Mont Tombe. Aubert convinced himself that this was a dream rather than a divinely ordained apparition, and the archangel had to appear three times before his wishes were taken seriously, scorching a hole in the bishop's skull with the radiance of his indicative finger. Aubert took the final message seriously, and founded an oratory on the site, consecrated in 709 and staffed by canons, several of whom were sent to Monte Gargano to obtain relics associated with St-Michel. The Revelatio is quite explicit in comparing Aubert's foundation with the 5C shrine of the Archangel Michael at Monte Sant'Angelo on the Gargano peninsula, pointing out that the church 'was not built on the summit, but was arranged as a crypt which would hold 100 people. By this St-Aubert hoped to reproduce the form of the sanctuary which the intervention of the archangel had laid out in the rock at Mont Gargan.'

Whatever the merits of this legendary foundation it was certainly the case that Mont-St-Michel was attracting a pilgrimage to the shrine of the archangel by 867, when we hear of a certain Bernard who had travelled to Jerusalem, Rome, Monte Gargano, and 'St-Michel-aux-deux-Tombes' (Mont Tombe and Tombelaine). In the same year Charles the Bald made over the county of the Cotentin to the Breton chief, Salomon, and so set in motion a territorial dispute which was to fracture relations between the Norse settlers of the areas to the east, and the emerging duchy of Brittany. The oratory on Mont-St-Michel was destroyed in the course of this dipute, and it was not until 933, with the concession of the bishoprics of Coutances and Avranches to Duke William Longsword, that the River Couesnon was established as the de facto border between Normandy and Brittany. Mont-St-Michel became in effect a Norman frontier post, a situation which

Mont-St-Michel

doubtless inspired the decision of Duke Richard I in 966 to introduce Benedictine monks from the abbey of Fontenelle (better known by its later medieval title of St-Wandrille) to the rock.

It was not until c 1017 however that abbot Hildebert II began the architectural expansion of the abbey, starting work on a new church above and to the east of the surviving 10C building. Although the crossing of Hildebert's church occupies the very summit of the rock, the current shape of Mont-St-Michel owes most to the decision of Abbot Ranulphe de Bayeux (1058–85) to situate the main conventual quarters to the north, supported on a series of massive substructures that once gave rise to a monumental three-storeyed arrangement, and provided the monks with a northern entrance to the church. The settlement problems this gave rise to probably caused the collapse of the nave north aisle in 1103, but the monastery to which Robert de Torigni was elected abbot in 1154 was undoubtedly an impressive one, and one whose restored nave was three bays longer than the present truncated version.

The great days of the pilgrimage to Mont-St-Michel were those of the later Middle Ages, and although the goal remained the same mighty rock, its ecclesiastical shape had changed, and with it the nature of its accommodation. During the early 13C Anglo-French struggle for Normandy the claims of King John found favour on the mount, and the abbey duly found itself a target for the French forces. A Breton army had allied itself to the French cause, and in 1203 set fire to the lower town of Mont-St-Michel, the conflagration spreading to the conventual quarter and destroying the greater part of Ranulphe's northern precincts. In reparation Philip Augustus financed the construction of a new northern complex between 1212 and 1228, pinned against the side of the rock in the same fashion as the earlier work, but on a scale and of a splendour which earned it the appellation—La Merveille. With this increased royal sensitivity to Mont-St-Michel's multi-farious role as pilgrimage centre, Benedictine abbey, and effective fortress, Abbot Richard Turstin (1237–64) found himself under pressure to fortify the lower town, and the first of the enceinte walls was built around the south and east faces of the rock.

The growth of this subsidiary town, offering food, shelter, and souvenirs to the growing bands of pilgrims, was a direct reflection of a relatively recent phenomenon—the recognition of Mont-St-Michel as one of the major pilgrimage sites of France, and a centre which might rival the attractions of the shrine of the Virgin at Chartres, or of Ste-Foi at Conques. By the mid 13C the rock had become one of the most popular sites in Europe, and St-Louis himself made the journey in 1256, to be met by abbot Turstin who had been accorded the privilege of wearing pontifical vest-ments. The prosperity this brought contrasts with the desuetude of the later 14C, when the catastrophic depopulation of France after the Black Death (1348) and a lax regime at the abbey, reduced a community of 42 monks in 1337 to no more than 20 in 1390.

Nonetheless the garrison was maintained at full strength, at a joint cost borne by the abbot and the king, and the Hundred Years War saw the strengthening of the upper walls and, following the English victory at Agincourt in 1415, the wholesale renewal of the town defences. The latter work was executed under Abbot Robert Jolivet, at the urging of the captain of the garrison, but Jolivet's faith in the efficacy of the new defences was clearly not of the same order as that of the soldiery, and with the English occupying virtually the whole of Normandy and establishing a forward base on Mont Tombelaine, Jolivet went over to the opposition in 1420. The abbot became adviser to the Duke of Bedford in Rouen, while the defence of Mont-St-Michel was left in the hands of a small standing army. The Romanesque choir of the monastic church collapsed in 1421, ironically between sieges, and a second siege of 1423 was successfully resisted with the aid of Breton mariners who managed to supply the mount by sea, under the nose of the English fleet. The appointment of Louis d'Estouteville as captain in 1425 perhaps marks the turning point in the defence of the mount, for it was d'Estouteville's brilliance as an engineer which allowed the completion of a vast new defensive complex, shielding the town from direct assault. The success of this might be judged from the attack of 1433 when, after setting fire to the town, an English army numbered by Thomas Le Roy at 20,000 was repulsed having managed to fracture no more than one, minor, breach.

Astonishingly, pilgrims continued to make the journey to Mont-St-Michel throughout this period, and the selling of safe-conducts became a useful money-spinner among the English garrisons of the southern Cotentin. The eventual expulsion of the English after the battle of Formigny in 1450 witnessed an explosion of visitors to the mount, as St-Michel became identified with the success of the French cause. Louis d'Estouteville had insisted on the appointment of his brother, Cardinal Guillaume d'Es-touteville, as abbot in 1444 and as archbishop of Rouen and bishop of Ostia (near Rome) Guillaume visited the abbey once, in 1452. It was a significant visit however and speeded work on the rebuilding of the choir, begun some six years earlier. Much of the money for this came from the impressive list of noble pilgrims who made the journey in the later 15C: Marie, wife of

Charles VII, in 1447; François I, Duc de Bretagne, in 1450; François II in 1460; King Louis XI in 1462, 1472, and 1473. But Guillaume's abbacy presaged the fallow centuries of non-residentiary abbots, and with this came decreasing popularity, dwindling revenues, and disrepair.

To some extent the religious life of the abbey was reinvigorated by the introduction of the Maurist reform in 1622, but little work was effected on the abbatial buildings, and the crumbling superstructure was denuded of the three western bays of the nave in 1776. By the time of the Revolution there was scarcely a monastic community left to target, and the abbey was transformed into a prison, accepting as its first inmates some 300 priests who had refused to accede to the civil reconstitution of the clergy. It was well suited to the purpose, and by the mid 19C was routinely pressed into service to house political prisoners of the calibre of Barbès, Blanqui, and Raspail. The abuse of a monument of capital importance soon became a cause for complaint however, and in 1836 Victor Hugo opened a campaign to end the use of Mont-St-Michel as a prison with the question: 'When will we in France understand the sanctity of these structures?' Nonetheless it was not until 1863 that the prison was closed, and 1874 that Mont-St-Michel was declared a 'Monument Historique', setting in train a major programme of restoration. This had the effect of renewing a considerable quantity of the earlier stonework, but it also saw the exterior profile of the main church significantly altered, with the rebuilding of the lantern tower and raising of a timber flèche under Victor Petitgrand in 1897. The last large-scale restoration was conducted by Yves Froidevaux between 1965 and 1966, when Notre-Dame-sous-Terre was consolidated and a garden laid out in the upper cloister. As such, and particularly with regard to the late 19C repairs, one needs to exercise caution in assessing the finer details of the medieval work, though the general shape and lay-out of the abbey buildings hold good.

THE TOWN. Mont-St-Michel was connected to the mainland by a high causeway in 1877, prior to which one either sailed, or travelled on foot at low tide, following the right bank of the River Couesnon from the south. An equally popular route with pilgrims arriving from the north involved calculating the tides so as to allow a minimum of two hours to make the crossing from Genêts, but the Grève is an unreliable partner and the route remains as inadvisable now as it was dangerous then. You enter the town by the only gap in the medieval ramparts, **La Porte de l'Avancée**, a triangular bastion overlooked by the early 16C **Corps de Garde des Bourgeois**, which acts as the outer layer of a concentric system of defences. The sea also floods the advance gate at high tide, leaving an attacking army relatively little time in which to construct the siege works necessary to penetrate the second line of defence. This is known as the Porte du Boulevard and in turn gives onto a third mighty gate, **La Porte du Roy**. Belonging to Louis d'Estouteville's early 15C reinforcement of the town this inner gate was originally sunk to the south with a moat, but has acquired an upper two-storey dwelling, known as the Logis du Roi, which accommodated the captain of the garrison. Breaking through this protective skin brings you onto **La Grande Rue**, the old main street of the lower town.

The street abounds with restaurants, cafés and cheap souvenir shops, a bustling narrow marketplace which can provide the modern visitor with as many gawdy mementoes as it once managed to foist on willing medieval pilgrims, if, that is, you manage to move along it. The buildings which house this commercial market were mostly rebuilt in the late 19C, but a few have retained their late medieval core, and warrant a cursory inspection. The

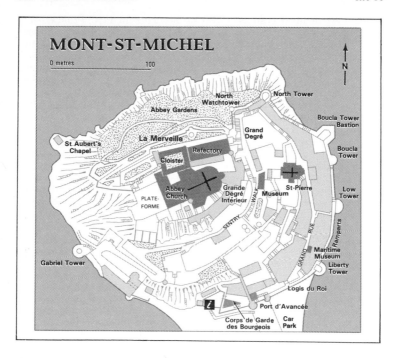

best are the Maison de l'Artichaut and Maison de la Sirène, both late 15C half-timbered townhouses, the lower of which stands above a passage giving onto the eastern ramparts.

Just before the Grande Rue begins to pitch more steeply and ascend to the abbey itself, you are channelled beneath the shadow of the parish church of **St-Pierre**, architecturally unprepossessing but a pleasant respite from the hustle below. The greater part of the present building is late 15C, the main piers having been laid on the bases of the 11C structure. The sculpture is more promising, with an impressive array of funerary slabs and a fine early 16C Virgin and Child in the south-east chapel. From the rear of the church you can cross the small terraced cemetery and climb up towards the Terrasse de la Gire, and beyond to the splendid **Chemin de Ronde**, the old sentry walk beneath the south flank of the abbey, capturing views south along the course of the Couesnon, or east to Avranches. This also brings you face to face with the outer defences of the abbey at the head of the **Grand Degré**, the heavily restored monumental stairway which connects the Grande Rue with the abbey proper.

THE ABBEY. It is now impossible to visit the abbey except as a member of a guided tour, and having bought a ticket you are expected to wait on the platform to the west of the main monastic church until there are sufficient numbers to form a party, usually 10–15 minutes. In summer it is possible to join an English, German, or Italian speaking guide (usually one per hour). By far the most stimulating way to spend your time here would be to take a Visite Conférence, which allows access to Notre-Dame-sous-Terre and l'Escalier de Dentelle, the late 15C outer stairway of the apse, otherwise excluded from the general circuit. These last around two hours, and encourage discussion, but are unfortunately only available during the spring and summer academic holidays. The following brief description of the abbey parallels the likely progress of the general tour, and is intended to be used in conjunction with the broader history of the foundation given above.

The Grand Degré brings you out against the northern flanks of the most imposing of the outer defences, the 14C **Châtelet**, built of alternate courses of pink and grey granite and opening onto a second covered staircase, the **Escalier du Gouffre**. This in turn connects with the early 13C **Salle des Gardes** (now the main ticket hall) from where medieval pilgrims would have passed to the right, into the Almonry or, if of higher rank, into the Salle des Hôtes above. Today's visitor does neither, and instead climbs the **Grand Degré Intérieur** towards the western platform. This takes you between the mid 13C abbot's quarters and the south flank of the choir, before twisting to the north and leading out on the western **Plate-Forme du Saut-Gauthier**. Until 1780 most of this terrace was occupied by the western three bays of the nave, terminated by a 12C twin-towered façade which had replaced the original narthex of c 1080, but the rank decline of the abbey in the years preceding the Revolution led to their demolition, and replacement by the present drab west wall.

You are also standing above the earliest of the surviving structures, **Notre-Dame-sous-Terre**, revetted against the western summit of the rock some time between 933 and 942, i.e. before the secular canons had been replaced by Benedictine monks. This is divided into two aisles by a thick wall, pierced by brick arches to measure out two bays, and gives onto a flat east end surmounted by a later tribune. It is a modest and tantalising structure, and one where the dedication of the altars to the Trinity and the Virgin suggests that the building was again seen as emulating the grotto of Monte Sant'Angelo on the Gargano.

The problems associated with the main monastic church, **l'Eglise Abbatiale du Mont-St-Michel**, are of a wholly different order, and might be posed in terms of function and appearance. Put simply the building has been stripped of its reliquary iconography, with barely a cult object to be seen, and a spareness in the interior has left the church little more than an architectural shell. The earliest part of the surviving building is the south elevation of the **nave**, that to the north having been rebuilt after the north aisle collapsed in 1103. Although Hildebert II undertook the building of a new church, starting with the choir shortly after 1017, it was not until the abbacy of Ranulphe de Bayeux (1058–85) that work began on the nave. This was to prove an influential design, and is beautifully realised with attached half-columns creating an emphatic bay rhythm, and giant pilasters which enclose the clerestory in a high relieving arch. The triforium is divided by angle-moulded arches into two major units, which have been further subdivided by narrower and plainer arches, to create a band of open arcading across the elevation and quicken the longitudinal rhythms. It is the earliest example of a type of treatment which was taken up in the transepts of St Albans after 1077, and surfaced in a number of important 12C buildings, most notably in the choir of Suger's St-Denis and at Sens cathedral.

The crossing and splendid lantern were entirely rebuilt by Victor Petit-grand between 1889 and 1897 and offer an abrupt transition between the Romanesque work to the west, and the Flamboyant vocabulary of the **choir**.

The early 11C choir collapsed in 1421, though as it has been shown that the crypt survived (making it possible to reconstruct the apse ambulatory groundplan of Hildebert's church) the reasons for this disaster remain obscure. Reconstruction was delayed until 1446, when a new crypt was laid out, and work on the choir proper began c 1450, though a lengthy late 15C hiatus meant that the structure was not completed until 1521. It is relatively austere, controlling the tracery in rectangular panels in the glazed triforium, or simplifying the tracery patterns of the window heads rather in the manner of St-Ouen at Rouen, but the loss of all the glass makes it difficult to judge the intended range of effects. The exterior is more exhilarating, but before passing outside you could take the opportunity to gaze on what little sculpture has survived in situ. The chapels to the north and south house early 16C bas-reliefs of the Expulsion and Harrowing of Hell, and Four Evangelists respectively, though the finest work is to be found in the second chapel to the north, where a set of five English 15C alabasters have been arranged as a retable. It is tragically little in a choir which was intended to assail the visitor with devotional imagery, and the absence should be borne in mind when examining the acres of stripped and polished stonework.

A door in the north-eastern bay of the nave leads across a small inner court, beyond which the western range of the **Merveille** has been pinned to the precipitous northern face of the rock. The established precedent is to take visitors directly into the monks' **cloister**, an indulgence which would have been regarded as preposterous in medieval times, but useful because it allows one to take stock of where the cloister sits in relation to the rest of the conventual buildings. Prior to the 1203 sack of the town the earlier monastic quarters were somewhat piecemeal and situated around the north-western angles of the church, as can be seen in the Promenoir des Moines and Salle de l'Aquilon. And the sheer complexity of the layout at Mont-St-Michel derives in part from the decision to retain some of this earlier accommodation, and when coupled with the need to provide crypts at various levels to act as support for the superstructure, has created a spiral labyrinth. The lower two storeys of the Merveille connect with these earlier crypts and passages, while the upper storey affords the monks entry to the church.

The planning of the Merveille is in fact best approached with a view to its social operations. It is a long, rectangular structure in three storeys, each storey consisting of two principal rooms, and was built quickly between 1212 and 1228, with the areas to the east being slightly earlier than those to the west. The east wing was given over to the provision of food, with the almonry at the bottom offering succour to poor pilgrims, the Salle des Hôtes above reserved for visitors of noble birth, and the uppermost refectory the preserve of the monks. It thus mirrors the medieval world view of the three layers of society. The west wing was purely monastic, with a basement cellar, intermediate Salle des Chevaliers acting as the scriptorium and warming room, and upper cloister. This last structure was logistically more significant than it now appears, as the three western windows which offer such splendid views of the Brittany coast originally gave onto the chapter house.

The cloister remains one of the finest early 13C monastic buildings in northern France, its spandrels encrusted with a virtuosic display of foliate carving which compares closely with that in the choir of Bayeux cathedral, or the parish church of Norrey-en-Bessin. Although the colonettes were replaced in the 19C the arrangement of the arcading in two layers is original, and creates a measured half-beat by syncopating the inner arcade, fracturing the rhythms and teasing the eye. To the east the vast hall of the **refectory** elaborates a far simpler geometry, and still retains the niche in its south wall from which an accented bible would be read aloud during meals.

The construction of this upper storey of the Merveille coincided with a series of modifications to the substructures supporting the north flank of the Romanesque church, and which are most readily seen in the chapel of **Notre-Dame-des-Trente-Cierges**, off the intermediate storey. This is one of two crypts built between 1030 and 1048 to provide a platform for the building of the transepts of the main church, that of St-Martin being to the south. The apse is Romanesque but, as is all too evident, the oblique angle by which the Merveille intersects with the earlier structures to the south necessitated the rebuilding of the end wall of Notre-Dame, and the chief interest now lies with its fragmentary 13C polychromy. To the west a long passage, known as the **Promenoir des Moines**, pushes you out towards the north-west angle of the Romanesque church façade. Elements of the walling here have been taken over from the corridor's previous incarnation as the site (in all probability) of Ranulphe de Bayeux's 11C refectory, but the damage caused by the 1103 collapse of the nave north aisle above led to a wholesale redesign. This was effected during the abbacy of Roger II (1106–26), and is renowned among architectural historians for its early use of ribbed vaulting, probably soon after 1120.

The complex interdependence, and capacity for grandeur, of the major corridors at Mont-St-Michel is best illustrated in the magnificent barrel-vaulted passageway which runs from north to south beyond the western end of the Promenoir des Moines. This descends as you move south, and acts as the main return, taking you past Notre-Dame-sous-Terre and into the old mortuary chapel of **St-Etienne**, dismally restored in 1976. The southern precincts are considerably less ambitious than their counterparts to the north, and are effectively divorced from Richard Turstin's mid 13C abbot's lodgings by the Grand Degré Intérieur. As such you hug the southern foundation walls of the nave, passing through the ossuary to the **Crypte St-Martin**, which unlike Notre-Dame-des-Trente-Cierges, remains wholly 11C, with simply decorated foliate capitals and spare mouldings. The return east passes through the aptly named **Crypte des Gros-Piliers**, the main support for the late medieval choir, and a structure whose role is strictly functional. Begun in 1446 with a minimum of architectural detail, the crypt is furnished with the same number of radiating chapels as the choir, but there is now little to stay for, and the north door takes you back towards the middle storey of the Merveille.

Here, to the east, the **Salle des Hôtes** was designed to act as a reception chamber for noble guests, witnessing the meeting of Louis IX and Abbot Richard Turstin in 1256, and Louis XI and Abbot Jean d'Estouteville in 1472. Even denuded of its full complement of tapestries it is perhaps the most elegant of all the monastic buildings—a spacious hall divided by a single row of columns, tall, airy, and light. And beyond, to the west, this notion of the ample hall was transformed into something much more grave, replacing the sleek axial rhythms of the Salle des Hôtes with the stately grandeur of a three-aisled design. This latter room is confusingly known as the **Salle des Chevaliers**, a title it was awarded in the 18C when the belief that it acted as a meeting place for the Order of St Michael gained ground. The order had in fact been founded at the Château d'Amboise in 1469 by Louis XI, and so far as is known never met at Mont-St-Michel. Even if it had it most certainly would not have been offered this particular hall, since the

Salle des Chevaliers was the monks' warming room, as well as acting as the scriptorium, and lay firmly within the conventual west wing of the Merveille.

The lowest storey of the Merveille is more modest, with a cellar to the west, and a vast twin-aisled **aumônerie** (almonry), the focus for so much peasant hope, to the east. The almonry was where alms were dispensed, where the greater number of pilgrims were fed and watered, and where accommodation might be offered. Reasonably enough this has now been fitted out as a general souvenir shop, and in leading you out at the western base of the Merveille offers a more interesting route back towards the Grande Rue through the abbey gardens. Alternatively you can return along the ramparts which, from the 13C north tower south-westwards, cling to the seaward flank of the rock, passing Louis d'Estouteville's splendid polygonal **Bastillon Boucle**. Eventually you will arrive at the Porte du Roy, but whichever route you take there remains, as ever, only one exit from Mont-St-Michel—the Porte de l'Avancée.

South of Mont-St-Michel the D976 hugs the Norman bank of the River Couesnon as far as the old frontier town of (9km) **Pontorson**. The early settlement acquired a strategic importance in 1031 when the local seigneur, Orson, built a bridge over the Couesnon, and as a target for Breton raiding parties the town became a significant factor in Duke William's 1064 campaign against the Bretons. An early legend ascribes the foundation of the town church of Notre-Dame to William, in thanksgiving for the eventual safe passage of his horsemen through the shifting sands of the Couesnon, and the church was certainly in the hands of the Dukes of Normandy in the following century, when Henry II made it over to Robert de Torigni at Mont-St-Michel.

Notre-Dame lies in the Place de l'Eglise, though sadly, along with the 16C Hôtel de la Ménardière on the Rue St-Michel, it is the only building of distinction still standing in an otherwise drab, roadside town. The west front is particularly fine—a rectangular massif in which the portal is recessed beneath a giant relieving arch, and flanked by two corner towers. This approach to the handling of a façade is reminiscent of the Anglo-Norman architecture of the English West Country, and like the nave is unlikely to be much earlier than c 1120. The latter was probably vaulted shortly after its initial construction, and certainly by 1150, with thickly moulded ribs supported on capitals whose diagonal abaci have been carved with shallow lozenges. The barrel-vaulted choir and south chapel are the earliest part of the exising church, and along with the crossing piers probably date from the second half of the 11C. These were modified between 1381 and 1418, when the crossing tower was raised and new window openings inserted in the choir.

The later medieval alterations run deeper than this however, and a splendid marble altar table of 1220 has been remounted against the east wall of the choir, close to where an early 15C arch was driven through the north choir aisle to communicate with the contemporary chapel of St-Sauveur. Here, against the east wall, one of the most notable late medieval survivals of south-western Normandy might just be detected in the wreckage of an ambitious stone retable, commissioned in 1502 by Robert Montlard. The various scenes depict the Passion of Christ, from the Triumphal Entry to the Resurrection, along with a prayerful Robert commending himself and his wife to Christ in the outermost panels of the lowest register. It is known locally as the altar of broken saints, in recognition of the brutal treatment it received during the Wars of Religion, and the damage is indeed catastrophic, with few heads surviving among the 19 smaller panels, and little to distinguish the great tripartite Crucifixion in what was clearly an intensely vivid cycle.

The church is the finest building in an area which has lost most of its better monuments, and the more stimulating route east would be to take the D30 through the flat pasture of the southern Avranchin to the market town of (15km) **St-James**. At the eastern edge of the town the last of the medieval ramparts towers above a gorge cut by the River Beuvron, and looks out over the *cour d'honneur* formed by the three surviving wings of the early 17C **Château de la Paluelle**. Many of the troops of Patton's 3rd Army who were killed during the Avranches Break-Out were buried in the war cemetery south-east of the town, set above one of the rises which mark the onset of that gently rolling landscape to the south of the valley of the Sélune. The damage caused by the German 7th Army's attempt to cut Patton's supply lines in the unsuccessful counter offensive of the 6–7 August 1944, is all too apparent among the smaller towns and villages of this area, and most devastatingly felt some 20km to the east, at **St-Hilaire-du-Harcouët**. The town was subsequently rebuilt in a workaday fashion, furnishing a number of promising squares with an unrelieved succession of stone mansion blocks. These centre on a particularly ugly late 19C church, whose twin-towered west front constitutes the major vertical accent in an otherwise flattened townscape, and has understandably been adopted as the local motif. The isolated late medieval bell tower of the earlier church still stands forlornly in a garden to the south, and having been decorated with frescoes by Marthe Flandrin in 1947 was briefly used as a baptistery, before once more falling into disrepair.

From here the D977 strikes north-east, taking you over the Sélune and onto the higher ground around (14km) the ancient fortress town of **Mortain**. The strategic potential of the site was first recognised by one of the Mauritanian legions employed by Rome to defend north-western Gaul, and a military camp was established on the southern slopes of the ridge during the 3C, becoming known as Mauritonium. Its early medieval significance depends from the collapse of a viable Carolingian administrative regime, and the emergence of three powerful feudal domains whose disputed borders ranged around the town—those of Normandy, Brittany, and Maine. Duke William Longsword constructed a castle above the valley of the Cance, and the county of Mortain was subsequently held by a member of the ducal family, most famously William the Conqueror's half-brother, Robert of Mortain.

Nothing survives of the town fortifications, and the closing of the Falaise-Mortain Pocket in August 1944 took a serious toll on the town, though the major ecclesiastical structures came through the bombardments largely intact. What was destroyed has been on the whole sensitively recon-structed, and from the Grande-Rue you can still survey a handsome small town, pinned against the steep flanks of a hill which to medieval pilgrims offered a first sight of Mont-St-Michel. But you need an exceptionally clear day to empathise with the raising of spirits that saw this promontory named Montjoie, though even a dull atmosphere can offer a breathtaking perspec-tive, westwards along the valley of the Sélune. In order to gain a foothold in this steep terrain the town is laid out as a series of parallel streets, clinging to the lateral contours of the land, and pivots around its principal monu-ment, the collegiate church of **St-Evroult**.

This stands on a terrace above the Grande-Rue, shaded by a tall bell tower whose otherwise sheer surfaces are broken by pairs of massively attenuated lancets. The college of canons was founded in 1082 by Robert of Mortain, and the south nave portal of their first church survives, bordered with continuous zig-zag moulding and uninterrupted by capitals. This is unlikely to be any earlier than c 1130 but was, unusually, retained by the canons after 1216, when they embarked on a wholesale rebuilding of the church. Architecturally this articulates a rigorous and simplified approach to 13C Norman design, transeptless, and with single, untraceried clerestory windows, an archaic triforium, and crude crocket capitals. It is hoped to remove the 19C vault (a plaster insert of 1856), and so reveal the great timber roof thrown over the high spaces in 1562. None of the earlier medieval fittings have been retained but the 15C choir stalls are among the finest in Normandy, glorying in a complete set of 24 carved misericords which include masks, musicians, good and bad canons, and Saints Crespin and Crespinien, patron saints of shoemakers, hard at work.

St-Evroult's most precious relic is housed in the treasury on the first floor of the tower (usually restricted to a single short opening at 15.00 daily), where you can see the early Christian **Chrismale** displayed. This is a 7C beechwood casket, covered by a series of gilded copper plaques which show Christ flanked by the archangels Michael and Gabriel, together with a third angel on the lid, and carries a runic inscription which translates as 'May God help Aeda who made this Chrismal'. It was used to store the Eucharistic host, and is certainly a relic of Celtic Christianity made, in all likelihood, at the monastery of Iona. Its appearance in Mortain, like that of the 10C gospel book illuminated in Winchester displayed alongside it, is probably due to the founder. As a leading figure in a conquest ostensibly undertaken to reform the English church, it would have been perfectly understandable if Robert felt no compunction over transferring a few ecclesiastical treasures to help launch his new foundation.

Robert was also indirectly responsible for the decision to site another significant religious house within the vicinity of the town, for shortly after 1105 Adeline, the sister of Robert's chaplain, Vitalis, founded **L'Abbaye Blanche** as a convent for nuns. This is no more than a kilometre upstream of Mortain in the gorge of the Cance, and reached along the D977.

The site is now dominated by a disproportionately large southern range built in the mid 19C as a seminary, though the simple outlines of an aisleless church and north cloister walk survive from earlier days. These formed part of the second complex to have been built here, and went up between 1180 and 1205. The main church consists of a square-ended sanctuary, transept, and three-bay nave, which are simply rib vaulted and lit by tall lancet windows at clerestory level. The east walk of the cloister is a later rebuild but the north gallery survives intact, with some rough, non-figurative carving carried on the granite capitals as the sole concession to architectural decoration. To the west of the church several subsidiary buildings escaped the worst ravages of the Revolution, the period between 1790 and 1822 seeing the demolition of the refectory, dormitory, kitchens, and warming house, and offer a glimpse at least of the wider provisions of the site. The groin-vaulted refectory and cellar of the lay-sisters is still there, along with the remnants of the chapter house, divided, according to the custom established at La Lucerne, into two aisles.

Mortain is also renowned for the beauty of the Gorge du Cançon, where the river cuts south through the granite to spill into the valley of the Sélune in a series of dramatic waterfalls. The easiest way to reach what are known as **Les Cascades** is to take the road below the Grande-Rue, the Rue Moulin Richard (or D205), where it winds down to cross the Cance. A footpath to the right climbs towards the Grande Cascade, the greater of the two waterfalls, and on to the village of Le Neufbourg. If, instead, you carry on up the road to the edge of the village, a short metalled track drops as far as the head of the **Petite Cascade**, a narrow gorge where the Cançon drops 37 metres, descending a ladder of small rocky pools. A path follows it down to where the views, upwards, are undeniably more interesting, enabling the cognoscenti to seek out those spots favoured by Corot when he returned to paint the gorge between 1845 and 1855.

East of Mortain the D907 switchbacks above the valley of the Sélune to Domfront, passing the old cider-making town of (9km) Barenton. A possible alternative to the direct route east would be to take the D217, where it cuts off to the left of the main road just beyond (9km) Rouelle, to the remote agricultural village of (6km) **Lonlay l'Abbaye**. As you approach the centre the farmhouses settle into a denser congestion of granite houses, ranged around the abbey choir and the banks of the Egrenne. A monastery was founded here in 1017 by Guillaume de Bellême, initially colonised by monks from St-Benoît-sur-Loire, and rapidly developed as one of the more powerful houses of southern Normandy, numbering Notre-Dame-sur-l'Eau at Domfront and Notre-Dame at Alençon among its dependent priories.

The church itself now presents a truncated silhouette, with a 13C crossing tower, acting as a sort of western tower-porch, giving entry to the **transepts**. The latter date from c 1100 and are articulated, notably to the south, by a splendid blind arcade at triforium level, and a series of magnificent capitals. These fall into two distinct groups—a set of limestone capitals beneath the crossing arches, treated in a flattened, almost chip-carved, manner; and the cruder, rounded forms of the granite capitals which adorn the transept proper.

The **choir** is undated, and appears to be mid to late 13C, despite the alteration to its character effected by the provision of a new clerestory after an English army set fire to the nave in 1418. Its severity recalls St-Evroult at Mortain, and in matters of detail compares closely with the choir of Hambye, but the principal interest now lies in the chapels. Since the recent restoration these have come to act as repositories for some very fine late medieval sculpture, including a damaged 15C polychromed statue of Mary Magdalen, and an excellent 14C relief of the Annunciation. And, unusually, a good set of 16C choir stalls has survived, situated to the east of the crossing and easily found from the now wrecked night-stairs which lead down from the south transept end wall.

The D22 is the most direct route from Lonlay to Domfront, and climbs first east and then south of the village, throwing off views of the watermeadows that surround the church before reaching (9km) **Domfront** via the lower town, known as Domfront-Gare. Here, shortly before 1020 and on the banks of the Varenne, Guillaume de Bellême was responsible for founding the most significant of Lonlay's early dependencies—the priory church of **Notre-Dame-sur-l'Eau**. The church has been badly treated, and in 1836 the four western bays of the nave and the aisles were demolished to make way for a new road. This has left the building sadly truncated, with a two bay aisleless nave (the original openings into the aisles were walled up after 1836), projecting transepts, and a single sanctuary bay giving onto an apse. The earliest construction is confined to the rump of the nave, and probably predates Duke William's annexation of Domfront and the surrounding Passais in 1050, which brought into Normandy what had previously been part of Maine.

The transepts, crossing, and choir, along with the handsome bell tower, date from c 1100, contrasting plain interior transept walls with the rhythmically varied blind arcading in two registers which embellishes the choir. The transepts were given two apsidal chapels, that to the north rebuilt in the 17C, which sit off-centredly beneath two large oculi—rare events in Normandy, and whose use can only otherwise be paralleled at Deux-Jumeaux. The church was restored in 1959, and this led to the discovery of a remarkable series of paintings in the south transept chapel, showing five unenthroned, though ostensibly seated, figures. The sixth niche is empty, and the presumption has been that the chapel was decorated with half a full college of Apostles. Alternatively they might represent fathers of the church, but like the late 14C limestone effigy of a knight to the west it is impossible to identify them precisely.

The massively fortified upper town has extended along the slopes to the south-east, but its distinctive medieval structure, squeezed within an irregular rectangle of rampart walls, is everywhere apparent. A later account holds that Domfront grew up around a hermitage established c 540 by St-Front, but whatever the merits of this assertion, the surviving documentary records mention nothing earlier than Guillaume de Bellême's construction of a wooden castle in 1010. This lay at the western extremity of a high sandstone ridge, where the River Varenne cuts a gorge some 61 metres deep, a ridge which soars above the surrounding Passais and which established Domfront as one of the great frontier towns of southern Normandy. Nothing survives of the early 11C castle, as in 1092 the town overthrew its seigneur, Roger de Montgomery, and sought the protection of William the Conqueror's youngest son, Henry Beauclerc. Domfront became Henry's power base in southern Normandy, and on the site of Guillaume's castle stand the ruins of the earliest of the great stone keeps Henry built, work starting in 1092 and accelerating through the late 1090s when Henry ruled Normandy while his brother, Robert Curthose, was on crusade.

The ruins are visible for miles, overlooking the ascent to the main town gates off the **Grande Carrefour**, which remain the obvious entrance to the old town. One of the machicolated portal towers still stands—at the opposite end of the town to the castle—and originally constituted one of 24 rampart towers with which the walls were progressively strengthened during the 13th and 14C. Thirteen of these survive, sandwiched between houses, or looming above cultivated terraces and embellished with flowering wall boxes. The main street into the town has long been known as the Grande-Rue, and retains a handful of 16C houses, but the finest domestic buildings are to be found on its continuation, the Rue du Docteur-Barrabé, with a splendid 15C townhouse at No. 40.

To the west the Rue St-Julien leads to the Place Poirie and the **château**, the former housing the 19C Hôtel-de-Ville, the latter perched high above the river to command a stunning view of the south-western approaches to Normandy. Only two walls of Henry's late 11C keep survive as the complex was largely demolished on the orders of Sully in 1608. By this time it was already in a poor state, having been aggressively damaged in 1574 when the Comte de Matignon laid siege to Gabriel de Montgomery, holed up in the castle with a posse of 150 armed Calvinists, and forced a surrender after cannon had reduced Montgomery's force to less than 15. The site is nevertheless impressive, bolstered in 1205 by Philip Augustus who added the eastern barbican and western bulwark towers, and graced to the north by the ruined chapel of **St-Symphorien**. Recent consolidation of the short aisleless nave, transepts, and apse of the chapel has tentatively suggested it is contemporary with Henry's keep, i.e. of the late 1090s, but in the 12C it was ordered as a dependency of Notre-Dame-sur-l'Eau and witnessed the baptism of Eleanor, daughter of Eleanor of Aquitaine, and grandmother of the future St-Louis. The castle was in fact a favourite residence of Henry II, and in the 1160s frequently hosted Eleanor of Aquitaine's brilliant court of troubadours and poets, becoming yet another centre in which elements of the dispute between Henry and Becket were played out. Becket spent the Christmas of 1166 in Domfront and met with Henry at Notre-Dame-sur-l'Eau, Henry having already agreed to lift his threat of expulsion against the Cistercian Order in England. And some four years later, in August 1170, a delegation of papal legates moved up to the castle itself in a final attempt to achieve a reconciliation between the two, patching up a truce in which Henry promised to make amends for having stampeded the prerogatives of Canterbury by agreeing the coronation of his eldest son, Henry (the young king), by Roger Pont-l'Evêque, the archbishop of York.

To the east of Domfront the high ground belongs to the pines of the Forêt des Andaines, a still sizeable tract of woodland extensively worked for its soft timber, and whose forest floor is broken by innumerable springs and lakes. One of these springs, in a rocky gully where the Vée cuts a path through the underlying sandstones and granites, is credited with near legendary healing powers and is now the centre of the best-known spa town in western France—**Bagnoles-de-l'Orne** (19km along the D908 and D335). It is an extremely pleasant spot, banked above a natural lake where you might hire 'pédalos' and splash beneath the pale walls of the casino, though for those in robust health the presence of thousands of elderly French visitors earnestly committed to prolonging life can seem intimidating.

The spring itself breaks from a rock downstream of the lake at 25 degrees, low in minerals but notably radioactive, and has acquired a reputation, among the French at least, for its efficacy in relieving circulatory disorders and preventing varicose veins. The water may be drunk but the essential treatment involves bathing and massage, all of which is conducted at the **Etablissement Thermal** on the Rue du Dr-Louvet. There is now no alternative to the Etablissement but it was not always so, and an entirely spurious legend holds that the tonic effect of these waters was first recognised at an unspecified but suitably medieval date. The story maintains that Hugues, Lord of Tessé, abandoned his ageing horse, Rapide, in the forest, only to be staggered several months later by Rapide's frisking home in the peak of health. Hugues retraced the horse's tracks to a forest spring, where he bathed himself and was similarly rejuvenated, sowing a tale which became the toast of the local hoteliers. There was little provision here prior to the late 18C however, when three bathing pools were set up, made of open wooden planking. These were arranged as a sequence of plunges in which the water passed first through the mens' pool, then the womens', and finally to a pool reserved for the poor, who apparently were not felt worth separating. The treatment was never short of testimonials however, and immediately behind the Etablissement Thermal two high rocks stand 4 metres apart, a gap known as the Saut du Capucin, in memory of a Franciscan monk who celebrated his reinvigoration by leaping between the pinnacles.

The architectural ambience of Bagnoles, and the neighbouring village of Tessé-la-Madeleine to which it is joined, is 19th and early 20C, though it has on the whole renounced the sort of architectural fantasies that so animated the great planned resorts of the coast. At the very centre of

Bagnoles, above the **Place de la République**, a flight of steps leads to the Art Deco church, privately built in 1934, which has crowned its western tower-porch with a spire and drum derived from Nash's All Saints, Langham Place. The interior is more seriously bizarre, with a nave elevation whose rounded piers and palm-like capitals are sprayed with roses, in an evident attempt to loosely evoke cherubic faces. There are some pleasant forest walks along the gorge which nominally separates Bagnoles from Tessé, and which takes you out into the open parkland surrounding the **Château de Tessé-la-Madeleine**. This is the one successful example of historicism in the resort, built in 1859 in an acutely observed mid 16C style, with as much an eye for the decorative brickwork of St-Germain-de-Livet as for the more fully advertised grandeur of Chambord.

La Ferté-Macé, 6km north-east along the D916, is Bagnoles' industrial big brother and much the better market town, renowned throughout Normandy for the annual tripe fair held at the end of each April. Excepting this the town attracts few visitors, leaving its handsome central square, the Place du Général LeClerc, to the locals. The Place is overlooked by the richly decorated twin-towered façade of **Notre-Dame**, a substantially late 19C parish church which provides the town with a theatrical backdrop for the Thursday market. A Romanesque bell tower has survived from an earlier priory immediately to the south of the church, having been extended as a freestanding chapel before it came to serve as a sacristy. The streets running off the square are now largely pedestrianised, and flanked by narrow 18C granite-faced houses which spill down the steeper slopes to the east, or hug the line of the ridge to the north. At the bottom of the hill the D908 picks up the thickly wooded country of the Normandy-Maine border, passing a picturesque late medieval manor house at Joué-du-Bois, before breasting the splendid eminence of (17km) **Carrouges**.

The great **Château de Carrouges** lies, somewhat surprisingly, beneath the hill-town, in a valley floor created by the youthful Udon. Its primary defence remains a moat, fed by the river, though as it now stands the castle is a creation of the 16th and 17C, when a small seigneurial residence was transformed into a mighty rural palace. The main blocks are arranged as an irregular rectangle, the four major façades broken by projecting wings or angle towers, and disposed around an internal courtyard. The process by which the present form was arrived at is complex, and for the purposes of this description the main entrance façade, where the moat is bridged and which faces west by north-west, will be referred to as the west range, that to its left as the north range, and so on.

The earliest extant building belongs to this west range—a machicolated tower attached to a secondary block which projects further westwards into the moat. This is known as the **Donjon**, and was constructed by Jean IV de Carrouges in the late 14C as a relatively straightforward defensive tower. The **north range** was begun after Jean de Blosset took control of Carrouges during the latter stages of the Hundred Years War, work starting c 1450 on a rectangular central block with two wings projecting at 45 degrees towards the moat, and an inner stair tower providing access to the two upper storeys. These two distinctive late medieval structures were not linked until c 1520, by which time the family of Jean le Veneur had acquired the château through marriage. A short connecting structure was added to de Blosset's magnificent gable-ended loggia, and the main entrance block was put in hand. The west range was completed during the Wars of Religion, when the projecting south-west angle was added, and finally, during the early

17C, this sprawling and hybrid L-shaped castle was closed around a courtyard by the building of the south and east ranges.

The various campaigns are unified by their use of similar materials and are arranged in three storeys throughout, with the main walls faced in a deepish pink brick, a stone plinth, sharply pitched roofs, and granite window embrasures. The arrangement of rooms and functions is predominantly 17C however, with the kitchens, cellars, and workshops at ground level, bedrooms, ante-chambers, salons, and dining rooms on the first floor, and the servants' quarters in the attic. This later reordering of the building means that the greater part of the interior decoration is equally 17C, with a virtually intact painted and panelled bedroom, known as the **Chambre Louis XI**, in the north-western angle tower. The so-called **Antichambre d'Honneur** (on the first floor of the 15C north wing) was also panelled and repainted, though an early 16C hunting scene was retained above the fireplace.

The succession of rooms which measure out the first floor of the **east wing** are the most unreconstructed of any in the château—a sweeping progress from room to room, free of the encumbering corridor which usually disfigures such arrangements. This prodigious suite leads, via the mostly post-facto portraits of the Salon des Portraits, to the main staircase. Unlike its counterpart in the north-east angle, the plaster and paint have here been pared back to reveal the underlying brickwork, a reflection of a late 20C fascination for geometry which clarifies Maurice Gabriel's early 17C design, but at a considerable cost. For the patina of 18C decoration concentrated around this angle has been irretrievably broken. The estates can be surveyed from the south and east wings and originally lay at the very edge of a great hunting forest, the Forêt d'Ecouves, and while this remains the largest oak forest in Normandy it has been latterly much diminished, the old western flanks given over to pasture. The densest forest covers the hills to the east of Carrouges, though you will catch glimpses of this along the wooded ridge which runs from Les Rochers du Vignage to La Roche-Mabile, before the D22 descends to the border with Maine at (26km) **ALENÇON**.

Lying deep in the belly of Normandy Alençon has built on its credentials as a frontier town, market centre, and ducal seat to become the chief town and préfecture of the département de l'Orne. The town in fact lies well to the south of the headwaters of the Orne, and grew above the north bank of the River Sarthe, astride the Bronze Age trade route running from the mouth of the Seine south to the Pyrénées. This spot was subsequently colonised c 300 BC by the Gallic Aulerces, leaving the settlement with the Latinised title of Alercum, but its experience of the early Middle Ages was uneventful and it took the conferment of a dukedom on its count in 1414, and 32 years of English occupation and enfeeblement between 1417 and 1449 to pitch the town into the mainstream of French political life. With the duchy passing into the hands of the crown on the death of Duke René in 1492, and liable to be shuffled among relatives as a royal appanage, the town was fortunate in sustaining Marguerite de Valois-Angoulême as its first royal overlord, René's widow and the sister of François I. Marguerite initiated a major programme of rebuilding, completing the churches of Notre-Dame and St-Léonard and establishing a convent of Poor Clares, as well as opening the town to commerce with Germany, Spain, and Italy. With a secure administrative and commercial base, Colbert selected Alençon as the manufacturing centre he hoped would satisfy the lucrative 17C passion for lace, thereby denting the virtual monopoly enjoyed by Venice. This was

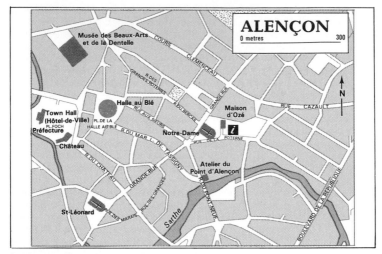

dedicated to producing a variant of Venetian lace, a pattern of c 1650 known as the 'Point d'Alençon', and became a considerable success. Indeed, along with its modern electrical industry and primary administrative role, the town still produces a phenomenally expensive fine lace from a factory owned, like that of Sèvres, by the State.

The centre of the town occupies the inward crook of a right angle formed by the rivers Briante and Sarthe, and is bounded, in a fitting display of regional power, by the Préfecture to the east and the town hall to the west. The latter stands in the breezy reaches of the **Place Foch**, a late 18C municipal riposte to the remaining towers of the seigneurial castle. Since the castle now houses the town jail you need good reason for a visit, but the vertical accents of the 15C barbican, and the earlier machicolated donjon beyond, lend a feudal note to an imposing square. The Rue Matignon leads from here to the **Halle au Blé**, the 19C corn exchange, with a large circular trading floor enveloped by two arcaded aisles. Though completed in 1812 it was badly damaged by fire in 1835, and did not receive its great iron and glass dome until 1865, when, as engineer, the aptly-named Croquefer topped out the weather vane. The exchange is now used as an exhibition hall and tends to concentrate on the more technically-minded displays, which are thought better seen against the flamboyance of its 19C engineering, leaving the purely pictorial shows to the **Musée des Beaux-Arts**.

This is situated in the old Jesuit college behind the Place Henri Besnard, whose 17C buildings it shares with the Bibliothèque Municipale. Its grander title is the Musée des Beaux-Arts et de la Dentelle, as besides its holdings of 16–19C paintings the museum houses a substantial collection of lace drawn from throughout Europe. The latter is accommodated on the second floor, with the ground floor largely given over to temporary exhibitions, and the first floor divided into three large rooms devoted to painting from 1600–1850, late 19C painting and sculpture, and the work of local artists respectively. It is the furthest room on the ground floor which holds the finest work however, with two 17C altarpieces by **Philippe de Champaigne** depicting the **Trinity** and the **Assumption of the Virgin**. The room is also graced by a number of 17C Dutch and Flemish works, with notable portraits by **Nicolas Maes** and **Thomas Wijck** but, inevitably, the most concentrated holdings are of French 19C painting. Among the better known names there is an unusual still-life by **Gustave Courbet**, opposite one of his more familiar, though badly glazed, landscapes, and a late and rather bleak seascape by **Eugène Boudin**. You should not entirely ignore the collection of local work however, mundane though much of this might be, for enlivening the dimmer recesses are a series of startling and well-worked portraits by **Jean-Jacques Montanteuil**.

The floor above is given over to an engaging exhibition of the design and manufacture of lace. It takes comparatively little time to realise that the actual process of making the fragile shawls and tablecloths, trimmings and veils, can lend a new meaning to the phrase 'labour-intensive', for with some of the finest pieces one square inch represents two days work. The collection is organised so that you can compare patterns favoured in Alençon, Chantilly, Bruges, and Venice, or most other lace-making centres for that matter. You can watch lace being made, or indeed buy lace, at the Atelier-Conservatoire du Point d'Alençon on the Rue du Pont-Neuf.

The **Bibliothèque Municipale** sits immediately opposite the main entrance to the museum, where it was installed in the 17C Jesuit seminary. For the non ticket-holder it is primarily worth visiting for its superb first-floor reading room, where the manuscripts and rare early printed volumes are shelved in 18C wooden casement presses rescued from the Charterhouse at Val-Dieu.

The Rue des Grandes Poteries and Rue du Bercail lead from the library and museum towards the commercial centre, with the **Place Lamagdelaine** lying at the heart of a network of streets mercifully undamaged in 1944, and recently pedestrianised. These present a pleasant variety of 18C granite houses and 16C timber dwellings, with a particularly fine 15C mansion, known as the **Maison du Petit Nègre** at No. 37 Grande-Rue. The centrepiece of the area is the church of **Notre-Dame**, begun c 1435 to the east, with the late 15C nave undertaken after the English were forced out of Normandy, and the addition of the justly famous western portal marking the culmination of the project between 1506 and 1516.

This latter work was instigated by Marguerite de Valois-Angoulême, duchess of Alençon, who commissioned Jean Lemoyne to design a processional entrance. Lemoyne's solution was as bold, and breathtaking, as Ambroise Havel's at St-Maclou de Rouen. The porch is three-sided and canted away from the west door, breaking up beyond the main arcade level in a trilogy of openwork gables which soar through the tracery and balustrades of the upper registers, to act as the stage for a piece of pure theatre. At the top of the central gable God the Father looks down upon the Transfigured Christ, ablaze in the presence of Moses and Elijah, while in the lower reaches Peter, James, and John look up as from the base of the mountain, John with his back turned to the street below. This unfettered illusionism had already found expression in the nave, where the flying buttresses sag as if bowed by the outward thrust of the high vault, but it had never before been employed so dramatically. The general spirit seems to possess even the minor (and heavily restored) elements, for the mullions of the aisle windows are sprung to meet at the head of the relieving arch as if they were the flattened section of an orange.

The interior lost its choir and transepts in a fire of 1744, and was given a second-rate replacement by Perronet, but the nave was happily untouched. This boasts a relatively simple five bay elevation, and is crowned by a

Vault over the nave at Notre-Dame, Alençon

tierceron vault whose complexity has been enhanced by a rare calligraphy of shallow bosses, finials, and monsters. The vault is almost certainly a design hangover from the choir, begun under English patronage, and an intriguing example of an essentially English vaulting technique crossing the Channel. The clerestory glass, by contrast, owes nothing to any earlier projections of the church, and would seem to reflect something of the cosmopolitanism encouraged by Marguerite.

All eleven windows survive, with the Tree of Jesse of 1511 in the great west window the earliest. The rest are by the master glaziers of Alençon and Le Mans, and open with a cycle of the Life of the Virgin in the south clerestory. From west to east these represent: the Presentation in the Temple, Marriage of Mary and Joseph (both by Pierre Fromentin, 1530–31), Descent from the Cross, Annunciation and Visitation (both by Berthin Duval, 1531), and the Dormition of the Virgin (attributed to the Fromentin shop, c 1540). The north clerestory narrates a short Old Testament cycle with, from west to east: the Creation, Expulsion, Sacrifice of Isaac (all Pierre Fromentin, c 1545–50), Crossing of the Red Sea (Michel Fromentin, 1535), and Raising of the Brazen Serpent (attributed to the Fromentin shop, c 1550). It is an exceptionally fine series, marked by an awareness of a century of Florentine art, particularly in the work of the Le Mans glazier, Berthin Duval, who borrows motifs from both Raphael and Lorenzo Ghiberti. The work of the Fromentin workshop has an altogether more popular edge, and, as with the compositions of Engrand Le Prince at Rouen and Gisors, often lifts familiar arrangements and motifs from German engravings, though the exposure seems to be to Holbein the Younger and Cranach rather than Dürer.

In addition to the church the Place Lamagdelaine is a pleasant spot from which to survey the **Maison d'Ozé**, where the Syndicat d'Initiative is housed in a former manor house and stable yard, built for the magistrate, Jean de Mesnil, in 1450. This was certainly the spot from which Marguerite de Valois-Angoulême surveyed the town, as along with her second husband, Charles de Valois, she made it her principal residence in Alençon after 1492.

From the Place the Grande-Rue runs south-west to another recipient of Marguerite's interest—the church of **St-Léonard**. Less obviously flamboyant than Notre-Dame, and denuded of all but a fragment of its 16C glass, it is now a rather simplified version of the original. Although it incorporates a 13C bay to the east of the apse, in what is now the vestry, the church is essentially that begun by René, Duc d'Alençon, in 1489 and completed by his widow, Marguerite, in 1505. The simplicity of the architecture—the sharp and spare mouldings, narrow clerestory, and large aisle chapels—serves as a foil for the huge stained glass windows of the chapels, but as the original glass has been replaced by a mediocre set of 19C windows the effect is sadly diminished.

To the east of the apse the Rue des Marais and its continuation, the Rue des Granges, are flanked by a fine range of 15–19C townhouses, and offer an attractive route back to the Grand Rue and the centre.

17

Mortagne and the Normandy Perche

ROAD (101km): Mortagne-au-Perche; D938, 17km Bellême; D7/D277, 12km Ste-Gauberge; D277/D11, 15km Rémalard; D920, 10km Moutiers-au-Perche; D918, 10km Longny-au-Perche; D290, 8km Autheil; 2km Tourouvre; C2, 12km Abbaye de la Trappe; D251, 4km Soligny-la-Trappe; D205, 11km Mortagne-au-Perche.

To a traveller intent on leaving the north and reaching out to the Beauce, the Perche must seem a meagre passage, darker and more remote than the Pays d'Ouche, sparser and more thinly spread. It is certainly geographically and culturally at odds with central Normandy, lying to the south of the earlier frontier lines, and allows the duchy to bite deep into Maine. The absorption of the northern Perche into Normandy during the 11C led to the division of the old county, so that the larger towns of Nogent-le-Rotrou and La Ferté-Bernard became a part of the Orléanais and Maine, respectively, although the Perche as a whole has something of the character of a land-locked island. The region is bound by its historical identity and a collective memory leads most to describe themselves as 'Percherons' before they might think of themselves as 'Normands' or 'du Maine'.

The memory is rooted in poverty and depopulation—the famines of the 17C encouraged thousands to emigrate to Canada, while the rural impoverishment of the 19C was countered by a further thinning out of the countryside. This in turn reflects the experience of those who try to wrest a living from the land, and the landscape of the Perche is not one to provide easy bounty. The underlying formations are limestone, but these are coated with a thick layer of flinty clay, and have been folded into a range of hills which can rise as high as 300 metres to the north. The whole of this area was once thickly forested, though the plains and river valleys were mostly cleared during the Middle Ages, leaving the more substantial tracts of woodland to cling to the higher ground. It is nonetheless still a region of great oak forests, and the felling of timber, along with the agriculture of the valleys, remains the mainstay of the local economy. This is supplemented by the breeding of Percherons, a famous breed of draught horse descended from the tournament stallions reared for the 12th and 13C seigneurial classes, and which were themselves a cross between the native strain and the Arabs introduced by returning Norman crusaders.

Given the geographical constraints of the Guide the suggested itinerary makes no pretence at covering the whole of the old county, confining itself to those areas within the borders of Normandy. It is a sparsely populated region, and one where hotels can be difficult to find, so for anyone intent on spending more than a few days in the Perche Nogent-le-Rotrou could make a good alternative to Mortagne as a general base. The latter is nevertheless much the most congenial centre from which to tour an area which remains both remote and beautiful.

MORTAGNE-AU-PERCHE. Commanding the north-western reaches of the Perche and the seat of its medieval counts, Mortagne is in the opinion of this author one of the finest small towns in France. It rises without a single outstanding building, houses neither a major nor a minor collection of art, and lacks the municipal flamboyance of neighbouring Alençon or Evreux. It instead supports two good hotels, an excellent Saturday market, a pair of spacious squares, sympathetically populated by well-used pavement cafés, one of the richest vernacular townscapes in Normandy, and a breathtaking situation overlooking the forests of the Perche. And if this is insufficient, the town is not only a splendid centre from which to explore the surrounding country, but for those whose horizons stretch beyond Normandy it also lies within easy reach of the great centres to the south, of Chartres and Le Mans.

There was a Roman settlement on the high, flattish mound which sustains the modern town, and legend ascribes the foundation of a monastery here to St-Eloi in 654, but it was not until the counts of the Perche raised a castle in the late 10C that Mortagne began to be recognised as a regional capital. The castle was destroyed in 997 by Robert, son of Hugh Capet, and once rebuilt as a royal seat the complex acquired a new name to match its new ownership, Fort Toussaint. Despite the construction of a sizeable enceinte wall during the 14C, little now survives of the medieval town, for most of what came through the Hundred Years War fell during the repeated sieges and assaults which dogged Mortagne in the course of the Wars of Religion. The last of the large-scale medieval structures fell in 1780, when all but a single gate of the enceinte wall was demolished. It is a sad loss, and the remaining urban fabric is substantially 16–18C, though its cohesion is largely due to the organic relationship observed between the later architecture and the medieval street pattern on the northern slopes of the mound.

The modern centre of Mortagne pivots around two squares, the Place de la République and Place du Général-de-Gaulle, which merge into each other along the highest ground the town can offer. To the south-east the Rue Ste-Croix conceals a cluster of 17th and 18C houses and courtyards, and to its rear, behind the 18C Hôtel-de-Ville, the **Jardin Public** offers a magnificent prospect of the Huisne valley and Forêt de Bellême, some 16km to the south.

The older town slopes northwards from here, to either side of the Rue

Notre-Dame and the smaller Places Notre-Dame and du Palais. The first of these is commanded by the church of **Notre-Dame**, begun in 1494 to a relatively controlled design, and completed in the 18C with a stupendous disregard for the conventional norms of ecclesiastical decorum. The building has in fact been variously disfigured, and the bizarre south-west tower was begun as a fortifiable belfry in 1535, the design being swiftly abandoned and the tower completed in the late 18C. A fire of 1887 caused considerable damage, destroying the upper stage of the belfry, and necessitating a major programme of restoration in the nave. This had the effect of robbing the stone of its natural lustre, a loss in a building which depends for its success on achieving contrasts between the purity of the arcade, and the richly carved complexity of the vault.

The church largely follows a design laid down in 1494 and seems to have been completed by 1535, without transepts or ambulatory but, as if in compensation, with unusually wide aisles which open onto a total of 15 chapels. This breadth is counterpointed by the vault which, relying on the imported forms of Alençon, takes up the English tradition of tierceron vaulting and transforms it into a fretwork of cusps, pendants, and deftly carved musicians. At a lower level the eye is forced outwards, laterally to the chapels or axially to the choir, and while the chapels contain an interesting array of 16–19C altarpieces, it is the **choir** which repays the greater attention. Mortagne was another beneficiary of the collapse of the Carthusian monastery of Valdieu, and the rich early 18C panels, doors, and stalls on show in the choir testify, once more, to the latterday splendour of that most aristocratic of monastic orders.

To the east of the apse the **Porte St-Denis** marks the limit of the medieval town, and is the sole remnant of Mortagne's fortifications, with a late 13C gate surmounted by a 16C lodge. The latter now houses the Musée Percheron, with a modest collection of material devoted to local history, behind its splendid foliate relief carving. Immediately to the north a door opens into the **Maison des Contes du Perche**, the larger 17C wing having been attached to a 15C donjon, which originally formed the late medieval residence of the counts. This in turn has come to accommodate the municipal library and **Musée Alain**. The latter is concerned with the life and work of the brilliant teacher, philosopher, pacifist, and journalist, Alain, who was born in Mortagne as Emile Chartier in 1868, and who bequeathed his personal papers to the town. The museum proper is based on the first floor, with a reconstruction of Alain's study at Vésinet immediately above. It is an impressive memorial to the energies of a man who taught throughout his life, and wrote a series of critiques which number among the seminal works of 20C philosophy. More sobering is the realisation that his life was barely half-run when, on the outbreak of the First World War, he enlisted in the French army, becoming a private at the age of 46 as a means of bringing a balance to his longstanding pacifism. The few letters on display are perhaps more telling than the newspaper articles, and show that he continued to correspond with some of the many adolescent students who passed through his hands, Simone Weil, André Maurois, and Maurice Schumann among them.

The second of these smaller squares, the Place du Palais, occupies the site of the nave of the 14C collegiate church of **St-André-de-Toussaint**. This was severely damaged during the Revolution, and demolished in the first decade of the 19C, its stone sold off to be reused as the dressing you continually encounter when walking through the town. The Palais de Justice was rebuilt within the old choir area, with the original **Crypte**

16C houses along the Ruelle aux Chevaux, Mortagne-au-Perche

St-André maintained as a cellar. This has been restored (if locked the librarian at the Musée Alain holds the keys) and though reduced to little more than two transverse aisles retains the octagonal bases and chamfered vaulting profiles to be expected of a major 14C church.

St-André lay towards the eastern perimeter of the medieval town, and in spite of the destruction of the larger buildings a more varied townscape has survived in this quarter than is the case on the high ground. The narrow alleys to the north include a fine 16C townhouse, the **Maison Henri IV**, on the corner of the Rue de Toussaint, and a superbly modulated rhythm of later housing along the Venelle de Vert Gallant. There is another grand 16C building north of the Palais de Justice, the **Maison du Doyen Toussaint**, which as its name suggests was built as the dean's residence. The south is equally worth exploring, with a terraced garden, along the **Ruelle aux Chevaux**, offering views over the 16C towers and later gables which clamber back towards the larger town squares.

To the south-east the Rue du Mail brings you onto the old Paris road and the Rue de Longny, where the modern hospital has grown up around a late 15C establishment run by the **Couvent de St-François**. This was founded as a convent of Poor Clares by Marguerite de Valois-Angoulême, Duchess of Alençon, in 1492. The chapel and cloister survived redevelopment, and provide the sort of peaceful setting in which one's health might actually improve. Both structures date from c 1500, with an aisleless chapel supporting a segmental wooden barrel vault, and a simple cloister surmounted by a beautifully braced timber lean-to roof. This latter would almost certainly have carried a plaster barrel vault, but the repinned timberwork is a splendid revelation. The chapel itself received a surfeit of attention during the late 19C, and elements of the 16C emblematic cycle which adorns the vault were entirely reinterpreted. When combined with the brasher colouring of the glass the effect is to dislocate the purposefully muted aesthetics of the building, but this is the only example of over-restoration in a town whose cycles of building, repair and maintenance are otherwise so sympathetically handled.

South of Mortagne the D938 offers a fast route to (17km) **Bellême**, swooping through the damp, rolling country with the finesse of a causeway. The town was once renowned as the great medieval fortress of the Perche, straddling a rocky spur above the Maine frontier, though its atmosphere is now that of a tranquil 18C market town. It was the focus of a celebrated assault in the winter of 1229, when the army of Louis IX and Blanche of Castille seized the castle from Pierre de Mauclerc, head of the Dreux-Bretagne family, and leader of the pro-English faction among the northern feudal baronage. Nothing survives of this castle but a 15C barbican, known as **Le Porche**, stands above the 11C foundations of its enceinte walls, and separates the Place de la République from the Rue de la Ville-Close. The post-medieval town grew among the ruins of the castle bailey—surrounded by its ramparts like a citadel. This became known as the **Ville-Close**, and its main street is enlivened by a sequence of 17th and 18C terraced elevations which descend to the Maison du Gouverneur, and adjacent **Hôtel de Bansard des Bois** (No. 26). The latter is a crisply detailed 17C town mansion, imaginatively arranged with a rear loggia taking advantage of the rectangular stretch of water retained from the castle moat. The Boulevard Bansard-des-Bois runs alongside what were once rampart walls, its grassy banks looking out over the surrounding country, before slipping right towards the old corn market in the Place au Blé. It is a tight circuit, with the Place au Blé practically one with the **Place de la République**, the centre of the town, and the site of the Thursday market—a sloping, triangular space bounded by the 15C 'Porche', 18C Mairie, and late 17C church of **St-Sauveur**.

There was a substantial 15C church on the site, but this was rebuilt between 1675 and 1710 and provided with a loosely classical western tower-porch. Much of the medieval fabric was retained however, and the broad nave and buttress chapels make an excellent foil for the richly decorated interior. As was the case at Mortagne, the Charterhouse at Valdieu contributed some fine 18C woodwork, here confined to the choir stalls and accompanying panelling which run behind the high altar. With the possible exception of Oudry's altarpiece of 1712, depicting the **Transfiguration**, no individual piece would be likely to feature in the standard texts on French 17th and 18C art, but the range and variety of the late 17C sculpture and painting works well when seen in the context of a low and broad church such as this. Before leaving you might also cast an eye to the ambitious **Font** of 1684, garlanded with swags of fruit and given not one, but three bowls.

To the north and west the rump of the **Forêt de Bellême** sustains a still majestic tract of woodland, with 2500 hectares of mature, and maturing, oak spread over undulating ground. It is easily entered and explored by bicycle or on foot, though a few metalled roads afford an armchair view by car. On the opposite flank, to the south, the D7 picks up the valley of the Coudre at (6km) La Chapelle-Souëf, where a left turn onto the D277 brings you to (6km) **Ste-Gauberge**. It is worth stopping en route at **St-Cyr-la-Rosière**, where the church houses a 17C painted terracotta tableau of the Entombment, and the terrace to the side offers a glorious view over the valley of the Rosière to the **Prieuré de Ste-Gauberge**.

As a minor dependency of St-Denis, the priory here received an aisleless church at roughly the same date as the nave of its ruling house was being completed—i.e. c 1250. The restoration programme of 1991 has reopened the church to the public, and at last allows a closer examination of a particularly interesting type of building—the purposely small foundation capable of drawing on the design vocabulary of great church Ile-de-France. This interest extends to the large 'composed windows' (two lancets surmounted by an oculus) which so illuminate the interior, but seems to have played a lesser role in formulating the simple use of space. A single storeyed, aisleless structure, the priory is more like a chapel, a similarity which would have been clearly felt before the 15C refurbishment removed the lower vault, and so opened out the space into a new timber roof. The 15C was kinder to the exterior however, and saw to the erection of a rather fine southern belfry tower. The conventual precincts were rebuilt in the 17C, and purchased privately after the Revolution, forming part of a farm which cannot be visited. But you can move down to the west, where a spacious two storeyed timber hall houses the **Musée des Arts et Traditions Populaires du Perche**. This holds an eclectic and well-exhibited collection of tools, photographs, memorabilia, and artefacts concerned with the rural industries of the Perche—cider-making, horse-breeding, and, most variedly, forest crafts.

From Ste-Gauberge you should head for the D11, which runs north past the fortified towns of the Beauvrière, to cross the Huisne at (15km) Rémalard. Beyond, the D920 rises and dips between the many small valleys which cut into the local ironstone, before settling beneath the picturesque hill town of (10km) **Moutiers-au-Perche**. Rising above the tiled roofs which clad the lower hillside, the church of **Notre-Dame-du-Mont-Harou** throws off magnificent views of the upper valley of the Corbionne, richly wooded and populated by numerous outlying farms. The building itself is one of the more engaging parish churches of the Perche, with a salacious array of 15C gargoyles, and a good 12C west portal. The interior evidently received a piecemeal series of frescoes in the early 16C, the remaining episodes being concentrated in the south chapel, just beyond the wooden scissor-bracing of the clock tower. To the west is a scene of the **Birth of John the Baptist**, but east of this, and by a different hand, are a **Kneeling Knight** and two enigmatic though related episodes, depicting a young man before a group of richly-dressed inquisitors. As the earliest cult image on display here is of St James the Pilgrim, the paintings may well represent a pilgrimage tale encountered on the road to Compostela.

The deep valleys hereabouts lie at the eastern limits of the Armorican massif, where its granites and ironstones meet the sedimentary strata of central Normandy. Being at the edge of an area submerged during the 'secondary' era has thrown up large pockets of sand, and the combination of narrow valleys, ironstone, and sand make the region notably less agricultural than elsewhere in the Perche. It is thickly wooded, and dotted with small settlements whose names recall the numerous foundries, forges, and charcoal villages which constituted the main livelihood here well into the 19C.

From Moutiers the D918 heads north-west, passing the one sizeable market town of the area, **Longny-au-Perche**, agreeably disposed around a large central square and overlooked by the 16C bell tower of the parish church of **St-Martin**. The main body of the church was begun shortly after 1472, with an ample nave and a single southern aisle, one of hundreds of fairly routine parish churches going up throughout France in the last quarter of the 15C. This nave has suffered in the course of a drastic 19C restoration, which replaced the roof and glass, and the interior is now chiefly interesting for the 15C polychromed statue of the Virgin and Child in the south aisle. A slightly later belfry was lavished on the building however, whose succinct sculptural programme is considerably more accomplished than anything to be found inside. The western face supports St Martin as the Bishop of Tours, flanked by personifications of Prudence and Temperance, while on the angle buttresses Fortitude and Justice complete the Cardinal Virtues. Above, in the pediment, a relief is devoted to St Martin dividing his cloak to give to a beggar, the physical embodiment of Charity, while again at the same level, but pushed out onto the angle buttresses, Faith and Hope make up the Theological Virtues. The coherence of the programme is perhaps more impressive than the quality of the sculpture, all of which dates from c 1530–40, though the equestrian portrait of St Martin stands out as a fine piece of carving.

The town became more widely celebrated in the 16C for a miracle-working statue of the Pietà, said to have been ordered from the cathedral yard at Chartres by the Carthusians of Valdieu. Having crossed the River Jambée at Longny, the cart carrying the statue became stuck on the rise to the west of the town, and refused to move, whatever repairs were made or strategies attempted. This was eventually perceived as a sign that the Virgin wished her image to remain above Longny, and shortly before 1536 a chapel, dedicated to **Notre-Dame-de-Pitié**, was put in hand to house the statue.

The chapel can be reached by a monumental flight of steps which take you above the Mortagne road and into the large cemetery surrounding the chapel. It is an exceptionally fine Renaissance building, given a surprisingly medieval twist in the treatment of the belfry, which lies at 45 degrees to the main axis. The tower was not completed until 1594, but the chapel proper seems to have been finished by 1549, when the western portal sculpture was completed. If the roundel depicting the **Sacrifice of Isaac** above this portal is representative of the general quality of the sculpture here, then one has the greatest reason to mourn the loss of the buttress figures during the Revolution. The interior falls short of this standard, and sadly the cult image itself has been crudely restored, though an upwards gaze is rewarded with a virtuosic display of decorated vaulting.

Between Longny and the Perche forest the D918 runs across the high plateau which separates the southwards flowing Huisne and Jambée from the valleys of the Avre and Iton, the latter emptying into the Eure. To the west, on either side of the N12, the villages of Autheuil and Tourouvre accommodate notable churches, that of (8km) **Autheuil** being reached most directly along the D290. This is purely Romanesque, although the west front has been heavily restored, and boasts a fine blind arcade, running from west to east at triforium level in the aisleless nave. The figurative sculpture is concentrated in the choir, with a superb grimacing demon on the north-east crossing pier, and a pair of relief panels around the apse arcade, contrasting the Agnus Dei with a dancing sprite, intoxicated with the Holy Ghost. There is also an impressive array of non-figurative capitals and moulded doorways, all of which are early 12C.

Just to the north the church at (2km) **Tourouvre** was clearly more modest, at least in the 12C, although this is now the larger of the two villages. There is in fact little more than the base of the western wall, and a couple of windows in the nave, to inform you of the Romanesque origins of the church, but the spaciousness of the 14C building which replaced it i impressive. A 15C Crucifixion group has been mounted along the south wall, and despite the widespread poverty which prompted the mass migrations to Canada during the 17C, the choir contemporaneously acquired a series of three large-scale paintings. These are decidedly odd, with a pair of sub-Guido Reni canvases depicting the Annunciation and Presentation in the Temple, between which an eclectic and clumsy Adoration of the Magi has deployed elements of the narrative conventions of three centuries across its picture space.

Tourouvre stands at the southern edge of the Forêts du Perche and de la Trappe. These have been extensively managed since the 12C and are still largely cultivated for their oak and ash, though certain areas have now been given over to Scots Pine. A network of forest roads extends across the woodland, and either the C2 from Tourouvre, or any left turn off the D918 between Ste-Anne and Randonnai, will bring you to the **L'Etoile du Perche**—the spot at the heart of the Perche forest where eight tracks meet. From here you might follow the signs to Bresolettes and Rond de la Trappe, and from Rond the sign 'vers D930', on the opposite bank of which the D251 leads to the **Abbaye de la Grande Trappe**—the spiritual home of Abbot de Rancé and the later Cistercian monastic reform movement. It is a complicated route (12km from Tourouvre) to what was always intended to be a remote site.

Little survives of the small Cistercian monastery founded here in 1140, and the current church and conventual precincts were built to an enthusiastically revivalist design by Tessier in the 1890s. You cannot enter the monastery proper, though its layout dominates the surrounding fields. A video film is shown at 16.00 each day to those interested in the life of a Trappist monk. Despite these restrictions the site is of considerable interest. The reform of La Trappe was undertaken during the late 17C, in the teeth of entrenched resistance from monks accustomed to the laxity of commendatory regimes. Between 1664 and 1700 Abbot de Rancé instituted a programme of strict monastic observance, manual labour, prayer, and silence, with the result that by the 1680s La Trappe had attracted an international community of monks, who numbered 300 by de Rancé's death, and became the centre of the European reform movement. The community still counted 100 brethren in 1789, to whom another thousand 'Trappist' monks in other Cistercian houses looked for spiritual guidance. These were led into exile during the Revolution by Dom Augustin de Lestrange, who divided the monks into smaller itinerant bands. None returned to France until 1814, by which time La Trappe had gone the way of Jumièges and St-Vigor at Bayeux. This necessitated the recolonisation of smaller monastic houses throughout France, but as the movement does not recognise the authority of any one senior house, but only the authority of each particular abbot, the repopulation of La Grande Trappe during the 1890s had no particular constitutional impact.

The D251 continues west of La Trappe to the pleasant village of **Soligny-la-Trappe**, easily straddling a steep rise which looks out over the country to the north of Mortagne. The grison-built parish church boasts a weathered 12C west portal, and commands much the widest views, picking up the sinuous profile of the D205, the back road which will return one to the warmer pleasures of Mortagne-au-Perche.

INDEX TO PEOPLE

INDEX TO PLACES

Note. Figures highlighted in bold are for main entries.

View of the crossing tower and nave, Jumièges

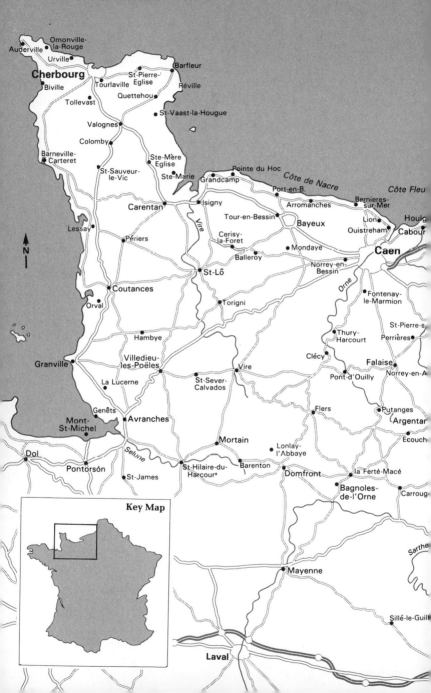

NORMANDY

Auderville
Omonville-la-Rouge
Urville
Cherbourg
Biville
Tourlaville
St-Pierre-Eglise
Barfleur
Réville
Quettehou
Tollevast
St-Vaast-la-Hougue
Valognes
Colomby
Barneville-Carteret
St-Sauveur-le-Vic
Ste-Mère Eglise
Ste-Marie
Pointe du Hoc
Grandcamp
Côte de Nacre
Côte Fleu
Port-en-B.
Arromanches
Bernieres-sur-Mer
Lessay
Périers
Carentan
Isigny
Tour-en-Bessin
Bayeux
Lion
Ouistreham
Houlg
Cabour
Cerisy-la-Foret
Mondaye
Caen
Balleroy
Norrey-en-Bessin
St-Lô
Orne
Coutances
Torigni
Fontenay-le-Marmion
Orval
St-Pierre-s
Perrières
Hambye
Thury-Harcourt
Granville
Villedieu-les-Poêles
Vire
Clécy
Falaise
Norrey-en-A
Pont-d'Ouilly
La Lucerne
St-Sever-Calvados
Genêts
Avranches
Flers
Putanges
Argentar
Mont-St-Michel
Mortain
Lonlay-l'Abbaye
Ecouch
Dol
Sélune
St-Hilaire-du-Harcourt
Barenton
Domfront
la Ferté-Macé
Carroug
Pontorsón
St-James
Bagnoles-de-l'Orne
Key Map
Sarthe
Mayenne
Sillé-le-Guill
Laval

N

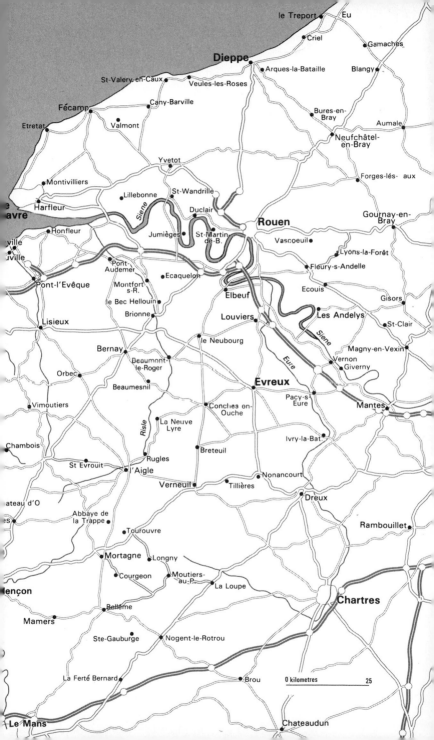